E-Activity and Intelligent Web Construction:

Effects of Social Design

Tokuro Matsuo
Yamagata University, Japan

Takayuki Fujimoto
Toyo University, Japan

Information Science
REFERENCE

Senior Editorial Director:	Kristin Klinger
Director of Book Publications:	Julia Mosemann
Editorial Director:	Lindsay Johnston
Acquisitions Editor:	Erika Carter
Development Editor:	Joel Gamon
Production Coordinator:	Jamie Snavely
Typesetters:	Milan Vracarich, Jr. and Deanna Jo Zombro
Cover Design:	Nick Newcomer

Published in the United States of America by
Information Science Reference (an imprint of IGI Global)
701 E. Chocolate Avenue
Hershey PA 17033
Tel: 717-533-8845
Fax: 717-533-8661
E-mail: cust@igi-global.com
Web site: http://www.igi-global.com/reference

Library of Congress Cataloging-in-Publication Data

E-activity and intelligent web construction: effects of social design /
Tokuro Matsuo and Takayuki Fujimoto, editors.
        p. cm.
  Includes bibliographical references and index.
  Summary: "This book presents the crux of the interdisciplinary concerns of meshing artificial intelligence and web technologies for maximizing the effectiveness of the available technologies, covering business value and e-innovation to 3D modeling and infrastructure construction"--Provided by publisher.
  ISBN 978-1-61520-871-5 (hbk.) -- ISBN 978-1-61520-872-2 (ebook) 1. Information technology. 2. Internet. 3. Artificial intelligence. I. Matsuo, Tokuro, 1978- II. Fujimoto, Takayuki, 1976-
  T58.5.E22 2011
  006.7--dc22
                          2011005918

British Cataloguing in Publication Data
A Cataloguing in Publication record for this book is available from the British Library.

All work contributed to this book is new, previously-unpublished material. The views expressed in this book are those of the authors, but not necessarily of the publisher.

Editorial Advisory Board

Table of Contents

Section 2
Analysis and Social Design

Section 3
Intelligent Web Construction and E-Support

Detailed Table of Contents

Section 1
Innovative Technologies in E-Activity

Chapter 1

Ippei Torii, Aichi Institute of Technology, Japan
Yousuke Okada, Aichi Institute of Technology, Japan
Manabu Onogi, Aichi Institute of Technology, Japan
Naohiro Ishii, Aichi Institute of Technology, Japan

The process of creating photorealistic 3-dimensional computer graphic (3DCG) images is divided into two stages, i.e., modeling and rendering. Automatic rendering has gained popularity, and photorealistic rendering is generally used to render different types of images. However, professional artists still model characters manually. Moreover, not much progress has been achieved with regard to 3-D shape data acquisition techniques that can be applied to facial modeling; this is an important problem hampering the progress of 3DCG. Generally, a laser and a highly accurate camera are used to acquire 3-D shape data. However, this technique is time-consuming and expensive. Further, the eyes may be damaged during measurements by this method. In order to solve these problems, we have proposed a simple method for 3-D shape data acquisition using a projector and Web cameras. This method is economical, simple, and less time-consuming than conventional techniques. In this chapter, we describe the setup of the projector and Web cameras, shape data acquisition process, image processing, and generation of a photorealistic image. As an example, we take a reconstructed photorealistic 3DCG image of vegetable "bitter melon," whose surface is extremely bumpy. Finally, we evaluate the error margin by this proposed method.

Chapter 2

Takanori Terashma, Miyagi University, Japan
Koji Makanae, Miyagi University, Japan
Nashwan Dawood, University of Teesside, UK

This chapter presents the implementation of a system that visualizes the construction process using 3D modeling data and schedule data to analyze construction planning. Past chapters emphasize the benefits of visual 4D planning which combines 3D CAD data and process schedule for work progress control. It rapidly shows the work performance with scheduled activity and it makes ease of construction planning and inspection. Consequently, it should increase the productivity and will reduce the rework. However, even a remarkable construction company won't adopt such a work style yet, because the lasting well organized way of working is not readily changed unless the new style has much more benefit than the effort and cost to adapt. There must be a system that integrates all outputs from each application to move the conventional work style into the new one. We thus aim at developing a system that integrates several types of data and enables the simulation of the construction progress by gradually showing 3D models according to the associated activity schedule. Proposed system in this chapter utilizes general data from several applications, such as AutoCAD and Microsoft Project, and allows deriving the same benefit as 4D-CAD without changing conventional work style.

Chapter 3
Alexandros Karakasidis, University of Thessaly, Greece
Vassilios S. Verykios, University of Thessaly, Greece

The contemporary era is characterized by a high degree of involvement of computers harvesting data in various aspects of everyday life. Merging these data would provide numerous benefits, such as in the field of medical research where new patterns for diseases could be unveiled or the effects of certain drug use could be investigated. However this is not a trivial task, since individual data holders may maintain data corresponding to the same real world entities without necessarily maintaining common and unique linkage identifiers. Additionally, these data may contain errors, rendering the integration process very difficult. All these issues encountered during merging data from heterogeneous sources refer to different aspects of the classical record linkage problem. Even though many solutions have been proposed towards addressing this problem, a new issue arises regarding the privacy of data which usually has to be protected during linkage. Sensitive information such as names and addresses, especially in cases of medical data management, should not be revealed to any participant of the merging procedure. This raises the need of creating new techniques for linking data that preserve the privacy of the subjects described by these data. This need has caused the inception of a new research area called privacy preserving record linkage. In this book chapter, we will attempt to present the state of the art of recent methods developed to address this problem, as well as a taxonomy and an evaluation of these approaches based on their salient features.

Chapter 4
Rei Itsuki, Hiroshima International University, Japan

This chapter picks up and explains some problems of system costs or specifications that we will face when trying to construct a traceability system by using RFID tags. The peripherals including RFID reader are even now expensive because they are not widespread in the market. Because of the sense of comparatively high price of the system cost and the dilemma to the specification, the impression that construction approach of the traceability system using RFID tags may be in the contemplation period is strong. In this chapter, these problems obtained from a market trend concerning the traceability in recent years and the result of reviews of the RFID tag applications or proof experiments. Next, the points of the future traceability system construction using these new technologies, especially about simple and handy type RFID reader using FPGA, are described.

Chapter 5

Distributed computing and Peer-to-Peer (P2P) systems have emerged as an active research field that combines techniques which cover networks, distributed computing, distributed database, and the various distributed applications. Distributed Computing and P2P systems realize Information Systems that scale to voluminous information on very large numbers of participating nodes. Data mining on large distributed databases is a very important research area. Recently, most work for mining association rules focused on a single machine or client-server network model. However, this traditional approach does not satisfy the requirements from the large distributed databases and applications in a P2P computing system. Two important challenges are raised; one is how to implement data mining for large distributed databases in P2P computing systems, and the other is how to develop parallel data mining algorithms and tools for the distributed P2P computing systems to improve the efficiency. In this chapter, a parallel association rule mining approach in a P2P computing system is designed and implemented, which satisfies the distribution of the P2P computing system well and makes parallel computing become true. The performance and comparison of the parallel algorithm with the sequential algorithm is analyzed and evaluated, which presents the parallel algorithm features consistent implementation, higher performance, and fine scalable ability.

Chapter 6

As the load of traffic increases in RFID middleware, RFID system can no longer manage the RFID tags. Because of the incapability of the RFID system to handle vast amount of RFID tags, there are possibilities that the data cannot be processed efficiently in the RFID middleware. Implementation of agent technology is useful for verification and validation in RFID system architecture, because intelligent agent is autonomous and has the capability to define specific verification process to increase efficiency and trustworthiness of the data in RFID middleware. Therefore, in this research, we have implemented the multi-agent based verification of data in RFID middleware. The results of the implementation have been encouraging based on the investigation and verification done on the simulation platform. As a result, the verification of RFID middleware system architecture is clearly understood and has been successfully implemented in RFID system.

Chapter 7

In intellectual collaborative works with participants talking between remote sites via WAN, CSCW have been used as general communication tools. Especially, the sharing of various high-quality digital contents such as various materials, computer graphics or visualization contents, and video streaming by between remote places is important to recognize or analyze to easily refer to these contents. However, the image magnification by general projector and large-sized display equipment is low-resolution, and sufficient quality of contents is not obtained. In this research, we have constructed tele-immersive collaborative environment with tiled display wall. In this environment, we have implemented an application to display high-resolution real video streaming on tiled display wall in a remote place. By using the application, we displayed the clear video image of remote place over a wide range. Then, we conducted experimental verification on the effect for eye-to-eye contact by changing the position of camera on frame of LCDs on tiled display wall, and collected much knowledge. Moreover, we have tried realistic display processing of high-resolution astronomical observation image and movie data, and it enabled observation of the entire image of observation data all over tiled display wall.

Section 2
Analysis and Social Design

Chapter 8

This study seeks to assess the relationship between Web infrastructure and Internet-based innovation as source of business value. To respond to this challenge, a conceptual model, grounded in the resource-based view (RBV) is developed. To test hypotheses, a sample comprising 1,010 Spanish firms is employed. The results show that, as hypothesized, Web infrastructure is not positively related to business value and that Internet-based innovation has a positive significant impact on business value. In addition, the results show no significant complementarity between Web infrastructure and Internet-based innovation.

Chapter 9

The Kaohsiung County unified broadband network project is the first and the largest broadband network deployment of the $1.5 billion M-Taiwan program. It is jointly funded by the Bureau of Industry Affairs of the Taiwanese central government and Tatung InfoComm, a wireless service provider. Hewlett Packard oversees the network construction. The network is in operation. The project has two parts: state-of-art infrastructure building and innovative applications deployment. In infrastructure building, there are two tasks: (1) converting all telephone systems in county owned facilities from the conventional circuit-switched PSTN to packet-switched VoIP; (2) building a large trial WiMAX broadband wireless mobile network. The VoIP phone system includes all government administration offices, affiliated agencies and more than 220 elementary, middle, senior, and vocational high schools in twenty seven (27) townships. The WiMAX broadband wireless mobile network consisting of 90 base stations, and covers 350 square kilometers of coastal areas with two-third of county's population of 1.25 million. The much cheaper WiFi hot zones in place of WiMAX base stations are installed in remote mountain range areas where the number of subscribers is relatively small. In addition to the M-government, the M-live, and the M-learning services promoted by the M-Taiwan program, several innovative location-based and law-enforcement services have also been deployed. We will give a description of the overall network architecture and services, and the rationale behind all the trade-offs made in the design process. We will also present the test results; that is, how the network performs. It should serve as a good reference for those who plan to build a similar network.

Chapter 10

Akihiko Nagai, Tokyo Institute of Technology, Japan
Koji Tanabe, Tokyo Institute of Technology, Japan

The worldwide market for semiconductor totaled nearly $2,594 billion in 2009. Japan is the world's second-largest semiconductors market after the U.S, with the huge size of $497 billion. On the other hand, compared to the world's semiconductor makers, Japan's vertically integrated (IDM) semiconductor makers are seen to have lost international competitive power through a horizontal integration in the distribution of semiconductor systems. Incidentally, the sales of Japanese IDM have placed it continuously among the world's three top-ranked semiconductor companies since 1980. This chapter first analyzes the features of the Japanese semiconductor market and the positioning of Japanese IDMs and semiconductor makers in other countries. In doing so, we analyze the relevance of the cooperation between Japanese IDMs and semiconductor distributors in the distribution system of the semiconductor market in Japan and the commercial practices of set makers. We also use those analysis results as the basis for considering the strategy and international competitive power of the distribution system of Japanese.

Chapter 11

Atsushi Tanaka, Yamagata University, Japan

In modern rapid technological change, how some innovation can diffuse all over is a very fascinating subject. In the past diffusion research, the case studies or analyses based on the economic theory have been dominant. The theory with the classification of adopter categories by E. M. Rogers is most famous and called a milestone for the former approach. There are rich case studies on why it has been accepted widely, however the fact that a more than forty-year-old theory still governs the world sounds a little curious. As you can see, recent progress of the Internet is amazing. The penetration of e-commerce and Web 2.0 applications have varied the form of purchases and the pattern of information propagation, respectively. As above, the importance of the relationships between individuals has grown higher. From that point of view, the field of complex networks has become very popular and revealed several important facts these years. In this chapter, some important matters of complex networks and their models are reviewed shortly, and then the modern diffusion of products under the information propagation using multiagent simulation is discussed. The remarkable phenomena like "Winner-Takes-All" and "Chasm" can be observed and one product marketing strategy is also proposed.

Section 3
Intelligent Web Construction and E-Support

It is pointed out that the 21st century is an era of knowledge creation where productivity of knowledge is more important than the productivity of things. Therefore, improvement of the productivity of knowledge is an urgent demand from public organizations i.e., industry, academia, and government, as well as personal individuals. As a method to achieve it, knowledge management systems have recently been studied and developed. However, there have been few cases that could successfully improve the productivity of knowledge; many systems have been installed but not used. One of the principal problems of the ordinary attempts is, I think, the unbalanced way for sharing the knowledge. For example, experts are required to voluntarily provide their professional knowledge to create and to maintain a knowledge-base with many efforts so that novices as free riders can readily exploit the knowledge-base without any efforts. In order to solve and/or to avoid this problem, I focused on informal communications by chance as places for sharing knowledge and my laboratory has been constructed various e-cocreation systems to support sharing and creating knowledge in the informal communications. This chapter introduces some of the research efforts conducted in the author's laboratory.

Computer-mediated communication (CMC) has been a 'hot' topic in computer-assisted language learning (CALL); however, its effectiveness remains uncertain. This article reviews the nature of CMC, pinpoints strengths and weaknesses of incorporating it into language learning, considers factors that may affect the quality of CMC, and identifies possible direction for future studies. The author argues that sound criteria are lacking for the evaluation of the effectiveness of CMC and attempts to identify a set of possible criteria for classroom-based studies drawing from literature in language teaching and learning. The author also urges engineers to consider these criteria when designing new software, so that end users can conveniently measure its effectiveness and record their own progress.

Chapter 14

Hidehiko Hayashi, Naruto University of Education, Japan
Akinori Minazuki, Naruto University of Education, Japan

This chapter presents an objective assessment method of image quality using visual evoked potentials (VEPs) to image engineer field based on multi-disciplinarily approach such as knowledge of neurobiology, or image recognition theory of computer vision. The multi-disciplinarily based objective assessment method applies Gaussian scale-space filtering in order to construct a scalar parameter to depict blur image. In the experiment, visual stimuli are provided, and the scalar parameter and subjects are detected VEPs. Their VEPs are recoded during observation of the checkerboard pattern reversal (PR) stimuli, and are analyzed to have a latency of about Negative 145 msec (N145) component. The result of the experiment was that latency of N145 components were long (about10-20 msec) when parameters were large vale (more blur). This result shows one example of availableness for the multi-disciplinarily based objective assessment of image quality by integrating the pattern reversal visual evoked potential (PR-VEP) and the scale-space theory.

Chapter 15

Hidehiko Hayashi, Naruto University of Education, Japan
Akinori Minazuki, Naruto University of Education, Japan

In this chapter, we propose a new method for improving detection probabilities of the defect inspection in quality control on the FRP product surface. Our proposed method has improved the detection probabilities by using the joint probabilities of dual attributes with correlation for multiple perceptions. In order to obtain the improving detection probability, three kinds of attributes such as size, aspect ratio, and color density are prepared in experiments. The experiments were performed by the paired comparison under constant stimuli. The result of our experiment qualitatively shows that the improving ratio of detection probabilities for dual attributes: P12, P23, P31 respectively rise approximately 21%, 26%, and 24% for the mean in the case of dual attributes experiments. In addition, detection probabilities to be obtained by our method for multiple perceptions such as using dual attributes experiment were improved approximately 28% in comparison with the detection probability of past single attribute. These results showed our method was effective in raising detection probability for multiple perceptions.

Chapter 16

Tetsuo Kosaka, Yamagata University, Japan
Takashi Kusama, Yamagata University, Japan
Masaharu Kato, Yamagata University, Japan
Masaki Kohda, Yamagata University, Japan

High recognition accuracy has been achieved for read speech with a large vocabulary continuous speech recognition (LVCSR) system. However, it is well known that rather poor performance is reported for spontaneous speech recognition. Compared with read speech, spontaneous speech has repairs, hesitations, filled pauses, unknown words, unclear pronunciation, and so on, and those phenomenon cause poor performance. In order to improve the recognition performance of spontaneous speech, we propose several methods of unsupervised adaptation for LVSCR and evaluate the methods by using diagonal-covariance and full-covariance hidden Markov models. In the adaptation procedure, both methods of language model (LM) adaptation and acoustic model (AM) adaptation are used iteratively. Several combination methods are tested to find the optimal approach. In the LM adaptation, a word trigram model and a part-of-speech (POS) trigram model are combined to build a more task-specific LM. In Japan, a large-scale spontaneous speech database "Corpus of Spontaneous Japanese (CSJ)" has been used as the common evaluation database for spontaneous speech and we used it for our recognition experiments. From the results, the proposed methods demonstrated a significant advantage in that task.

Chapter 17

E-learning has altered, and will continue to affect teaching and learning contexts in universities and tertiary education worldwide, including in Taiwan. Many universities in Taiwan have moved to offer courses that include both face-to-face and e-learning, but very little research has been undertaken on student perspectives. The issue about whether e-learning can bring benefits to improve student learning or students will face more challenges is concerned by many researchers or educators. This chapter explores the benefits and challenges of e-learning support from a student perspective in a national research-oriented university in Taiwan. An interpretive paradigm with quantitative and qualitative methods was adopted as the basis for the research methodology. This chapter outlines the findings from a survey of nearly 400 different college students and focus group discussions with over thirty students about their perceptions and experiences of e-learning in blended learning courses. SPSS were used to analyze the data of the questionnaires and interviews. The findings suggest that students experience benefits and challenges relating to their personal perception of e-learning, learning attitude, personal expertise with ICT use, and access to the requisite technology. Students perceived the benefits of e-learning as arising from being able to preview and follow up on face-to-face lectures and to discuss ideas and issues with peers and instructors given that class sizes are large, typically over a hundred students. Respondent students indicated e-learning might help them change their learning attitudes to become more active and diligent learners and also improve their personal time management and organizational ability. However, the findings from questionnaires and interviews also identified students face personal and technological challenges. The researcher expects the findings can contribute to enhance the university e-learning practice and improve instructor teaching and student learning in e-learning. The university and instructors need to identify the perceived benefits and challenges of e-learning and provide practical support for student learning. Students also need to change their perceptions and learning attitude to e-learning.

Toshiyuki Maeda, Hannan University, Japan
Tadayuki Okamoto, Ehime University, Japan
Yae Fukushige, Osaka University, Japan
Takayuki Asada, Osaka University, Japan

We present an e-mail based mobile communication system for interactive lecture support. This system consists of: attendance management subsystem, attendance history management subsystem, short examination management subsystem, questionnaire subsystem, and assignment delivery subsystem. Both students and teachers mainly use only e-mail functions, and it can access the server. This system can be used regardless of terminal models, only if mail can be sent and received through the Internet. In this chapter, the outline of this system is described, and the functions and effects are discussed.

Preface

As the Internet develops, it is becoming an increasingly prosperous network for many types of activity and support. This book introduces and discusses the innovative Information Technologies, their applications, and e-activity, including: applied AI techniques, social scientific methodologies, interface, network and distributed computing, and several other techniques. The book also focuses on their theories and practices in points of emerging technologies and analysis of human activities in WWW.

In the research on the Internet technology and WWW issues, most of them are focused on just techniques and technologies without the analysis of human behavior. However, when the system is developed, it is important for us to know the business strategy, trends of activities, cultures, and other viewpoints, including human and society. As a result, such proposed techniques have a strong impact when the systems are useful for users.

The purpose of this book is to help learners, researchers, system managers, and business mangers grasp and analyze an appropriate perception of the present situation of Web research. The technical contribution of this book provides the innovative theory and practice of Web intelligence, AI and the Internet, and applied Web technology with a sociological viewpoint. The book also includes the concept about e-activity and its application based on human cognitive mechanism, social analysis, and information design. It discusses analyses of existing/current Web technology including sociological standpoint and outlines the basic direction for future Web engineering techniques.

Tokuro Matsuo
Takayuki Fujimoto
Yonezawa, Japan
March 1, 2011

Section 1
Innovative Technologies in E–Activity

Chapter 1
Inexpensive, Simple and Quick Photorealistic 3DCG Modeling

Ippei Torii
Aichi Institute of Technology, Japan

Yousuke Okada
Aichi Institute of Technology, Japan

Manabu Onogi
Aichi Institute of Technology, Japan

Naohiro Ishii
Aichi Institute of Technology, Japan

ABSTRACT

The process of creating photorealistic 3-dimensional computer graphic (3DCG) images is divided into two stages: modeling and rendering. Automatic rendering has gained popularity, and photorealistic rendering is generally used to render different types of images. However, professional artists still model characters manually. Moreover, not much progress has been achieved with regard to 3-D shape data acquisition techniques that can be applied to facial modeling. This is an important problem hampering the progress of 3DCG. Generally, a laser and a highly accurate camera are used to acquire 3-D shape data. This technique is time-consuming and expensive. The eyes may be damaged during measurements by this method. In order to solve these problems, this chapter proposes a simple method for 3-D shape data acquisition using a projector and Web cameras. This method is economical, simple, and less time-consuming than conventional techniques. This chapter describes the setup of the projector and Web cameras, shape data acquisition process, image processing, and generation of a photorealistic image. As an example, the authors take a reconstructed photorealistic 3DCG image of Japanese vegetable "bitter melon," whose surface is extremely bumpy. The authors evaluate the error margin of this technique. They also verify the accuracy of this method by comparing the photograph of a face with its rendered image.

DOI: 10.4018/978-1-61520-871-5.ch001

1. INTRODUCTION

Recent progress of 3-Dimensional Computer Graphics (3DCG) has made photorealistic images. The 3DCG is researched in various fields according to the purposes, and is one of the main research themes (Lee, Terzopoulos & Waters, 1995; Young, Beeson, Davis, Rusinkrewicz & Ramamoorthi, 2007). The process to express photorealistic images is divided into the modeling which defines and creates the data of 3-D irregular object shape, and the rendering which outputs a final picture from the modeling data. The rendering is comparatively easy for automatic creation and it can generate photorealistic images from complicated form easily. However, modeling has to be performed by an expert handwork, and its efficient improvement is slow. Highly precise 3-D irregular modeling is an important problem of 3DCG. Conversional slit ray projection method (An, Woodward, Delmas, Gimel'farb & Morris, 2006; Araki et al.,1995; Narasimhan, Koppal & Yamazaki, 2008) research is difficult to apply to measurement data for the creation of computer graphics. Also, destroyed polygons are a hindrance to creating computer graphics. The aim of the modeling is to reconstruct the shape without the noise. In this chapter we have proposed a new system of shape reconstruction based by slit ray projection method. To acquire the data of the object is developed as follows.

1. The projection method that can measure delicate ups and downs precisely.
2. Image processing and regularization images methods to calculate shape data.
3. Computation of value method to coordinates value at the vertex point.
4. Application to 3-D irregular objects modeling and accuracy enhancement.

Concretely, the projection method with an inexpensive web cameras and the projector device is developed in the first step (1), the line extrac-tion, the noise processing, the line thinning, and regularization of several cameras images are developed in the second step (2), computation of value is developed in the third step (3), and application to 3-D irregular object modeling and accuracy enhancement are developed in the fourth step (4).

2. RELATED WORK

Achieving highly precise geometric modeling is an important challenge in 3DCG. Conventional methods such as stereo imaging and 3-D scanning are used for 3-D modeling,. Stereo imaging makes use of a stereo camera that can simulate binocular vision, which is often called binocular stereo. Binocular stereo algorithms producing a dense 3-D data set have been developed and applied for face reconstruction (Chan, Delmas, Gimel'farb & Leclercq, 2005; Enciso, Fidaeo, Noh & Neumann, 1999; Leclercq et al., 2004; Scharstein & Szeliski, 2002; Woodward & Delmas, 2004). The 3-D scanning involves and use of a laser scanner and a CCD camera. In 3-D scanning, the vertical planes of an object are measured using the laser scanner by the 2-D scanning method, in which a method of measuring the objects shape of carrying the cross section is developed (Lee et al, 1995; Zhang, Sim & Tan, 2004). Unfortunately, the price of 3-D scanning equipment makes this approach impractical for most lab situations (Woodward, An, Gimel'farb & Delmas, 2006). As an another approach of 3-D modeling, a photometric stereo is developed, which uses three lights sources (Faugeras, 1993; Kette & Schuluns, 1998). However, conventional methods have some disadvantages. Stereo imaging is difficult to use under varying light conditions, because the shadow of the object is misinterpreted by the turbulence light. In 3-D scanning, we can acquire large high-density data by only one scan in short time. Then, a large amount of memory is required because it is necessary to scan the object in all directions. In 3-D scanning, the object size in the passage direction is misinterpreted when the speed and direction of object change in the measurement domain.

3. WORKFLOW OF OBJECT MODELING

A slit ray projection method is a simple and well known one to reconstruct the objects in the computer. It is expected in the method that the line is horizontal from anywhere when the horizontal line is projected to the plane. However, the line has been often curved when this line is projected to complex ups and downs, which is observed from the upper part. Then, the difference of the reconstructed object with the web camera, and the shape of the real object will be needed to compare and analyze between them. In this section, we develop a more accurate method than the conventional slit ray projection method.

3.1. Environment

The basic devices required for scanning in this method are a projector and three web cameras. The projector and three web cameras must be set up in the position as shown in Figure 1. The projector

and three web cameras should be set up based on the lens. In this chapter the light environments include room without direct sunshine and strong light from other.

3.2. Calibration with Standard Slit Ray Lines and Standard Position

Before object scanning, we defined slit ray lines of on the computer. The line generated by the computer is projected on the standard position. Any color can be used for the standard slit ray lines and the scan slit ray line. In this chapter, we use blue for both lines. We also measure the distances between the projector's lens and the standard position (lc), between the web cameras and the standard position (ln), between the height of the center of the projector lens and the web camera (hc), and between a camera and another camera (lh). Then, we obtain a static image with the web camera and map the standard position on the global coordinate space to the camera coordinate one, which is called calibration. In this method, we defined the camera coordinate space $(0, 0)$ as the original point on the standard position that passes over the lowest point. We show Equation (1) in the below. (x, y) shows in the millimeter on global coordinate. $(\Delta x, \Delta y)$ and $(\Delta X, \Delta Y)$ are

Figure 1. Projector and web camera setup. Left shows side view, while right shows top view.

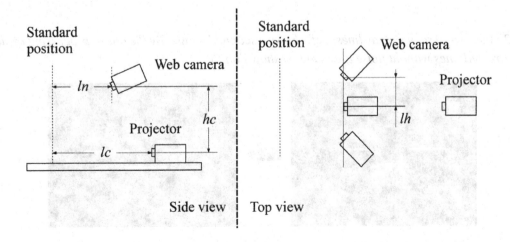

slope of linear function to solve ratio of global coordinate and camera coordinate. So, (Δx, Δy) is in millimeter scale, which is on global coordinate. It shows the length between two standard slit ray lines. (ΔX, ΔY) is in pixel scale, which is on camera coordinate. Then, (X_i, Y_i) is variables, which is changed from pixel scale to millimeter scale. I is used to define (0, 0). In this chapter we arranged standard slit ray lines for 7mm intervals.

$$\begin{pmatrix} x \\ y \end{pmatrix} = \begin{pmatrix} \dfrac{\Delta x}{\Delta X} X_i \\ \dfrac{\Delta y}{\Delta Y} Y_i \end{pmatrix} + I \qquad (1)$$

3.3. Generation and Projection of Scan Slit Ray Lines

We generate a scan slit ray line projected to the object with the projector based on information of the standard slit ray lines set in the preceding section. The direction of movement and the color of the scan slit ray lines should be the same as that of the standard slit ray lines. Here, sequential scanning is used to reduce processing complexity and mutual interference by multiplying the standard slit ray lines. It is necessary for the web camera to capture every line scanned. This operation is performed at very high speeds, which reduces eye strain. The danger of the scan slit ray lines passing over the eyes is not as great as that posed by

a laser beam; however, the examinee must close his/her eyes when a picture is being taken. Only the scan slit ray line is extracted from the image data and all additional information is discarded. The image by the web camera is converted RGB (Red, Green, Blue) color space into HSV (Hue, Saturation, Brightness) color space. In this chapter, we treat hue as an angle. i.e., hue change from 0 to 360. It analyzes the hue angle of all pixel and defines average angle as threshold H_t. Hue angle H_{ij} ($0 < H_{ij} < 360$) from each pixel is got from obtained graphics data. If H_{ij} satisfied $360 - H_t < H_{ij}$ and $H_{ij} < H_t$, the pixel of H_{ij} is *True*, if not, it is *False*. After that, it analyzes saturation and brightness of all pixels. Saturation S_{ij} ($0 < S_{ij} < 255$) and brightness V_{ij} ($0 < V_{ij} < 255$) from each pixel is obtained from graphics data. If S_{ij} and V_{ij} satisfied $250 < S_{ij} < 255$ and $140 < V_{ij} < 240$, the pixel of S_{ij} and V_{ij} is *True*, if not, it is *False*. If all the values of H_{ij}, S_{ij}, and V_{ij} are *True*, the pixel is made white, while if not, it is made black. Furthermore, the noise in the direction of the x-axis can be removed that deviated from the scan slit ray line greatly using continuing on an image. Line thinning is performed in order to increase the clarity of the extracted line. The thickness of the line is set to 1 pixel by deducing the average of the point of the topmost part and the lowermost part of the line. We show the result of image processing in Figure 2.

Figure 2. Analysis of scan slit ray lines. Left shows a scanned image. By the above processing of slit ray lines, corrected lines without noise are made as shown on the right.

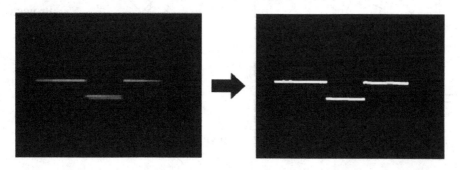

3.4. Regularization of Several Camera Images

We get values of θ and ls in Figure 4 using Equation (2) from parameters lc, ln, and lh. This is the calibration to use more than two cameras. After that, we regularize images from camera A (Figure 3(a)) and camera B (Figure 3(b)). We correct the image in camera B (Figure 3(b)) from Equations (3) and (4). (X, Y, Z) is coordinate of a 3-D vertex point on the global coordinate space. (u, v) are coordinates of point projection in pixels. (cx, cy) is a principal point (that is usually at the image center). fx and fy are focal lengths expressed in pixel-related units. The joint rotation-translation matrix $[R|t]$ is called a matrix of extrinsic parameters. k_1 and k_2 are radial distortion coefficients, p_1 and p_2 are tangential distortion coefficients, where equation $r^2 = \dfrac{x}{z}^2 + \dfrac{y}{z}^2$ holds. We have

shown the correct data as an image in Figure 3(c). Then, we synthesize the image in camera A to correct the image (the image in camera B) based on the point of maximum y-scale to get an image in Figure 3(d). Camera C is regularized as well as camera B. Thus, the image of camera A is restructured and regularized from the images of camera B and C.

$$ls = \frac{ln}{\cos(\arctan\frac{lh}{ln})} = \frac{lh}{\sin(\arctan\frac{lh}{ln})} \qquad (2)$$

$$\begin{pmatrix} x \\ y \\ z \end{pmatrix} = R \begin{pmatrix} X \\ Y \\ Z \end{pmatrix} + t \qquad (3)$$

Figure 4. Computation of coordinate values. The point P shows a point of slit ray line projected on the object.

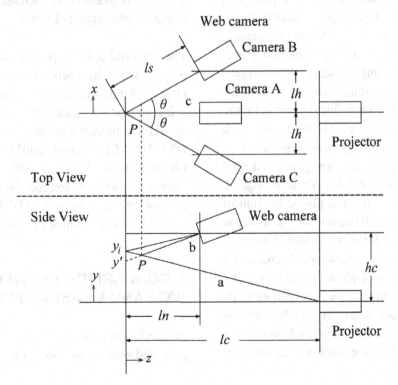

Figure 3. Image processing to correct two cameras. These are examples of nose figure on the face. Image (a) is from Camera A and image (b) is from Camera B. Image (c) is corrected from that of (b). From images (a) and (c), a regularized image (d) is obtained.

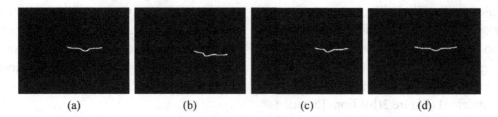

(a)   (b)   (c)   (d)

$$\begin{pmatrix} u \\ v \end{pmatrix} = \begin{pmatrix} fx\left[\left\{\frac{x}{z}\left(1+k_1r^2+k_2r^4\right)\right\}+\frac{2p_1xy}{z^2}+p_2\left\{r^2+2\left(\frac{x}{z}\right)^2\right\}\right]+cx \\ fy\left[\left\{\frac{y}{z}\left(1+k_1r^2+k_2r^4\right)\right\}+p_1\left\{r^2+2\left(\frac{y}{z}\right)^2\right\}+\frac{2p_2xy}{z^2}\right]+cy \end{pmatrix}$$

$$(4)$$

3.5. Computation of Coordinate Values

The scanned data must be sampled along the x-axis, and the amount of data must be determined. In this chapter, we sampled every 1 pixel i.e., we sampled width resolution as accurately as possible. After that we have to convert camera coordinate space scan slit ray lines into global coordinate space using standard slit ray lines. They calculate the coordinates on the basis of the analyzed images. We show this scheme in Figure 4. The values of $lc, ln, hc,$ and lh have already been measured. The scan slit ray lines projected from the projector, become a real image at point y_i on the standard position. Point y_i is also measured. However, when the object is placed in front of the standard position, it becomes a real image at point P of the object. It holds the same as the point observed by point y' on the standard position by the web camera. The straight line of a, b, and c is linear function, therefore it is easy to estimate an intersection coordinate (x_P, y_P, z_P). We show its coordinate in Equation (5) and a schematic diagram in Figure 4 for the coordinates calculation.

The global coordinate $(0, 0, 0)$ defines the center point of the standard slit ray lines that passes over the lowest point.

$$P = \begin{pmatrix} x_P \\ y_P \\ z_P \end{pmatrix} = \begin{pmatrix} \dfrac{x_i(y_i ln + lchc - y_i lc)}{y_i ln + lc(hc - y')} \\ \dfrac{y_i(y' ln + lchc - y' lc)}{y_i ln + lc(hc - y')} \\ \dfrac{lcln(y_i - y')}{y_i ln + lc(hc - y')} \end{pmatrix}$$

$$(5)$$

3.6. Conversion of Modeling Data to Polygonal Data

The acquired 3-D shape data are converted to polygonal data by a general software application. Objects in the form of polygons is represented by using a standard modeling technique in 3DCG, as they can be easily edited. Then, we adopt the DXF-3DFACE (Ochiai, 2003) file format. The file structure of DXF simplifies the process of mapping data to polygon coordinates. Since many software applications support DXF, it is possible to import DXF data from one application to another.

4. COMPARISON BETWEEN ACTUAL DATA AND MEASUREMENT DATA

In this chapter, we verify the accuracy of our proposed method by using a geometric form. A geometric form is a solid model used for sketches etc., whose sizes are known. The accuracy of acquisition data is evaluated by using a geometric forms in Figure 5. In this chapter describing an experiment about accuracy evaluation, values of parameters *lc*, *ln*, *hc*, and *lh* which can easily be changed, are set as shown in Table 1. We used three cameras which were made for general use, in which the resolution (800×600) and angles (60 degrees) are fixed. The purpose of this experiment is to compare accuracies between actual data and the measured by the proposed method using cameras here, so the parameters are fixed. It is necessary to measure the dimensions of a known object and verify them with the acquired data to measure the accuracy of the proposed method. We show the processing images in Figure 6. The actual dimensional values and the measurement data acquired by number of cameras (a camera means only camera A, two cameras means camera A and camera B, three cameras means camera A, camera B and camera C) are shown in Table 2. The scale of Table 2 is in millimeter and the values show those of z-axis and y-axis from global coordinate (0, 0, 0) to vertex point. From experiments by using the number of the camera, the accuracy of the shape data has increased. As a result, we succeeded in the analysis of a clearer

scan slit ray lines. As the volume of data on the object side is amplified, more accurate 3-D shape data will be confirmed.

5. APPLICATION TO 3-D IRREGULAR OBJECTS

We aim to get 3-D irregular objects shape data. According to experiments with simple objects by using the number of cameras, the accuracy of the shape data has been increased. Since the scan slit ray lines on 3-D irregular objects is often lost, so it is difficult to scan using one camera. Then, the distance between the object and the camera is reduced in the computation. Therefore, three cameras are used, to counterbalance the losses of slit ray lines. We use a bitter melon in Figure 7 as an example of 3-D irregular objects. The bitter melon has innumerable ruggedness on the surface, and doesn't have the rules for position. The results

Table 1. Parameters used in the experiment

Parameters	*lc*	*ln*	*lh*	*hc*
Values (mm)	730	450	14	22

Figure 5. Drafting (left) and dimensions (right) of a geometric form

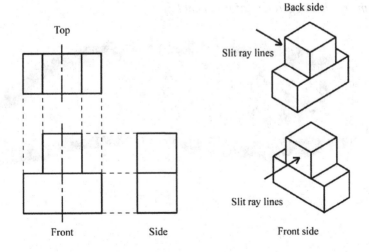

Figure 6. Examples of processing images of geometric form. The upper figures are regularized to the lower figures by the procedures in the section 2.5.

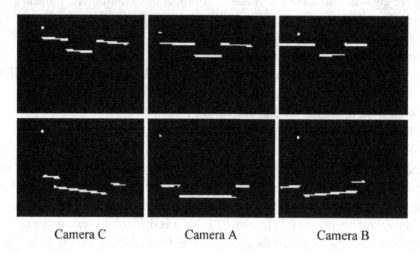

Camera C   Camera A   Camera B

Table 2 Comparison with actual and measurement data: Point Z means z-axis from global coordinate and others mean y-axis from global coordinate in mm.

	Point Z	**Point 1**	**Point 2**	**Point 3**
Actual size	95.000000	254.000000	95.000000	32.000000
A camera	97.289247	252.837490	96.130645	33.250734
Two cameras	96.197642	253.797867	94.513023	32.546014
Three cameras	95.120138	254.212251	95.190119	32.240153
	Point 4	Point 5	Point 6	Point 7
Actual size	307.000000	7.000000	56.000000	134.000000
A camera	305.918502	6.898537	54.178345	133.156354
Two cameras	306.502746	6.976744	55.849264	133.803582
Three cameras	306.976736	6.979416	55.973589	133.954030

Figure 7. Some innumerable ruggedness of bitter melon

and images of reconstruction 3-D shape data are shown in Table 3 and 3-D object in Figure 10 and Figure 11 in Appendix. The scale of Table 3 is shown in millimeter and the number is value of z-axis from global coordinate space (0, 0, 0) to vertex point.

6. APPLICATION TO FACIAL MODELING

We apply our method to facial modeling (Akimoto, Suenaga & Wallace, 1993; Bickel, Lang, Botsch, Otaduy & Gross, 2008; Essa, 1994). Facial modeling is one of the most difficult process during 3DCG production pipeline. So it is valuable to realize rapid facial modeling system. Experimental results of facial modeling is shown in Figure 8. We used Subdivision Surface (Zorin, 2006) to revise and secure smoothing. Further, we adopted UV Mapping (Sander, Snyder, Gortler & Hoppe, 2001; Tarini, Yamauchi, Haber & Seidel, 2002) technology to texture the modeling object. Because it is a method of mapping generated one image to the object. First, mesh parameterization is done from the 3 dimensional modeling object. Next, mesh of two dimensions is generated. We resample the texture mesh from the photograph of face. We map sampled photograph to modeling object, and render it in Figure 9 by photorealistic rendering technology like ray tracing. The procedure adopted here, makes the best use of the advantage of facial

Table 3. Sample of 3-D shape data by three cameras (camera A, camera B, and camera C). All values show y coordinate in mm.

	Point A	Point B	Point C	Point D
Actual size	120.000000	273.000000	230.000000	327.000000
Three cameras	120.310000	273.390000	229.470000	326.610000
	Point E	Point F	Point G	Point H
Actual size	251.000000	311.000000	93.000000	147.000000
Three cameras	251.190000	311.330000	92.740000	146.810000
	Point I	Point J	Point K	Point L
Actual size	198.000000	239.000000	287.000000	341.000000
Three cameras	198.370000	238.650000	287.160000	340.770000

Figure 8. Results of facial modeling using our method. The facial images are rotated by 30 degrees from the leftmost image. The lower show wireframes correspondent to the upper rendered images.

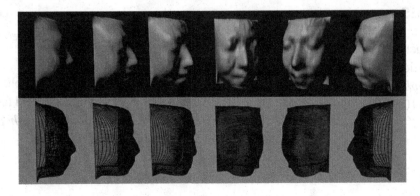

Figure 9. From the leftmost image: modeling data, a photograph for UV mapping, mesh parameterization image, and final rendered image. By mapping the center mesh parameterization image to the left model, the final modeling figure is made on the right.

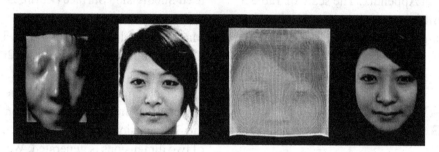

modeling and human body modeling (Doyle & Philips, 1989; Frick, Leonhardt & Starck, 1991; Gray, 1985; Guenter, 1992).

7. CONCLUSION

In this chapter we proposed a more accurate system of shape reconstruction based on slit ray projection method. It includes image processing, regularization of image, computation of coordinate value, and reconstruction of 3-D shape data. As a result, we can get a satisfactory result ±0.5mm as accuracy with three cameras. Next, we will contemplate the reduction of the data capacity and propose a simper method. The technology will be applied to facial modeling and animation because this method is safety and simple. The simplicity of our method will be applied to many objects modeling.

REFERENCES

Akimoto, T., Suenaga, Y., & Wallace, R. (1993). Automatic creation of 3D facial models. *IEEE Computer Graphics and Applications, 13*(5), 16–22. doi:10.1109/38.232096

An, D., Woodward, A., Delmas, P., Gimel'farb, G., & Morris, J. (2006). Comparison of active structure lighting mono and stereo camera systems: Application to 3D face acquisition. *ENC '06: Proceedings of the Seventh Mexican International Conference on Computer Science*, (pp. 135-141). Washington, DC: IEEE Computer Society.

Araki, K., Shimizu, M., Noda, T., Chiba, Y., Tsuda, Y., & Ikegaya, K. (1995). A high-speed and continuous 3d measurement system. *Machine Vision and Applications, 8*(2), 79–84. doi:10.1007/BF01213473

Bickel, B., Lang, M., Botsch, M., Otaduy, M. A., & Gross, M. (2008). *Pose-space animation and transfer of facial details.* ACM SIGGRAPH Symposium on Computer Animation, (pp. 57-66).

Chan, M., Delmas, P., Gimel'farb, G., & Leclercq, P. (2005). *Comparative study of 3D face acquisition techniques: Computer analysis of images and patterns.* (LNCS 3691), (pp. 740-747).

Doyle, J., & Philips, J. (1989). *Manual on experimental stress analysis* (5th ed.). Society for Experimental Mechanics.

Enciso, R., Li, J., Fidaeo, D., Noh, T. Y., & Neumann, U. (1999). Synthesis of 3d faces. *Proceedings of the International Workshop Digital and Computational Video*, Florida.

Essa, I. A. (1994). *Visual interpretation of facial expressions using dynamic modeling*. Unpublished doctoral dissertation, MIT.

Faugeras, O. (1993). *Three-dimensional computer vision*. Cambridge, MA: The MIT Press.

Frick, H., Leonhardt, H., & Starck, D. (1991). *Human anatomy* (*Vol. 1*). Stuttgart, Germany: Thieme Medical Publishers.

Gray, H. (1985). *Anatomy of the human body* (29th ed.). Philadelphia, PA: Lea Febiber.

Guenter, B. (1992). *A system for simulating human facial expression: State of the art in computer animation* (pp. 191–202). Springer-Verlag.

Kette, R., & Schluns, K. (1998). *Computer vision–three-dimensional data from images*. Springer-Verlag.

Leclercq, P., Liu, J., Chan, M., Woodward, A., Gimel'farb, G., & Delmas, P. (2004). Comparative study of stereo algorithms for 3D face reconstruction. *Proceedings of the Conference of Advanced Concepts for Intelligent Vision Systems*, (pp. 690-704).

Lee, Y., Terzopoulos, D., & Waters, K. (1995). Realistic modeling for facial animation. ACM Conference on SIGGRAPH (ACM Computer Graphics), (pp. 55-62).

Narasimhan, S., Koppal, S., & Yamazaki, S. (2008). *Temporal dithering of illumination for fast active vision*. European Conference on Computer Vision, 4, (pp. 830-844).

Ochiai, S. (2003). *DXF handbook*. Tokyo, Japan: Ohmsha Ltd.

Sander, P. V., Snyder, J., Gortler, S. J., & Hoppe, H. (2001). *Texture mapping progressive meshes*. ACM SIGGRAPH Symposium on Computer Graphics.

Scharstein, D., & Szeliski, R. (2002). A taxonomy and evaluation of dense two-frame stereo correspondence algorithms. *International Journal of Computer Vision, 47*(1), 7–42. doi:10.1023/A:1014573219977

Tarini, M., Yamauchi, H., Haber, J., & Seidel, H. P. (2002). *Texturing faces*. Parco. Graphics Interface.

Woodward, A., An, D., Gimel'farb, G., & Delmas, P. (2006). A comparison of 3-D facial reconstruction approaches. *Proceedings of the IEEE International Conference on Multimedia and Expo*, (pp. 9-12). Canada.

Woodward, A., & Delmas, P. (2004). Toward a low cost realistic human face modeling and animation framework. *Proceedings of the International Conference on Image and Vision Computing*, (pp. 11-16). New Zealand

Young, M., Beeson, E., Davis, J., Rusinkiewicz, S., & Ramamoorthi, R. (2007). *Viewpoint coded structured light*. IEEE Conference on Computer Vision and Pattern Recognition, (pp. 1-8).

Zhang, Y., Sim, T., & Tan, C. T. (2004). Rapid modeling of 3D faces for animation using an efficient adaptation algorithm. *Proceedings of the 2nd International Conference on Computer Graphics and Interactive Techniques in Australia and South East Asia*, (pp. 173-181).

Zorin, D. (2006). *Modeling with multiresolution subdivision surfaces*. ACM SIGGRAPH 2006 Course, (pp. 30-50).

APPENDIX

Figure 10. From left to front view, top view and side view of complex rendered objects. The upper figures show rendered images, while the lower figures show their wireframes.

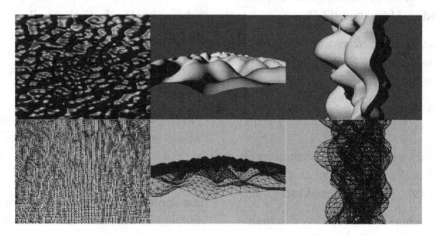

Figure 11. The upper figures show partial expanded images of the lower rendered figures

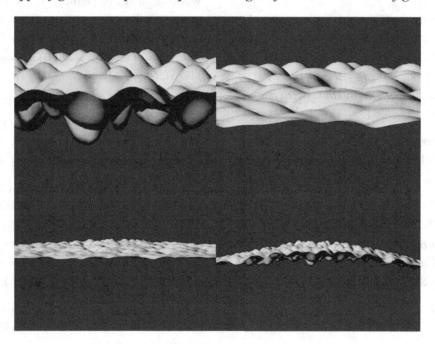

Chapter 2
Development of a 4D Visualization Tool for Construction Planning

Takanori Terashma
Miyagi University, Japan

Koji Makanae
Miyagi University, Japan

Nashwan Dawood
University of Teesside, UK

ABSTRACT

This chapter presents the implementation of a system that visualizes the construction process using 3D modeling data and schedule data to analyze construction planning. Previous papers have emphasized the benefits of visual 4D planning that combines 3D modeling data and process schedule data for work progress control. The proposed methodology offers rapid visualization of work performance with scheduled activity and facilitates construction planning and schedule inspection. Consequently, it should increase productivity and reduce rework. However, even major construction companies will not adopt such a work style, because the existing, well-organized way of working would not be readily changed unless the new style is proven to afford benefits that outweigh the effort and cost required to adapt to the style. The advanced CAD system, for example, is able to simulate the assembly process, and the advanced 3D graphic designer is able to animate the arrangement of objects. Even though each software provides multiple functionalities, the applications in practical use are all independent and specific, such as CAD for designing 3D models, and a project manager for scheduling and analyzing. Therefore, a system that integrates all outputs from each application is required to move from the conventional work style to the new one. This chapter, thus, aims to develop a system that integrates several types of data and enables the simulation of the construction progress by gradually showing 3D models according to the activity schedule. It is also possible to attach material data to each object and to display related information

DOI: 10.4018/978-1-61520-871-5.ch002

like cost and object properties. The system assumes the following requirements: (1) to import and display the 3D modeling data, (2) to import the project schedule, (3) to link each model and activity, (4) to give the material data on each object to enhance reality, and (5) to show cost accumulation. These functions are supposed to be realized such that the system utilizes the resources previously reserved. Therefore, the system should be able to import a DXF format file for 3D modeling data and access the MDB format database for the project schedule, including costs. The MDB file is originally a database that Microsoft Access creates. Microsoft Project, which is probably the most widely used software for project management, is also able to export the project data in this format. These functions are implemented with Microsoft Visual C++ and DirectX SDK. Although the system displays inaccurate models partially because of the misinterpretation of the DXF file, all of the demands listed above are satisfied currently. The authors of this chapter are now at the stage of implementation of further functions, that is, to display not only structures but also other elements such as the temporal space on the site, the route of delivery vehicles, and the work area of the temporally used heavy machinery, all for the sake of the visualization and analysis of the entire construction site.

1. INTRODUCTION

Previous papers have emphasized the advantages of architectural methodologies that use 4D data that associate three-dimensional modeling data with constructional timing. In recent times, the construction industry has aimed to rationalize the production system by deriving the benefits afforded by the integration of procedures ranging from designing to construction, and therefore, promoting the use of a 3D CAD system. The aim of recent 3D CAD technology is to provide a platform to unify several types of data that project members share, including data related to design, construction, and facilities; earlier CAD technology could only provide data related to the intended design at an early planning stage or a consistent drawing at the final planning stage. Technical issues at the construction stage are considered from the early design stage. Combining design with production in such a manner, called production design, allows the user to rapidly show the work progress and the completed amount of work as well as to reduce rework and redesign at the post-process stage since visualization at an early stage helps identify technical problems. Such a methodology requires various types of applications, including a CAD system, to design, plan,

manufacture, and manage the process. However, it should be noted that the interchangeability of shared data between the software is not sufficiently high, and thus, the efficiency of the entire project is not improved considerably. The product model is being developed as a good solution for interoperation among different systems. Product model is a generalized data model that expresses three-dimensional shapes and information about the attributes of each element that composes a structure. The data set can be shared by various systems or applications when it is created as a product model, as shown in Figure 1.

Despite the advantages of the abovementioned method, even major construction companies do not adopt such a work style. In fact, two-dimensional drawings are still widely used for design drawing and construction planning. Although a 2D drawing is sufficient for a designer, it is hardly possible for less-experienced people to visualize the 3D aspect from the 2D drawings, and besides, it is not suitable to simulate or analyze the problems on a PC. It appears that the conventional way of working will not change easily unless the new style can be clearly shown to afford benefits that outweigh the effort and cost required to adapt to this style.

Figure 1. Data sharing using product model

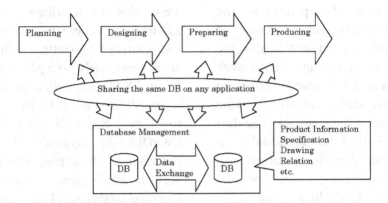

Considerable cost is involved in deriving the benefits of the new methodology in order to, for example, produce a new set of data structures such as the product model, simulate the assembly process on an advanced CAD system in addition to designing, or animate the arrangement of objects on a high-performance 3D graphic designer. Even though each software provides multiple functionalities, the applications in practical use are all independent and specific, such as CAD for designing 3D models and a project manager for scheduling. Therefore, a system that integrates all outputs from each application is required to move from the conventional work style to the new one.

This study proposes a system that integrates data created by several applications, whereas other studies have suggested the integration of applications. The main part of this system is the visualization of process control using a 3D shape linking the schedule. Visualization in this case includes not only showing a construction state but also simulating the entire construction field by using heavy machinery and material carriers along with their route and the situation of temporary stores, in order to examine the entire construction plan in advance. Although all required data is created by different applications, the proposed system offers the functionality to link associated data from each dataset, and thus, it provides the same advantages as 4D CAD without the necessity of

creating a product model or any other new type of data structure. Therefore, users can concentrate only on using the generic application specified for each purpose, such as CAD and Microsoft Project (MS-Project), in the usual manner.

This chapter describes the implementation of software that simulates the work progress by visualizing the given drawing data and linking them with schedule data.

2. DESIGNING THE CONSTRUCTION VISUALIZING TOOL

2.1 Software Specification

It is assumed that the system needs to perform the following functions. It integrates imported resources by linking related matter.

1. Reading drawing data
2. Reading schedule data
3. Linking parts and schedule
4. 3D visualization
5. Displaying work progress at any point of time
6. Displaying the accumulation of cost
7. Setting parts material
8. Saving/reading work

Functions 1 and 2 involve the import of application data created by other applications. The other functions involve the data processing of imported data. Work in function 8 implies the work on the proposed system and not the work in a construction project. It is quite reasonable to expect the proposed system to utilize the drawing data created by AutoCAD and the schedule data created by MS-Project to follow the actual situation. Its appearance should be like that of a general Windows application; further, a user should be able to operate the 3D model by a mouse.

2.2 Reading Drawing Data

AutoCAD creates two types of data, DWG and DXF. DWG is binary-type data, and DXF is text-type data that is easier to handle in various applications. DXF is the Drawing Interchange File Format; its specification is published, and it is widely used for data exchange between applications that deal with models or drawings. The proposed system should be able to process a DXF file.

Each DXF file consists of seven sections: HEADER, CLASSES, TABLES, BLOCKS, ENTITIES, OBJECTS, and THUMBNAILIMAGE.

The ENTITIES section contains information about the shape. Processing the data in this section is important for visualizing the model. There are entities that describe a specific figure such as a circle or a curve, with a layer name and the coordinates of the vertices in this section. There are approximately 40 types of elements defined for the ENTITIES section, as shown in Figure 3. Shapes defined in ENTITIES are usually one of four types—REGION, 3DFACE, 3DSOID, and LWPOLYLINE; typically, the LWPOLYLINE shape is used. The implementation of the processing of the drawing data is currently limited to these four types of shapes. VPORT and LAYERS in the TABLE section are also essential. VPORT is used for determining the line of sight, and LAYERS is used for fetching the layer name list for the shapes. All parts that compose the structure belong to one of these layers. We assume that the parts data, which is related to a construction, is drawn on a layer. When a layer is linked to a process in the entire construction plan, all parts drawn on the same layer are linked to the process together. Therefore, the animation that changes a process by process equivalent to changing layer by layer.

2.3 Reading Schedule Data

It is assumed that the process schedule is developed on MS-Project; actually, the system requires a file exported by MS-Project, which is in the Mi-

Figure 2. System overview

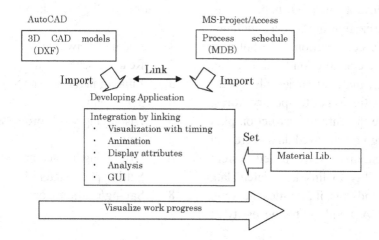

Figure 3. Seven sections in DXF file and entity list in the ENTITIES section

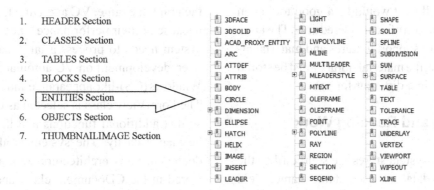

1. HEADER Section
2. CLASSES Section
3. TABLES Section
4. BLOCKS Section
5. ENTITIES Section
6. OBJECTS Section
7. THUMBNAILIMAGE Section

3DFACE
3DSOLID
ACAD_PROXY_ENTITY
ARC
ATTDEF
ATTRIB
BODY
CIRCLE
DIMENSION
ELLIPSE
HATCH
HELIX
IMAGE
INSERT
LEADER

LIGHT
LINE
LWPOLYLINE
MLINE
MULTILEADER
MLEADERSTYLE
MTEXT
OLEFRAME
OLE2FRAME
POINT
POLYLINE
RAY
REGION
SECTION
SEQEND

SHAPE
SOLID
SPLINE
SUBDIVISION
SUN
SURFACE
TABLE
TEXT
TOLERANCE
TRACE
UNDERLAY
VERTEX
VIEWPORT
WIPEOUT
XLINE

crosoft Access (MS-Access) format. The system accesses the elements stored in the database via an ODBC (Open Data Base Connectivity) driver. The software is unable to operate a MS-Project file directly since the ODBC driver for MS-Project is not provided. The exported MS-Access-type file contains several databases, and one of them has a table that contains the process schedule. The table has fields that describe the task name, process start date, finish date, and cost. The proposed system can read them and modify them directly since it uses ODBC and can execute an SQL command.

2.4 Linking Parts and Schedule

It is necessary to link task names written in the schedule data and modeling data. A task name should be reasonable name since it is given for process management. Modeling data are created on the same layer for each process flow. The linking operation is as follows: choose one entry from the task name list and one from the layer name list, and then link them. This operation is repeatedly carried out as many times as required by the process flow. A user should be able to save and reproduce these links because the number of processes will be considerable when the building structure is huge.

2.5 Visualization

When the system reads a DXF file, coordinates are fetched for each part and constructed as a set of meshes. Each mesh is made up of triangles; hence, the displayed model is composed of a number of triangles because of the display mechanism of the hardware. A triangle mesh exhibits the best performance on the hardware considered for the proposed system.

Displayed model after linking layer and schedule shows the situation of work progress at any given point of time. Some parts are already constructed, others are ongoing, and the others are not yet started. They are distinguished by color.

The scene that displays the construction can be operated by a computer mouse, and it is possible to examine the scene from any angle and from any distance.

2.6 Setting Parts Material

A DXF file has a factor using for colors, but it is not always used because it is not really necessary at the designing stage. Therefore, the system uses only mono color with gradation; however, the color differs according to the completion status. The displayed scene may have more reality when each part has the material attribute. It is apparently important to animate the design for process examination or analysis. If the proposed system accomplishes this, it would be a good tool even for the presentation of a considered area. The DXF format does not support textures and material attributes; hence, the material library must be stored by the system in a different format.

2.7 Saving and Reading Work

The proposed system stores the source files, the name of the database used, table name, field names, links of task names, and layer names in a text file. Each factor is separated by a certain text separator. When this file is read, the work that user did is duplicated again according to the text file.

3. IMPLEMENTATION OF THE SYSTEM

3.1 Development Environment

Software code is developed on Visual C++ (VC) with DirectX SDK. Other language options are

Visual Basic or Java, and OpenGL or Java3D for the graphic engine. VC and DirectX are selected because of their performance since the proposed system needs to process a large dataset. Moreover, development on VC automatically offers a Windows (OS)-like appearance and user interface. The FormView class is selected as the base class so that additional functions and their icons can be placed easily. The system is also based on document-view architecture. Imported data are stored in the CDocument class, and the CView class takes control of the appearance of imported data. Although details are described afterwards, the specified class designed for each data type will be instantiated when the system imports the data source file. These data are imported into classes declared in the CDocument class, and the CView class refers to them when they are rendered. The relation among the classes is shown in Figure 4. Principal functions are described in the following subsections.

Figure 4. Structure of classes

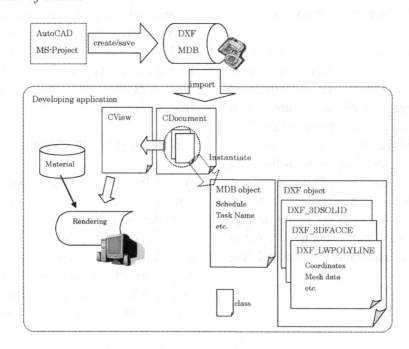

3.2 Importing Source Files

When the system imports shapes, it seeks the DXF file line by line to find the ENTITIES section, and it instantiates a class that is associated with each entity style as it finds the shape's definition within the section. Each class stores coordinates, layer name, and so on. Imported shapes are rendered as a set of meshes made by defining these coordinates. Layer names are listed in an array (actually vector class), and classes are listed in an array together with the shape styles such as LWPOLYLINE or 3DSOLID. All parts belong to one of the layers. A set of parts drawn on the same layer is considered to be the parts that a particular construction process needs.

The required schedule data is a MS-Access format database; its extension is MDB, which is the database scheduled in MS-Project and exported. The system is connected to the MDB file via an ODBC driver; the system chooses the schedule table and the fields for task name, starting date, finishing date, and cost. Screen shots of this operation are shown in Figure 5.

3.3 Visualization

After the model data and schedule data are imported, layer names and task names will be listed. Part names are listed under the layer name. The linking layer name and the task name are selected with a mouse click, and then they are right-clicked for linking. Then, the layer, including construction parts, that has to be scheduled appears under the process name. Figure 6 shows this operation. If any date is given afterwards by user, the parts that have not started by that date are not displayed, the ones that under construction are displayed in red, and the ones completed by that date are displayed in blue. If the date in changed automatically with a certain interval, the process progress would be animated as shown in Figure 7. The resource list is shown on a tab. Click the other tabs to view other information such as the work progress, cost, and the materials list, as shown in Figure 8. The scene can be changed either by the gradation of the display colors or by the material attribute. When the tab is set at materials list, the parts and the material can be linked with the same operation as that used for liking parts and a task.

4. DISCUSSION

The proposed system can currently import model data and schedule data, visualize them and create an animation according to the process plan with materials if the library is well organized, and display cost accumulation related to work progress. The construction status along the time axis can visually be confirmed. All processes from beginning of construction to the end are able to

Figure 5. Selection of a table (left) and fields (right)

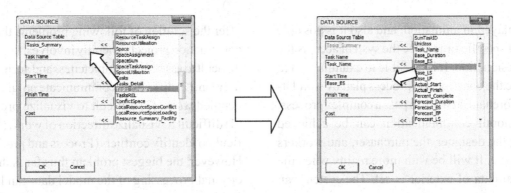

Figure 6. Linking of layer and activity

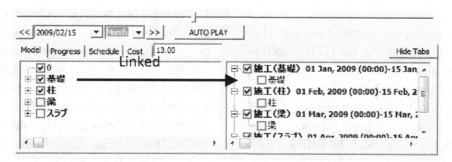

Figure 7. Animation of construction progress

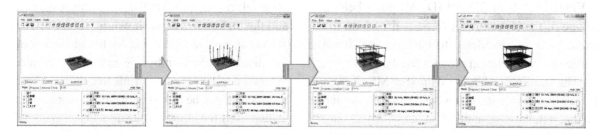

Figure 8. Changing tab to show cumulative cost (left) and work progress (right)

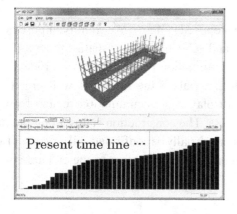 

be displayed in animation, and also it is possible to do at specific time since the system accepts the time designation. It is possible to examine and to analyze the construction process plan by simulating beforehand at work to pass a complex process, and smooth communication can be achieved among the designer, the purchaser, and workers on the site. It will be with more reality when the material data of exterior is set. The system can

offer the solution of following problems that any construction project generally involves, that is, (1) difficult to assess the completeness and accuracy of the plan, (2) difficult to communicate progress and detailed work, (3) difficult to visualize progress, (4) difficult to visualize direction of work, (5) difficult to identify conflicts (Process and products). However, the biggest problem thus far is that the original processing of the model data can hardly support all the elements that the DXF format defines. The proposed system renders only a few types of shapes as of now. Taking advantage of a third-party SDK for DXF, e.g., Open Design Alliance's OpenDWG (http://www.opendwg.org/), is probably a realistic choice. A material library is also important to make the model realistic, but this requires considerable work.

As a further work, we plan to implement a function that can visualize temporarily used heavy vehicles in the scene in order to examine their movements and to examine where the building materials are stored and how and where they are carried. The given MS-Project data usually contains such information. We aim to derive the benefits of 4D CAD using resource files that are generally used at a production site.

5. REFERENCES

Dawood, N., Scott, D., Hobbs, B., & Mallasi, Z. (2005). The virtual construction site (VIRCON) tools: An industrial evaluation. *ITcon, 10*.

Dawood, N., Sriprasert, E., Mallasi, Z., & Hobbs, B. (2001). Development of an integrated information resource base for 4D/VR construction process simulation & visualization. *Proceedings of CONVR 2001*.

Dawood, N., Sriprasert, E., Mallasi, Z., & Hobbs, B. (2002). 4D visualisation development: Real life case studies. *Proceedings of CIB W78 Conference*.

Japan Civil Engineering Consultants Association. (2008). *Readers of product model*.

Kang, L. S., & Jee, S. B. (2006). 4D system for visualizing schedule progress of horizontal construction project including earthwork. *Proceedings of CONVR 2006*.

Kano, N. (2009). Construction simulation trend. *Japan Construction Method and Machinery Research Institute, 708*, 18–24.

Kano, N., Hosoda, M., Kagawa, Y., Tamura, N., & Miyamoto, T. (2003). Virtual construction site-visualized simulation for construction sites. *Proceedings of 19th Symposium on Construction and Production*, (pp. 95-102).

Kano, N., Yao, T., & Hosoda, M. (2002). Virtual construction site-development of a prototype system and the issues. *Proceedings of 18th Symposium on Construction and Production*, (pp. 67-72).

Kawanai, Y. (2005). *The present position of product model*. 7th Workshop of Japan Construction Information Center.

Nagao, M., Fukushima, K., Sone, H., Fujii, Y., Matsuba, Y., & Tsunakawa, T. (2005). Cost estimate and possibility of cost control due to production design-using 3D-CAD in production design. *Journal of Architecture and Building Science, 21*, 373–377.

Vries, B., & Harink, M. J. J. (2007). Generation of a construction planning from a 3D CAD model. *Automation in Construction, 16*, 13–18. doi:10.1016/j.autcon.2005.10.010

Yabuki, N., & Makane, K. (2005). Product model and 3D/4D CAD. *Proceedings of Japanese Society of Civil Engineers, 90*(5), 23–25.

Yabuki, N., & Shitani, T. (2005). Development and application of a three dimensional product model for prestressed concrete bridges. *Proceedings of Japanese Society of Civil Engineers, 784*, 171–187.

Chapter 3
Advances in Privacy Preserving Record Linkage

Alexandros Karakasidis
University of Thessaly, Greece

Vassilios S. Verykios
University of Thessaly, Greece

ABSTRACT

The contemporary era is characterized by a high degree of involvement of computers harvesting data in various aspects of everyday life. Merging these data would provide numerous benefits in various fields, such as in the field of medical research, where new patterns for diseases could be established. However, this is not a trivial task, since among other reasons, separate data holders maintain data corresponding to the same real world entities without necessarily maintaining common and unique linkage identifiers. Additionally, these data may contain errors, rendering the integration process very difficult. The aforementioned reasons encountered during merging data from heterogeneous sources comprise some important aspects of the classical linkage problem.

However, even though many solutions have been proposed towards addressing this problem, a new side effect rises regarding the privacy of the data which usually has to be protected during linkage. Sensitive information such as names, addresses, and illnesses, especially in cases of medical data, should not be revealed without further evidence to any participant of the merging procedure. This raises the need of creating new techniques for linking data while, at the same time, the privacy of the subjects described by these data is preserved. This need led to the evolvement of a new research area called privacy preserving record linkage. This chapter will attempt to present the state of the art of the methods proposed to address the privacy preserving record linkage problem and provide a taxonomy of these techniques based on their core characteristics.

DOI: 10.4018/978-1-61520-871-5.ch003

1 INTRODUCTION

Nowadays, both public and private organizations maintain databases consisting of information for every one of us. Very often these organizations need to integrate these data. The reasons for such an action may vary from scientific purposes to performing market surveys. In any case, however, the privacy of the individuals described by these data should not be compromised.

An important field of application of data integration concerns the sector of public health and safety. Gathering information for medical research would have as a result to facilitate research towards establishing patterns for diseases. Moreover, being able to combine all this independent information could lead to the creation of a public safety early warning system as Clifton et al. (Clifton et al., 2004) and Bhowmick et al. (Bhowmick, et.al, 2006) describe. The ability of building such a system would also be useful as a component for other systems for conducting surveys either for commercial or scientific reasons.

Very often, companies need to merge their data in order to redefine their marketing policies. In such a situation, the matching parties may not wish to reveal their databases to each other for competitive reasons. Additionally, customer information should not be freely exchanged since this is considered as a privacy violation. All these aspects comprise part of a hot problem known as privacy preserving record linkage.

It would be useful to distinguish the difference between private record linkage and private data mining. While in private record linkage the aim is to obfuscate data maintaining at the same time their usability in order to perform data integration, in private data mining the aim is to preserve privacy of personal information during the data mining process (Verykios et al., 2004). In other words, privacy preserving record linkage is a step prior to privacy preserving data mining.

At this point we would like to recommend for the novice reader for this domain, fundamental works concerning both the classical and the private record linkage field. More specifically, considering the classical record linkage problem we suggest the works of Herzog et al. (Herzog et al., 2007) and Elmagarmid et al. (Elmagarmid et al., 2007). We also suggest the work of Christen (Christen, 2008) which contains details regarding Febrl, a record linkage toolbox. Concerning the private record linkage field, the interested reader should consider the works of Clifton et al. (Clifton et al., 2004), Du et al. (Du et al., 2000) and Kantarcioglou et al. (Kantarcioglu et al., 2008).

2 BACKGROUND

To introduce the reader to the problem of privacy preserving record linkage, we will provide in this section some elementary materials regarding the issues which need to be addressed for its viable solution.

2.1 Preliminaries

Let us take a first look at the challenges involved in addressing the privacy preserving record linkage problem. First of all, identically to the classical record linkage problem, the databases that are going to be integrated do not share common primary keys. Therefore specific steps regarding linkage keys to be selected have to be employed as described in (Trepetin, 2008).

Record linkage is the process of identifying the same real world entity in two or more separate databases. The first problem rising in such a situation is that these databases do not have the same primary keys, a fact that forces us to examine other ways for joining. First of all, unique linkage identifiers may be used such as the SSN. Since there might be errors or formatting discrepancies between the matching databases, these identifiers could be examined for similarity used some predefined metric, able to assess if they refer to the same real world entities.

The absence of such identifiers leads us to our second option of comparing combinations of non-unique linkage identifiers. Such values include name, city address, etc. are descriptive for a real world entity when combined together, but when they are solely used may be common to many database entries. Finally, the last option dictates testing between non-unique variables allows the assessment of matching accuracy the linkage system may achieve.

It is self evident that when using low quality identifiers for integration purposes, data quality issues are very likely to be encountered. The most common problems involve mistypings which may occur in any kind of field, misspellings usually within string fields as names and addresses, false age calculations or zip codes in numeric fields and so on. Therefore the methods used for such a task should be able to dirty data for identifying same entities.

However, all these techniques assume that all matching parties have access to all data, in order to assess similarities. This means that organizations involved in the linkage process should exchange plain text information, leading any attempt towards data integration to privacy breaches raising not only ethical but also legal issues: certain legislation, such as the EU Data Privacy Directive, render each company responsible for maintaining the privacy of its stored data and any evident leaking might lead the data holder to face prosecution. For all these purposes mentioned before, it is self evident that performing data linkage while preserving privacy is an important problem that needs to be taken seriously into consideration.

2.2 Problem Definition

Being more formal, we could say that privacy preserving record linkage is the problem where two data holders wish to integrate their data in a way that the only extra information gained by each party will exclusively concern matching records.

No information should be revealed to the opposite data holder regarding non matching records.

However this is not a trivial task to achieve. While information has to be hidden from the opposite matching participant, data used for linkage should still be usable and exhibit high quality. By simply enciphering identifiers may ensure security but will not provide for performing approximate matching. In a similar context, when matching is performed, the amount of information participants reveal to each other should be minimal. As less information as possible should be revealed between the parties in order to perform privacy preserving record linkage. Finally, matching cost is another important factor in a private record linkage framework. The methods developed will be applicable to large volumes of data requiring therefore minimal computational time and resources.

In general, the big picture of the private record linkage process is illustrated in Figure 1. Initially, the databases wishing to merge their records perform standardization of individual records in order for these record to obtain similar characteristics. Next, sensitive data within records are transformed or encrypted in order to be deidentified. After deidentification takes place, the records of the matching parties are either delivered to a trusted third party to perform the matching or they are exchanged, for comparison to take place using certain comparison functions. These comparison functions while not being aware of the actual data, they should be able to determine the matching status of each deidentified pair of records. Finally, the comparison results are returned to the matching parties for evaluation.

3 TAXONOMY AND EVALUATION METRICS

At this point we provide to the reader some information concerning the core characteristics of private record linkage approaches and criteria

Figure 1. Private record linkage process

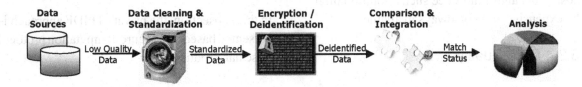

based on them in order to evaluate the behavior of each algorithm.

3.1 Taxonomy

To better understand the characteristics of the proposed methods we will categorize them based on their core characteristics. In specific, we can divide the methods proposed for solving this problem into two main categories. The first category consists of solutions that solely focus on matching fields. These can be characterized as privacy preserving string matching algorithms. The second category comprises of methods which aim at providing a solution at the problem itself. These solutions can be characterized as privacy preserving record matching approaches

Regarding the way matching is achieved in a privacy preserving context; we separate linkage methods presented in this chapter in four categories. In the first category fall the methods which perform linkage by simply comparing hashes. The second category comprises of methods in which comparing occurs by means of string tokens. The third category consists of methods which use scalar products for computing similarities. Finally, in the fourth category we present a statistical method where merging is provided by means of phonetic codes.

3.2 Evaluation Metrics

In order to examine the methods proposed for addressing the private linkage problem we will use some assessment criteria common for all the matching algorithms presented.

3.2.1 Security

The first and most important criterion to be evaluated is the security a record linkage algorithm provides. According to the security model assumed in each case an analysis follows trying to examine what privacy is maintained by each method.

3.2.2 Information Leakage

A similar evaluation parameter is information leakage. This term refers to amount of information revealed by the matching parties in order for the algorithm to operate properly. The difference between information leakage and security is that a security issue refers to algorithmic flaws, while information leakage is required by the algorithm in order to function. A typical example occurs with algorithms which assume that both matching parties have agreed in advance over the matching keys or schemas.

3.2.3 Cost

The need for private record linkage usually occurs between large organizations holding millions of records. As such, the time and space required for an operation of this size are critical. The developed algorithms should be both time and space efficient. However, these are not the only parameters affecting the operational cost. Sometimes, a third party has to be employed in order for the algorithm to operate properly. This is a factor that increases the cost of the algorithm since such a solution might be expensive and not always available.

3.2.4 Data Quality

One of the most important problems with the large amount of data available for linkage concerns their quality. Since linkage is performed among heterogeneous databases, it is obvious that the two matching parties will not share common primary keys. Moreover, it is highly unlikely that unique identifiers (like SSN) exist in both parties. Therefore, fields as name and surname have to be used, increasing the possibility of false mismatch due to errors such as mistypings, abbreviations etc. This renders the ability of performing approximate matching crucial for such an application.

3.2.5 Field Matching Issues

Since linkage is performed over various types of fields, it is interesting to examine the ability of each algorithm to hide sensitive data of any type. In specific, some algorithms are aimed exclusively towards private string matching, while others may require the ability to form hierarchies in order to perturb values.

4 MATCHING ALGORITHMS

In this section we present current state of the art in the field of private record linkage. Current work is categorized using the taxonomy earlier provided.

4.1 Field Matching Techniques

Developed field matching techniques mainly focus on matching individual fields. In this section we will present approaches aiming towards this direction.

4.1.1 Scalar Based Solutions

In this subsection, the private TFIDF approach is presented based on a secure computation protocol of scalar products.

4.1.1.1 Secure String Distance Metrics

Ravikumar et al. (Ravikumar et al., 2004) suggest in their approach ways of providing privacy to string distance metrics, specifically TFIDF and Euclidean distance by relaying computations on secure distance protocols. In the case of TFIDF the authors assign the computation to a calculation secure scalar product protocol. However, in such a situation, both matching parties should either share frequency statistics concerning common words or private approximate frequency statistics. Considering the case of Euclidean Distance, the problem is expressed as the calculation of a scalar product of two vectors which is proven to depend on a secure set intersection protocol.

The suggestion of Ravikumar et al. is interesting since instead of creating a new privacy aimed metric, they try to add privacy to well known ones with broad applicability in approximate matching. Moreover, regarding the transformations described, neither algorithm demands excessive space or computational time. In terms of security both presented approaches rely on SMC protocols rendering them secure.

However the use of an SMC layer for achieving privacy makes the whole protocol dependable on the algorithm to be chosen to implement computational functionality securely, mainly in terms of computational cost. Moreover, some privacy issues may be posed regardless of the SMC layer posed. Considering the TFIDF metric alteration, in the case of using a common statistics list, the question posed is how to create this common list from the two parties without revealing sensitive information. In the other alternative suggested, where each party maintains a separate frequency list, the weight calculation might be inaccurate. Additionally, extra information has to be revealed between parties during the phase where they agree on the fields they will use as linkage keys, a procedure which is independent of the underlying SMC protocols.

4.1.2 Token Based Solutions

The token based solution hosted in this subsection benefits by combining a token based approach with a broadly used hashing scheme.

4.1.2.1 Bloom Filters with Bigrams

Schnell et al. (Schnell et al., 2009) have used Bloom Filters in their approach which they combine with n-grams to take advantage of their approximate matching properties. In specific, each of the matching parties constructs a BF for each linkage key and inserts the corresponding bigrams. The matching parties then exchange the filters they created and perform a binary AND operation with their own. Finally a similarity score is calculated using the Dice coefficient based on the number of common bits of each participant's Bloom Filter.

The method proposed by Schnell et al. combines the security offered by Bloom Filters when used with a secure hash function with the agility of using bigrams for approximate matching. Their approach manages to exhibit security and approximate matching properties. Moreover, this method is neither space nor computationally intensive, rendering it applicable to real world conditions.

On the other hand, due to the use of bigrams, this method is aimed exclusively towards string fields. The use of identifiers such as age cannot benefit from such an approach. Finally, as with many algorithms described in this chapter, this approach require that there is a prior agreement made by the participants regarding their schemas, leading them to reveal information to each other over the structure of each one's database.

4.2 Record Matching Techniques

Record matching techniques do not only focus on linking fields. Their aim is to provide means for matching entire rows in a privacy preserving manner.

4.2.1 Hash Based Solutions

In this subsection we present approaches based on the comparison of hashed values.

4.2.1.1 Hybrid Scheme

In their work, Inan et al. (Inan et al., 2008) propose the use of a hybrid scheme for record linkage. Their approach combines blocking for reducing candidate pairs and secure multi party computation methods for calculating field similarities. In specific, this protocol assumes three parties: two data holders who hold the linkage data and a querying participant who also performs the matching. Initially value generalization hierarchies (VGH) are constructed at each party to form categories. These categories are both used to deidentify data and for blocking based on their generalized values. This way non matching candidate pairs are eliminated. Considering fields that cannot be blocked, the protocol performs an SMC step. For instance, for securely calculating the Euclidean distance between two fields the authors suggest the use of homomorphic encryption.

This approach manages to perform approximate matching both due to the generalization scheme used in the blocking step of the protocol and due to the multiparty computation performed at the next step. These two approaches also provide for security in the proposed method and are applicable to any type of matching field.

The blocking step reduces the matching cost by eliminating the candidate pairs. This however can be useful only in cases where the linkage fields can form hierarchies. In other case, the cost is equal to the SMC protocol used. This protocol assumes the existence of three parties, something which is not always applicable to real world applications. Finally, the two databases have to agree on the hierarchies to be used for anonymization, thus revealing information to each other about each ones internal structure.

4.2.1.2 Private Multiparty Matching

Lai et al. (Lai et al., 2006) have used Bloom Filters for achieving private matching in a multiparty setting. Bloom Filters (BF) are data structures with a wide field of applications. As such, research in privacy preserving record linkage has used them a means of privacy assurance.

They suggest in their approach a secure multiparty computation protocol in which, each party inserts all its records into a BF. Afterwards, each participant partitions its own BF and sends a segment to the other participants of the protocol. Then, the received segments are ANDed and finally, the partial results are exchanged. Each record is then checked against the BF. If the membership test is successful, it is considered to be matching.

This protocol differs from the others in the sense that the computation is totally distributed. The use of the Bloom Filters itself and the fact that each party retrieves only parts of the other participants are factors which assure privacy. This method can be applied to any type of field since entire records are encoded. Regarding its cost it is low, since the creation of a BF is a quite fast procedure and the comparisons are carried out using bitwise operators.

However, this fact mandates that all of the linkage parties have identical schemas. Moreover, it is obvious that such an approach is very sensitive to data with low quality and unable to perform approximate matching.

4.2.1.3 Hash Pseudonyms

Van Eycken et al. (Van Eycken et al., 2000) propose the creation of a single hash pseudonym for maintaining privacy. Their approach suggests that both parties will merge the linkage identifiers, such as name, address, birth date, SSN in order

to create a single string. Then, this string will be hashed using a secure hash function creating a temporary hash pseudonym. The hashed pseudonym is hashed again using a public key encryption algorithm in order to prevent malicious users performing dictionary attacks by combining fields and hashing them using the secure hash function.

This scheme is secure since no information will be revealed to either site regarding the complete dataset and an eavesdropper cannot easily infer information due to the double hashing scheme. Moreover, it is cost effective, since for each set of linkage keys each site has to perform only two encryptions: one for the pseudonym hash and one with the public key encryption algorithm. Additionally, this method allows for any type of identifier to be encoded and used for linkage.

However, this method suffers from some drawbacks. First of all, this approach does not allow for approximate matching. Since secure hashing algorithms are very sensitive, a single alteration in a field (e.g. name mistyping) will lead to a totally different hash pseudonym, making the whole method very sensitive to field errors. Finally, the participating organizations have to reveal information regarding the schemas of their databases, in order to achieve common formats for the fields to merge. Since birth dates for instance, might be stored in a variety of ways, the participants should agree beforehand in a common way of representing the keys to be used for creating the pseudonym.

4.2.1.4 Enciphered Permutations

The approach of Song et al., (Song et al., 2000) takes into consideration the problem of approximate matching. They suggest that various permutations of the linkage identifier should be computed and then each of them encrypted. Thus, during the linkage procedure if an encrypted identifier matches one of the encrypted permutations, then there is a match since the permutation occurred due to a typographical error.

The advantages of this method include security and the ability to perform approximate matching. A secure hash function is used to encipher the identifier permutations exploiting again the fact that even with a minor identifier alteration a secure hashing algorithm will produce a totally different hash. Approximate matching is achieved by computing the permutations of the identifiers. This method mainly applies to string linkage keys. Identifiers such as SSNs may also be used successfully.

The main drawback of this method is that it is practically impossible to predict and precompute all kind of different errors that might occur within a matching field. However, even if it was possible to predict all possible permutations, the computational cost would be huge regarding real world applications where thousands of records have to be linked. Regarding the information that has to be revealed in order for the protocol to operate, again both parties have to exchange schema information in order to adapt their fields. This step is necessary since there is no assurance that linkage fields will contain the same level of information.

4.2.1.5 Precomputed Scores

Du et al. (Du et al., 2000) suggest a similar solution for securely answering approximate queries. According to their proposal, all comparison results between linkage identifiers should be precomputed. In specific, when the linkage field is a high quality identifier such as the SSN which ranges from 0000000000 to 9999999999, a matrix consisting of 10^{10} positions has to be used. Considering the case of alphanumeric fields such as *name*, the approach is similar: all possible permutations are precomputed and each of them is enciphered. Again, a table is created and for each cipher combination a score is assigned which indicates the similarity of the unencrypted permutation. The authors also discuss in their work various aspects regarding the setup of such a protocol.

Such an approach achieves to perform approximate matching for both textual and numerical fields. However, as Trepetin indicates in his survey,

this approach features major drawbacks limiting its applicability to cases featuring identifiers with limited range of values. First of all, an unrealizable amount of storage is required if all of the linkage keys were to be stored even for a single alphanumeric field such as a surname. Second, despite the use of cryptographic functions, Trepetin shows that this approach is not so secure. In specific depending on the way the comparison matrix is created, this method is susceptible to Known Plain Text attacks. Also in this case, information has to be revealed between the linkage participants regarding database schema information in order to establish common linkage identifiers.

4.2.2 Scalar Based Solutions

In this subsection we present approaches that have as common ground the use of scalar products for assessing matching similarity.

4.2.2.1 Blocking Aware Linkage

The work presented by Al Lawati et al. (Al Lawati et al., 2005) introduces a secure blocking method for achieving high performance private record linkage. For string comparisons, the authors adopt the method also used by Ravikumar et al. (Ravikumar et al., 2004) for secure TFIDF distance computations using secure hash signatures and employing a third party for the matching process. In their work, three blocking methods are explored, all of which use the token blocking scheme and the Jaccard metric for comparing binary values of the hash signatures. The first approach, called simple blocking, is the most efficient in terms of privacy. To perform simple blocking the matching parties arrange their records in blocks, encrypt them with signatures and deliver them to the matching party for integration. The second method called record-aware blocking aims at further increasing matching performance. In this method the record id is coupled with the hash signature. In the third approach presented, frugal third party blocking, the candidate matching records are computed without the intervention of the third party using a secure set intersection protocol. The reason for this is to reduce the cost of transferring entire datasets to the third party.

This work is comparable to the approach of Ravikumar et al. in terms of security, cost and ability of approximate matching, since they both use the TFIDF distance metric for linkage key comparison. The introduction of blocking techniques reduces the linkage cost. The alternatives presented provide a tradeoff between privacy and cost, according to the analysis provided by the authors. According to it, the lowest information leakage occurs when no blocking is used, while the highest in the record-aware case. Additionally the need of a third party for the linkage process also increases the cost while the absence of a schema matching technique also provides for information leakage between the two matching parties.

4.2.2.2 Embedding Spaces
Scannapieco et al. (Scannapieco et al., 2007) presented a privacy preserving protocol which performs approximate matching on data. Their approach also offers schema privacy. In their approach Scannapieco et al. transform their records into a metric space while preserving the distances between record values. For this purpose the SparseMap method was employed since it features secure characteristics. Their method can be summarized as follows. The two matching parties agree on a distance function to be used and one of them generates a set of random strings which shares it with the other. Data from each source are embedded into the metric space using the agreed distance function forming vectors. These new data structures are finally sent to the third party to perform the comparison. To achieve secure schema matching, Scannapieco et al. assume that the third party, also used for data matching, holds a global schema. The schemas of each matching party are then mapped to the global schema.

This approach is the most complete regarding the criteria set at the beginning of this chapter.

It manages to maintain privacy for both data and schema without revealing any information. It does not require high computational costs or massive storage spaces making it efficient for large datasets. It performs approximate matching since a distance function is used to compare the linkage identifier. All these features however come at a cost: the need to employ a third party for performing comparisons and for holding the intermediate schema information.

4.2.2.3 Complex Plain Linkage
Yakout et al. (Yakout et al., 2009) present an approach based on the one introduced by Scannapieco et al. (Scannapieco et al., 2007). The proposed method uses Scannapieco's vector representation of data, but does not require the presence of a third party for performing private linkage. Again, the matching keys are encoded to vectors. This time however, complex numbers are calculated to create a plain within which a blocking algorithm is used to provide candidate pairs. To achieve this, they author consider an adjustable width moving slub within a complex plain. The complex numbers that fall within the slub's area are considered to be likely matched. Finally, the actually matching pairs are computed using a scalar product protocol based on randomized vectors. Their protocol relies on a security parameter which reflects on the amount of computed hyperplane to reveal. The authors adopted this approach in order to avoid expensive cryptographic computations.

This protocol is actually an improvement of the embedding spaces approach introduced by Scannapieco et al. It features the same characteristics, such as the ability for approximate matching, but overcoming the need for a third party for comparing the computed vectors. Regarding the security offer, the matching parties in the scheme of Yakout et al. reveal some of the private information to each due to the scalar product computation protocol. However the amount of this information can be controlled by adjusting the size of the security parameter earlier described.

4.2.3 Token Based Solutions

In this subsection we present methods which use tokens and specifically n-grams for assessing the similarity in a privacy preserving environment.

4.2.3.1 Dice Coefficient Deidentification

The approach suggested by Churches et al. (Churches et al., 2004) indicates the use of a scheme which combines hashing with powersets of bigrams. Bigrams are overlapping substrings of size two of a given word. According to their approach, for a given identifier a sorted list like structure is created initially consisting of a single bigram belonging to the word to be used as a linkage identifier, ending with all the bigrams comprising the word. Each list element is hashed in order to be deidentified, while extra information is maintained in order to be used in the comparison functions: the number of bigrams contained in the hash and the number of total bigrams comprising the original identifier. When it comes to comparing records, all matching hash values are examined, and using the extra information held the dice coefficient is calculated to produce a similarity score.

This n-gram based method manages to achieve approximate matching during linkage procedure. Also, its cost is not significantly high, especially compared to the enciphered permutations and the precomputed scores method. An evaluation regarding the cost of this method can be found in (Verykios et al., 2009). Moreover, it is obvious that this method is aimed towards string comparisons, since splitting a number e.g. the age of a person into bigrams does not offer anything to the linkage procedure. However, the main weak point of this approach is security.

First of all, similarly to the previous cases, the matching parties have to reveal to each other the schemas of the databases and the contents of each field in order to agree on the linkage keys to be used. Moreover, the extra information maintained by each powerset which is publicly available may partially reveal information about the enciphered

identifier. As Trepetin indicates, this may be easily achieved using frequency analysis of the most common bigrams of the English language.

4.2.4 Phonetics Based Solutions

Herein we present a method which takes advantage of phonetic codes for performing linkage operations while preserving privacy at the same time.

4.2.4.1 Private Phonetic Codes

Karakasidis et al. (Karakasidis et al., 2009) propose in their work a scheme using phonetic codes. Data holders encode their linkage identifiers using phonetic codes. Next they generate random phonetic codes and mix them with the ones form the actual dataset. Then, they send their data to a third party which performs matching based on the phonetic codes. The matching results are returned to the participants. Then participants sent to each other the matching records.

The proposed approach is secure, since neither of the data holders is aware of the other party's data and the third party does not know which of the data sent reflect original values. Moreover, since phonetic codes diminish the dimensions of the encoded data, they do not exhibit the one to one property making them suitable for privacy aware applications. The cost of the protocol is low, since phonetic algorithms are very fast. Approximate matching is achieved since using phonetic codes may address in many cases typographical and spelling errors.

However the existence of a third party may pose some difficulties in some applications since such a setup might not always be available. Moreover, phonetic codes are not suitable for numerical values, making this approach unsuitable for linking numbers. Finally, again, the two parties should have pre agreed on the fields on which matching will be performed.

5 OTHER ISSUES

In this section we discuss issues very closely related to private record linkage. In specific we present work that has been made regarding blocking and private schema matching.

5.1 Private Blocking

Consider our usual scenario where two organizations one holding m records and the other holding n records wish to integrate their data. Since there are no common linkage keys, linkage will be performed over k matching keys. Instantly this rises the amount of comparisons to be performed to $k*m*n$. It is obvious that it is very expensive to exhaustively compare all candidate pairs. Therefore there is the need to quickly eliminate pairs that are not likely to match. Blocking is the process of eliminating candidate pairs before proceeding to the linkage procedure.

In the case of private matching, we are specifically interested in private blocking, where less likely candidate pairs will be pruned but without revealing information concerning actual data. Currently, two methods have been proposed towards this direction. The first one by Inan et al. (Inan et al., 2008) suggests the use of hierarchies for reducing the cost of the SMC protocol used for their linkage method. While this method manages to reduce the cost, the nature of the data used should be suitable for forming hierarchies. The second one suggested by Al-Lawati et al. (Al Lawati et al., 2005) proposes various levels of blocking in exchange of privacy. In this case, in order to achieve efficiency, privacy should be compromised. It is evident that research within this field is not over yet towards achieving a privacy preserving blocking scheme.

5.2 Private Schema Matching

Most of the methods presented in this chapter assume that the linkage participants have agreed on using the same schema. However in real world applications this rarely is the case. Usually, both parties have different schemas meaning that even in the case of private record linkage information has to be revealed regarding the schema and the size of the databases. In certain circumstances however this is not the desired solution, for example when rival companies wish to exchange data.

Thus, attempts were made to achieve private schema matching. This case differs from the classical problem of schema integration in the sense that no information has to be revealed to either of the parties. The only available solution towards this direction was suggested by Scannapieco et al. (Scannapieco et al., 2007) and Cruz et al. (Cruz et al., 2007). They both propose the use of a global schema where the schema of each party's database will be mapped. Despite this approach, it is evident that private schema matching remains an open problem.

6 CONCLUSION

In this chapter we tried to present the state of the art regarding privacy preserving record linkage. The attempts made to solve the problem have tried to address it suggesting solutions combining techniques from various domains. The techniques presented in this chapter range from classical record linkage methods enhanced by SMC protocols for presenting privacy, to custom solutions developed specific for this problem. While there has been some advance regarding approximate private matching there are still issues to be resolved such as the absence of robust techniques to provide private blocking and private schema matching. As such, there is not yet available a viable solution well applicable to real world conditions which will successfully address all of the problem's major aspects such as security, efficiency and data quality.

REFERENCES

Al-Lawati, A., Lee, D., & McDaniel, P. (2005). *Blocking-aware private record linkage*. IQIS 2005, International Workshop on Information Quality in Information Systems, 17 June 2005, Baltimore, Maryland, USA (SIGMOD 2005 Workshop)

Bhowmick, S. S., Gruenwald, L., Iwaihara, M., & Chatvichienchai, S. (2006). Private-iye: A framework for privacy preserving data integration. In ICDEW '06: *Proceedings of the 22nd International Conference on Data Engineering Workshops* (ICDEW'06), Washington, DC: IEEE Computer Society.

Christen, P. (2008). Febrl: An open source data cleaning, de-duplication and record linkage system with a graphical user interface. *KDD, 2008,* 1065–1068.

Churches, T., & Christen, P. (2004). Blind data linkage using n-gram similarity comparisons. *PAKDD, 2004,* 121–126.

Clifton, C., Kantarcioğlu, M., Doan, A., Schadow, G., Vaidya, J., Elmagarmid, A., & Suciu, D. (2004). Privacy-preserving data integration and sharing. In DMKD '04: *Proceedings of the 9th ACM SIGMOD Workshop on Research Issues in Data Mining and Knowledge Discovery*, (pp. 19-26). New York, NY: ACM.

Cruz, I. F., Tamassia, R., & Yao, D. (2007). Privacy-preserving schema matching using mutual information. In *Proceedings of the 21th Annual IFIP WG 11.3 Working Conference on Data and Applications Security* (DBSec '07). Redondo Beach, CA. July 2007.

Du, W., & Atallah, M. (2000). *Protocols for secure remote database access with approximate matching*. 7th ACM Conference on Computer and Communications Security (ACMCCS 2000), The First Workshop on Security and Privacy in E-Commerce. November 2000, Athens.

Elmagarmid, A. K., Ipeirotis, P. G., & Verykios, V. S. (2007). Duplicate record detection: A survey. *IEEE Transactions on Knowledge and Data Engineering, 19*(1), 1–16. doi:10.1109/TKDE.2007.250581

Herzog, T. N., Scheuren, F. J., & Winkler, W. E. (2007). *Data quality and record linkage techniques*. Springer.

Inan, A., Kantarcioglu, M., Bertino, E., & Scannapieco, M. (2008). A hybrid approach to private record linkage. In *Proceedings of the 24th International Conference on Data Engineering*, 7–12 April 2008; Cancun, Mexico. (pp. 496-505). Los Alamitos, CA: IEEE.

Kantarcioglu, M., Jiang, W., & Malin, B. (2008). *A privacy-preserving framework for integrating person-specific databases*. Privacy in Statistical Databases Conference, (pp. 298-314).

Karakasidis, A., & Verykios, V. S. (2009). Privacy preserving record linkage using phonetic codes. In BCI '09: *Proceedings of the 4ᵗʰ Balkan Conference in Informatics*. Thessaloniki, Greece, 2009, (pp.101-106).

Lai, P. K. Y., Yiu, S. M, Chow, K. P., Chong, C. F., &Hui, L. C. K. (2006). An efficient Bloom filter based solution for multiparty private matching. *Security and Management*, 286-292

Ravikumar, P., Cohen, W., & Fienberg, S. E. (2004). *A secure protocol for computing string distance metrics*. WPSADM 2004.

Scannapieco, M., Figotin, I., Bertino, E., & Elmagarmid, A. K. (2007). Privacy preserving schema and data matching. In SIGMOD '07: *Proceedings of the 2007 ACM SIGMOD international conference on Management of data*. (pp. 653-664). New York, NY: ACM.

Schnell, R., Bachteler, T., & Reiher, J. (2009). Privacy-preserving record linkage using bloom filters. *BMC Medical Informatics and Decision Making, 9*(1), 41. doi:10.1186/1472-6947-9-41

Song, D.-X., Wagner, D., & Perrig, A. (2000). *Practical techniques for searches on encrypted data*. IEEE Symposium on Security and Privacy. Berkeley, CA, May 14–17, 2000.

Trepetin, S. (2008). Privacy-preserving string comparisons in record linkage systems: A review. *Information Security Journal: A Global Perspective, 17*, 253-266.

Van Eycken, E., Haustermans, K., Buntinx, F., Ceuppens, A., Weyler, J., & Wauters, E. (2000). Evaluation of the encryption procedure and record linkage in the Belgian National Cancer Registry. *Archives of Public Health, 58*, 281–294.

Verykios, V. S., Bertino, E., Fovino, I. N., Provenza, L. P., Saygin, Y., & Theodoridis, Y. (2004). State-of-the-art in privacy preserving data mining. *SIGMOD Record, 33*(1), 50–57. doi:10.1145/974121.974131

Verykios, V. S., Karakasidis, A., & Mitrogiannis, V. K. (2009). Privacy preserving record linkage approaches. *International Journal of Data Mining. Modelling and Management, 1*(2), 206–221.

Yakout, M., Atallah, M., & Elmagarmid, A. (2009). *Efficient private record linkage*. 2009 IEEE International Conference on Data Engineering, (pp. 1283-1286).

ADDITIONAL READING

Directive 95/46/ec of the European parliament and of the council of 24 October 1995 on the protection of individuals with regard to the processing of personal data and on the free movement of such data," Official Journal of the European Communities of 23, vol. L, no. 281, p. 31, November 1995.

Philip, S. (Ed.). (2008). *Aggarwal, Charu C.; Yu (Vol. 34)*. Privacy-Preserving Data Mining Models and Algorithms, Advances in Database Systems.

Chapter 4
Construction of Traceability System by Using Simple and Handy Type RFID Reader

Rei Itsuki
Hiroshima International University, Japan

ABSTRACT

This chapter picks up and explains some problems on system costs or specifications faced when trying to construct a traceability system by using RFID tags. The peripherals including RFID reader are even now expensive because it is not widespread in the market. Because of the sense of comparatively high price of the system cost and the dilemma to the specification, the impression that construction approach of the traceability system using RFID tags may be in the contemplation period is strong. This chapter shows these problems obtained from a market trend concerning the traceability in recent years and the result of reviews of the RFID tag applications or proof experiments. Next, the points of the future traceability system construction using these new technologies, especially about simple and handy type RFID reader using FPGA are described.

1. INTRODUCTION

In recent years, there are various actions to try to construct a traceability system by using the radio frequency identification (RFID) tag (Finkenzeller, 1999; Takaragi, et al., 2001), reflecting minia-

DOI: 10.4018/978-1-61520-871-5.ch004

turization, price-reduction and diversification of them. Establishment of automatic identification method itself have become very important problem and very popular in various application field, especially in case of supermarkets or traffic fee. In the supermarket, there are so many commercial products to calculate the total amount of purchase in a short time correctly. In the transportation system, there are so many stops or stations to calculate the fee in the same way. Barcode system is one of the most popular automatic identification methods in the world. Historically thinking, magnetic card system would have follow after that (Husemann, 1999). Surprisingly, RFID has also used in the application field from relatively early on, especially in a payment system. Cash card or credit card system has a need for strength for repeated use. In the field of traffic fee system, displacement from magnetic card to plastic car (RFID card) has pushed forward in a positive manner, because of security reasons, for examples, actions against counterfeiting or illegal train-ride. In the field of food distribution management system, the BSE problem (Dickinson & Bailey, 2002; Cyranoski, 2001) has been shocking and tragic news. There are many experimental or suitable traceability systems for practical use to emphasize the importance of securing food safety (opera, 2003).

In the process of the examination of these traceability system constructions, various problems in specifications or systems cost concerning RFID tag applications have become clear. For the cost of system construction, the price of RFID tag first is come up. Although RFID tag shows the tendency to miniaturize and to reduce the price (RFID news, 2003), the current state is tens of times in the price so far compared with the bar code widely used in the market.

Moreover, for peripherals equipments that include RFID readers, they are much expensive than that of barcode because it is not widespread in the market. In addition, the standstill feeling of the introduction examinations that aim at the standardization trend is also incontrovertible along with diversify of RFID tags. On the other hand, for the specification that assumes application to various application fields, there are a lot of dilemmas between the miniaturization, multi-functionalization or generalization of RFID tags and distance of call, price or implementation cost. Because of the reason why the sense of comparatively high price to system cost and the dilemma

to specifications, constructions of the traceability system that apply RFID tags are strongly in the impression of contemplation period.

This report first describes market trends concerning the traceability in recent years, results of review in RFID tag applications to various applications, and problems obtained from the result of the proof experiments. Next, a technical current tackling to these problems is described. In addition, it explains the method of constructing a simple, small reader using FPGA (Field Programmable Gate Array) (Estrin, et al., 2002) as a point of the future traceability system construction.

2. MARKET TREND IN TRACEABILITY

In recent years, the market highly pays attention to the traceability system (Cleland-Huang, et al., 2007). One of the reasons of this will be diversification of the commercial distribution market. Growing rate of Internet access around the world has accelerated the speed of unfettered spread of information. Consumers have been able to obtain much fresh information of commercial products and this accelerates the cycle speed from appearance of new products or services to popularization of them. The Internet has also accelerated the speed of globalization. Some commercial products have easily transported from country to country.

Laws pertaining to the collection, reutilization, and disposal of various products, such as industrial machinery, semiconductor materials, plastic articles, have been revised and the management of such products has intensified. In order to improve production efficiency, further reduce inventories and production shipping costs, and maintain and improve customer satisfaction, particularly in the fields of production and distribution, information management has intensified in the supply chain (SC), the business process that covers products from production to sale. When supply chain management (SCM) (Simchi-Levi, et al., 2003;

Lee & Billington, 1992; Pooler & Pooler, 1997) intensifies, production efficiency rises and large quantities of inexpensive products pour onto the market. On the other hand, once these products are used, how should they be collected, reutilized, and disposed of, and how should they be managed? This has become a major issue for the market and government. Furthermore, this trend is not limited to the usual machinery, semiconductors, and plastics but is intensifying for products such as food and livestock feed as well. The clear-cut management of the location of production, fertilizer and livestock feed being used, and distribution channel, in other words the improvement of traceability, is regarded as important (Itsuki, et al., 2003; Soga, et al., 1999).

According to the above market trend, there are various actions to try to construct the traceability system using the RFID tag. With RFID tags, data in tags can be read and written without contact. In the sense that they transfer data, they can also be called data carriers. Although non-contact IC technology, such as that of RFID tags, is relatively more expensive than bar code technology, it has been used for cargo tracking control in the field of logistics (Frazelle, 2001), because data reading and writing are rarely affected by a dirty or damaged surface and alignment accuracy is not required. Taking information management technology that employs these RFID tags and introducing it into the field of supply chain management is expected not only to make production activities more efficient and labor-saving but to be a highly significant step toward achieving a recycling-oriented society. Recently, with the aforementioned cost reductions, applications into a variety of fields in the general consumer market have been examined. The activity of Auto-ID Center that centered on M.I.T. (MIT) was succeeded to two groups. One is the EPC global (Traub, et al., 2005) that promotes technical activities and the other is the Auto-ID Lab (Schuster, et al., 2010) that promotes standardization activities. Especially, the latter tries the standardization of a series of activity of

doing efficient SCM by appending the RFID tag to the article in SC, and managing information on the article collectively at some centralized control centers. In Japan the Ubiquitous ID Center is aiming to identify items by machine, using a Ubiquitous ID Chip (an RFID chip containing a microcomputer) that controls and makes determinations (Sakamura, 2009).

It is said that "RFID meets the Internet" (Roussos, et al., 2009; Estrin, et al., 2002). Both the diffusion of small, low-cost, and higher-range passive RFID and the widely use of the Internet or Intranet have conduced to the situation. The diffusion of the Intranet has broken down barriers between the legacy system and the global system. Large-scale RFID application systems have been constructed to trace and track individual commercial products (Mo, et al., 2009). Especially, standardization systems like the EPC global Network have backed up the construction of large-scale system.

And, in order to accelerate the usability for taking much information of the individual products into the Internet or the traceability systems, wireless sensor network systems have been used together (Bose, 2009). The wireless sensor network uses various sensors corresponding to purpose and low power consumption wireless network. For the former technology, a low-cost, high performance, and small sensors have been manufactured by the development of the new technology like the MEMS (Micro Electro Mechanical System). On the other hand, for the latter technology, ZigBee (Wheeler, 2007) has become popular recently.

3. PROBLEMS IN CONSTRUCTING TRACEABILITY SYSTEM

Though a lot of various proof experiments using RFID tags have been conducted in the market as mentioned above, there are many systems which materialization for the real application are not advanced after the examination on paper and the experiment of proof. Then, taking the materialization examination of the traceability system as an example in this chapter, various problems for system cost of tag application system construction and for specifications are put in order.

3.1. Problems in RFID Tag Application Systems

(1) Specification of RFID Tag

A physical specification of the RFID tag is different in each vender and that the data format to be a key to article information managed by RCM is still different in each vender or each standardization promotion group although it has been expected as a new technology for the product information management. The application of the RFID tag has been remarkable from the production site as a medium to manage information on the product so far. A technical improvement and a further miniaturization concerning the RFID tag advance after the latter half of 1990's, and, consequently, it tends to the price cutting. The problem in application on the size and the cost side is being canceled and application to the management object of, for instance, a large amount of consumer goods management etc. from which application has been put off up to now is reexamined. In addition, as the range of the application examination spreads, comparatively cheap RFID tag has come to be equipped with the readout function or the rewriting function which is equipped with only expensive RFID tag up to now. Application of the RFID tag to the production site is paid attention as a medium to manage information of the product. However, there are some problems that united management cannot be done even if it is the same kind of product if same kind of RFID tag is not used because the specification is different under the present situation depending on the vender for the RFID tag, for instance, used frequency, built-in data, it's format, and addition functions like rewriting or multi readouts at same time, etc.

(2) Price of RFID Tag

The price of the RFID tag is still more expensive than that of the bar code in case that the RFID tag is located as a tool only to assign a number to the recycling objects or to relate traceability information that centers on circulation information to the number. Although how use the RFID tag is examined through various experimental proofs now, the price of the RFID tag is often considered as a bottle neck of system construction at the stage where the materialization of the system is examined after the experimental proof. Some application like the smart dust project will use huge number of RFID tags (Warneke, et al., 2001). In this project, tags' location itself is more important than the information of the article which the tag is attached.

(3) Specification of Reader/Writer

It is necessary to use a RFID reader/writer which reads tags ID information or writes necessary information to tags when RFID tag is used, as well as the case to use the bar code. There are many types of readers/writers, which are built-in type, hand-held portable data terminal type or built in device type by using the offered module. The variety of them is limited under the present situation compared with bar-code reader/writer, it is difficult to get one which is fit to the application. Differing from the bar code, RFID tag is expected as an interface to a familiar computing for general consumers in ubiquitous society, it is requested from the reader/writer to be more friendlier for the consumers. There are impossibilities for general consumers to carry about a current size reader of portable type and to confirm commercial farms in the supermarket. For instance, it is necessary to make an environment to be able to obtain a reader of the cellular phone or pedometer size easily.

(4) Cost of Reader/Writer

Not only reader/writer's specification but also the price is a big problem to be considered. Most of readers/writers are expensive enough which cost tens of thousands of yen-several hundred thousand yen or more under the present situation. It may be possible to assign comparatively expensive budget to readers/writers repeatedly used. However, if the prototype system cannot be constructed by obtaining readers/writers at a low price at the introduction examination stage, it may be difficult to develop the market quickly.

(5) Application Field

In the present state, there are not so many applications which bring out RFID tag merits enough. With the exception of some country-level applications, relatively-small number and size of applications are in practical use, for example, traffic fare card systems which treat money directly, important document management systems for compliance (Figure 1), bibliotheca management systems in a library for clear reduction of labor cost, and economic development project systems in a local area which doesn't need much development money, etc.

In Figure 1, First of all, those who browse important documents have to certify themselves by using their own name tags before they enter the document filing room. The RFID tag is mounted on their name tag, and they certify

Figure 1. Document management system

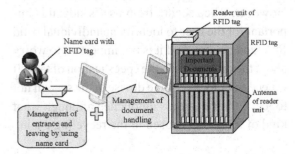

themselves by their ID in tags. The RFID reader and the antenna are mounted on the bookshelf where important documents are kept. RFID tags are mounted on each of the document or the document file kept on the inside of the room. These RFID tags correspond to anti-collision and close-range reading. For instance, 1 or 2 mm separated two tags can be read correctly. Therefore, the manager of the documents can verify and record which document and a document folder is in the bookshelf now in a short period of time. When a person gets out a certain document or document folder, the action is detected by the reader and the tag ID and the time of it are recorded with ID of the person's name tag. When the document is returned, the person's ID, ID of the document, and the return time are similarly recorded.

3.2. Problems in System Development

Here, the case where the traceability system is constructed by chiefly using RFID tags is assumed, and the problem in the system construction is concisely considered.

(1) Large Scale Distribution of Information Gathering Base

The first problem is that information gathering bases distribute on a large scale and therefore an enough information gathering from each base and unitary management of collected information are difficult. Especially, a lot of food shops exist because it has stuck to people's lives. The part of products is collected by the collection trader though the most part sold in the shop circulates to the general consumer home. It is difficult to manage all information from production to sales.

(2) Unifying the Information Management

The second problem is to give administrative information to a collected material to manage it when it is collected and in addition the information given first is succeeded to when the collection thing arranges in the process of the collection. The collected material is carried between two or more traders while it is collected and is re-processed, and ｡is soled in the collection route. It is indispensable to manage data in a comprehensive manner by relating individual collection information in the recycling chain for the relevant information to be managed through a series of recycling business.

(3) Unifying the System Management

The third task is to construct the SCM support system while adjusting participation person's interests in the supply chain. Originally, the retail shop should be correspondent to an administrative measure. However, it takes much time and cost when an individual shop's having individually responded. At the same time, it takes much time to consolidating these recycling data. On the other hand, when seeing from collection trader's side, they try to acquire a lot of shops even a little because doing a lot of collections leads to their profit improvement. It is easy to advance the shop acquisition if the collection trader enters with a certain incentives for the shop. Some collection traders are reporting on the collection amount data that the shop is originally sure to be managing. It takes much time and load for the collection trader to correspond to many shops. It is important to reduce the overall cost for SCM by facilitating correspondence to the legal system. In the independent construction of each recycling trader of the SCM support system, it costs an after all similar as for any trader a system construction cost and the load doesn't decrease. Moreover, it doesn't lead to the reduction of the load in individually corresponding for the legal system.

The mechanisms which extracts necessary data for the legal system from the managed collection data and which is able to refer necessary data in a view point of the administrative side are needed.

(4) Method of Attaching RFID Tags on Commodities

The fourth task is a managing and activating method of gathering data. The purpose of SCM here is to manage accurate collection data, and to use it to expand the business scale by the efficiency improvement of the recycling business. It is necessary to maintain the freshness of the collection material especially for food, to raise the commercial value of the recycling thing, and to give the consumer the sense of security on the other hand according to the accuracy of the SCM. The additional feature is necessary that not only maintains the collection data by the SCM support system but also totals the variable situation of freshness and the amount of the collection material from the collection data and presents.

(5) Uniting of Complex Marketing Channel and RFID Tag

The sixth task is a better use of the RFID tag that is the technology paid attention to in a current market. It is examined that RFID tag is attached to parts in the production process for the efficiency improvement of SCM, and is used to manage production information (Itsuki, et al., 2003). When the application of the RFID tag to SCM would advance in the future, various RFID tags with different specification will be used in the market. However, when seeing from user's side, it is important for the user to identify an individual solid for management, and it is not important to worry about the difference in the specification of tags. It is necessary to take some devise in the system not to leave their business untouched although what kind of RFID tag is used in the recycling chain.

4. TECHNICAL POINTS FOR TRACEABILITY SYSTEM CONSTRUCTION

This chapter describes the approach that will become needed or effective when thinking about the case to construct the traceability system by using electronic tag. It also describes especially in terms of RFID reader.

4.1 Approaches Involving End Users

In order to enlarge the RFID market, it is good to involve end users. Generally speaking, the market dimensions are enlarged when character of information, class of information, information system and persons involved are increased (Figure 2). In Figure 2, as the information and telecommunications technology upgrades, it comes to be able to transmit large quantities of data at higher speed in short time. As a result, it comes to be able to handle voice, still image, and animation. In addition to the past character base data, it comes to be able to use multimedia functions. Web system becomes more attractive for enterprises and users, and the number of users increases in a synergistic manner. Moreover, web

sites which handle information that crosses number of web sites, so-called "Web 2.0" or "Mush Up" have come out. When merchandise information handled on the Internet increases, a new style and more detailed marketing will become possible in a short time by logging the information.

In addition, when RFID tags or sensors are used together, it comes to be able to figure out not only static but also dynamic information of merchandises which the position and numeric information change actually hour by hour. It is a stage so-called "Internet of Things" (Roussos, et al., 2009). When the consuming public are involved in the market place by using a simple, inexpensive and small RFID reader (Figure 3), and they can retrieve information about commercial products they want. A handy type reader like a past bar-code reader has ten keys and the liquid crystal display. Numeric information can be input and be confirmed on site. But the size of the reader comparatively grows bigger and the price rises adhering to the high performance. When ten keys and the liquid crystal display are daringly omitted, a comparatively cheap, very small, and pocket size reader can be constructed with only the push-button for being possible to read RFID and the LED lamp for the confirmation of

Figure 2. Evolution step of information system

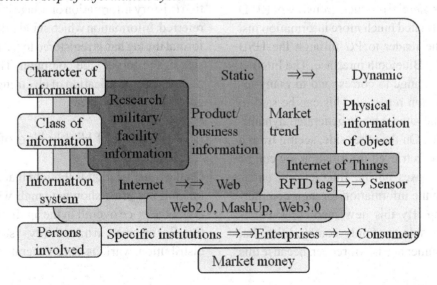

Figure 3. Simple and small RFID reader

Small RFID reader   Handy reader now

Figure 4. RFID oriented Web system

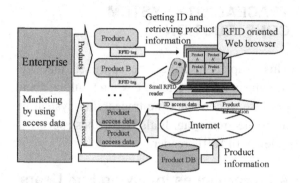

the reading operation in Figure 3. Of course, it is also possible to provide these functions for the cellular phone. However, it is easily thought the cellular phone will become large in size, and become expensive under the present situation. And easiness that general consumers can use will be lost.

Figure 4 shows a new web system image which is assumed to use the above-mentioned small reader. The consumers read tag IDs of RFID tag which is attached to commodities in the market to a small reader. For instance, a small leader might be able to connect it with the personal computer through the USB interface or the Bluetooth interface. Web a browser is installed in PC. The browser can multilaterally retrieve merchandise information which relates to a certain tag ID on the Internet. Users can be retrieve information of several commercial products from IDs of RFID tags and also related much more information just connecting the reader to PC through the USB interface or the Bluetooth interface. The Internet browser will change to correspond to many-to-many information retrieval. This can be said to be a new portal site which is generated dynamically in the PC. On the other side, seeing from a enterprise side, retrieved information log can be stored in databases on the Internet and enterprises can use the information for their commercial marketing. By this new marketing, enterprises will be able to supply commodities that match to consumer needs. Moreover, because this

becomes an advantage for the consumer, they will be able to reduce the precaution feeling to being recorded their commodity retrieving information except individual information on the Internet.

4.2 Approaches in Terms of RFID Tag

(1) Approach in Standardization Interface of RFID Tag

The specification of the RFID tag paid attention to in a current market is different depending on tag makers, and a lot of kinds of electronic tag exist. So, an on-line standardization interface of RFID tag seemed to be effective. By connecting with the management side computer or furthermore severs through the network, necessary information (history information or image information) is referred. Information which standard specification format the tag has is registered to the management side or the server side computer. The difference of physical specification of electronic tags can be absorbed on the system.

(2) Approach of Highly Use of RFID Tag

On the other hand, it is thought that the approach making tag price showing small when thinking about the price overall in the application is effective. For instance, in traceability system in the food distribution, various data generated by relating the quality data from the sensor function to ID information on electronic tag in the marketing channel is unitary managed by using RFID tag with some sensor function in Figure 5. In Figure 5, static recycle data like date, time, or etc. are stored in RFID tag or in database related to RFID tag ID. On the other side, dynamic data which is measured by using some sensors are stored in the database by relating it to tag ID. The price ratio of electronic tag is substantially reduced by assuming reference information managed on the computer side to be more additional value information based on ID information on electronic tag.

(3) Other Approaches

It is necessary to obtain critical mass of RFID tags easily and at a low price. For instance, the allocation administrative task of IP addresses for the Internet connection has been consigned to Internet service providers (ISPs). Following this example, a mechanism and traders who sell RFID tags that each vender manufactured to engineering enterprises, software houses or general consumers are necessary.

Figure 5. Utilization of RFID tag with sensor

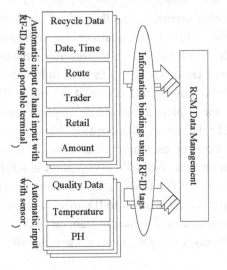

4.2. Approaches from Reader/ Writer's Viewpoint

(1) Approach for Familiar Reader/Writer Development

It only has to provide the function for RFID tag to bar-code reader/writer of a current image if thinking about a progressive replacement of the merchandise control by using bar code that has been used up to now, or fix use of reader/writer. However, if thinking about more convenient or more familiar purpose of use, it is better to think some mechanism which makes reader/writer with final use image easily by assembly style. It seems to be reasonable to design or develop RFID reader to combine with suitable antenna, program that materializes necessary minimum specification, programmable LSI that materializes it and interface necessary for the basic I/O. Though it is not easy to modify a reader module, it is possible, for instance, to achieve it by using the technology such as ASIC (Application Specific Integrated Circuit) and FPGA (Field Programmable Gate Array) (Wittig & Chow, 1996) to arrange the reader for target use (Figure 6). In Figure 6, reader/writer module generates high frequency to do readout processing and ID reception from RFID tag. The program to control this module is implemented on the microcomputer or FPGA. Tag IDs which are read from the RFID tag can be recorded on FPGA, too. Moreover, if the I/O interface such as USB interfaces and Bluetooth interfaces is implemented on circuit board, the tag IDs can be easily forwarded to PC. It is also able to pass along and have use of a new application program which would be developed by using a Software Development Kit (SDK) on the PC.

These are technologies originally to offer target LSI by reasonable price for the application as not mass-produced. It is thought that there is enough possibility that reader/writer which has the function of the purpose of use and is smaller and cheaper than a past portable data terminal

Figure 6. Basic design for RFID tag reader using FPGA

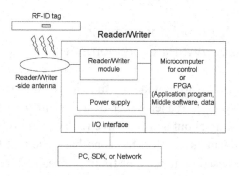

Figure 7. Basic system construction procedure with FPGA

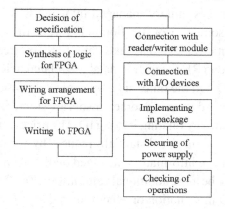

type can be achieved by combining with a small basic module, basic I/O device and the power supply. Moreover, the outline of the procedure when the system using such FPGA is actually constructed is shown in Figure 7. Because FPGA is a logical hardware, it needs to do logical synthesis after deciding an application software specification and internal wiring arrangements for FPGA. After writing the logical program for controlling RFID module to FPGA, the FPGA would be connected with the RFID module and I/O devices to PC. Putting them in appropriate small package and securing of power supply, a small and simple RFID tag reader will come to completion.

(2) Other Approaches

There is a necessity of multi function reader/writer which can correspond to different electronic tag as concerning reader/writer. Although it may not be general-purpose, it can be examined that the construction of the reader/writer which can correspond to two or more purposes hardly changing the face by applying the programmable LSI technology like above-mentioned.

5. PROTOTYPE MAKING OF SMALL RFID READER

Here, it explains the content that confirms a necessary basic function when the small RFID tag reader is constructed by using FPGA according to a basic examination of paragraph 4.2

(1) Mounting of Reader Control Program on FPGA

RFID tag reader is usually constructed by connecting a reader module and a reader side antenna to a computer such as a personal computer so far. If the program that controls the reader module can be mounted on FPGA, it comes to no need to use the computer together with the reader, and certain miniaturization and cost reduction of the reader can be achieved. So, installing the reader module control program to built-in FPGA board with the configuration circuit by using VHDL that was typical hardware description language (HDL: Hardware Description Language) and the operation experiment was done. The experiment program reads ID information in RFID tag memory (ROM) first of all. And it turn on a LED lamp if the ID is mach to ID information memorized beforehand in the program on FPGA. It was confirmed to be able to send the pulse signal by using FPGA that was able to control the reader module. And moreover, it was able to be confirmed for the reader module to operate normally as a result, and to be able to read ID information in RFID tag memory.

(2) Scale of Internal Logic Elements Usage of FPGA

FPGA used in this experiment has comparatively small scale of logic elements. When the experiment program above-mentioned had been installed in FPGA with the logic elements of about 600, the logic element used was about 5%. It will be possible to install two or more applications on the FPGA at a time if programs are relatively small.

6. CONCLUSION

In this chapter, by taking the traceability system as an example, it explained various problems on the system cost or on the specification that faced when it tried to construct the traceability system by using RFID tag. In addition, a current approach for these problem solutions and the future view were described. Especially, by switching the point of view to reader/writer construction from RFID tag, directionality for the construction of a small, cheap reader/writer which had used FPGA was described. In the experiment for making a small reader that used FPGA for trial purposes, the control program of the reader module was installed in FPGA and the reader module was operated. And readability of ID information on RFID tag was confirmed. Though it is necessary to do the further experiment that unifies a special bay board making, a small power supply, and the computer connection interface, etc. to achieve a practicable miniaturization, the prospect was able to be obtained that FPGA was able to be used for miniaturization/reducing the cost of RFID tag reader/writer effectively.

REFERENCES

Bose, R. (2009). Sensor networks- motes, smart spaces, and beyond. *IEEE Pervasive Computing / IEEE Computer Society [and] IEEE Communications Society, 8*(3), 84–90. doi:10.1109/MPRV.2009.55

Cleland-Huang, J., Settimi, R., Romanova, E., Berenbach, B., & Clark, S. (2007). Best practices for automated traceability. *IEEE Computer, 40*(6), 27–35.

Cyranoski, D. (2001). Japan's first BSE case fuels fears elsewhere. *Nature, 413*, 337. doi:10.1038/35096710

Dickinson, D. L., & Bailey, D. V. (2002). Meat traceability: Are U.S. consumers willing to pay for it? *Journal of Agricultural and Resource Economics, 27*(2), 348–364.

Estrin, D., Culler, D., Pister, K., & Sukhatme, G. (2002). Connecting the physical world with pervasive networks. *IEEE Pervasive Computing / IEEE Computer Society [and] IEEE Communications Society, 1*(1), 59–69. doi:10.1109/MPRV.2002.993145

Finkenzeller, K. (1999). *RFID handbook: Radio-frequency identification fundamentals and applications*. John Wiley & Sons.

Frazelle, E. H. (2001). *Transportation and distribution management, supply chain strategy: The logistics of supply chain management* (pp. 169–223). McGraw-Hill.

Husemann, D. (1999). The smart card: Don't leave home without it. *IEEE Concurrency, 7*(2), 24–27. doi:10.1109/4434.766959

Itsuki, R., Shibata, H., Ikkai, Y., & Komoda, N. (2003). The autonomous Information System design for item management using rewritable RFID tags in supply chain. *Proceedings of 2003 IEEE International Conference on Emerging Technologies and Factory Automation* (ETFA 2003), (pp. 27-34).

Lee, H. L., & Billington, C. (1992). Managing supply chain inventory: Pitfalls and opportunities. *Sloan Management Review, 33*, 65–73.

Mo, J. P. T., Sheng, Q. Z., Li, X., & Zeadally, S. (2009). RFID infrastructure design: A case study of two Australian RFID projects. *IEEE Internet Computing, 13*(1), 14–21. doi:10.1109/MIC.2009.18

Opara, L. U. (2003). Traceability in agriculture and food supply chain: A review of basic concepts, technological implications, and future prospects. *Food. Agriculture & Environment, 1*(1), 101–106.

Pooler, V. H., & Pooler, D. J. (1997). *Purchasing and supply management creating the vision.* Chapman & Hall. RFID news. (2003). Hitachi unveils smallest RFID chip. *RFID Journal.* Retrieved January 31, 2011, from http://www.rfidjournal.com/article/view/337/1/1

Roussos, G., Duri, S. S., & Thompson, C. W. (2009). RFID meets the Internet. *IEEE Internet Computing, 13*(1), 11–13. doi:10.1109/MIC.2009.19

Sakamura, K. (2009). *Ubiquitous ID technologies 2009.* Retrieved January 31, 2011, from http://www.uidcenter.org/ wp-content/themes/wp.vicuna/pdf/UID910-W001-090511_en.pdf

Schuster, E. W., Brock, D. L., & Allen, S. J. (2010). *Global RFID: The value of the EPCglobal network for supply chain management.* Springer.

Simchi-Levi, D., Kaminsky, P., & Simchi-Levi, E. (2003). *Designing and managing the supply chain concepts, strategies, and case studies.* McGraw Hill.

Soga, S., Hiroshige, Y., Dobashi, A., Okumura, M., & Kusuzaki, T. (1999). Products lifecycle management system using radio frequency identification technology. *Proceedings of 1999 IEEE International Conference on Emerging Technologies and Factory Automation* (ETFA'99), (pp. 1459-1468).

Takaragi, K., Usami, M., Imura, R., Itsuki, R., & Satoh, T. (2001). *An ultra small individual recognition security chip* (pp. 43–49). IEEE MICRO, Nov.-Dec.

Traub, K., et al. (2005). *The EPCglobal architecture framework.* Retrieved January 31, 2011, from http://autoid.mit.edu/CS/files/folders/specifications/entry5.aspx

Warneke, B., Last, M., Liebowitz, B., & Pister, K. S. J. (2001). Smart dust: Communicating with a cubic-millimeter computer. *IEEE Computer, 34*(1), 44–51.

Wheeler, A. (2007). Commercial applications of wireless sensor network using ZigBee. *IEEE Communications Magazine, 45*(4), 70–77. doi:10.1109/MCOM.2007.343615

Wittig, R. D., & Chow, P. (1996). One chip: An FPGA processor with reconfigurable logic. *Proceedings of IEEE Symposium on FPGAs for Custom Computing Machines*, (pp. 126-135).

Chapter 5
Parallel Computing for Mining Association Rules in Distributed P2P Networks

Huiwei Guan
North Shore Community College, USA

ABSTRACT

Distributed computing and Peer-to-Peer (P2P) systems have emerged as an active research field that combines techniques which cover networks, distributed computing, distributed database, and the various distributed applications. Distributed Computing and P2P systems realize information systems that scale to voluminous information on very large numbers of participating nodes. Data mining on large distributed databases is a very important research area. Recently, most work for mining association rules focused on a single machine or client-server network model. However, this traditional approach does not satisfy the requirements from the large distributed databases and applications in a P2P computing system. Two important challenges are raised, one is how to implement data mining for large distributed databases in P2P computing systems, and the other is how to develop parallel data mining algorithms and tools for the distributed P2P computing systems to improve the efficiency. In this chapter, a parallel association rule mining approach in a P2P computing system is designed and implemented, which satisfies the distribution of the P2P computing system well and makes parallel computing become true. The performance and comparison of the parallel algorithm with the sequential algorithm is analyzed and evaluated, which presents the parallel algorithm features consistent implementation, higher performance, and fine scalable ability.

DOI: 10.4018/978-1-61520-871-5.ch005

I. INTRODUCTION

Distributed computing deals with hardware and software systems containing multiple processing node or storage element, or multiple programs, running under a loosely or tightly controlled regime. Currently, distributed computing and Peer-to-peer (P2P) systems have emerged as an active research field that combines techniques which cover networks, parallel computing, distributed database, and the various distributed applications. Different from traditional client-server model, a host node in a distributed P2P system has significantly changed the way of information store, sharing, distribution, communication, search and computing. Distributed P2P systems realize information systems that scale to voluminous information on very large numbers of participating nodes (Melucci, 2005; Guan & Chueng, 2000; Wang, 1999; Guan & Li, 1996; Datta, 2005; Guan, 1995; Mehyar, 2005; Guan & Li, 1997; Kamvar, 2005; Guan & Cheung, 1997; Sobolewski, 2006; Guan, 1996; Guan & Sun, 1993; Gao, 2009).

Data mining is a very important research area for database applications, knowledge discovery in databases and data streams, and search engines. The subject can be loosely defined as finding useful patterns or exceptions from a large collection of data. An association rule is an expression $X \Rightarrow Y$, where X is a set of attributes and Y is a single attribute. Intuitively, it means that in the rows of the database if the attributes in X have value "true", Y tends to have value "true" too. The *association rules mining* is to design an efficient algorithm for finding such rules from a database. Recently, most work for mining association rules focused on a single machine or traditional client-server network model. However, this traditional approach does not satisfy the requirements from the large distributed databases and applications in a P2P computing system (Gao, 2009; Kowalczyk, 2003; Agrawal, 1993; Tan, 2006; Hipp, 2000; Guan & Li, 1995; Han, 2006; Guan & Cheung, 1996; Zytkow, 1998). Two important challenges

are raised, one is how to implement data mining for large distributed databases in P2P computing systems, and the other is how to develop parallel data mining algorithms and tools for the distributed P2P computing systems to improve the efficiency (Guan & Yu, 2006; Agrawal, 1996; Guan & Li, 1995; Guan & Ip, 2007; Fa, 2006; Guan, 1996; Sun, 2009; Guan & Ip, 1998; Yang, 2008; Guan & Sun, 1992; Kargupta, 2008). In this chapter, a parallel association rule mining approach in a distributed P2P computing system is designed and implemented. First, an overview is given in the section I. Next, a formal specification and some definitions for mining association rules are presented in the section II. Then, a ring P2P computing system architecture is proposed in the section III. Following that, a parallel algorithm for mining association rules on large scale distributed databases in the P2P computing system is designed and implemented in the section IV. An example and analysis are discussed in the section V. The performance and comparison of the parallel algorithm with the sequential algorithm is evaluated in the section VI. Lastly, a summary is addressed in the section VII.

II. FORMAL SPECIFICATION AND DEFINITIONS FOR MINING ASSOCIATION RULES

The formal specification and definitions are presented in this section. Some definitions are given in the section A and the principles of association rules mining are given in the section B.

A. Some Definitions

Definition 1 (*itemset*): Let D be a database consisting of binary vectors of length n generated by a set of attributes $J = \{J_1, J_2..., J_n\}$. An *itemset* $I = \{I_1, I_2..., I_m\} \subseteq J$ is a subset of attributes. By definition, any non-empty subset of an *itemset* is also an *itemset*.

Definition 2 (*satisfy*): Let X be a subset of items of I. A transaction t *satisfies* X iff $\forall I_i \in X$, $t[i] = 1$.

Definition 3 (*k-itemset* and *length of itemset*): An *itemset* I is called a *k-itemset* if it consists of exactly k attributes. We say that the *length* of the *itemset* is k.

Definition 4 (*association rule*): Let X, $Y \subseteq I$ be two subitemsets in I. An *association rule* is an expression $X \Rightarrow Y$, where $X \cap Y = \emptyset$.

Definition 5 (*support*): The itemset X has *support s* in the database D iff $s\%$ of the transactions of D satisfy X, and it is represented as $s(X)$.

Definition 6 (*association rule with a confidence*): An association rule $X \Rightarrow Y$ holds in the database D with the *confidence c* ($0 \leq c \leq 1$) iff at least $c\%$ of the transactions of D that satisfy X also satisfy Y, where the *confidence c* is defined as the ratio $s(X \cup Y) / s(X)$. The rule is represented as the notation $X \Rightarrow Y \mid c$.

Definition 7 (*large itemset* and *small itemset*): A *large itemset* I of D is an *itemset* that has the *support s* above a certain threshold, called *minimum support*, for the transactions of D. An itemset that does not meet the *minimum support* is a *small itemset*.

Definition 8 (*set of large itemsets* and *set of small itemsets*): A *set of large itemsets* of D is a set of *itemsets* where all itemsets have the *support s* above the *minimum support* for the transactions in D. We take the symbol L^k as the *set of large itemsets* with the *length k*. All the other combinations of itemsets that do not meet the *minimum support* are *sets of small itemsets*.

B. Principles of Association Rules Mining

The principle of association rules mining is to find all the rules that satisfy a user-specified *minimum support* and *minimum confidence*. This problem can be decomposed into two subproblems:

1. Generate a *collection* of all *sets of large itemsets L*, that is $L = \cup_i L^i$, $i = 1, 2,..., k$, and k is the largest length of all sets of *large itemsets*.

2. For a given *large itemset* $l^k = \{I_1, I_2,..., I_k\}$, $k \geq 2$, generate all rules (at the most k rules) that use items from the itemset l. The antecedent of each of these rules will be a subset X of l such that X has k-1 items, and the consequent will be the itemset l^k - X. To generate a rule $X \Rightarrow I_j \mid c$, where $X = \{I_1, I_2...I_{j-1}, I_{j+1}..., I_k\}$, take the support of l and divide it by the support of X. If the ratio is greater than c then the rule is satisfied with the confidence factor c; otherwise it is not.

Once *collection* of all *sets of large itemsets L* has been determined, the solution to the second subproblem is rather straightforward.

III. A RING P2P COMPUTING SYSTEM ARCHITECTURE

We construct a ring topology as a basic P2P computing system architecture. The first walk-in node is assigned as the node *1*, the second walk-in node is assigned as the node *2*, ..., and the last walk-in node is assigned as the node *n* and is connected to the node *1*. Assume *n* very large scale databases are distributed in the P2P computing system, each of them is residing at one node and it is called as a local database D_i, that is the *i*th local database D_i is located at the node i ($i=1,2,...,n$). The ring topology has good *scalable* feature. When the numbers of the nodes are changed, a ring topology can be easily extended or changed dynamically, which means just the identify of the node *i* or *n* is updated. The ring P2P computing system architecture is shown in Figure 1.

Figure 1. A ring P2P computing system architecture

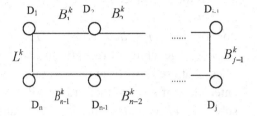

IV. PARALLEL ASSOCIATION RULES MINING IN P2P COMPUTING SYSTEMS

Recently, there have been considerable research results in the algorithms for mining association rules (Gao, 2009; Kowalczyk, 2003; Agrawal, 1993; Tan, 2006; Hipp, 2000; Guan & Li, 1995; Han, 2006; Guan & Cheung, 1996; Zytkow, 1998), however almost of them are designed and implemented in single machine or traditional client-server model which do not satisfy the requirements for distributed P2P computing systems.

Mining association rules for large scale distributed databases located in a P2P computing system needs to solve the following main issues: (1) calculate and collect local large itemset on each node independently; (2) communicate and combine all local large itemsets among all nodes of a P2P computing system efficiently; (3) generate a globe large itemset for all distributed databases integrally; (4) has a good performance and efficiency; (5) can execute the same implementation code on each node of a P2P computing system; (6) can be scalable to satisfy the nodes' changes of a P2P computing system. Based on the above considerations, we design a parallel algorithm for mining association rules in a ring P2P computing system. The algorithm features the same implementation is executed in parallel on all nodes and only necessary information is transmitted among the P2P computing system, it is also with fine scalability when the number of the nodes is

changed in a P2P computing system. The detail design is proposed and investigated in this section.

A. Notations Used in the Parallel Algorithm

At first, we present some notations used in the parallel algorithm of the P2P computing system in following Table 1.

B. Design and Implementation of a Parallel Algorithm for Finding the Set of Large itemsets in the P2P Computing System

The algorithm assumes each D_i ($i=1,2,...,n$) is located on one node i in the P2P computing system.

In the design of the algorithm, the main goals which are cited as the (1)-(6) issues in the beginning of this section are achieved by taking the following five strategies: The first is that each node generates its *set of local candidate of k-itemset* C_i^k, then transmits and combines them among the P2P computing system to generate a *set of combined local candidate of k-itemsets* B_i^k until a *set of global large k-itemset* L^k is generated at the node n. This approach reduces the cost of data communication among these nodes as much as possible. The second is to take L^k as a new C_i^k, that is to take L^k as a seed and use it to scan and generate new *set of local candidate of k+1-itemset* C_i^{k+1}. This approach reduces the cost to scan and generate C_i^k at each node as much as possible. The third is that the implementation of the algorithm on each node is the same, which satisfies the distribution of the P2P system. The fourth is all processes of this algorithm are executed in parallel on each node, which improves the performance. The last one is there is no limitation for the size of the P2P computing system, that is the number of nodes n and the index i is flexible and changeable, which reaches a scalable purpose. The following is the main design of the

Table 1. Notations used in the algorithm

D_i	*Local database* residing on node *i*.
C_i^k	*Set of local candidate of k-itemset* at node *i* (after pass *k* scan); each member of this set c_i^k has two fields: 1) itemset, $c_i^k.itemset$; 2) *support* count, $c_i^k.count$.
$c_i^k[m]$	The *m*th member of c_i^k .
$c_i^k[m].item_j$	The *j*th item contained in $c_i^k[m].itemset$.
C^k	*Set of global candidate of k-itemset* (after pass *k* scan); each member of this set c^k has two fields: 1) itemset, $c^k.intemset$; 2) *support* count, $c^k.count$.
B_i^k	*Set of combined local candidate of k-itemset* (after pass *k* scan) till the node *i*; each member of this set b_i^k has two fields: 1) itemset, $b_i^k.itemset$; 2) *support* count, $b_i^k.count$.
L_i^k	*Set of local large k-itemset* with *minimum support* at node *i* (after pass *k* scan); each member of this set has two fields: 1) itemset; 2) *support* count.
L^k	*Set of global large k-itemset* with *minimum support* (after pass *k* scan); each member of this set has two fields: 1) itemset; 2) *support* count.
L	*Collection of all sets of global large k-itemset.*
l^k	A *global large k-itemset* which has two fields: 1) itemset, $l^k.itemset$; 2) *support* count, $l^k.count$.
s^{k-1}	*Subset of a global large k-itemset*, each member of this subset has two fields: 1) itemset, $s^{k-1}.itemset$; 2) *support* count, $s^{k-1}.count$.

parallel algorithm and some comments are provided as the explanations.

```
main begin
    /* during the scan 1, that is
when k = 1 */
    k = 1;
    for each node i do in parallel
        begin
            C_i^k = gen_initial_local_
cand(D_i, ∅); /* generate initial C_i^1
on each node. */
        end for
    /* the process executed on the
node 1 in parallel */
    if (i = 1) then B_i^k = C_i^k ; /* take
C_1^1 as an initial set of combined
local candidate of 1-itemset B_1^1 . */
        send B_i^k to succeeding node;
        receive C_n^k from node n;  /*
at this moment, C_n^k = L^1. */
        C_i^k = C_n^k ;  /* take C_n^1 as
new seed of C_1^1 . */
        send C_i^k to succeeding node;
    /* during the scan k, that is
when k ≥ 2 */
        for (k = 2; C_i^{k-1} ≠ ∅; k ++)
dobegin C_i^k = gen_local_cand(D_i, C_i^{k-1});
            B_i^k = C_i^k ;
            send B_i^k to succeed-
ing node;
            receive C_n^k from node
n;  /* at this moment, C_n^k = L^k. */
```

$C_i^k = C_n^k$; /* take the C_n^k as a new seed of C_i^k . */

send C_i^k to succeeding node;

end for

/* the process executed on the node i in parallel, $1 < i < n$ */

else if ($1 < i < n$) **then** *receive* B_{i-1}^k from antecedent node $i - 1$;

/* combine B_{i-1}^1 with its C_i^1 to generate B_i^1 which becomes *set of combined local candidate of 1-itemset from node 1 to node i* */

$B_i^k = com\_local\_cand(B_{i-1}^k , C_i^k)$;

send B_i^k to the succeeding node $i + 1$;

receive C_{i-1}^k from antecedent node $i - 1$; /* at this moment, $C_{i-1}^1 = L^1$ */

$C_i^k = C_{i-1}^k$; /* take the C_{i-1}^k as new seed of C_i^1 . */

/* send the new seed of C_i^1 around the ring */

while ($i < n - 1$) **dobegin** send C_i^k from node i to node $i+1$;

end while

/* during the scan k, that is when $k \geq 2$ */

for ($k = 2$; $C_i^{k-1} \neq \emptyset$; k ++) **dobegin** $C_i^k = gen\_local\_cand(D_i, C_i^{k-1})$;

receive B_{i-1}^k from antecedent node $i - 1$;

/* combine B_{i-1}^k with its C_i^k to generate B_i^k which becomes the *set of combined local candidate of k-itemset from node 1 to node i* */

$B_i^k = com\_local\_cand(B_{i-1}^k , C_i^k)$;

send B_i^k to the succeeding node $i + 1$;

receive C_{i-1}^k from antecedent node $i - 1$; /* at this moment, $C_{i-1}^k = L^k$ */

$C_i^k = C_{i-1}^k$; /* take the C_{i-1}^k as new seed of C_i^k . */

/* send the new seed of C_i^k around the ring */

while ($i < n - 1$) **dobegin** send C_i^k from node i to node $i+1$;

end while

end for

end else if

/* the process executed on the node n in parallel */

else if ($i = n$) **then** *receive* B_{i-1}^k from antecedent node $i - 1$;

/* combine B_{i-1}^1 with its C_i^1 to generate B_i^1 which becomes the *set of global candidate of 1-itemset for all D_i*. */

$B_i^k = com\_local\_cand(B_{i-1}^k , C_i^k)$;

/* generate the *set of global large 1-itemset L^1* with *minimum support*. */

$L^k = gen\_large(B_i^k)$;

$C_i^k = L^k$; /* L^1 becomes a seed as a new C_n^1 . */

send the new seed C_n^1 to the node 1;

/* during the scan k, that is when $k \geq 2$ */

for ($k = 2$; $C_i^{k-1} \neq \emptyset$; k ++) **dobegin** $C_i^k = gen\_local\_cand(D_i, C_i^{k-1})$;

receive B_{i-1}^k from the antecedent node $i - 1$;

```
            /* combine  B_{i-1}^k  with
its  C_i^k  to generate B_i^k  which becomes
the set of global candidate of k-
itemset for all D_i.  */
            B_i^k = com_local_cand(
B_{i-1}^k,  C_i^k);
            /* generate the set
of global large k-itemset L^k with
minimum support. */
            L^k = gen_large( B_i^k );
            C_i^k = L^k; /* L^k be-
comes a new seed and take L^k as a new
C_n^k. */
            send the new seed of
C_i^k to the node 1;
        end for
        /* generate L which is the
collection of all set of global large
k-itemset L^k */
        for (i = 2; i = k; i++)
dobegin L = ∪_{i=2,3,...,k} L^i ;
        end for
```

```
    end else if
end main begin
```

The functions used in the algorithm are defined in the Table 2.

```
gen_initial_local_cand function for
generating set of initial local
candidate
```

The generation function for the set of initial local candidate *gen_initial_local_cand* takes local database D_i and an empty set as parameters. It scans the D_i, each item of the transactions in the D_i is examined and the *support* for each item is counted. It generates a *set of initial local candidate of 1-itemset* C_i^1, and C_i^1 is sorted in lexicographic order. The function is implemented as follows:

```
begin
    C_i^1 = ∅;
    forall transactions t ∈
```

Table 2. Functions used in the algorithm

Function name	Description of functions
send(data, source node, destination node)	The *source node* sends the *data* to the *destination node*.
receive(data, source node, destination node)	The *destination node* receives the *data* from the *source node*.
gen_initial_local_cand(D_i, ∅)	Scan the local database D_i and generate a *set of initial local candidate of 1-itemset* C_i^1.
gen_large(B_i^k)	Generate the *set of global large k-itemset L^k* with *minimum support*.
gen_local_cand(D_i, C_i^{k-1})	Scan the local database D_i and generate the *set of local candidate of k-itemset* C_i^k.
com_local_cand(B_{i-1}^k , C_i^k)	Combine the antecedent B_{i-1}^k with the *set of local candidate of k-itemset* C_i^k on node *i* to generate its *set of combined local candidate of k-itemset* B_i^k which is the *set of combined local candidate of k-itemset* from node 1 to node *i*.
sort(C_i^k)	C_i^k is sorted and become in lexicographic order.

```
D_idoif t[j] = 1  then do C_i^1[j].itemset =
C_i^1[j].itemset ∪ t[j];
            C_i^1[j].count = C_i^1[j].count +
1;
    end  forall
    C_i^1 = sort(C_i^1);
end
```

The *gen_initial_local_cand* function is executed in parallel on all nodes of the P2P computing system.

```
gen_local_cand function for generat-
ing set of local candidate
```

The generation function for the set of local candidate *gen_local_cand* takes local database D_i and the current set of local candidate of k-1-itemset C_i^{k-1} as parameters. In fact, the C_i^{k-1} is just the precedent (in *k-1th* scan) *set of global large k-1-itemset L^{k-1}*. The function returns a superset of the set of all *k-itemset* as a new *set of local candidate of k-itemset C_i^k* and the following is a brief description.

Let $C_i^{k-1}[m].item_j$, $C_i^{k-1}[n].item_j \in C_i^{k-1}$, j = 1, 2,..., *k-1*. First, this function executes a *join* operation of one extension for the set C_i^{k-1}, and the *join* operation can be described by several embedded SQL statements as follows:

select $C_i^{k-1}[m].item_1$, $C_i^{k-1}[m].item_2$, ..., $C_i^{k-1}[m].item_{k-1}$, $C_i^{k-1}[n].item_{k-1}$ **into** C_i^k **from** $C_i^{k-1}[m]$, and $C_i^{k-1}[n]$ **at** site i**where** $C_i^{k-1}[m].item_1 = C_i^{k-1}[n].item_1$, ..., $C_i^{k-1}[m].item_{k-2} = C_i^{k-1}[n].item_{k-2}$, $C_i^{k-1}[m].item_{k-1} < C_i^{k-1}[n].item_{k-1}$;

Then, this function scans the local database D_i, and the *support* for each itemset of C_i^k is measured and counted. The procedure is described as follows:

```
forall  transactions t ∈ D_idoforall c_i^k
∈ C_i^k doif c_i^k.itemset ⊆ tthen c_i^k.count =
c_i^k.count + 1;
        end  forall
    end  forall
```

Just like the *gen_initial_local_cand* function, the *gen_local_cand* function is executed in parallel on all nodes of the P2P computing system.

```
com_local_cand function for generat-
ing set of combined local candidate
```

The generation function for the set of combined local candidate *com_local_cand* takes two parameters. One is its antecedent *set of combined local candidate of k-itemset B_{i-1}^k*, and the other is the *set of local candidate of k-itemset C_i^k*. The function combines B_{i-1}^k with C_i^k on node *i* to generate the *set of combined local candidate of k-itemset B_i^k* which is the *set of combined local candidate of k-itemset* from node 1 to node *i*. This is a combination of a *union* operation with *count* operation to the set B_{i-1}^k and the set C_i^k and it is implemented as follows:

```
forall  itemsets  c_i^k ∈ C_i^k  and  b_{i-1}^k
∈ B_{i-1}^k  do
        b_i^k.itemset = b_{i-1}^k.itemset ∪
c_i^k.itemset;
        b_i^k.count = b_{i-1}^k.count + c_i^k.count
;
    end  forall
```

The function *com_local_cand* is also executed in parallel on all nodes of the P2P computing system.

gen_large function for generating *set of large itemset*

The generation function for the set of large itemset *gen_large* takes the *set of combined local candidate of k-itemset* B_i^k as a parameter, where B_n^k is the *set of global candidate of k-itemset* at node *n*. It returns a *set of global large k-itemset* L^k with *minimum support*. That is to assure that all itemsets of the members of L^k with their counts of *support* are more than the *minimum support*. The function is implemented as follows:

```
Lᵏ = Ø ;
    forall bₙᵏ ∈ Bₙᵏ doif  ( bₙᵏ.count ) ≥
minimum supportthenLᵏ = Lᵏ ∪ bₙᵏ ;
    end  forall
```

C. Algorithm to Generate Association Rules

As soon as *set of global large k-itemset* L^k has been obtained, the *collection of all sets of global large k-itemset L* is determined at the end of the above parallel algorithm. As such, we can execute a function to generate all association rules for all distributed databases of the P2P computing system immediately. The algorithm for generating association rules is described as follows:

```
for  (j = 2;  j =k;  j++)  dobegin-
forall  global large j-itemset l ʲ
∈ Lʲdoforall subset of global large
j-itemset s ʲ = {global large j-1-
itemset ⊂ l ʲ} doμ = support(l ʲ) /
support(l ʲ - s ʲ) ;
                    if  (μ ≥ minimum
confidence)  then
                        The rule s ʲ
⇒ l ʲ - s ʲ | c holds and output it;
        end
```

V. ANALYSIS AND EXAMPLE

In this section, an example is given to interpret the calculus and communication procedures by using the above algorithm for mining association rules in the P2P computing system. Assume three databases are distributed in three nodes as following Table 3, where "X" represents the attribute of the database and "i_j' represents the jth tuple at the node i.

Assume that the minimum support is 60% for all distributed databases. The following is the updated situation for each scan step by step, where, $c_i^k.item$ is an abbreviation of $c_i^k.itemset$, that is the itemset in the *set of local candidate of k-itemset* at node *i*; $c_i^k.c$ is an abbreviation of $c_i^k.count$, that is the *support* count for the itemset; and $b_i^k.item$ is an abbreviation of $b_i^k.itemset$, that is the itemset in the *set of combined local candidate of k-itemset* at node *i*; $b_i^k.c$ is an abbreviation of $b_i^k.count$, that is the *support* count for the itemset; and $l^k.item$ is an abbreviation of $l^k.itemset$, that is the itemset in the *set of global large k-itemset* (with *minimum support*); $l^k.c$ is an abbreviation of $l^k.count$, that is the *support* count for the itemset.

A. After the First Scan

The *set of local candidate of 1-itemset* at node *i*, C_i^1. (Table 4) The *set of combined local candidate of 1-itemset* at the node *i*, $c_1^1.item$. (Table 5) The *set of global large 1-itemset* (with *minimum support*), L^1. (Table 6)

B. After the Second Scan

The *set of local candidate of 2-itemset* at node *i*, C_i^2. (Table 7) The *set of combined local candidate of 2-itemset* at the node *i*, $c_1^2.item$. (Table 8) The

Table 3. Three Distributed Database example

	A	B	C	D	E	F	G
1_01	1	0	1	0	1	0	1
1_02	1	1	1	1	1	1	0
1_03	1	1	1	0	1	0	0
1_04	1	1	0	0	0	0	1
1_05	1	1	1	0	1	1	0
1_06	0	1	0	0	0	1	0
1_07	1	1	1	0	1	1	0
1_08	1	0	0	0	1	0	1
1_09	1	1	1	0	1	1	0
1_10	1	1	1	0	1	1	1
	A	B	C	D	E	F	G
2_01	1	1	1	0	1	0	1
2_02	0	1	1	0	1	1	1
2_03	1	1	1	0	1	1	1
2_04	0	1	1	1	0	1	1
2_05	1	0	1	0	0	0	1
2_06	1	1	1	0	1	1	1
2_07	1	1	1	0	1	1	0
2_08	1	1	1	0	1	0	1
2_09	1	1	0	0	1	1	1
2_10	1	1	1	0	1	1	0
	A	B	C	D	E	F	G
3_01	1	1	1	0	1	1	1
3_02	1	1	1	0	0	1	1
3_03	1	1	0	0	1	1	1
3_04	1	1	1	1	1	1	0
3_05	1	1	1	0	0	1	1
3_06	1	1	1	0	1	1	1
3_07	1	1	1	0	1	1	1
3_08	1	1	1	0	1	1	0
3_09	1	1	1	0	0	1	1
3_10	1	1	1	0	1	0	1

Table 4.

$c_1^1.c$	$c_2^1.item$	$c_2^1.c$	$c_3^1.item$	$c_3^1.c$	B_i^1
{A} 9	{A}	8	{A}	10	
{B} 8	{B}	9	{B}	10	
{C} 7	{C}	9	{C}	9	
{D} 1	{D}	1	{D}	1	
{E} 8	{E}	8	{E}	7	
{F} 6	{F}	7	{F}	9	
{G} 4	{G}	8	{G}	8	

Table 5.

$b_1^1.item$	$b_1^1.c$	$b_2^1.item$	$b_2^1.c$	$b_3^1.item$	$b_3^1.c$
{A}	9	{A}	17	{A}	27
{B}	8	{B}	17	{B}	27
{C}	7	{C}	16	{C}	25
{D}	1	{D}	2	{D}	3
{E}	8	{E}	16	{E}	23
{F}	6	{F}	13	{F}	22
{G}	4	{G}	12	{G}	20

Table 6.

$l^1.item$	$l^1.c$
{A}	27
{B}	27
{C}	25
{E}	23
{F}	22
{G}	20

set of global large 2-itemset (with *minimum support*), L^2. Table 9)

C. After the Third Scan

The *set of local candidate of 3-itemset* at node i, C_i^3. (Table 10) The *set of combined local candidate of 3-itemset* at the node i, $c_1^3.item$. (Table 11) The *set of global large 3-itemset* (with *minimum support*), L^3. (Table 12)

Table 7.

$c_1^2.c$		$c_2^2.item$	$c_2^2.c$	$c_3^2.item$	$c_3^2.c$	B_i^2
{AB}	7	{AB}	7	{AB}	10
{AC}	7	{AC}	7	{AC}	9
{AE}	8	{AE}	7	{AE}	7
{AF}	5	{AF}	5	{AF}	9
{AG}	4	{AG}	6	{AG}	8
{BC}	6	{BC}	8	{BC}	9
{BE}	6	{BE}	8	{BE}	7
{BF}	6	{BF}	7	{BF}	9
{BG}	2	{BG}	7	{BG}	8
{CE}	7	{CE}	7	{CE}	6
{CF}	5	{CF}	6	{CF}	8
{CG}	2	{CG}	7	{CG}	7
{EF}	5	{EF}	6	{EF}	6
{EG}	3	{EG}	6	{EG}	5
{FG}	1	{FG}	5	{FG}	7

Table 8.

$b_1^2.item$	$b_1^2.c$	$b_2^2.item$	$b_2^2.c$	$b_3^2.item$	$b_3^2.c$
{AB}	7	{AB}	14	{AB}	24
{AC}	7	{AC}	14	{AC}	23
{AE}	8	{AE}	15	{AE}	22
{AF}	5	{AF}	10	{AF}	19
{AG}	4	{AG}	10	{AG}	18
{BC}	6	{BC}	14	{BC}	23
{BE}	6	{BE}	14	{BE}	21
{BF}	6	{BF}	13	{BF}	22
{BG}	2	{BG}	9	{BG}	17
{CE}	7	{CE}	14	{CE}	20
{CF}	5	{CF}	11	{CF}	19
{CG}	2	{CG}	9	{CG}	16
{EF}	5	{EF}	11	{EF}	17
{EG}	3	{EG}	9	{EG}	14
{FG}	1	{FG}	6	{FG}	13

D. After the Fourth Scan

The *set of local candidate of 4-itemset* at node i, C_i^4 . (Table 13) The *set of combined local candidate of 4-itemset* at the node i, $c_1^4.item$. (Table 14) The *set of global large 4-itemset* (with *minimum support*), L^4. (Table 15)

E. After the Fifth Scan

The *set of local candidate of 5-itemset*, C_i^5; and the *set of combined local candidate of 5-itemset*, B_i^5; and the *set of global large 5-itemset*, L^5 all become φ, the algorithm is terminated. The *collection of all sets of global large k-itemset*, for the example is $L = \{L^2, L^3, L^4\}$.

As soon as the *set of global large k-itemset* with *minimum support* is obtained, the association rules

Table 9.

$l^2.item$	$l^2.c$
{AB}	24
{AC}	23
{AE}	22
{AF}	19
{AG}	18
{BC}	23
{BE}	21
{BF}	22
{CE}	20
{CF}	19

for all distributed database of the P2P computing system can be extracted from the *collection of all*

Table 10.

$c_1^3.c$	$c_2^3.item$	$c_2^3.c$	$c_3^3.item$	$c_3^3.c$	B_i^3
{ABC}	6	{ABC}	6	{ABC}	9
{ABE}	6	{ABE}	7	{ABE}	7
{ABF}	5	{ABF}	5	{ABF}	9
{ABG}	2	{ABG}	5	{ABG}	8
{ACE}	7	{ACE}	6	{ACE}	6
{ACF}	5	{ACF}	4	{ACF}	8
{ACG}	2	{ACG}	5	{ACG}	7
{AEF}	5	{AEF}	5	{AEF}	6
{AEG}	3	{AEG}	5	{AEG}	5
{AFG}	1	{AFG}	3	{AFG}	7
{BCE}	6	{BCE}	7	{BCE}	6
{BCF}	5	{BCF}	6	{BCF}	8
{BEF}	5	{BEF}	6	{BEF}	6
{CEF}	5	{CEF}	5	{CEF}	5

Table 11.

$b_1^3.item$	$b_1^3.c$	$b_2^3.item$	$b_2^3.c$	$b_3^3.item$	$b_3^3.c$
{ABC}	6	{ABC}	12	{ABC}	21
{ABE}	6	{ABE}	13	{ABE}	20
{ABF}	5	{ABF}	10	{ABF}	19
{ABG}	2	{ABG}	7	{ABG}	15
{ACE}	7	{ACE}	13	{ACE}	19
{ACF}	5	{ACF}	9	{ACF}	17
{ACG}	2	{ACG}	7	{ACG}	14
{AEF}	5	{AEF}	10	{AEF}	16
{AEG}	3	{AEG}	8	{AEG}	13
{AFG}	1	{AFG}	4	{AFG}	11
{BCE}	6	{BCE}	13	{BCE}	19
{BCF}	5	{BCF}	11	{BCF}	19
{BEF}	5	{BEF}	11	{BEF}	17
{CEF}	5	{CEF}	10	{CEF}	15

Table 12.

$P.item$	$P.c$
{ABC}	21
{ABE}	20
{ABF}	19
{ACE}	19
{BCE}	19
{BCF}	19

Table 13.

$c_1^4.c$	$c_2^4.item$	$c_2^4.c$	$c_3^4.item$	$c_3^4.c$	B_i^4
{ABCE}	6	{ABCE}	6	{ABCE}	6
{ABCF}	5	{ABCF}	4	{ABCF}	8
{ABEF}	5	{ABEF}	5	{ABEF}	6
{BCEF}	5	{BCEF}	5	{BCEF}	5

sets of global large k-itemset L immediately by using the algorithm addressed in the section IV.C.

VI. PERFORMANCE AND COMPARISON

In this section, we compare the performance of our parallel algorithm with the sequential Apriori algorithm (Kowalczyk, 2003; Agrawal, 1993; Tan, 2006; Hipp, 2000; Guan & Li, 1995; Han, 2006; Guan & Cheung, 1996; Zytkow, 1998; Guan & Yu, 2006; Agrawal, 1996; Guan & Li, 1995; Guan & Ip, 2007; Fa, 2006; Guan, 1996). The sequential Apriori algorithm makes all scans for each database on each node to generate the set of *large k-itemset* for each local database, which is actually a set of *local large k-itemset* without

Table 14.

$b_1^4.item$	$b_1^4.c$	$b_2^4.item$	$b_2^4.c$	$b_3^4.item$	$b_3^4.c$
{ABCE}	6	{ABCE}	12	{ABCE}	18
{ABCF}	5	{ABCF}	9	{ABCF}	17
{ABEF}	5	{ABEF}	10	{ABEF}	16
{BCEF}	5	{BCEF}	10	{BCEF}	15

Table 15.

$l^4.item$	$l^4.c$
{ABCE}	18

any combination information to other node, then it transmits all sets of *local large k-itemset* to next node one by one until to last node. Some items in the set of *local large k-itemset* on the node *i* do not belong to the *set of global large k-itemset* L^k eventually which is really used to create the association rules. We still take the example in the section V, if using the sequential algorithm, refer to the above subsection B., after the second scan, {BG}, {CG}, {EF} and {EG} are the items of *large 2-itemset* for the database on the node 2, however they do not belong to the *set of global large 2-itemset* L^2. The same situation happens on the node 3, {BG}, {CG}, {EF} and {FG} are the items of *large 2-itemset* for the database on the node 3, they also do not belong to the L^2 eventually. Similarly refer to the subsection C., after the third scan, {BEF} is the item of *large 3-itemset* on the node 2, and {ABG}, {ACF}, {ACG}, {AEF}, {AFG} and {BEF} are the items of *large 3-itemset* on the node 3, however all of them do not belong to the *set of global large 3-itemset* L^3. Refer to the subsection D., after the fourth scan, {ABCF} and {ABEF} are the items of *large 4-itemset* on the node 3, however they are not in the *set of global large 4-itemset* L^4. All of these items are

not useful to create the association rules, and the time for calculating, generating and transmitting these items is wasted.

Our parallel algorithm avoids this kind of situation. Refer to the subsection B. of the section IV and the example in the section V., first of all, on each node, the parallel algorithm combines the information from previous node with current node to calculates B_i^k (the *set of combined local candidate of k-itemset*) and makes all these items become necessary items for generating L^k (the *set of global large k-itemset*), which avoids above wasted items being generated and transmitted in the network. Secondly, after each scan, it takes current L^k as a seed for next scan to generate new C_i^{k+1} (the *set of local candidate of k+1-itemset*) on each node, which avoids unnecessary scans for generating no useful items. Thirdly, it is executed in parallel on all nodes to generate B_i^k at the same time, which improves the performance well. Lastly, it is the most important that the implementation of our parallel algorithm for all nodes is the same, when a node joins the P2P computing system, it takes the same function and working load as others. This approach has following advantages: it satisfies not only the distribution but also the random walking in/out features of a P2P computing system; it balances the working load of each node in the P2P computing system; it saves the synchronous time for the communication of each node; it is easy for the maintenance and reuse of the software.

For our last several experiments, we keep the database constant and varied the number of nodes in a P2P computing system. The size of each database is fixed at the number of the attributes is 16 and the number of records is 1000. Actually, for our parallel algorithm addressed in this chapter, there is no limitation for both the size of attributes and records of each database, the fixed size here is only used for the evaluation purpose to compare the parallel and sequential approaches. Figure 2 shows the results of running both parallel and sequential algorithms on configurations of up to 32 nodes in the P2P computing system, where the *X* axis represents the number of nodes and the *Y* axis represents the execution time, the time unit is second, and the *speedup rate = (Sequential time - Parallel time) * 100% / Sequential time.* As the results shown in Figure 2, the *speedup rate* is 9.30% for 4 nodes and 20.67% for 32 nodes, which means our parallel approach has a very good speedup performance, especially when the size of a P2P computing system becomes larger and there are more nodes in.

VII. SUMMARY

In this chapter, a parallel association rule mining approach in a P2P computing system is proposed, the parallel algorithm is designed and implemented with the following good features:

1. The consistent implementation: the implementation of the algorithm for all nodes in a P2P computing system is the same so that it satisfies the distribution of the P2P computing very well and makes parallel computing become true.

2. Good performance: the algorithm is designed and implemented in parallel over all nodes in a P2P computing system which reaches higher efficiency.

3. Fine *scalable* ability: when the size of a P2P computing system is changed, that means the numbers of nodes are changed, it is only needed to update the identify *i* or *n*. The ring topology can be conveniently changed to satisfy the *scalability*.

Discovering and analyzing data dependencies is of primary importance among the goals for reasoning from large data set. Data mining for large scale distributed databases in P2P computing systems requires more efficient parallel or distributed algorithms (Guan & Yu, 2006; Agrawal, 1996; Guan & Li, 1995; Guan & Ip, 2007; Fa, 2006; Guan, 1996; Sun, 2009; Guan & Ip, 1998; Yang, 2008; Guan & Sun, 1992; Kargupta, 2008). Parallel data mining applications in a P2P computing system may play a key role in the next generation of large scale distributed databases, file sharing networks, mobile ad hoc networks and search engines.

REFERENCES

Agrawal, R., Imielinski, T., & Swami, A. (1993). Database mining: A performance perspective. *IEEE Transactions on Knowledge and Data Engineering, 5*(6), 914–925. doi:10.1109/69.250074

Agrawal, R., & Shafer, J. C. (1996). Parallel mining of association rules. *IEEE Transactions on Knowledge and Data Engineering, 8*(6), 962–969. doi:10.1109/69.553164

Datta, S., Giannella, C., & Kargupta, H. (2005). *K-means clustering over peer-to-peer networks.* In the 8th International Workshop on High Performance and Distributed Mining. IEEE.

Figure 2. Performance and comparison

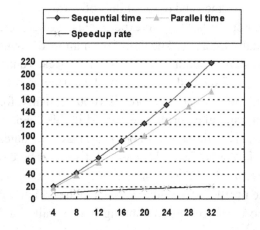

Fa, T., Pi, C., & Peng, Y. (2006). Multiple labels associative classification. *Knowledge and Information Systems, 9*(1), 109–129. doi:10.1007/s10115-005-0213-x

Gao, J., Jiang, G., Chen, H., & Han, J. (2009). *Modeling probabilistic measurement correlations for problem determination in large-scale distributed systems.* In International Conference. on Distributed Computing Systems (pp. 623-630). Montreal, Quebec, Canada: ICDCS.

Guan, H. (1995). Technical approaches of real-time control based on multiprocessor systems. *IEE International Computing & Control Engineering Journal, 6*(2), 75–78. doi:10.1049/cce:19950203

Guan, H. (1996a). Construction and implementation of the parallel computing model of DBP learning algorithm. *Journal of Software, 7*(2), 111–118.

Guan, H. (1996b). *Technical approaches for supporting multimedia communication in a distributed network of multiple servers.* In 1996 IEEE International Conference on Commuincation Systems (pp. 1483-1487). Singapore. IEEE.

Guan, H., & Cheung, T. (1996). *A belief logic system and associative plan method based on goal.* In 1996 IEEE International Conference on Systems, Man and Cybernetics (pp. 2653-2658). IEEE.

Guan, H., & Cheung, T. (2000). Efficient approaches for constructing a massively parallel processing system. *Journal of Systems Architecture, 46,* 1185–1190. doi:10.1016/S1383-7621(00)00019-9

Guan, H., Cheung, T., Li, C., & Yu, S. (1997). *Parallel design and implementation of SOM neural computing model in PVM environment of a distributed system.* In IEEE the 1997 Advances in Parallel and Distributed Computing Conference (pp. 26-31). APDC. IEEE.

Guan, H., & Ip, H. (2007). A study of parallel data mining in a peer-to-peer network. *Concurrent Engineering: Research and Applications, 15*(3), 281–289. doi:10.1177/1063293X07083088

Guan, H., Ip, H., & Zhang, Y. (1998). Java-based approaches for accessing databases on Internet and a JDBC-ODBC implementation. *IEE International Computing & Control Engineering Journal, 9*(2), 71–78. doi:10.1049/cce:19980204

Guan, H., & Li, C. (1995). *An associative plan method based on goal and construction of a belief logic system.* In 1995 IEEE International Conference on Intelligent Control & Instrumentation (pp. 358-363). Singapore, IEEE.

Guan, H., & Li, C. (1997). Generalized stochastic petri net technology modelling MPP system. *MINI-MICRO Systems, 18*(3), 34–41.

Guan, H., Li, C., & Chan, W. (1995). *A parallel implementation of BP neural network on a multiple processor system.* In 1995 IEEE International Symposium on Artificial Neural Networks. Taipei, Taiwan: IEEE.

Guan, H., Li, C., & Cheung, T. (1996). *A generalized stochastic petri net approach for modeling multi-processor parallel processing system.* In IEEE 2nd International Conference on Algorithms & Architectures for Parallel Processing (pp. 413-420). Singapore.

Guan, H., & Sun, Y. (1992). The parallel programming techniques based on transputers. *MINI-MICRO Systems, 13*(9), 1–8.

Guan, H., & Sun, Y. (1993). Design and implementation of a reconfigurable system of multi-transputer network. *Journal of Computers, 16*(7).

Guan, H., Yu, S., & Ip, H. (2006). *A parallel algorithm for mining association rules in a distributed system. In the 3rd International Workshops on Software Development Methodologies of Distributed Systems* (pp. 23–30). IEEE.

Han, J., & Kamber, M. (2006). *Data mining: Concepts and techniques* (2nd ed.). Morgan Kaufmann.

Hipp, J., Guntzer, U., & Nakaeizadeh, G. (2000). *Algorithms for association rule mining-a general survey and comparison.* In the 36th ACM SIGKDD International Conference on Knowledge Discovery and Data mining. ACM.

Kamvar, S., Schlosser, M., & Garcia-Molina, H. (2003). T*he eigentrust algorithm for reputation management in p2p networks.* In the 12th International Conference on World Wide Web (WWW) (pp. 640-651). IEEE.

Kargupta, H., Han, J., Yu, P., Motwani, R., & Kumar, V. (Eds.). (2008). *Next generation of data mining.* Taylor & Francis.

Kowalczyk, W., Jelasity, M., & Eiben, A. (2003). *Towards data mining in large and fully distributed peer-to-peer overlay networks.* In BNAIC'03 (pp. 203-210).

Mehyar, M., Spanos, D., Pongsajapan, J., Low, S., & Murray, R. (2005). *Distributed averaging on a peer-to-peer network.* In IEEE Conference on Decision and Control. IEEE.

Melucci, M., & Castiglion, R. (2005). *A weighing, framework for information retrieval in peer-to-peer networks.* In 16th International Workshop on Database and Expert Systems Applications (pp. 374-378). Copenaghen. IEEE.

Sobolewski, M., & Kolonay, R. M. (2006). Federated Grid computing with interactive service-oriented programming. *Concurrent Engineering, 14*(1), 55–66. doi:10.1177/1063293X06064148

Sun, Y., Yu, Y., & Han, J. (2009). *Ranking-based clustering of heterogeneous information networks with star network schema.* In 2009 ACM SIG-KDD International Conference on Knowledge Discovery and Data Mining (KDD'09). Paris, France: ACM.

Tan, P.-N., Steinbach, M., & Kumar, V. (2006). *Introduction to data mining.* Pearson Addison-Wesley.

Wang, Z., Guan, H., Niu, J., & Hung, S. (1999). *An online slack stealing algorithm for jointly scheduling aperiodic and periodic tasks in fixed-priority preemptive system.* In the 20th IEEE Real-time Systems Symposium (pp. 60-64). Phoenix.

Wikipedia. (2010). *Data mining.* Retrieved from http://en.wikipedia.org/wiki/Data_mining

Wikipedia (2010). *Distributed computing.* Retrieved from http://en.wikipedia.org/wiki/Distributed_computing

Yang, Q., & Wu, X. (2008). 10 challenging problems in data mining research. *International Journal of Information Technology Decision Making, 5*(4), 597–604. doi:10.1142/S0219622006002258

Zytkow, J. M., & Quafafou, M. (1998). *Principles of data mining and knowledge discovery.* (LNAI 1510).

Chapter 6
Multi–Agent Based Formal Verification of Data in RFID Middleware

Muhammad Tarmizi Lockman
Universiti Teknologi Malaysia, Malaysia

Ali Selamat
Universiti Teknologi Malaysia, Malaysia

ABSTRACT

As the load of traffic increases in RFID middleware, RFID system can no longer manage the RFID tags. Because of the incapability of the RFID system to handle vast amount of RFID tags, there are possibilities that the data cannot be processed efficiently in the RFID middleware. Implementation of agent technology is useful for verification and validation in RFID system architecture because intelligent agent is autonomous and has the capability to define specific verification process to increase efficiency and trustworthiness of the data in RFID middleware. Therefore, in this research, the authors have implemented the multi-agent based verification of data in RFID middleware. The results of the implementation have been encouraging based on the investigation and verification done on the simulation platform. As a result, the verification of RFID middleware system architecture is clearly understood and has been successfully implemented in RFID system.

1. INTRODUCTION

Radio frequency identification (RFID) is a technology that can identify and detect something. RFID tag can be applied by embedding it into an item, animal, or a person for identification and tracking. It works with automatic identification method that retrieves data using RFID tags or transponders. Many of business activities and operations have been using a conventional system to manage their assets. This can affect their performance and quality of services (QOS). In

DOI: 10.4018/978-1-61520-871-5.ch006

fact, with the rapid growth of business operation and management, RFID has taken advantages to introduce the fast and cost saving tools for asset management and solve the identification problem. Thus, we could reduce the processing time and human involvement in the conventional system by implementing detection and product management using RFID. Therefore, in this chapter, we propose an integration of agent based verification in RFID middleware using formal method for processing the data and modeling the verification in order to meet the system specification and requirement. Figure 1 shows the RFID building block as presented in the RFID certification textbooks (Harold et al., 2007; Klaus, 2003; Weinstein, 2005; Selamat and Lockman, 2009). The RFID building block shows how the reader can read tag information in the radio communication interface. This environment can be a part of RFID system (Harold et al., 2007).

In recent years, RFID middleware has again attracted great attention due to its technology advancements, security concern and competitive business environment. There is a research that has been done using agent based for RFID middleware (Cui and Chae, 2007). It uses agent to design the load balancing system. Software agent is a technology that provides autonomous, flexible and dynamic computational entities in solving problems (Timothy and Scott, 2000; Yan et al. 2004). This is because according to (Gerhard, 2000), agents work in a goal oriented environment in which they have the ability to sense, communicate and achieve the given task at a specific time. Therefore, by applying agents in the RFID system specifically in the RFID middleware architecture, it will manage to enhance the performance of RFID data verification.

In this research, an agent technology is applied in the extended design of RFID System that has the potential to increase the performance of system management processes. The goal of this research is to investigate the capability of agent to check and verify the RFID middleware architecture especially on the communication protocols in data transaction which includes the format of the RFID data and the reliability of the data transfer. The structure of the chapter is as follows. In Section 2, we describe the related works and the overview of RFID middleware, RFID application and multi-agent. Next, Section 3 presents the taxonomy of RFID system, followed by Section 4 that explains how multiple agents are interconnected with each other. Then, Section 5 explains the formal verification approach that is

Figure 1. RFID building block

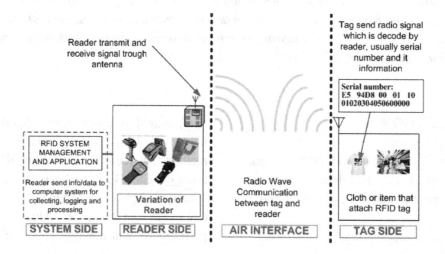

used in the research and finally, in Section 6, we conclude our findings

2. RELATED WORK

The related work of RFID middleware is described as follows:

2.1 Overview of RFID Middleware

RFID systems are implemented to fulfill enterprise system needs. To help ensuring RFID service alignment, a suitable enterprise architecture approach is required. Weaknesses in current IT architectures, for example, centralized data processing, delays in processing and point solutions, make the system less capable to handle vast amount of RFID data used in retail operations and real-time decision making at the edges of the system. Successful RFID systems implementation requires multi-agent distributed architectures for verification and validation. The concept of service and agent is complementary because they need each other to perform their roles (Foster et al., 2005).

The data that will be stored in the database before being filtered and processed by RFID middleware requires verification process. This is to maintain and increase the efficiency of the system to handle vast amount of different data that has been scanned, before RFID middleware filters and processes the data. By implementing verification here, RFID middleware will operate at the optimum and efficient level for filtering and processing data to the system repository. This is important in order to avoid problems in data management, time management and data loss at the RFID middleware. Verification and validation are depending on the purpose of the system as shown in Figure 2.

Referring to Figure 2, the architecture of the system, verification process can be implemented when the RFID tag has been scanned by the RFID fixed or mobile reader. This is because the segregation of data is important here to avoid entrust of data and data loss before going to the RFID middleware. Issues such as counterfeiting and authentication need to be handled by verifying the tag on the reader and validating the original data to confirm that the tag is valid on the system and is the one that we want to read. In EPC Network, RFID middleware is one of the most important components (EPCglobal, 2011). EPC Network is designed and implemented to enable all the objects to be linked together. Figure 3 shows the architecture of the EPC Network. EPC Network is composed of five components: tags,

Figure 2. Architecture of RFID system

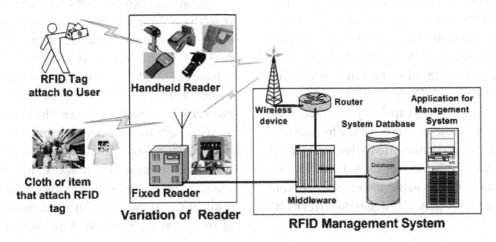

Figure 3. Architecture of EPC network

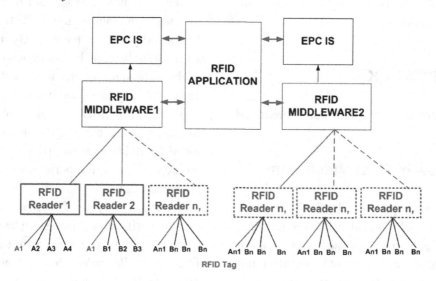

readers, RFID middleware, RFID Application and EPC Information Service

RFID middleware is a middleware software designed to process collection of tags coming from one or more reader devices. RFID middleware performs filtering, aggregation and tag management. These functions are required in order to handle the congestion of data read in the system. It forms extremely large quantities of data that is generated through the continuous interrogation of tags.

In a typical RFID system, each RFID middleware receives tags information from the connected readers. The information depends on the number of readers connected to it and the number of tags collected from those readers. If RFID middleware has too many connected readers or collects too many tags, it may make the RFID middleware response to be delayed or broken down during the detection of RFID tag. If RFID middleware is idle or has enough capability to process the workload, this problem can be solved by redistributing the readers connected to the heaviest loaded middleware to other lighter loaded middleware. In order to provide a stable and reliable working environment, agent should be considered for RFID

middleware, so that the collection of RFID data sources can be evenly distributed.

2.2 Overview of Multi-Agent

In recent years, agent technology has been rapidly developed in order to fulfill the needs of new conceptual tools for modeling and developing of complex software systems (Nardine et al., 2006). The agent approach is suitable for designing and modeling of crucial system by representing their behavior, components and interactions between them. An agent is a computer system located in an environment, which is capable to make autonomous action in order to achieve its design objectives. An agent has the ability to describe a software abstraction, an idea or a concept and provides a convenient way to explain complex software entity. Moreover, agent is capable to act with certain degree of autonomy in order to accomplish task on behalf of its user. The main aspects of agents are their autonomy, which is capable to perceive reason and act in their surrounding environments, as well as to cooperate with other agents to solve complex problems (Changhong, et al. 2002). At the lower level, agent follows set of rules that are predefined by user. However, when the agent applies these rules, they are able to learn and adapt them to their environment, in terms of user requests and the resources that are available to the agent.

In the RFID System, for instance, we have applied a group of agents known as Multi Agent (MA) to reach goals that are difficult to be achieved by an individual agent. The MA is self-motivated, as agents are able to learn from their experience, sharing task, communicate and collaborate with each other in order to achieve their internal goals. Thus, this technology is recommended in complex system design and development in which agents provide higher level of abstraction. In RFID System, we have divided the agents into several categories with substantial tasks; RFID physical Agent, RFID communication agent and RFID top layer agent

3. TAXONOMY OF THE VERIFICATION OF RFID SYSTEM

Verification of each RFID system can be part of the physical layer, communication layer and top layer in which applications operate on them. The Physical layer is important for the RFID system because operation of the hardware such as reader and tag are in this layer. The ability of RFID for identification is important to specify based on their length of coverage and to classify whether the RFID reader type is passive RFID or active RFID. Agent based technology should be managed by different reader that has been used in the RFID system.

The communication layer is important in any RFID system. It has attracted a large proportion of academics and researchers to improve the speed and accuracy of tag identification. In the communication services, the media access control protocol needs to specify verification and validation by using algorithm and protocol to communicate. Identification, authentication and privacy are also included in this layer. The

Top layer is the upper layer of RFID system that consists of the integration services for the RFID system and the RFID application, which perform their role as the RFID system implemented. This services layer usually refers to middleware of the system that provides data filtering, aggregation and routing to the appropriate enterprise systems. Verification agent could be implemented here so that it can reside on readers or servers before data can be identified. There are a number of players in the integration layer market based on the RFID survey (Macmillan-Davies, 2006). The application is depending on the system's function whether for identification or tracking. When tracking a person or item attached with the RFID tag, the system usually only reads the user identity (UID) on the tag and compares it with the UIDs that are stored in the database for validation process. Information about the tag can be read by the reader that has been installed at the recognized area for tracking and identification

4. MULTI AGENT INTERCONNECTION

In this chapter, a case study of RFID middleware is selected because it has the potential to support our multi agent verification. Basically, in RFID system, there are four modules based on the RFID system process. The first module is RFID layer agent that specifies verification and validation from RFID bottom layer (physical layer) to the upper layer (application layer). This layer includes hardware operations where the tag and reader are handled by the agent. The second module is RFID communication services agent. This module is responsible to handle and manage interconnection and communication activities that use algorithm and protocol to communicate. The third module is RFID integration services agent. This agent is responsible to manage the system integration for data services, which is usually the middleware software of RFID that supports data

Figure 4. A Multi-agent architecture RFID system

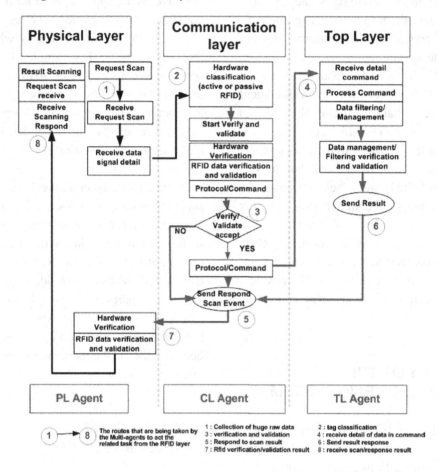

management for filtering, aggregation, routing and integration at the back end of the system. Finally, the last module is the RFID application agent. This module is responsible to display the result that the system needs. Information about the activities of item identification and tracking are handled by the agent to ensure applications in RFID system run well. Figure 4 shows the multi-agent interconnection for RFID system that can be implemented.

4.1 Physical Layer Agent (PL Agent)

RFID reader requests information about the item scanned. The information from the reader is the scanned RFID tags containing item information and the serial number (UID) of item that reader

has scanned. At the RFID Physical layer, PL agent manages the data scanned by requesting the scanning event of the tag and passes it to the Communication layer so that the CL agent can verify the data. Then, PL agents respond the scanned result by doing hardware verification to confirm that the reader has requested the validated data from the RFID system.

4.2 Communication Layer Agent (CL Agent)

The data received from the PL agent follows the CL agent feature of verification. It is important to avoid loss and damage of data before passing it to the RFID middleware. Here, the data is scanned again to perform the verification of event that has been specified by the CL agent. Then, it is verified and validated for confirmation and the process follows the RFID command protocol for that event. Since the locations of these RFID tags attached to items are already known, we can easily refer to each set of tags by their serial numbers or user Identity (UID) addresses according to the locations where user or reader scans them. This is because each UID is unique and the system knows the difference of the RFID tags from the verification of the UID at the communication layer. Here, RFID middleware supports objects checking in and out, reading, writing, filtering, grouping and routing of data generated by RFID readers. Within this layer, the expected agent application is developed so that readers can communicate with each other through the interactions and coordination of agents. Figure 5 shows RFID Agents based reader-tag checking scheme.

These agents are part of the CL agent that determines which reader will perform the read process for data verification and validation on the backend of system database. Reader 1 and Reader 2 perform the scanning event at the same time. The agent creates check in event for read process of each tag that is detected and read by the RFID reader. For each tag that is success-

Figure 5. RFID agents based reader-tag checking scheme

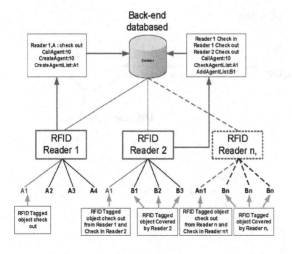

fully read, the agent creates agent list for the tag's read event to make the system verification process fast the next time it is executed. Reader 2 is always in the check out state because Reader 1 is the reader that performs read event. This can avoid collision between the RFID readers during the process of data read. It is similar to the implementation of media access control protocol such as tree or aloha algorithm in this communication layer to increase efficiency of the data process. When Reader 1 is finished reading it, agent creates the check out event to inform that any reader can start to read. So Reader 2 can now perform the check in event for the data process.

4.3 Communication Layer Agent (CL Agent)

Finally, at the Top layer agent where the RFID application for the system resides, information about the item that the reader has scanned is filtered and managed for validating the scanning event at the beginning of the process. It can be identified and tracked by sending it to the system for data management. Then, the result of the identification is submitted to the system and the reader will get the result of the scanning, which is the data that is successfully read. Interconnection between CL agent and TL agent is required here to confirm that the RFID data is verified by following the action that the agent has justified. This is because communication layer and top layer are the critical parts of RFID data verification and validation for RFID middleware to perform their functions efficiently.

5. FORMAL VERIFICATION

During the verification stage, the proposed formal verification uses the concurrency workbench of the new century CWB-NC model checker in order to ensure the effectiveness of the agent validations. The CWB-NC model checker can check property of the system specification. After the verification process, the formal verification tests the results whether the system is in the correct condition. The model checker provides identification if the model fails and needs to be modified in order to overcome the uncertainties. But if the error is not found, the model checker may refine the model and make it reliable to the specification. The verification process will continue until all states are completely checked.

Figure 6 shows RFID system properties specification. This RFID system property is based on RFID system operation environment. For the specification that we have stated,, there are commonly user identity (UID) or serial number on the tags that are the main criteria for RFID tag which can be read first before we can get the information on the tags. PL agent will get UID from RFID tag at the RFID physical layer. Then, verification and validation occur to authenticate and route the information on the tags to the CL agent. The detail of information on the tags is received and here the data in command form of UID is routed to the next RFID layer that has been managed by TL agent. Result of UID command is responded by the reader to determine whether the UID is successfully read or not. If it is successfully read, the tag information will be managed by the RFID system whereas the UID of tags will be verified for another property that has been specified. Finally,

the system is ready for the next UID verification and validation. The specification requirement can be formulated as follows:

```
Start initial State
IF NOT scan trace = STOP
     OR {Physical Layer agent (PL
agent) receives information UID;
Communication layer agent (CL agent)
receives UID from Physical layer
agent (PL agent);
END;  }
        OR {PL agent sends to CL
agent;
CL agent receives UID from PL agent;
END;   }
     THEN
Requirement is violated;
End requirement;
```

The architecture of the multi-agent and model verification used to check and verify the model of the RFID system is shown in Figure 6 and 7, respectively. Based on the interactions of multi-agents in Figure 7, we have further verified the agent's interaction as shown in Figure 4. The physical layer agent (PL agent) sends the input data of RFID tags with the details containing a tag serial number or user identity (UID) and information of data to be routed to RFID communication layer and

Figure 6. States of RFID system specification for UID checking

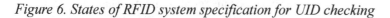
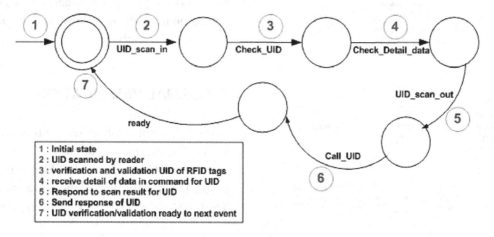

to be verified by the PL agent. The information is verified and validated by RFID Agents based on the reader-tag check scheme in terms of protocol and syntax of command of the input data as shown in Figure 5. The message received from the PL agent with the specified syntax can be accepted by the RFID system. If the contained information is detected to be invalid, the system sends an acknowledgement to the PL agent to rescan the RFID tags again until it is in correct format. Otherwise the tags are blocked and considered void. If the information is valid, the PL agent transmits the details of the tags to communication layer agent (CLA) while formal verification checks for the suitable data in the RFID tags before going to the top layer. At the same time, the CLA sends the acknowledgement to the PL agent stating that the command response of information is successfully delivered and verified.

The RFID system database is updated after the CL agent has completed the verification process. The TL agent plays an important role in ensuring that the data transaction is manageable and releasable during the delivery of the tags information. At the early state, the RFID informa-

tion command message has to be verified by the PL agent in order to ensure that the requirement follows the specification given by the system. If the specification of the particular state has not been satisfied, the PL agent generates a counter-example for the error. It decides whether the systems need to do a refinement or an automatic tag information will be sent to the RFID system. The RFID system uses the CWB-NC model checker in order to evaluate the validity of the data and verify the correctness of the data by checking the information contained in the RFID tags. In RFID system, the load of traffic always increases at its RFID middleware. Usually, RFID middleware reacts by reducing the number of data and distributing it to other RFID middleware, which the data that enters them during the scanning and reading of the RFID tags is low. This operation requires longer time to solve the problem especially by increasing the time of RFID middleware operation. Our approach that implements multi-agent in RFID system can help the RFID middleware to do only their specific filtering operation without doing verification of data contained in RFID tags. This is because informa-

Figure 7. The interactions of multi-agents in RFID system layer

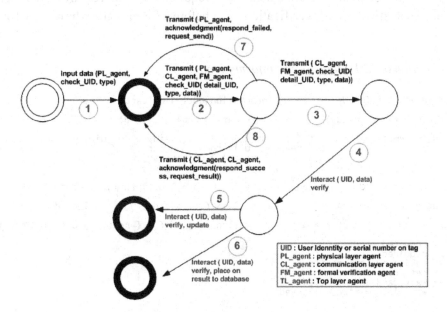

tion on the RFID tags includes the serial number or user identity (UID), data type and data information about the item that must be verified to avoid counterfeiting of information especially the tags that contain privacy information. Another reason is to reduce congestion during the scanning and filtering of tags in RFID middleware and optimize the efficiency of RFID system operation. This can be shown when the time consumed by RFID middleware to verify the RFID tags that enter the RFID system application decreases. The classical verification method can be performed by running more testing at each level of software life cycle. As a result, we have discovered more errors at each level and it is considered too late to detect the errors as our system is a time critical system. We aim to find the errors at the earlier stages to fulfill the requirement analysis and high level design which are concentrated at the early stages of the system. Formal specifications and verification help significantly in ensuring that the protocols operate correctly. Therefore, we feel that a formal specification and verification of the RFID middleware properties of the mechanism is useful. We have developed a formal specification of the data using the CWB-NC automaton model.

For the formal verification of data, we use invariant assertion and simulation (refinement) techniques. The specification of verification information in RFID tag before the tag is read by reader until the information is gathered at the system is as shown in Figure 8. The property that we have specified in our specification must satisfy the correct property as mentioned at the specification follows:

```
"prop correct = required_cardtag ^
required_uid ^ delivered_information
^ return_cardtag ^ wait_cardtag_col-
lected ^ wait_information_ collected
".
```

The specification of verification of RFID tags to find information in basic operation is shown in Figure 6 and can be written as the formal model as shown in as shown in Figure 9. In the case of RFID middleware that has heavy load of traffic entering to the system, we must specify it with different specification. Here, we show the specification of a system that has basic operation and is delayed.

At the simulation of our specification based on the property that has been specified as shown in Figure 9, we can show that the specification has satisfied the formal model that we have proposed. This is because the system meets the user requirement, in this case is the basic RFID system requirement that requires UID detection first before information can be received by the system.

Figure 8. Verification of RFID tags to find information

```
prop required_id = A G ( {ready} -> ( ( {-information_out} ) U {cardtag_in} ) )

prop required_uid = A G ( {ready} -> ( ( {-information_out} ) U {uid} ) )

prop delivered_information = A G ( ( ( {cardtag_in} /\ ( {-ready} ) U {uid} )
                             -> ( {-ready} ) U {information_out} ) \/
                             ( {uid} /\ ( {-ready} ) U {cardtag_in} )
                             -> ( {-ready} ) U {information_out} )

prop returned_cardtag = A G ( {cardtag_in} -> ( ( {-ready} ) U {information_out} ) )

prop wait_cardtag_collected = A G ( {cardtag_out} -> ( ( {-ready} ) U {coll_cardtag} ) )

prop wait_information_collected = A G ( {information_out} -> ( ( {-ready} ) U {coll_information} ) )

prop correct = required_cardtag
            /\ required_uid
            /\ delivered_information
            /\ returned_cardtag
            /\ wait_cardtag_collected
            /\ wait_information_collected
```

Figure 9. Simulation of our specification based on the property that has been specified based on verification of RFID tags to find information

System with basic operation:-

```
proc Machine = ready -> cardtag_in -> uid -> information_out -> InformationGiven
proc InformationGiven = coll_information -> cardtag_out -> CardtagReturned
proc CardtagReturned = coll_cardtag -> Machine
```

System with delay operation:-

```
proc Machine = ready -> cardtag_in -> uid -> information_out -> informationGiven
proc informationGiven = delay -> information_back -> cardtag_out -> CardtagReturned
             [] coll_information -> cardtag_out -> CardtagReturned
proc CardtagReturned = delay -> cardtag_back -> Machine
             [] coll_cardtag -> Machine
```

Figure 10 shows the simulation result of the specification of verification information in RFID.

7. CONCLUSION

In this chapter, we have proposed an agent based approach to verify data in RFID system, especially in the RFID middleware. Agent based technology is helpful when it is used to determine the verification of the RFID data in the RFID system that consists of several layers, from physical layer to top layer. We have shown the multi-agent interaction for RFID system. We have also verified the information sent by agent using formal verification. As a result, the multi-agent can increase the efficiency of the RFID system by implementing verification in RFID layer and RFID middleware operation. For the future work, some RFID network simulations using other formal verification methods for RFID middleware will be studied and used to find better technique that has efficient qual-

Figure 10. Simulation for specification of verification information in RFID

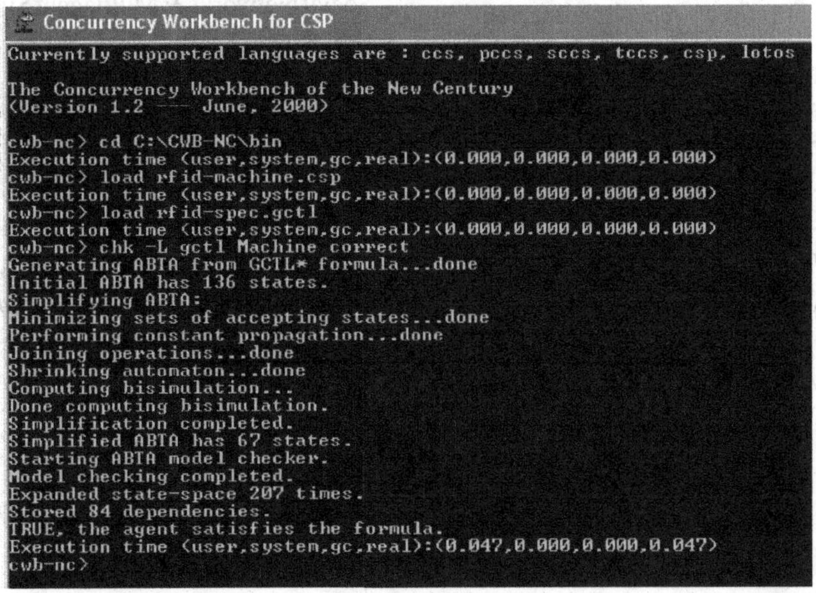

ity of service (QOS) for RFID system, especially for the system that requires efficient management of huge amount of RFID tags.

8. ACKNOWLEDGMENT

This work is supported by the Fundamental Research Funding Scheme (FRGS) under the Ministry of Higher Education (MOHE), Malaysia and Research Management Center, Universiti Teknologi Malaysia (UTM).

9. REFERENCES

Changhong, L., Minqiang, L., & Jisong, K. (2002). *Cooperation structure of multi-agent and algorithms*. In IEEE International Conference on Artificial Intelligence Systems, 2002. (ICAIS 2002), (pp. 303–307).

Cui, J. F., & Chae, H.-S. (2007). Agent-based design of load balancing system for RFID middleware. *Proceedings of the 11th IEEE International Workshop on Future Trends of Distributed Computing Systems (FTDCS'07),* IEEE USA.

EPCglobal Inc. (2011). *Electronic product code.* Retrieved from http://www.epcglobalinc.com/

Foster, I., Jennings, N. R., & Kesselman, C. (2005). Brain meets brawn: Why grid and agents need each other. In Kudenko, D., Kazakov, D., & Alonso, E. (Eds.), *Adaptive agents and multi-agent systems II. (LNCS 3394)* (pp. 19–23). Heidelberg, Germany: Springer.

Gerhard, W. (2000). *Multi agent system–a modern approach to distributed artificial intelligence.* Cambridge, MA/ London, UK: The MIT Press.

Harold, G., Clampitt, H. G., & Jones, E. C. (2007). *RFID certification textbook, 3rd ed.* American RFID Solution, LLD, USA.

Klaus, F. (2003). *RFID handbook: Fundamentals and applications in contactless smart cards and identification* (2nd ed.). England: John Wiley & Sons Ltd. USA.

Lacey, T. H., & Deloach, S. A. (2000). *Automatic verification of multi-agent conversations.* The Midwest Artificial Intelligent & Cognitive Science Conference, (MAICS2000), AAAI Press, USA.

Macmillan-Davies, C. (2006). *Radio frequency identification (RFID) survey.* Booz Allen Hamilton.

Nardine, O., David, R., & Christopher, W. (2006). *Dynamic model checking for multi agent systems* (pp. 43–60). Berlin/Heidelberg, Germany: Springer-Verlag.

Selamat, A., & Lockman, T. (2009). Multi-agent verification of RFID system. In N. T. Nguyen, R. Katarzyniak, & A. Janiak (Eds.), *Challenges in computational collective intelligence* (pp. 255-265). Berlin/Heidelberg, Germany: Springer-Verlag. 1st International Conference on Computational Collective Intelligence - Semantic Web, Social Networks & Multiagent Systems, Wroclaw (Poland).

Weinstein, R. (2005). RFID, a technical overview and its application to the enterprise. *Proceedings of IEEE IT, 7*(30) 27–33. IEEE USA.

Yan, W., Kian, L. T., & Jian, R. (2004). PumaMart: Parallel and autonomous agents based internet marketplace. [f]. *Electronic Commerce Research an Application, 3*(3), 294–310. doi:10.1016/j.elerap.2004.01.003

Chapter 7
Tele–Immersive Collaborative Environment with Tiled Display Wall

Yasuo Ebara
Osaka University, Japan

ABSTRACT

In intellectual collaborative works with participants between remote sites via WAN, CSCW have been used as general communication tools. Especially, the sharing of various, high-quality digital contents such as various materials, computer graphics or visualization contents, and video streaming by between remote places is important to recognize or analyze to easily refer to these contents. However, the image magnification by general projector and large-sized display equipment is low-resolution, and sufficient quality of contents is not obtained. In this research, the author has constructed a tele-immersive collaborative environment with a tiled display wall. In this environment, the author has implemented an application to display high-resolution real video streaming on a tiled display wall in remote place. By using the application, the author displayed the clear video image of remote place over a wide range. Then, the author conducted experimental verification on the effect for eye-to-eye contact by changing the position of camera on frame of LCDs on tiled display wall, and has collected a lot of knowledge. Moreover, the author has tried realistic display processing of high-resolution astronomical observation image and movie data, and it has enabled observation of the entire image of observation data all over tiled display wall.

DOI: 10.4018/978-1-61520-871-5.ch007

1. INTRODUCTION

Collaborative works between multi-field researchers using computer graphics and visualization techniques become important in order to utilize these large-scale data effectively, and can support human insight and interpretation. In order to realize remote collaborative works smoothly with participants at remote sites via WAN, Computer Supported Cooperative Work (CSCW) tools, such as e-mail, WWW browser, or video-conference systems have been used as general applications (Luczak, 2002).

Recently, various software such as video-phones for remote communication with PCs (Personal Computers) are now provided by number of users, and the demands for these tend to increase each year. However, the screen size to display video image used in these software is small. We consider that these are insufficient for displaying the existence of remote participants because the resolution of video image is low. Moreover, it is considered that non-verbal communication such as eye-to-eye contact is important, in addition to the existence of remote participants by transmission of a video in real time to realize remote communication with high-presence via WAN (Finn, 1997; Grayson, 2003).

In order to realize the sharing of high-quality information with video-conference system and enormous quantity of visualization contents, the use of large-scale display system with tele-immersion technology (Towles, 2002; Sadagic, 2001; Park, 2000) is effective, and it is considered to use display equipment such as a projectors and large-scale monitors. However, how a grainy image is displayed on large-sized screen depends on resolution specification of the display equipment.

We focus on the tiled display technology (Renambot, 2004; Ni, 2006; Nirnimesh, 2007) that realizes large-scaled display with two or more LCDs, and we tried to display a high-resolution video image on the large-scale display as an effective wide-area screen system to solve these issues. We have constructed a tele-immersive environment with tiled display wall to realize remote collaborative works with high-resolution video streaming and visualization contents.

2. RELATED WORK

Tele-immersion is defined as a new type of tele-communication media in which virtual reality has been incorporated into video-conference systems (Towles, 2002; Sadagic, 2001; Park, 2000 Schreer, 2005; Craig, 2009). The goal of tele-immersion is to enable users in physically remote spaces to interact with one another in a shared space that mixes both local and remote realities, and allows participants to share a mutual sense of presence.

In the 3D tele-immersion system, a user wears polarized glasses and a head tracker as a view-dependent scene is rendered in real-time on a large stereoscopic display in 3D (Gibbs, 1999; Kauff, 2002; Kelshikar, 2003; Towles, 2003; Blundell, 2005). Ideally, there exists a seamless continuum between the users' experience of local and remote space within the application. A technique has been developed which creates a 3D model from a human image captured by multi-viewpoint cameras. Video images depend on participant's direction of eyes in remote places at real time, as examples of studies on eye-to-eye contact in remote communication with video image (Sadagic, 2001) indicate. A technique has developed to merge virtual head images which create computer graphics on video images of heads in order to form HDM (Head Mount Display) to reconstruct eye-to-eye contact in a virtual communication environment with HDM (Takemura, 2005). However, these technologies are necessary to obtain position information of heads in real time to apply independent video image for each participant, and application of sensors on heads is fundamental. Therefore, it is difficult to have a conversation face to face, and this causes interference from smooth communication between participants.

Recently, IPT (Immersive Projection Technology) such as the CAVE system (Cruz-Neira, 1993; Froehlich, 2001) has become popular, and tele-immersive virtual environments are constructed by using IPT. In addition, when several immersive projection environments have been connected through a high-speed network, the real-world oriented 3D human image is also required as a remote communication with high-presence tools between remote places (Leigh, 1997). In order to realize such a demand, video avatar technology has been studied (Ogi, 2006; Schroeder, 2006). The video avatar is a technique to represent a human image with high-presence by integrating the live video image of the human into the 3D virtual world. However, collaborative works in IPT environment require deflection glasses and HMD. In such a condition, it is usually difficult to carry out face-to-face communication because the participant can't make eye-to-eye contact with others; i.e. it interferes with nonverbal communication.

On the other hand, a 3D display environment using a merged video image obtained from the multi-viewpoint videos merging system set up in the actual space has been developed (Ando, 2005). By using the system, we have examined how well two estimators can establish eye-to-eye contact with a gazer on the auto-stereoscopic display during a face-to-face communication and proved that two estimators could realize eye-to-eye contact in each direction (Ebara, 2006). However, we have considered that it is difficult to realize remote communication with high-presence by the restriction of space which can move in collaborative work since the auto-stereoscopic display indicates an unfocused 3D video image by positions. Therefore, we consider that the technology to display more realistic information is effective in order to realize remote communication with high-presence.

In order to solve these issues, we have studied to use the tiled display wall to display a high-resolution video image on the large-scale display. In this research, we have constructed tele-immersive collaborative environment with scalable tiled display wall.

3. TILED DISPLAY WALL

3.1. Tiled Display Technology

Tiled display wall is a technology to display a high-resolution image on the large-sized screen with two or more LCD panels in order to construct effective large-sized display system. Much research has been developed for tiled display wall and remote displays by using distribute rendering technique.

For example, Chromium have designed and built a system that provides a generic mechanism for manipulating streams of graphics API commands (Humphreys, 2002). It can be used as the underlying mechanism for any cluster graphics algorithm by having the algorithm use OpenGL to move geometry and imagery across a network as required. In addition, Chromium's DMX extension allows execution of multiple applications and window control. However, it has a single source, and its design is not suitable for data streaming over a long-distance network.

Moreover, CGLX (Cross-Platform Cluster Graphic Library) is a flexible, transparent OpenGL-based graphics framework for distributed high performance visualization systems in a master-slave environment (CGLX Project). The framework was developed to enable OpenGL programs to be executed on visualization clusters such as a high-resolution tiled display wall and to maximize the achievable performance and resolution for OpenGL-based applications on such systems.

We apply SAGE (Scalable Adaptive Graphics Environment) (Renambot, 2004; Renambot, 2006; Jeong, 2006) developed by Electronic Visualization Laboratory (EVL) to deliver streaming pixel data with virtual high-resolution frame buffer to a number of graphical sources for tiled display wall. SAGE is a graphics streaming architecture for supporting collaborative scientific visualization environments with potentially hundreds of mega-pixels of contiguous display resolution. In collaborative scientific visualization, it is crucial to share high-resolution visualization image as well as high quality video between participants at local or remote sites. The network-centered architecture of SAGE allows collaborators to simultaneously run various applications on local or remote clusters, and share them by streaming.

3.2. System Configuration

We have constructed tiled display wall environment consisting of 1 master node, 8 display nodes, and 16 LCD panels.

The tiled display wall LCDs are located at 4 x 4 arrays as shown in Figure 1. These appliance specifications are shown in Table 1. Master node and all display nodes are connected by a gigabit Ethernet network.

4. APPLICATION FOR REMOTE COLLABORATIVE ENVIRONMENT WITH TILED DISPLAY WALL

4.1. Remote Communication by Using High-Resolution Real Video Streaming

We have implemented an application of high-resolution real video streaming with SAIL. Pixel information obtained from IEEE1394 camera is rendered as a video image by gl-Draw Pixels on the tiled display wall. We have located a small IEEE1394 camera at the center of tiled display wall in order to realize remote communication with high-presence such as face-to-face by capturing the scene of each participant at the front.

Figure 2 shows the configuration of the experimental network environment. In this experimental network, Kyoto and Tokyo sites are connected to

Figure 1. Tiled display wall environment

Table 1. Machine specification

Master node	
CPU Memory VGA OS	Intel Xeon (Quad Core) 1.6[GHz] (x2). 8,192[MB] RAM. GLADIAC776G SUSE 10.1 (Linux 2.6.16.21-0.25-smp)
Display node (x8)	
CPU Memory VGA OS	Intel Core2 Duo 1.86[GHz] 1,024[MB] RAM. NVIDIA Quadro FX 560 SUSE 10.1 (Linux 2.6.16.21-0.25-smp)
LCD panel (EIZO FlexScan S170 (x16)	
Size	17 inch (1280x1024)
IEEE1394 Camera (Point Grey Research: Flea)	
Resolution Speed	1024x768 30[fps]

the Internet using VPN (IPSec) routers. Each tiled display wall is connected to the VPN routers using fast Ethernet (100Mbps) network. Each video image captured by small IEEE1394 camera located at the center of tiled display wall is transmitted to remote master node, and its video image is displayed on remote tiled display wall. In addition, we have used a voice communication application by voice communication Audio Library (voCAL) (Kukimoto, 2004) to promote smooth, remote collaborative work in the tiled display wall. The voCAL provides a multipoint network connection without the use of MCU or IP multicast.

Figure 3 show a video image captured by an IEEE1394 camera transmitted via WAN, and displayed on a remote tiled display wall. The

Figure 2. Network configuration between Kyoto and Tokyo

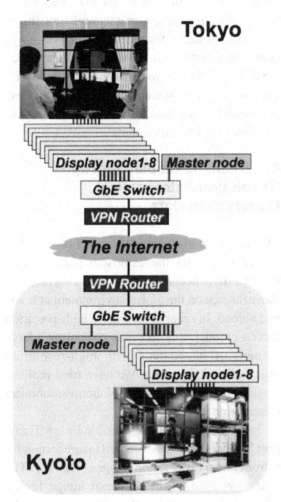

resolution of each display result is 5120 x 4096 pixels. Each video image is enlarged in a transverse direction. From these results, we showed that the existence of a participant and ambiance in a remote place displayed real video with high-presence on local tiled display wall environment.

4.2. Experiment on Eye-To-Eye Contact in Remote Communication with Tiled Display Wall

In a usual video-conference system, the camera is located at the top or sides of display, and as a result, the participants' gazes slide in opposite different directions. The direction of the participant's eyes is pointed at the remote participant displayed on the screen, although the setting enables pointing the camera at local participant. Therefore, it is difficult to have a conversation face-to-face, and this interferes with smooth communication between participants of remote places.

In contrast, the tiled display wall enables free position of the camera by using a frame of LCD panel. In this research, we have examined experimental verification on the effect for eye-to-eye contact by changing the position of camera on frame of LCDs on tiled display wall.

As experimental environment, a gazer and an estimator in remote places sit 1.5 [m] away from each tiled display wall and watch each video im-

Figure 3. High-resolution real video streaming image (Resolution: 5120 x 4096 pixels)

Video image from Tokyo on TDW of Kyoto   Video image from Kyoto on TDW of Tokyo

age on tiled display wall as shown in Figure 4. The display resolution of the video image in each remote place is configured at 2560 x 2048 pixels. In this experiment, a camera at gazer side is put in any of positions A-D. Gazer changes the direction of their eyes in random order in 9 directions every 10 seconds at the condition of each position. An estimator discriminates gazer's direction of eyes in the display video image on the tiled display wall. The number of discriminations by each estimator is 20 times for each position (A-D), and the camera position is changed every 10 times repeatedly. Moreover, an estimator provides answers to how one feels eye-to-eye contact for a gazer in video image on tiled display wall in discrimination of gazer's direction of eyes at each time.

From experimental results, we found to have a high tendency to discriminate the gazer's direction of their eyes in case that camera is located at close position for direction of eyes that an estimator faces on the front. In addition, the accuracy rate when the camera is in the bottom position was lower than the case of the top position. From

Figure 4. Gazer and estimator

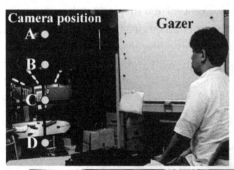

the above results, we showed experimentally that because each participant is able to change direction of eyes to a camera in a natural way, this is an important factor for realization of eye-to-eye contact in remote communication. In future works, we will examine the comparison experiment with the case of usual screen environments and experimental verification in actual remote communication between participants.

4.3. Realistic Display for High-Resolution Astronomical Observation Data

The research of Space Weather Forecast has started to predict the explosion phenomenon, called a flare, occurring on the sun's surface and the influence on the global environment at home and abroad. In order to establish a high-precision forecast model, it is necessary to analyze a large amount of phenomena with high-resolution observation image data. We have tried realistic display processing of high-resolution astronomical observation image data.

In general, FITS (The Flexible Image Transport System) is used as standard image format for astronomical observation images (Wells, 1981). It is now used as the universal image format which enables it to handle ordinary data in the field of astronomy, such as astronomical spectra and event data of current X-ray observations. We have tried realistic display of image data by FITS format on tiled display wall. ImageViewer is attached in SAGE as the image viewer application. However, ImageViewer is not supported display in FITS format. We have improved ImageViewer to display images in FITS format. In this research, the observation data (FITS format, resolution 4096 x 4096) by the Solar Magnetic Activity Research Telescope (SMART), located in Kwasan and Hida Observations, Kyoto University, is used as image data. In this experiment, observation data saved in the local site is transmitted via WAN, and displayed on the tiled display wall in remote places.

An example of astronomical observation data by realistic resolution on the tiled display wall is shown in Figure 5. Moreover, Figure 6 shows an example of multi-display of astronomical observation images on the tiled display wall. As these results show, this enabled us to observe the entire image of observation data all over the tiled display wall. We consider that it is possible to promote new intellectual discoveries from observation data by cooperative works, as it can observed by multiple users at the same time in this environment.

In addition, it is possible, by reducing a large amount of image data, to display expanded and reduced scale at free positions in this environment. We consider that the possibility of the analysis for these observation images by various techniques can be expected. The construction of new environment according to user requirements will be examined in the future.

5. EXAMPLE OF APPLICATION FIELDS

The fields of education, medical care, and entertainment are considered as effective applications of the remote collaborative environment with tiled display wall. In this research, as used in the field of education, we have executed the cooperative class using multi LCDs in group work, and tiled display wall in the entire discussion to display materials by students. In addition, distance learning with tiled display wall has been executed in cooperation with the class given at the same time in other buildings, as shown in Figure 7. It has been understood that the study on an effective display method for the video image and materials is important, even though each student used it effectively for the presentation and the discussion through the environment. Moreover, we expect the active use of the electronic blackboard of the tiled display wall, but only if the screen the teacher and the students own can be put on tiled display wall by easy operation that doesn't need the full-time maintenance.

Figure 5. Realistic display of astronomical observation image (4096 x 4096 pixels)

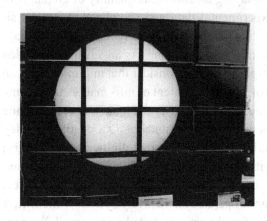

Figure 6. Multi-display of astronomical observation images

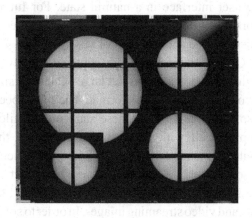

Figure 7. Distance learning with tiled display wall

Through this evaluation, the demands for displaying an enormous quantity of graphs with experimental data and visualization images simultaneously in order to realize remote collaborative works is rising. As an advantage of tiled display wall, we consider that multiple users can look at a high content of information at the same time. However, it is difficult to execute while viewing various contents data on tiled display wall when users operate the interactive control with a mobile terminal. Therefore, it is important to the development of the user interface that it can be operated interactively by users while always viewing the screen of tiled display wall. We consider if a user could control movement, rotation, scaling and hand-written annotation for contents data on tiled display wall by holding or wearing the user interface in a natural state. For future work, we will propose and implement the mechanism for the achievement of this system.

On the other hand, the contents data with high-resolution also has the large-scale data size according to the image format. The high-speed display processing of these data on the tiled display wall with the system resource of the contents management server becomes difficult in some cases. In addition, it has a big effect on the simultaneous display of other contents, like data and video streaming images. In order to solve the issue, the distributed rendering mechanism to execute efficient display processing to display node connected with each LCD in tiled display wall is necessary. Moreover, we consider that the display technique to realize continuous display of the time series data and simultaneous display of 3D contents data by the different observing point as available application of multi-screen in tiled display wall is important in the future.

6. CONCLUSION

In this research, we have constructed a tele-immersive environment with a tiled display wall and considered the possibility to construct an environment for remote collaborative works by implementation of various collaborative applications such as effective display of high-resolution video streaming and visualization contents.

In addition, we have examined the possibility of high-presence remote communication which eye-to-eye contact can realize with each other by locating a small IEEE1394 camera at each position with frame of LCDs in tiled display wall and have collected much knowledge.

REFERENCES

Ando, T., Mashitani, K., Higashino, M., Kanayama, H., Murata, H., & Funazou, Y. (2005). Multiview image integration system for glassless 3D display. *SPIE, 5664*(1), 158–166. doi:10.1117/12.596849

Blundell, B. G., & Schwarz, A. J. (2005). *Creative 3-D display and interaction interfaces: A trans-disciplinary approach*. Wiley-Interscience. doi:10.1002/0471764078

CGLX Project. (2010). Retrieved from http://vis.ucsd.edu/~cglx

Craig, A., Sherman, W. R., & Will, J. D. (2009). *Developing virtual reality applications: Foundations of effective design*. Morgan Kaufmann.

Cruz-Neira, C., Sandin, D. J., & DeFanti, T. A. (1993). Surround-screen projection-based virtual reality: The design and implementation of the CAVE. *SIGGRAPH, 93*, 135–142.

Ebara, Y., Nabuchi, T., Sakamoto, N., & Koyamada, K. (2006). *Study on eye-to-eye contact by multi-viewpoint videos merging system for tele-immersive environment*. IEEE International Workshop on Network-based Virtual Reality and Tele-existence, (pp. 647-651).

Finn, K. E., Sellen, A. J., & Wilbur, S. B. (1997). *Video-mediated communication*. Lawrence Erlbaum Assoc Inc.

Froehlich, B., Deisinger, J., & Bullinger, H. J. (2001). *Immersive projection technology and virtual environments*. Springer.

Gibbs, S. J., Arapis, C., & Breitender, C. J. (1999). TELEPORT-towards immersive copresence. [Springer-Verlag]. *Multimedia Systems, 7*, 214–221. doi:10.1007/s005300050123

Grayson, D. M., & Monk, A. F. (2003). Are you looking at me? Eye contact and desktop video conferencing. *ACM Transactions on Computer-Human Interaction, 10*(3), 221–243. doi:10.1145/937549.937552

Humphreys, G., Houston, M., Ng, Y., Frank, R., Ahern, S., Kirchner, P., & Klosowski, J. T. (2002). *Chromium: A stream-processing framework for interactive rendering on clusters*. The 29th Annual Conference on Computer Graphics and Interactive Techniques SIGGRAPH '02, (pp. 693-702).

Jeong, B., Renambot, L., Jagodic, R., Singh, R., Aguilera, J., Johnson, A., & Leigh, J. (2006). *High-performance dynamic graphics streaming for scalable adaptive graphics environment*. ACM/IEEE Conference on Supercomputing 2006, (p. 24).

Kauff, P., & Schreer, O. (2002). An immersive 3D video-conferencing system using shared virtual team user environments. *Proceedings of the 4th International Conference on Collaborative Virtual Environments*, (pp. 105-112).

Kelshikar, N., Zabulis, X., Mulligan, J., Daniilidis, K., Sawant, V., & Sinha, S. et al. (2003). *Real-time terascale implementation of teleimmersion*. International Conference on Computation Science, (pp. 33-42).

Kukimoto, N., Ebara, Y., & Koyamada, K. (2004). Voice communication library for collaborative virtual environment. (IPSJ Technical report, 109).

Leigh, J., DeFanti, T. A., Johnson, A. E., Brown, M. D., & Sandin, D. J. (1997). Global tele-immersion: Better than being there. *Proceedings in ICAT, 97*, 10–17.

Luczak, H. (2002). Computer supported collaborative work -making information aware. *International Journal of Human-Computer Interaction*. Lawrence Erlbaum Assoc Inc.

Ni, T., Schmidt, G. S., Staadt, O. G., Livingston, M. A., Ball, R., & May, R. (2006). *A survey of large high-resolution display technologies, techniques, and applications*. The IEEE Conference on Virtual Reality 2006, (pp. 223-236).

Nirnimesh, H. P., & Narayanan, P. J. (2007). Garuda: A scalable tiled display wall using commodity PCs. *IEEE Transactions on Visualization and Computer Graphics, 13*(5), 864–877. doi:10.1109/TVCG.2007.1049

Ogi, T., & Sakai, M. (2006). Communication in the networked immersive environment. *ASIAGRAPH, 2006*, 67–72.

Park, K. S., Kapoor, A., Scharver, C., & Leigh, J. (2000). Exploiting multiple perspectives in tele-immersion. *Proceedings of Immersive Projection Technology Workshop*.

Renambot, L., Jeong, B., Jagodic, R., Johnson, A., Leigh, J., & Aguilera, J. (2006). *Collaborative visualization using high-resolution tiled displays*. CHI 06 Workshop on Information Visualization and Interaction Techniques for Collaboration Across Multiple Displays.

Renambot, L., Rao, A., Singh, R., Jeong, B., Krishnaprasad, N., & Vishwanath, V. … Johnson, A. (2004). *SAGE: The Scalable Adaptive Graphics Environment*. Workshop on Advanced Collaborative Environments.

Sadagic, A., Towles, H., Holden, L., Daniilidis, K., & Zeleznik, B. (2001). *Tele-immersion portal: Towards an ultimate synthesis of computer graphics and computer vision systems.* 4th Annual International Workshop on Presence, (pp. 21-23).

Schreer, O. Kauff, P. & Sikora, T. (2005). *3D video communication: Algorithms, concepts and real-time systems in human centred communication.* Wiley.

Schroeder, R., & Axelsson, A. (2006). *Avatars at work and play: Collaboration and interaction in shared virtual environments (computer supported cooperative work).* Springer.

Takemura, M., & Ohta, Y. (2005). *Generating high-definition facial video for shared mixed reality.* IAPR Conference on Machine Vision Applications, (pp. 422-425).

Towles, H., Chen, W., Yang, R., Kum, S., Fuchs, H., & Kelshikar, N., et al. (2002). *3D tele-collaboration over Internet.* International Workshop on Immersive Telepresence.

Towles, H., Kum, S., Sparks, T., Sinha, S., Larsen, S., & Beddes, N. (2003). *Transport and rendering challenges of multi-stream 3D tele-immersion data.* NSF Lake Tahoe Workshop on Collaborative Virtual Reality and Visualization.

Wells, D. C., Greisen, E. W., & Harten, R. H. (1981). FITS: A Flexible Image Transport System. *Astronomy & Astrophysics, 44,* 363–370.

Section 2
Analysis and Social Design

Chapter 8
E–Innovation as Source of Business Value in Firms

Pedro Soto-Acosta
University of Murcia, Spain

Ricardo Colomo-Palacios
Universidad Carlos III de Madrid, Spain

Euripidis N. Loukis
University of the Aegean, Greece

ABSTRACT

This chapter seeks to assess the relationship between Web infrastructure and Internet-based innovation as sources of business value. To respond to this challenge, a conceptual model, grounded in the resource-based view (RBV) is developed. To test hypotheses, a large sample consisting of Spanish firms is employed. The results show that, as hypothesized, Web infrastructure is not positively related to business value and that Internet-based innovation has a positive significant impact on business value. In addition, the results show no significant complementarity between Web infrastructure and Internet-based innovation.

INTRODUCTION

Recently, much debate about the value of IT and e-business has been raised. The technology itself will rarely create superiority. For that reason, some research studies found that IT spending rarely correlates to superior performance (Carr, 2003; Brynjolfsson and Hitt, 2000; Soto-Acosta and Meroño-Cerdan, 2009). However, even though competitors may copy an IT infrastructure, relative advantage can be created and sustained where the

technology leverages some other critical resource. A number of such complementary resources have been identified by previous studies, such as size, structure, culture, and so on, that could make it difficult for competitors to copy the total effect of the technology (Kettinger et al, 1994; Hempel, 2003; Arvanitis 2005; Loukis et al, 2009). This complementarity of resources is a corner stone of the resource-based view (RBV) and has been offered as an explanation of how IT has largely overcome its paradoxical nature and is contributing to business value (Bhatt and Grover, 2005; Clemons and Row, 1991).

DOI: 10.4018/978-1-61520-871-5.ch008

Innovation can be defined as the search for, the discovery and development of new technologies, new products and/or services, new processes and new organizational structures (Carneiro, 2000; Meroño-Cerdan et al., 2008b). Many researchers (e.g. Hamel 2002) emphasized the role of IT as an enabler of product and process innovation. Thus, IT may be source of competitive advantage through innovation. Web-based tools allow information and knowledge exchange, as well as work execution by integrating information, documents and employees. Thus, for instance, intranets can be used to distribute and share individual experience and innovation throughout the organization (Bhatt et al, 2005). In this sense, research is starting to focus on analysing how the web is and will change innovation within and between companies (Sawhney and Prandelli, 2000).

Consequently, to respond to these challenges, this chapter develops a conceptual model, grounded in the RBV, to analyze the relationship between Web infrastructure and Internet-based innovation as source of business value at the level of an individual firm. The analysis employs a large sample of companies from different industries for hypothesis testing.

The chapter consists of six sections and is structured as follows: The next section reviews the relevant literature. In Section 3, hypotheses are developed. Following that, the methodology used for sample selection and data collection is discussed. Then, data analysis and results are examined. Finally, the chapter ends with a discussion of research findings, limitations and concluding remarks.

LITERATURE REVIEW

The RBV of the firm (Barney, 1991; Schulze, 1992; Hoopes et al, 2003) is a well established theoretical framework from the strategic management domain which provides a solid foundation to differentiate between IT resources and IT capabilities and

study their separate influences on performance (Santhanam and Hartono, 2003).Based on this analysis, Bharadwaj (2000) suggested that if firms can combine IT related resources to create unique IT capabilities, they can improve their performance. IS researchers have followed this consideration of IT capability because competition may easily result in the duplication of investment in IT resources, and companies can purchase the same hardware and software to remove competitive advantage (Santhanam and Hartono, 2003). In this respect, research offers a useful distinction between IT resources and IT capabilities. The former is asset-based, while the latter comprises a mixture of assets formed around the productive use of IT.

In general, IT resources are not difficult to imitate; physical technology is by itself typically imitable. If one firm can purchase these physical technologies and thereby implement some strategies, then other firms should also be able to purchase these technologies, and thus such tools should not be a source of competitive advantage (Barney, 1991). However, firms may obtain competitive advantages from exploiting their physical technology in a better (and/or different) way than other firms, even though competing firms do not vary in terms of the physical technology they possess. IT resources are necessary, but not a sufficient condition, for competitive advantages (Clemons and Row, 1991). IT resources rarely contribute directly to competitive advantage. Instead, they form part of a complex chain of assets (IT capabilities) that may lead to better performance. Thus, some researchers have described this in terms of IT capabilities and argue that IT capabilities can create uniqueness and provide organizations a competitive advantage (Bhardwaj, 2000, Bhatt and Grover, 2005; Mata et al., 1995; Santhanam and Hartono, 2003).

The evaluation of the organisational performance impact of ITs is also an important issue within the area management information systems (Soto-Acosta, 2008). In this sense, firm performance has been principally measured by subjective measures (e.g., Lederer et al. 2001; Soto-Acosta and Meroño-Cerdan 2008; Zhu and Kraemer 2005) or by using financial measures (e.g., Meroño-Cerdan and Soto-Acosta 2007; Zhu and Kraemer 2002). The first normally uses senior executives as the key informants on the subjective measures of firm performance. Given the fact that IT investments may provide benefits after a certain period but increase operating costs in the short term, the locus of impact, that is, the business process, should be the primary level of analysis. As a result, some researchers have given up on trying to correlate financial results with IT investments and suggest focusing on the actual processes that IT is supposed to enhance (Mukhopadhyayet al. 1995). These arguments lead to the conclusion that a process approach should be used to explain the generation of IT value from a resource-based perspective, and this is the approach adopted in the present study. The present research uses the effectiveness of online procurement to measure e-business value. The business value of this process is discussed here.

E-procurement, or buying online, can potentially provide distinct value propositions to the firm. These come from the reduction of procurement and inventory costs, as well as strategic networks with suppliers that allow effective and efficient supply chain management (SCM). With regard to procurement costs, Kaplan and Sawhney (2002) indicated that buying in e-marketplaces considerably reduces transaction costs. With regard to strategic links and SCM, Internet technologies can enhance SCM decision making by enabling the collection of real-time information, and access to and analysis of this data in order to facilitate collaboration between trading partners in a supply chain. In this sense, Frohlich and Westbrook (2002) showed the importance of linking customers and suppliers together in tightly integrated networks. As a result of e-procurement, the collection of real-time information on demand is possible

and, more importantly, products and services are delivered quickly and reliably when and where they are needed (Frohlich, 2002).

DEVELOPMENT OF HYPOTHESES

This section develops hypotheses for the present study, drawing on the existing information systems and e-business literature. Three relationships will be explored: Web infrastructure and business value, Internet-based innovation and business value, and the complementarity of Web infrastructure and Internet-based innovation as source of business value.

Web Infrastructure and Business Value

Firms obtain competitive advantages on the basis of corporate resources that are firm specific, valuable, rare, imperfectly imitable, and not strategically substitutable by other resources (Barney, 1991). IT resources are easy to duplicate, and, hence, IT resources per se do not provide competitive advantages (Santhanam and Hartono, 2003). Although IT infrastructure is argued to be valuable, it is not a source of competitive advantage (Bhatt and Grover, 2005). Thus, IT infrastructure will rarely lead to superior performance. Similarly, Web infrastructure is not difficult to imitate. In general, Internet technology is by itself imitable. If one firm can purchase certain Internet technologies and thereby implement some strategies, then other firms should also be able to purchase these technologies, and thus such tools should not be a source of competitive advantage. Furthermore, as the diffusion of the Internet continues, the ability of proprietary IT to be a source of competitive advantage continues to be eroded. These arguments suggest that Web infrastructure may not have a significant impact on business value. Thus, the following hypothesis is proposed:

Hypothesis 1: There is no relationship between Web infrastructure and business value

Internet-Based Innovation and Business Value

Investing in IT is not a necessary nor sufficient condition for improving firm performance, since IT investments might be misused (Tallon et al., 2000). In this sense, IT assets cannot improve organizational performance if they are not used appropriately. However, when used appropriately IT is expected to create intermediary effects, such as IT being embedded in products and services and streamlined business processes (Ravichandran and Lertwongsatien, 2005). That is, IT may facilitate product/service innovation and process innovation which can be expected to have an influence on business value. IT may be source of competitive advantage through innovation. Thus, since Web-based tools allow innovation through information and knowledge exchange, as well as work execution by integrating information, documents and employees (Meroño-Cerdan et al., 2008a), the following hypothesis is formulated:

Hypothesis 2: There is a positive relationship between Internet-based innovation and business value

The Complementarity of Web Infrastructure and Internet-Based Innovation

Although there is research that posit a direct relationship between IT and firm performance (Bharadwaj, 2000; Santhanam and Hartono, 2003), others have questioned the direct-effect argument and emphasized that ITs are likely to affect firm performance only when they are deployed to create unique complementarities with other firm resources (Clemons and Row, 1991; Powell and Dent-Micallef, 1997).

The RBV highlights the role of complementarity as a source of value creation in e-business, though it is not the only source as suggested by Amit and Zott (2001). As mentioned earlier, Web infrastructure is not difficult to imitate and per se do not provide competitive advantages. However, having a proper Web infrastructure may facilitate the internal processing of online operations and this way influence positively firm performance. That is, the fact of possessing an adequate Web infrastructure can be critical for efficient information and knowledge sharing as well as for the formation of virtual teams to execute the innovation process (Adamides and Karacapilidis, 2006; Kessler, 2003). The following hypothesis incorporates these expectations:

Hypothesis 3: The complementarity between Web infrastructure and Internet-based innovations explains variations in business value

METHODOLOGY

Data

The data source for the present study is the e-business W@tch survey 2003, an initiative launched by the European Commission for monitoring the adoption of IT and e-business activity. The field work of the survey was conducted by Ipsos Eco Consulting on behalf of the e-business W@tch and was carried out using computer-aided telephone interview (CATI) technology. Telephone interviews with decision-makers in enterprises were conducted in March and November 2003. The decision-maker targeted by the survey was normally the person responsible for IT within the company, typically the IT manager. Alternatively, particularly in small enterprises without a separate IT unit, the managing director or owner was interviewed.

The population considered in this study was the set of all enterprises which are active at the national territory of Spain and which have their primary business activity in one of ten sectors considered (see Table 1). The sample drawn was a random sample of companies from the respective sector population with the objective of fulfilling strata with respect to business size. A share of 10% of large companies (250+ employees), 30% of medium sized enterprises (50-249 employees) and 25% of small enterprises (10-49 employees) was intended. The number of firms totalled 1,010. 91.1% of firms were small and medium-sized enterprises (less than 250 employees) and each sector considered had a share of around 10% of the total sample.

With regard to respondents' titles, 54.4% were IS managers, nearly 20% were managing directors, and 12.1% were owners. The dataset was examined for potential bias in terms of the respondents' titles. Since respondents included both IT managers and non-IT managers, one could argue that IT managers may overestimate e-business value. To test this possible bias, the sample was divided into two groups: IS managers (head of IT/DP and other IT senior managers) versus non-IS managers (owner, managing director, strategy development and others). One-way ANOVA was used to compare the means of factor scores between the two groups. No significant differences were found, suggesting that the role of the respondents did not cause any survey biases.

Measures of Variables

Measurement items were introduced on the basis of a careful literature review. Confirmatory factor analysis (CFA) was used to test the constructs. Based on the CFA assessment, the constructs were further refined and then fitted again. Constructs and associated indicators, as well as prior research support, are listed in the Appendix and discussed below.

- **Business value.** As discussed earlier, the present research uses the effectiveness of e-procurement for measuring business value. That is, business value is assessed through the business impact of purchasing online.
- **Web infrastructure construct.** This construct represents the adoption of physical Internet technologies. In this sense, respondents were required to assess the presence of four Internet tools: website, Intranet, Extranet and LAN (local area network).
- **Internet-based innovation.** This construct represents the introduction of product/service and process innovations directly related to or enabled by Internet-based technology.

Since correctly measuring is important, tests of reliability and validity for the three constructs were performed. The validity of the construct is established by relating a measuring instrument to a general theoretical framework in order to

Table 1. Statistics for reliability and validity tests

Measures	Items	Reliability	Convergent validity	Discriminant validity
		(Cronbach alpha)	(correlation of item with total store-item)	(factor loading on single factors)
E-business value	3	0.767	0.841; 0.828; 0.811	0.673; 0.719; 0.521
Web infrastructure	5	0.724	0.669; 0.749; 0.676; 0.707; 0.659	0.625; 0.747; 0.718; 0.685; 0.690
Internet-based innovation	2	0.862	0.929; 0.929	0.862; 0.862

determine whether the instrument is tied to the concepts and theoretical assumptions they are employing. In order to obtain evidence of construct validity, convergent validity and discriminant validity are assessed. For the first one, the item-to-total correlation is examined. The lower limit is 0.4. Discriminant validity is checked by a factor analysis. Each variable must have a factor loading in a single factor over 0.5. The results (Table 1) confirm that each construct is unidimensional and factorially different and that all items employed for operationalizing a particular construct load on a single factor. The reliability is the accuracy or precision of a measuring instrument, that is, the extent to which the respondent can answer the same or practically the same value each time. The internal reliability was assessed by calculating the Cronbach's alpha. It can be also observed that acceptable values (above 0.70) are obtained in all cases. Relatively high values of reliability and validity imply that the instruments used in this study are adequate. As shown in Table 1, tests of reliability and validity for the scales presented acceptable values in all cases.

EMPIRICAL RESULTS

To test the hypotheses, business industry and business size were introduced as control variables in order to avoid unexpected effects on e-business value. The former identified whether the business was operating at the manufacturing, services or commercial industry and was coded as a dummy variable. The latter was measured as the total number of employees and was coded as a continuous variable.

The basic econometric relationships may be specified as follows:

$$DV = f(WI, IBI, WI * IBI, \varepsilon) \qquad (1)$$

where WI denotes Web infrastructure; IBI stands for Internet-based innovation; and WI * IBI

represents the interaction effect between Web infrastructure and Internet-based innovation. DV denotes the dependent variable (e-business value). More specifically, the regression equation is:

$$DV = \alpha + \beta_1 WI + \beta_2 IBI + \beta_3 WI * IBI + (Firm\text{-}Size + IndustryDummies) + \varepsilon \qquad (2)$$

Where α is the intercept; the βi's are coefficients; and ε is the residual term that captures the net effect of all unspecified factors. The model includes both main and the interaction effect between Web infrastructure and Internet-based innovation. Mathematically, the interaction effect can be expressed by taking the first derivative of Equation (2):

$$\frac{\partial DV}{\partial WI} = \beta_1 + \beta_5 IBI \qquad (3)$$

High Web infrastructure-oriented firms exhibit stronger relationship between Internet-based innovation and business value than low Web infrastructure-oriented businesses.

The analysis was performed in 3 steps. The dependent variable was initially regressed on the control variables in step 1. Then, in step 2, Web infrastructure and Internet-based innovation were added. Finally, in step 3 the interaction effect was included. To examine the adequacy of using regression analysis, tests were conducted to assess the normality of residuals and the homogeneity of variance of residuals (Hair et al. 1998). No significant violations of these assumptions were observed.

Regression results are summarized in Table 2. Results in model 1 confirmed that the one of the control variables employed (business industry) explains the dependent variable. Model 2 showed that the direct effect of Web infrastructure and Internet-based innovation upon business value was significant as the increment in the squared multiple correlation coefficient ($R2$) was statistically significant. The effect for Internet-based innovation upon e-business value was positive and statistically significant, while for Web infrastructure the relationship was not significant. Finally, Model 3 showed no significant interaction between Web infrastructure and Internet-based innovation (the increment in R2 was not significant). Thus, support for hypotheses H1 and H2 was provided, whereas hypothesis H3 was rejected.

DISCUSSION

This chapter develops a conceptual model, grounded in the resource-based view (RBV) firms, which analyzes the complementarity of Web infrastructure and e-business capabilities as source of business value at the level of an individual firm. Moreover, it is intended to offer results more widely applicable than studies of Internet leaders or IT industry companies. In this sense, this study attempts to offer an explanation to why there are cases where firms engage in e-business without deriving any benefits.

The results showed that Web infrastructure is not positively related to business value. This finding indicates that, since competitors may easily duplicate investments in IT resources by purchasing the same hardware and software, IT

resources per se do not provide better performance. This can be explained through the RBV, because IT is not considered a resource that is difficult to imitate; IT is by itself typically imitable. This result supports the findings of recent research (Batt and Grover, 2005) that did not find evidence of a positive link between IT quality and firm performance. Similarly, Powell and Dent-Micallef (1997) showed that IT by itself cannot be a source of competitive advantage. Thus, our results confirm that Internet technology by itself will rarely create business value.

Furthermore, results demonstrate that there is a positive relationship between Internet-based innovation and business value. This finding supports existing empirical research (Bharadwaj, 2000; Santhanam and Hartono, 2003), which found that firms create competitive advantages though intermediary effects, such as IT being embedded in products and services and streamlined business processes, which in turn affect higher levels of firm performance.

Finally, the empirical results did not offer support for the complementarity of Web infrastructure and Internet-based innovation. The RBV highlights the role of complementarities between resources as a source of business value. Researchers such as Steinfield et al. (1999) suggest that business value can come from synergies between

Table 2. Web infrastructure, Internet-based innovation and business value

	Model 1	Model 2	Model 3
Manufacturing industry	-0.148	-0.100	-0.094
Commercial industry	0.016	0.059	0.064
Number of employees	0.115	0.077	0.075
Web infrastructure (WI)		0.104	0.177
Internet-based innovation (IBI)		0.302**	0.372**
Interaction (WI * IBI)			-0.218
F-value	2.363	4.119**	3.500**
Adjusted R^2	0.019	0.068	0.091
Δ in R^2		0.057**	0.002

Significance levels: *$0.01 < p \leq 0.05$; **$p \leq 0.01$.

online and offline presence. In this sense, using case studies, they showed the lack of exploitation of these synergies in SMEs. However, this chapter shows that the complementarity argument of the RBV as a source of business value is not found for Web infrastructure and Internet-based innovation. Therefore, it can be concluded that having a more complete Web infrastructure is not critical for the influence of Internet-based innovation on business value.

CONCLUSION, LIMITATIONS AND FUTURE RESEARCH

In recent years, much debate about the value of IT and e-business has been created, due to the gap between e-business investment and the lack of empirical evidence on e-business value. Thus, today IS researchers face pressure to answer the question of whether and how e-business creates value. This study developed a conceptual model, grounded in the RBV of the firm, to analyze the relationship between Web infrastructure and Internet-based innovation as source of business value at the level of an individual firm. The analysis employed a large sample of companies from different industries for hypothesis testing. Broadly, this research offers several contributions: (1) it tests the RBV logic, arguing that not all IT resources are source of competitive advantage; (2) it demonstrates that Web infrastructure is not positively associated with e-business value and that Internet-based innovation is positively related to e-business value.; (3) it shows that the interaction effect of Web infrastructure and Internet-based innovation on e-business value is not significant.

While this study presents some interesting findings, it has some obvious limitations which can be addressed in future research. First, the sample used was from Spain. It may be possible that the findings could be extrapolated to other countries, since economic and technological development in Spain is similar to other OECD Member countries.

However, in future research, a sampling frame that combines firms from different countries could be used in order to provide a more international perspective on the subject. Second, the e-business value measures are subjective in the sense that they were based on Likert-scale responses provided by managers. Thus, it could also be interesting to include objective performance data for measuring e-business value. Third, the key informant method was used for data collection. This method, while having its advantages, also suffers from the limitation that the data reflects the opinions of one person. Future studies could consider research designs that allow data collection from multiple respondents within an organization.

REFERENCES

Adamides, E. D., & Karacapilidis, N. (2006). Information Technology support for the knowledge and social processes of innovation management. *Technovation, 26,* 50–59. doi:10.1016/j.technovation.2004.07.019

Amit, R., & Schoemaker, P. J. (1993). Strategic assets and organizational rent. *Strategic Management Journal, 14*(1), 33–46. doi:10.1002/smj.4250140105

Arvanitis, S. (2005). Computerization, workplace organization, skilled labour and firm productivity: Evidence for the Swiss business sector. *Economics of Innovation and New Technology, 14*(4), 225–249. doi:10.1080/1043859042000226257

Barney, J. B. (1991). Firm resources and sustained competitive advantage. *Journal of Management, 7,* 99–120. doi:10.1177/014920639101700108

Bharadwaj, A. S. (2000). A resource-based perspective on Information Technology capability and firm performance: An empirical investigation. *Management Information Systems Quarterly, 24*(1), 169–196. doi:10.2307/3250983

Bhatt, G. D., & Grover, V. (2005). Types of Information Technology capabilities and their role in competitive advantage: An empirical study. *Journal of Management Information Systems*, *22*(2), 253–277.

Bhatt, G. D., Gupta, J. N. D., & Kitchens, F. (2005). An exploratory study of groupware use in the knowledge management process. *Journal of Enterprise Information Management*, *8*(1), 28–46. doi:10.1108/17410390510571475

Brynjolfsson, E., & Hitt, L. M. (2000). Beyond computation: Information Technology, organizational transformation and business performance. *The Journal of Economic Perspectives*, *14*(4), 23–48. doi:10.1257/jep.14.4.23

Carneiro, A. (2000). How does knowledge management influence innovation and competitiveness? *Journal of Knowledge Management*, *4*(2), 87–98. doi:10.1108/13673270010372242

Carr, N. (2003). IT doesn't matter. *Harvard Business Review*, (May): 41–49.

Clemons, E. K., & Row, M. C. (1991). Sustaining IT advantage: The role of structural differences. *Management Information Systems Quarterly*, *15*(3), 275–292. doi:10.2307/249639

Devaraj, S., & Kholi, R. (2003). Performance impacts of Information Technology: Is actual usage the missing link? *Management Science*, *49*(3), 273–289. doi:10.1287/mnsc.49.3.273.12736

Frohlich, M. T. (2002). E-integration in the supply chain: Barriers and performance. *Decision Sciences*, *33*(4), 537–555. doi:10.1111/j.1540-5915.2002.tb01655.x

Frohlich, M. T., & Westbrook, R. (2002). Demand chain management in manufacturing and services: Web-based integration, drivers and performance. *Journal of Operations Management*, *20*(6), 729–745. doi:10.1016/S0272-6963(02)00037-2

Hair, J. F., Anderson, R. E., Tatham, R. L., & Black, W. C. (1998). *Multivariate data analysis with readings*. New Jersey: Prentice-Hall.

Hamel, G. (2002). *Leading the revolution*. New York, NY: Plume.

Hempell, T. (2003). *Do computers call for training? Firm-level evidence on complementarities between ICT and human capital investments*. (ZEW Discussion Paper No. 03-20, Mannheim).

Hoopes, D. G., Madsen, T. L., & Walker, G. (Eds.). (2003). Guest editors' introduction to the special issue: Why is there a resource-based view? Toward a theory of competitive heterogeneity. *Strategic Management Journal*, *24*(10), 889–902. doi:10.1002/smj.356

Kaplan, S., & Sawhney, M. (2000). E-hubs: The new B2B marketplaces. *Harvard Business Review*, *70*(1), 71–79.

Kessler, E. H. (2003). Leveraging e-R&D processes: A knowledge-based view. *Technovation*, *23*, 905–915. doi:10.1016/S0166-4972(03)00108-1

Kettinger, W. J., Grover, V., Guha, S., & Segars, A. H. (1994). Strategic Information Systems revisited: A study in sustainability and performance. *Management Information Systems Quarterly*, *18*, 31–58. doi:10.2307/249609

Kowtha, N. R., & Choon, T. W. I. (2001). Determinants of website development: A study of electronic commerce in Singapore. *Information & Management*, *39*(3), 227–242. doi:10.1016/S0378-7206(01)00092-1

Lederer, A. L., Mirchandani, D. A., & Sims, K. (2001). The search for strategic advantage from the World Wide Web. *International Journal of Electronic Commerce*, *5*(4), 117–133.

Loukis, E., Pazalos, K., & Georgiou, St. (2009). An empirical investigation of the moderating effects of BPR and TQM on ICT business value. *Journal of Enterprise Information Management*, *22*(5), 564–586. doi:10.1108/17410390910993545

Mata, F. J., Fuerst, W. L., & Barney, J. B. (1995). Information Technology and sustained competitive advantage: A resource-based analysis. *Management Information Systems Quarterly, 19*(4), 487–505. doi:10.2307/249630

Meroño-Cerdan, A. L., & Soto-Acosta, P. (2007). External Web content and its influence on organizational performance. *European Journal of Information Systems, 16*(1), 66–80. doi:10.1057/palgrave.ejis.3000656

Meroño-Cerdan, A. L., Soto-Acosta, P., & Lopez-Nicolas, C. (2008a). Analyzing collaborative technologies' effect on performance through intranet use orientations. *Journal of Enterprise Information Management, 21*(1), 39–51. doi:10.1108/17410390810842246

Meroño-Cerdan, A. L., Soto-Acosta, P., & Lopez-Nicolas, C. (2008b). How do collaborative technologies affect innovation in SMEs? *International Journal of e-Collaboration, 4*(4), 33–50. doi:10.4018/jec.2008100103

Mukhopadhyay, T., Kekre, S., & Kalathur, S. (1995). Business value of Information Technology: A study of electronic data interchange. *Management Information Systems Quarterly, 19*(2), 137–156. doi:10.2307/249685

Powell, T. C., & Dent-Micallef, A. (1997). Information Technology as competitive advantage: The role of human, business, and technology resources. *Strategic Management Journal, 18*(5), 375–405. doi:10.1002/(SICI)1097-0266(199705)18:5<375::AID-SMJ876>3.0.CO;2-7

Ravichandran, T., & Lertwongsatien, C. (2005). Effect of Information Systems resources and capabilities on firm performance: A resource-based perspective. *Journal of Management Information Systems, 21*(4), 237–276.

Santhanam, R., & Hartono, E. (2003). Issues in linking Information Technology capability to firm performance. *Management Information Systems Quarterly, 27*(1), 125–153.

Sawhney, M., & Prandelli, E. (2000). Communities of creation: Managing distributed innovation in turbulent markets. *California Management Review, 42*(4), 24–54.

Schulze, W. S. (1992). *The two resource-based models of the firm: Definitions and implications for research* (pp. 37–41). Academy of Management Best Papers Proceedings.

Soto-Acosta, P. (2008). The e-business performance measurement in SMEs. *International Journal of Enterprise Network Management, 2*(3), 268–279. doi:10.1504/IJENM.2008.018781

Soto-Acosta, P., & Meroño-Cerdan, A. (2009). Evaluating Internet technologies business effectiveness. *Telematics and Informatics, 26*(2), 211–221. doi:10.1016/j.tele.2008.01.004

Soto-Acosta, P., & Meroño-Cerdan, A. L. (2008). Analyzing e-business value creation from a resource-based perspective. *International Journal of Information Management, 28*(1), 49–60. doi:10.1016/j.ijinfomgt.2007.05.001

Steinfield, C., Mahler, A., & Bauer, J. (1999). Electronic commerce and the local merchant: Opportunities for synergy between physical and Web presence. *Electronic Markets, 9*, 51–57.

Tallon, P., Kraemer, K., & Gurbaxani, V. (2000). Executives' perceptions of the business value of Information Technology: A process-oriented approach. *Journal of Management Information Systems, 16*(4), 137–165.

Wu, F., Mahajan, V., & Balasubamanian, S. (2003). An analysis of e-business adoption and its impacts on business performance. *Journal of the Academy of Marketing Science, 31*(4), 425–447. doi:10.1177/0092070303255379

Zhu, K., & Kraemer, K. (2002). E-commerce metrics for net-enhanced organizations: Assessing the value of e-commerce to firm performance in the manufacturing sector. *Information Systems Research, 13*(3), 275–295. doi:10.1287/isre.13.3.275.82

Zhu, K., & Kraemer, K. (2005). Post-adoption variations in usage and value of e-business by organizations: Cross-country evidence from the retail industry. *Information Systems Research, 16*(1), 61–84. doi:10.1287/isre.1050.0045

Zhu, K., Kraemer, K., & Xu, S. (2003). Electronic business adoption by European firms: A cross-country assessment of the facilitators and inhibitors. *European Journal of Information Systems, 12*(4), 251–268. doi:10.1057/palgrave.ejis.3000475

APPENDIX

Measures

Constructs & Indicators	Description	Literature support
Web infrastructure WI1 WI2 WI3 WI4	Does your company have a website? (Y/N) Does your company use an Intranet? (Y/N) Does your company use an Extranet? (Y/N) Does your company use a LAN? (Y/N)	*Soto-Acosta & Meroño-Cerdan (2008;Zhu et al. (2003);Zhu & Kraemer (2005)* *Kowtha & Choon (2001);Soto-Acosta & Meroño-Cerdan (2008);Zhu et al. (2003);Zhu & Kraemer (2005)* *Kowtha & Choon (2001);Soto-Acosta & Meroño-Cerdan (2008);Zhu et al. (2003);Zhu & Kraemer (2005)* *Soto-Acosta & Meroño-Cerdan (2008);Zhu & Kraemer (2005)*
Internet-based Innovation IBI1 IB2	Have any of your product or service innovations over the past 12 months been directly related to or enabled by Internet-based technology? Have any of your company process innovations over the past 12 months been directly related to or enabled by Internet-based technology?	*Adamides and Karacapilidis, (2006);Hamel(2002);Kessler (2003)* *Adamides and Karacapilidis, (2006);Hamel(2002);Kessler (2003)*
Business value: e-Procurement effectiveness IP1 IP2 IP3	What effect has online procurement on the procurement costs? (1-5) What effect has online procurement on your relations to suppliers? (1-5) What effect has online procurement on the costs of logistics and inventory? (1-5)	*Soto-Acosta & Meroño-Cerdan (2008);Wu et al. (2003);Zhu et al. (2003);Zhu & Kraemer (2005)* *Tallon et al. (2000);Soto-Acosta & Meroño-Cerdan (2008); Teo & Pian (2003);Wu et al. (2003);Zhu et al. (2003);Zhu & Kraemer (2005)* *Soto-Acosta & Meroño-Cerdan (2008);Wu et al. (2003);Zhu & Kraemer (2005)*

Note. Y/N, dummy variable; 1-5, five-point Likert-type scale.

Chapter 9
Kaohsiung County Unified Broadband Mobile Network

Ran-Fun Chiu
Hewlett Packard Laboratories, USA

Yuan-Sen Yeh
Tatung InfoComm Company, Taiwan

Chiu-hsing Yang
Kaohsiung County Government, Taiwan

ABSTRACT

Since 2005, the Taiwanese government has invested over $1.2 billion into the M-Taiwan program to bolster Taiwan's broadband mobile communications industry and modernize its IP network infrastructure. In addition to building a nation-wide IP fiber backbone and providing R&D grants for developing new technologies and novel applications, it has also co-funded the constructions of four large-scale test networks, and the Kaohsiung County unified broadband mobile network is the largest one. The network construction has three major tasks: (1) building a large scale wireless mobile network with WiMAX as the core technology and supplementing with Wi-Fi where the deployment of WiMAX is not feasible; (2) converting all telephones in the county's government offices and schools from the conventional PSTN circuit-switched systems to VoIP to unify the two separated voice and data networks to one common IP network; and (3) deploying a host of new application services that include services promoted by the M-Taiwan program and county specific services. This chapter gives an overview of the system architecture, the employed technologies, the application services, the test results, and the challenges.

1. INTRODUCTION

The majority of metropolitan wireless networks have been Wi-Fi based (Lawson, 2006; Huang, 2006). After the Taiwanese government success- fully launched the construction of the world's largest Wi-Fi metropolitan network at Taipei city in 2003, it started a much larger, multi-facet M-Taiwan program in 2005 by choosing the emerging WiMAX as the key wireless technology and in combination with VoIP to leapfrog to the 4th generation (4G) cellular network (WiMAX M-

DOI: 10.4018/978-1-61520-871-5.ch009

Taiwan, 2007). Since then it has invested more than $1.2 billion into the program which include building a fiber IP backbone network covering the whole island, providing R&D grants to local companies to develop both new technologies and novel applications, and co-funding the constructions of four large-scale test networks in three counties and one city. The Kaohsiung County unified broadband network is jointly funded with Tatung InfoComm Company, a private wireless service provider (WISP). The Kaohsiung County government makes its public properties available to network hardware installations, and it is also the major user of the network.

The network consists of four major subsystems: (1) a mobile WiMAX wireless network that includes 90 base stations covering the county's most densely populated coastal area of 350 square kilometers with 2/3 of its population; (2) Wi-Fi hot zones in three remote mountain range townships to provide remote class rooms, on-line job training and Internet services to local indigenous residents to close the city/country digital gap; (3) a broadband IP network with a combination of optical fibers, DSL and radio links, SIP proxy servers, SIP border controllers, and media gateways that interconnect the wireless networks, the Internet and all government offices, affiliated agencies and schools across county's 27 townships to provide VoIP and Internet data services; and (4) a comprehensive set of application services that include M-government (mobile government services, mobile law enforcements), M-life (mobile commerce, video conferences, remote home-cares), and M-learning (mobile libraries, mobile outdoor learning) that are promoted by the M-Taiwan program and several additional enhanced services such as M-portal, enhanced mobile law enforcement, remote classroom, and extended VoIP services. These subsystems are described in the following sections.

2. MOBILE WIMAX WIRELESS NETWORK

In 2006, the National Communications Commission (NCC) of Taiwan allocated the frequency band of 2.5 GHz to 2.69 GHz for mobile WiMAX transmission. In 2007, NCC granted three 30-MHz channels from 2.5 GHz to 2.59 GHz in an open-bid procedure to six licensees, three in northern Taiwan and three in southern Taiwan. For reducing co-channel interferences, each licensee further divided its 30 MHz channel into three equal segments, 10 MHz each. The antenna of a base station has three sectors; each sector operates in one of the frequency segments. The frequency reuse plan is shown in Figure 1.

The physical layer of mobile WiMAX follows the OFDMA (Orthogonal Frequency Multiple Access) specification defined in the IEEE 802.16e-2005 standard (IEEE 802.16-2004, 2004; IEEE 802.16e-2005, 2005). It operates in a TDD (Time Division Duplex) mode; that is, the time domain of the 10MHz channel is divided into fixed-size time frame intervals in which the base station (BS) and the mobile stations (MS) transmit alternatively in time. The key time frame parameters and both the maximum downlink (from BS to MS) and the maximum uplink (from MS to BS)

Figure 1. M-Taiwan mobile WiMAX frequency reuse plan

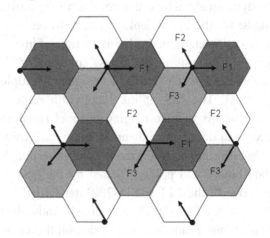

Table 1. Mobile WiMAX time frame parameters and maximum DL/UL transmission rates

Parameters		Uplink	Downlink
System bandwidth		10MHz	
FFT Size		1024	
Null Sub-Carriers		184	184
Pilot Sub-Carriers		120	280
Data Sub-Carriers		720	560
Sun-Channels		30	35
Symbol Period, Ts		102.9 microseconds	
Frame Duration		5 millisecond	
OFDM Symbols/Frame		48	
Data OFDM Symbols		44	
Modulation	Code Rate	Downlink Rate, Mbps	Uplink Rate, Mbps
QPSK	½ CTC, 6x	1.06	0.78
	½ CTC, 4x	1.58	1.18
	½ CTC, 2x	3.17	2.35
	½ CTC, 1x	6.43	4.70
	¾ CTC	9.5	7.06
16QAM	½ CTC	12.67	9.41
	¾ CTC	19.01	14.11
64QAM	½ CTC	19.01	*14.11*
	2/3 CTC	25.34	*18.82*
	¾ CTC	28.51	*21.17*
	5/6 CTC	31.68	*23.52*

transmission bit rates with different levels of modulation and coding are shown in Table 1.

The transmission time allocation for downlink and uplink traffics in each time frame interval can be dynamically adjusted according to the traffic loads; for the initial deployment, however, it is set to a predetermined value at the time of installation. The basic media access control (MAC) scheme is DAMA (Demand Assigned Multiple Access). The MS uplink bandwidth request mechanisms include ranging channel (random access in the ranging channel), piggyback (piggybacking the bandwidth request with other uplink data burst), and polling (polled by the BS) as described in the IEEE 802.16-2004 standard (IEEE 802.16-2004, 2004). The scheduled bandwidths in the transmission bursts in the downlink and the uplink are described in the DL-Map and the UL-Map respectively by the BS in the downlink transmission at the beginning of each time frame.

For performance improvement, smart antenna technologies, including beam-forming, space-time code (STC) and MIMO, are also supported. Mobility is a crucial requirement for this network. The requirements from the Bureau of Industrial Affaires, which co-funds the project, call for MS moving at a minimum speed of 60 KM/hr without application interruption within the coverage of the same antenna sector, a maximum of 150 ms interruption during handover between sectors within the same base station, and 300 ms interruption during handover between different base stations (ITRI, 2008).

The overall system architecture is essentially the same as that specified by the WiMAX Forum (WiMAX Pt. I, 2006). It consists of base stations, ASN (Access Service Network), and CSN (Connectivity Service Network). There are 90 base stations installed around the southeast coastal region where 2/3 of the county's residents live. The locations of these base stations are shown in dark circles in Figure 2.

The traffics of these base stations are back-hauled with a combination of 5.8 GHz radio links and optical fibers to the WISP's network center where the ASN gateway resides. The CSN gears that include DHCP server, AAA server and MIP (Mobile IP) home agent are also located in the network center. The network center serves as a network hub providing inter-connections to other networks. We will discuss more about the network center in later sections.

3. WI-FI HOT ZONES

Sanmim, Maolin, and Taoyuan are three indigenous townships in the county's sparsely-populated,

Figure 2. WiMAX and Wi-Fi base station locations

○ WiFi Hot Zone

● WiMAX Base Station

remote, northeast mountain range region. They are chronically in severe shortage of resources in education and healthcare. Because of the lack of local job opportunities, many of the adults have to go to the coastal cities to seek low-paying temporary works to support their families, leaving their young children and old parents behind. To mitigate this dire situation, Wi-Fi hot zones are installed in the mountain villages to provide remote class rooms, on-line job training, e-leaning, and free internet access to all of its local residents in the hope of giving better education to the children, better job training to the adults, and closing the digital gap between the coastal cities and the mountain villages.

Figure 3 shows a typical mountain village Wi-Fi network. There are two public offices in the village: one is the village administration office and the other is the police station. They are 222 meters apart. A Wi-Fi AP (base station) is installed in each of the offices. Each AP has two radio transceivers: One that complies with the IEEE802.11a standard interconnects the two APs; the other that complies with the IEEE802.11b/g standard serves the village subscribers. The AP at the administration office has an ADSL connection to the Internet. Thus, the Internet data of a subscriber that is associated with police station AP will be routed via the 802.11a link to the administration office AP, then to the ADSL line to get on to the Internet. Whereas, the Internet data of a subscriber associated with the administration office AP will be routed to the ADSL line directly. The two APs can sufficiently serve the whole village as shown in the embedded figure in Figure 3.

Eleven (11) village hot zones are installed, which cover all major villages in the three townships. Their geographic locations are indicated in light circles in Figure 2.

Figure 3. A village hot zone

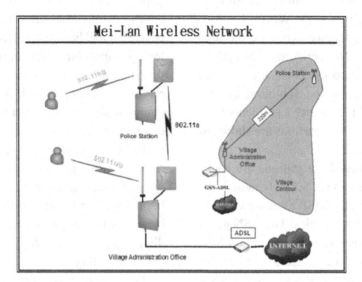

4. VOIP BROADBAND IP NETWORK

4.1 Basic Technologies

The signaling protocol specified for M-Taiwan VoIP is SIP (Session Initiation Protocol) (BoIA, 2007), which is an application protocol residing on the top of UDP, TCP, SCTP (Stream Control Transmission Protocol), or TLS (Transport Layer Security Protocol). It is used to establish or terminate multimedia communications. SIP functions are the determinations of user location, availability, and capabilities, and session setup and management. For a complete VoIP system, it also requires other protocols, such as RTP, RTSP (Real Time Stream Protocol), MEGACO (Media Gateway Control Protocol), and SDP (Session Description Protocol).

SIP is a simple text-based, request/response protocol (Rosenberg & Schulzrinne, 2002). A SIP message begins with a start-line, which is either a request-line for a request message or a status-line for a response message, followed by a number of message headers. At the end of the message headers comes an optional message body, usually a SDP message describing the media and media parameters to be used for the media session (Rosenberg & Schulzrinne, 2002; Hautakorpi et al., 2008).

A request-line has three fields: Method followed by Request-URI (the on-record URI of the called party), followed by SIP-Version. A status-line has also three fields: SIP-Version, Status-Code, and Reason-Phrase, in that order.

The commonly used Methods are REGISTER – for an IP phone to register its contact information to its Proxy server; INVITE, ACK, CANCEL for setting up sessions; and, BYE for termination sessions. The Status-Code has six categories: the 1xx category indicating provisional; 2xx, success; 3xx, redirection; 4xx, client error; 5xx, server error; and 6xx, global failure.

Figure 4 shows how to establish a call session between two SIP-enabled IP phones, and how to terminate it.

Before making a call, both SIP-enabled IP phones must register their respective contact information to their proxy servers, Sandy's IP phone to the taipei.com proxy and Raphael's IP phone to the kaohsiung.com proxy. Contact information can be an IP address or a full qualified URI.

Figure 4. Call session establishment and termination

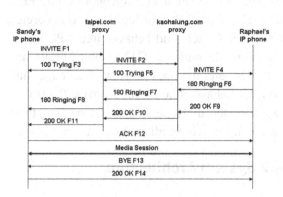

Figure 5. SIP to PSTN call flow

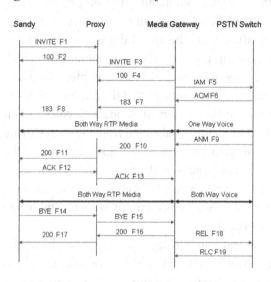

In this example, Sandy's IP phone makes the call. It sends an INVITE request message (F1) to the taipei.com proxy server with the on-record URI of Raphael's IP phone in the Request-URI field of the request-line, and its own contact information in a message header. A SDP message is also included in the message body with media type, media format, and connection information. The taipei. com proxy server finds Raphael's domain proxy server kaohsiung.com and forwards the INVITE message to it (F2) (Rosenberg & Schulzrinne, 2002). The taipei.com proxy server then sends a status message back to Sandy's IP phone with Status-Code value, 100, and Reason-Phrase, Trying (F3). The kaohsiung.com proxy server does the same procedure, forwarding the INVITE request message to Raphael's IP phone (F4) and sending a Trying status message to the taipei.com proxy server (F5). After Raphael's IP phone receives the INVITE message, it sends a Ring status message to the kaohsiung.com proxy server (F6), and it is further relayed back to Sandy's IP phone (F7, F8) to inform Sandy that Raphael's phone is ringing. When Raphael picks up the phone, his IP phone sends an OK status message to the kaohsiung.com proxy server (F9) with its contact information in a message header. Again, the OK status message is further relayed to Sandy's IP phone (F10, F11). Sandy's IP phone then sends an ACK message (F12) directly to Raphael's IP phone using the

contact information carried in the received OK status message. A media session is then setup by the two IP phones to start a conversation.

Either side can terminate the session. In this example, Raphael hangs up the phone first. His IP phone sends a BYE request message (F13) to Sandy's IP phone, and Sandy's IP phone sends back an OK status message (F14) in response. The session is then terminated.

A SIP enabled IP phone connected to IP network must be able to talk to a conventional phone connected to a PBX or the PSTN (Public Switched Telephone Network) and vice verse. It requires a media gateway to bridge the calls between these two types of networks.

Figure 5 shows the signaling messages exchanges between the SIP enabled IP phone and the media gateway, and between the media gateway and the PSTN switch.

The SIP call flow between Sandy's phone and the media gateway is similar to that of the previous example. The signaling protocol between the media gateway and the PSTN switch, however, is ISUP (ISDN User Part) (Camarillo, Roach, Penfield, Hawrylyshen, & Bhatia 2002; Q.764, 1999). To initiate a call, the media gateway sends an Initial Address Message (IAM) (F5) to the

PSTN switch, containing the origination point code, the destination point code, the circuit identification code, the dialed digits, and optionally, the calling party number and name. The switch responds with an Address Complete Message (ACM) (F6) to indicate that the remote end of the trunk has been reserved. A one way voice circuit is subsequently established from the switch to the gateway to pass the ring-back tone. When the called party picks up the phone, the switch sends an Answer Message (ANM) (F9) to the gateway, and a two-way voice circuit is then established for the call.

When Sandy hangs up her phone, the media gateway sends a Release (REL) message (F18) to the PSTN switch indicating that the calling party had hanged up the phone. The switch sends back a Release Complete (RELC) message (F19) to the gateway to indicate the called party is disconnected. When a call is initiated from the PSTN side, the direction of the signaling flow is reversed.

One other media gateway to PSTN signaling protocol used in Kaohsiung County's VoIP network is the ITU-Q.931 over the D channel of a primary rate ISDN (Q.931, 1998). The great majority media gateway to PSTN signaling protocol used in Kaohsiung County's VoIP network,

Figure 6. Kaohsiung county broadband mobile network system architecture

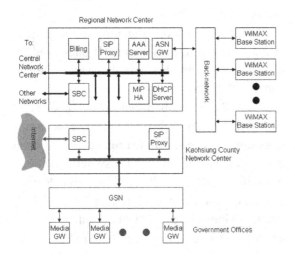

however, is the FXO/FXS interface, the signaling between a POT (Plain Old Telephone) and a PBX or a telephone central office. The FXO (Foreign Exchange Office) end behaves like a POT with signaling like on-hook, DTMF dialed digits, and off-hook, and the FXS (Foreign Exchange Subscriber) behaves like a central office (CO) with signaling like dial tone, ring-back tone, busy tone, ring tone, which we all are very familiar with.

4.2 System Architecture

The overall system architecture of the Kaohsiung County broadband mobile network is shown in Figure 6. The WiMAX subsystem on the up-right corner has been described in Section 2. In this section we will concentrate on the VoIP subsystem.

The VoIP subsystem architecture has a hierarchal structure. The first layer is the media gateways in every government office. The second layer is the county's network center where reside the set of switching gears and servers, including the proxy server, to support the county's VoIP services. The third layer is the WISP's regional network center where the mobile WiMAX network, Kaohsiung and other counties' networks interconnect. The fourth layer which is not shown in Figure 6 is the WISP's central network center where all regional networks interconnect.

Before the installation of the VoIP system, every government office in Kaohsiung County had either a PBX or a key telephone system connected to local telephone company's central office for local and long distance voice communications. To construct the new VoIP system, a media gateway is installed in each of the offices as shown in Figure 6. The media gateways are connected to Kaohsiung County's network center through a packet switched GSN network.

Figure 7 shows the VoIP network configuration in one of the county offices. The media gateway is inserted into the existing voice network between the PBX and the lines to the central office. The signaling protocol between the PBX and the media gateway is the same PBX signaling before, which is either FXO/FXS or Q.931 (Q.931, 1998). The signaling protocol between the media gateway and the PSTN lines is also kept the same PSTN signaling as before. Local calls are still routed through the PSTN lines to the local telephone company's central office; long distance calls, however, are routed through the GSN packet network to the county network center using SIP protocol.

Depending on where the called party is, the call may be further routed to the WISP's regional network center (the called party is on the WiMAX network, for example), or routed to a media gateway in another office, or the Internet. A SIP border controller (SBC) (Hautakorpi et al., 2008) is placed between the county's VoIP network and the Internet to control and protect access from the Internet.

5. APPLICATION SERVICES

To provide useful application services is the sole purpose of building a network infrastructure. Application services can improve citizens' living standard, increase the governments' efficiencies, protect the environment, and create employment opportunities. Moreover, innovative applications development is a lucrative high tech industry that every industrial country in the world is striving for. Therefore, application service is an important element of the M-Taiwan program.

Figure 7. Office VoIP configuration

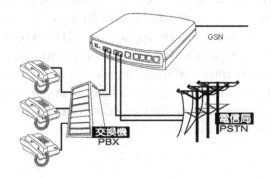

The unified broadband mobile network will support all existing M-Taiwan application services. In addition, a set of new enhanced services have been developed for Kaohsiung County to take advantage of the increased capabilities of the new network. These services are described in the following sections.

5.1 M-Taiwan Application Services

The M-Taiwan program has been funding and promoting three categories of application services: M-government, M-life, and M-learning (WiMAX M-Taiwan, 2007).

M-government includes (1) mobile government services – mobile on-line information retrievals, application submissions and payments; (2) mobile law enforcement services – police surveillance cameras, police information wireless network; (3) mobile traffic services – traffics monitoring and report; (4) mobile health service – on ambulance emergency medical treatments.

M-life includes (1) mobile commerce; (2) video conferences; (3) video/audio message services; (4) video phones; (5) on-line games; and (6) remote home-cares.

M-learning includes (1) mobile libraries; (2) mobile on-campus security enhancement; and (3) mobile outdoor learning.

5.2 M-Portal

The M-Portal consolidates all information regarding tourism, street and highway traffics, business activities, and cultural events in one portal. For example, the portal reminds visitors when the fragrant peach is in season, provides on-line brochures of the most popular tourist attractions such as the chapter umbrellas in Meinong Township, the Ear Festival celebrated by indigenous tribes, and the Zen experiences in Fo Guang Shan Monastery. The M-portal also gives detailed information of all current cultural activities in major entertainment venues such as the Weiwuying Centre for the

Arts, the Kio-A-Thau Art Village, the Fangshan National Dr. Sun Yat-sen Memorial Hall, and the Da-Dong Art Centre as well as the schedules of the Taiwanese Opera Train and the puppet shows. All vacation resorts in the county are listed on the portal with their nearest attractions, nearest shops, accommodation choices, and transportation details.

5.3 Mobile Law Enforcement

Surveillance cameras are installed in all major street intersections sending back digital images to the police control center to track down stolen cars automatically, and help police to manage busy street traffics and record traffic violations. Handheld WiMAX communications devices are provided to patrol polices to access information of suspected automobiles and individuals from police's central database.

5.4 Internet Connections for Remote Indigenous Townships

Remote classroom, on-line job training, and free Internet access are provided for the three indigenous townships. For example, in the deep mountain range at an altitude of 1,350 meters, the traditionally hard-reaching Baoshan Primary School, also known as the highest primary school in Taiwan, now can offer its 14 students and faculty members unlimited education resources via fiber and wireless networks.

5.5 Extended VoIP Services

The Kaohsiung County government's VoIP services are extended to local hospitals, restaurants, hotels, resorts, specialty shops, enterprises, and tourists to boost the county's tourism industry.

5.6 Gravel Truck Control and Management System

Gravel and sand mining from county's river beds contributes not only to the local economy but also to the maintenance of healthy water ways. However, uncontrolled excavation can damage the overall hydrologic system and jeopardize the safety of bridges. Moreover, the overloaded gravel trucks pose a grave hazard to the highways and a serious safety threat to other vehicles and residents along the highways. The county government deployed a mobile real-time gravel truck management system that integrates GPS, mobile communication, and digital map. The control center collects various data of each truck, including current location, travelling path, speed, travelling time and load.

5.7 Broadband Teleconference Legal Consultation Services

To mitigate the difficulties encountered with on-line web-based applications, the new network enables the county government to offer legal consultation services through teleconference. Residents can join the conference to obtain real time answers to their questions.

5.8 Mobile Multimedia Advertisement

More than 100 multimedia screens are installed throughout Kaohsiung County, such as MRT (subway) stations. The contents, which change with respect to both time and locations, are controlled by a centralized system through wireless communications. The application of 2D barcodes allows audiences to take pictures of their interested advertisements with their mobile phones. Mobile phones will then interpret the barcode and take the audiences to the product's websites or audiovisual blogs where they can shop on-line.

6. PERFORMANCE TESTS AND CHALLENGES

The Kaohsiung County broadband mobile network is in operation. The final acceptance tests conducted include three categories: (1) network performance, (2) operation performance, and (3) VoIP performance (ITRI, 2008; IEEEE 1012, 1998; IEEE 730, 2002; IEEE 829, 1998; P862, 2001; C-IE-5011_0, 2007; C-IT_5040_0, 2007; C-IS-2045_0, 2007; LP002, 2007).

6.1 Network Performance

Network performance test is mainly to check if the performance of the network meets the specifications of the original contract plan, which include the transmission frequency and output power of a base station, the cell size, the total coverage rate of the planned service area, the maximum offered user bandwidth - both upstream and downstream, and handover time for a roaming mobile station. The following is a summary of the test results:

The mobile WiMAX network covers 79% of the population in the original planned service area. The radius of a cell is about 250 meters in the urban area, 500 meters in the suburban area, and 2 kilometers in the rural area. The average capacity of a base station is 33.2 Mbps in the down-stream and 12.2 Mbps in the up-stream. The average bit rates of a stationary mobile station are 8.5 Mbps in the down-stream and 3.9 Mbps in the up-stream. While the mobile station moves at 60 Km/h, the down-stream bit rate reduces to 1.68 Mbps, and up-stream to.98 Mbps. At a speed of 30-50 Km/h, the handover times are 90 ms for intra-base-station, and 145 ms for inter-base-station. The service interruption times are 110 ms for intra-base-station and 470 ms for inter-base-station.

6.2 Operation Performance

Operation performance test is to verify if the mobile WiMAX network reaches its contractual initial operation goals, which include effective number of subscribers, the maximum number of concurrent users a base station can support, the maximum of concurrent users the overall system can support, and the related operation supporting systems. The test results are summarized as follows:

The lacking of WiMAX CPE devices was the biggest problem in achieving the operation performance goal. There were no PCs or any other handheld mobile devices with a built-in WiMAX transceiver card available in the market place. In fact, the only thing available was an external module plugging into a PC's USB interface, which severely limits the number of potential subscribers. The initial plan calls for a moderate 3300 initial subscribers, but even this low number is hard to achieve. However, the network itself works fine. A base station can support 110 concurrent subscribers in the uplink, and 312 subscribers in the downlink, based on the formula described in (ITRI, 2008). The overall system can support 8,706 concurrent subscribers in the uplink and 24,793 concurrent subscribers in the downlink. There are three operation support systems: network management and control system, billing and customer information system, and customer problems reporting system. All of them are in full operation.

6.3 VoIP Performance

The VoIP performance test has three parts: VoIP functions, VoIP system capacity, and VoIP interoperation. VoIP functions and VoIP system capacity include maximum number of simultaneous calls supported, proxy registration upper limit, BHCA (Busy Hour Call Attempts), and voice quality. VoIP interoperation is to test the interoperability with the Bureau of Industry Affairs' VoIP platform. The tests and their results are summarized as follows:

- VoIP- maximum number of simultaneous calls supported: 500;
- VoIP-proxy registration upper limit: 5000;
- Interoperation with the Bureau of Industry Affairs' IP Platform: Pass;
- WiMAX VoIP basic functions: Pass;
- WiMAX VoIP voice quality (end to ASN-GW): MOS=4.29;
- WiMAX VoIP voice quality (end to trunk GW): MOS=4.29;
- WiMAX VoIP- voice quality (end to end): MOS=4.27;
- Fixed line VoIP basic functions: Pass;
- Fixed line VoIP voice quality (end to end): MOS=4.32;
- Video phone: Pass;
- Wi-Fi phone call establishment: Pass;
- Web call (selecting an icon on a web page to make a call and conduct conversation): Pass;
- Interactive Voice Response (IVR) basic system: Pass;
- IVR call transfer to operator or voice mail: Pass;
- IVR FAX document request (requesting the IVR system to FAX a document): Pass;
- Web Call system capacity (capable of supporting 4 simultaneous calls): Pass;
- IVR system capacity (capable of supporting 4 users simultaneously): Pass
- IVR management (managing audio recording and audio file storage): Pass;
- IVR voice message functions (managing voice message recording and storage): Pass;
- IVR FAX document request management (document production and storage): Pass.

The MOS (Mean Opinion Score) test is based on the ITU P.862 standard (P.862, 2001). MOS with a value of 5 means the voice quality is perfect; with a value of 4 means the voice quality is fair, good enough for conducting a normal conversation, with a value of 3 or below the voice quality is unintelligible.

6.4 Challenges

We have encountered numerous technical problems during the network construction, especially having to work with a lot of old telephone equipment without proper documentations. With time and patience, we have been able to solve these problems one by one. The biggest challenge, however, is to find places for base station installations without resistances and protests from the surrounding neighborhood residences, because somehow radio wave is perceived as a health hazard. Despite all the public relations with data proving otherwise, the resistances persist.

7. CONCLSION

The WiMAX chip sets are becoming available and affordable from multiple vendors. CPE manufactures are integrating them into their designs. When these CPEs become available in the market place, the number of subscribers will increase exponentially. Tatung Infocomm plans to expand the network and start commercial operation soon. As for Kaohsiung County, the Kaohsiung County unified broadband mobile network will bring to the county the following benefits: It will provide affordable high bandwidth mobile services to the county's residents, businesses, and government agencies. It will increase the county's competitiveness, and enhance the county's international image. It will serve as a platform for innovative contents, applications, and new business models developments to benefit the county's large fishery industry and general consumers. Local based services (LBS) and hot zones will boost the county's tourist business, especially in the indigenous townships, which will create local jobs and improve their standard of livings. Most important, it will become a large driving force to the local wireless communications and IT high-tech industries in new products and services developments.

8. ACKNOWLEDGMENT

We would like to thank many distinguished experts from the Bureau of Industrial Affairs, the Industrial Research Institute, and the M-Taiwan Technical Review Board for their technical assistances and guidance. We are grateful to Dr. Nan-Ming Yeh, Mr. I Hsiung Huang and Mr. Kao Ping Huang of the Kaohsiung County government for their strong supports throughout the project. We are particularly indebted to the whole HP and Tatung teams for the great work they have accomplished.

REFERENCES

BoIA (Bureau of Industry Affairs). (2007). *M-Taiwan application promotion plan – VoIP application service interoperation specification.* Taiwan: Ministry of Economy.

C-IS2045_0. (2007). *Broadband wireless communication base station transmission equipment technical specifications.* National Communications Commission (NCC), Taiwan. C-IT-5040_0. (2007). *Broadband wireless communication base station conformance test specifications.* National Communications Commission (NCC), Taiwan.

Camarillo, G., Roach, A. B., Peterson, J., & Ong, L. (2002). *Integrated services digital network (ISDN) user part (ISUP) to session initiation protocol (SIP) mapping.* (IETF RFC 3398).

Chiu, R., Yeh, Y., & Chi, S. (2009). *Kaohsiung county broadband mobile network. IWEA2009/ACIS-SNPD2009 proceedings. C-IE-5011_0.* (2007). *Broadband wireless communication system conformance test technical specifications. National Communications Commission.* Taiwan: NCC.

Handley, M., Jacobson, V., & Perkins, C. (2006). *SDP: Session Description Protocol.* (IETF RFC 4566).

Hautakorpi, J., Camarillo, G., Penfield, R., Hawrylyshen, A., & Bhatia, M. (2008). *Requirement from SIP (Session Initiation Protocol) session border control developments.*

HP Technology INC. (2008). *Three mystic mountain M-Kaohsiung contract project management and acceptance procedure, system integration plan.* Taiwan: Kaohsiung County Government, Fengshan, Kaohsiung County.

HP Technology INC. (2009). *Three mystic mountain M-Kaohsiung contract project management and acceptance test report.* Taiwan: Kaohsiung County Government, Fengshan, Kaohsiung County.

Huang, M. (2006). *Wireless Taipei, the future is now – The birth of the world's first wireless capital.* Taipei City Government Publication.

IEEE 829. (1998). *IEEE standard for software test documentation.* IEEE Standard.

IEEE 1012. (1998). *IEEE standard for software verification and validation.* IEEE Standard.

IEEE 730. (2002). *IEEE standard for software quality assurance plans.* IEEE Standard.

IEEE 802.16-2004. (2004). *Air interface for fixed broadband wireless access system.* IEEE Standard for Local and metropolitan area networks.

IEEE 802.16e-2005. (2005). *Air interface for fixed and mobile broadband wireless access systems.* IEEE Standard for Local and metropolitan area networks.

ITRI (Industrial Technology Research Institute). (2008a). *Network, operation, and VoIP acceptance test procedure standard.* Taiwan: Bureau of Industry Affairs, Ministry of Economy.

ITRI (Industrial Technology Research Institute). (2008b). *Application service acceptance test procedure*. Taiwan: Bureau of Industrial Affairs, Ministry of Economy.

Johnston, A., Donovan, S., Sparks, R., Cunningham, C., & Summers, K. (2003a). *Session initiation protocol basic call flow examples*. (IETF RFC 3665).

Johnston, A., Donovan, S., Sparks, R., Cunningham, C., & Summers, K. (2003b). *SIP public switched telephone network-PSTN call flows*. IETF RFC 3666.

LP002. (2007). *Low power transmitter electrical specifications. National Communications Commission*. Taiwan: NCC.

Lawson, S. (2006). *Can metro Wi-Fi beat cellular?* PC World.

P.862. (2001). *Perceptional evaluation of speech quality (PESQ): An objective method for end-to-end speech quality assessment of narrow-band telephone network and speech codecs*. International Telecommunication Union (ITU) recommendation.

Q.737. (1997). *Specifications of signaling system no. 7 – ISDN supplementary services*. International Telecommunication Union (ITU) recommendation.

Q.764. (1999). *Signaling system no. 7: ISDN user part signaling procedure*. International Telecommunication Union (ITU) recommendation.

Q.931. (1998). *ISDN user-network interface layer 3 specification for basic call control*. International Telecommunication Union (ITU) recommendation.

Rosenberg, J., & Schulzrinne, H. (2002a). Session initiation protocol – locating SIP servers. (IETF RFC 3263).

Rosenberg, J., & Schulzrinne, H. (2002b). *An offer/answer model with the session description protocol* (SDP). (IETF RFC 3264).

Rosenberg, J., Schulzrinne, H., Camarillo, G., Johnston, A., Peterson, J., Sparks, R., ... Schooler, E. (2002). *Session initiation protocol*. (IETF RFC 3261).

WiMAX. (2006a). *Mobile WiMAX - part I: A technical overview and performance evaluation*. WiMAX Forum.

WiMAX. (2006b). *Mobile WiMAX – part II: A comparative analysis*. WiMAX Forum.

WiMAX. (2007). *M-Taiwan program – a WiMAX ecosystem*. WiMAX Forum.

Chapter 10
The Role of Semiconductor Distributors in the Japanese Semiconductor Market

Akihiko Nagai
Tokyo Institute of Technology, Japan

Koji Tanabe
Tokyo Institute of Technology, Japan

ABSTRACT

In 2009, the global semiconductor market was worth $219.6 billion. Japan has the third largest semiconductor market at $38.3 billion, behind America and China. Japan has a unique semiconductor distribution system based on close relations between semiconductor distributors and major IDMs (integrated device manufacturers), electronics manufacturers, and automobile manufacturers. Because of this, it is difficult for overseas semiconductor manufacturers and fabless semiconductor companies to enter the market. Semiconductor distributors play a significant role in Japan's semiconductor distribution system. The semiconductor market here has four main characteristics. These characteristics are the reason why Japan's semiconductor distribution system has developed the way it has.

I. INTRODUCTION

Japan's semiconductor market is worth $38.3 billion dollars. It is the world's third largest semiconductor market. This market has four main characteristics that, upon analysis, explain why Japan has developed such a unique semiconductor distribution system.

The semiconductor distribution system in Japan is based on very close relationships between major Integrated Device Manufacturers (IDMs), electronics manufacturers, automobile manufacturers, and the semiconductor distributors themselves.

DOI: 10.4018/978-1-61520-871-5.ch010

II. MATERIALS AND METHOD

In earlier research on the semiconductor industry in Japan, Ogawa (2007), Miwa (2001), and Yunogami (2004) investigated the importance of System LSI as the main semiconductor components that determine functionality in electronic devices. Fujimoto (2007), Sakakibara (2005), and Yoshimoto and Shintaku (2005) also hinted at the importance of System LSI as an element of integral architecture, at which Japanese Industry excels. These studies show the importance of relationships between major IDMs and electronics manufacturers, but System LSI comprises only about 30% of the Japanese semiconductor manufacturers' production, so it does not explain the general-use semiconductor market, which is also strong.

Due to the increase in Japanese exports in the electronics industry since 1980, there has also been much interest and research on the relationship between Japan's semiconductor market and electronics manufacturing industry from outside of Japan. Drysdale, Peter (1995), Johnson et al. (1989), Lawrence et al. (1990)(1993), Srinivasan (1991), and Okimoto et al. (1984), investigated the fact that Japan has its own semiconductor industry as a source of its competitiveness in electronics manufacturing. Satake (1994)(1996) investigated the relationship between the closed nature of the semiconductor industry and government support for R&D, based on the macro market-lockout theory. As well, Baldwin, Richard (1994) and Borrus et al. (1988a)(1988b) examined the fact that many Japanese electronics manufacturers also have their own semiconductor divisions, and are able to procure all major semiconductor components in-house, as a reason for the closed nature of the semiconductor industry. However, none of these studies addresses the issue for general-purpose semiconductors, which is also a strength for Japanese semiconductor manufacturers. In this research, we clarify some of the reasons that this market is essentially closed by studying characteristics of the market, rather than performing an analysis of the market.

III. FOUR MAIN CHARACTERISTICS

Figure 1 shows growth trends in Japan's semiconductor industry and, as in the rest of the world,

Figure 1. Japan's semiconductor market (Unit: Billion US $) (Source: SIA (Semiconductor Industry Association http://www.sia-online.org/))

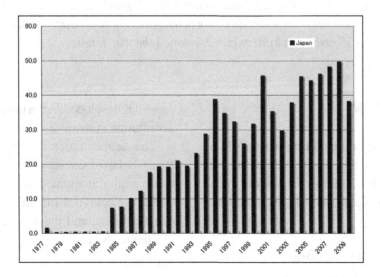

growth in the domestic market tends to follow a four-year "silicon cycle".

The driving force behind Japan's semiconductor market is demand from electronics manufacturers and automobile manufacturers.

Japan's semiconductor market has four characteristics.

The first is that the semiconductor market is driven by demand from electronics and automobile manufacturing, the second is that Japan's major IDMs are competitive in general-purpose semiconductors, the third is that the major IDMs are divisions of major electronics manufacturers, and the fourth is that there is a semiconductor distribution system in Japan. Table 1 shows trends in the market shares of the Japanese semiconductor market held by domestic and foreign manufacturers, with the domestic share being about 2/3 in 2004.

III.1 First Characteristic

The first characteristic is the high global share that Japanese manufacturers have in electronics and automobiles. The total sales amount is also very large. The companies that manufacture these kinds of products are like an anchor of strong demand for Japanese semiconductors. In the past, 60 to 70% of semiconductor demand in Japan's electronics industry was for industrial use. Nowadays nearly 60% of demand is for consumer use. The demand for semiconductors used in electronics appliances continues to grow because of rapid advances in electronics, higher performance, and miniaturization.

Table 1. Domestic semiconductor and foreign semiconductor share

Semiconductors	1991	1995	2004
Domestic	83.8%	69.8%	64%
Foreign	16.2%	30.2%	36%
Market size (billions US $)	15.2	38.8	45.5

(Source: United States Tariff Commission (USTC), Department of Commerce)

Figure 2 shows trends in production and export in electronics devices. Exports have been mainly stable since 2002, supported by production which has also been stable.

In 2007 Japan's electronics and engineering products totaled $30 billion dollars for consumer use and $70 billion dollars for industrial use.

Table 2 shows a breakdown by product category. In 2007 Japan produced 45 million mobile handsets, 46.7 million digital cameras, 7.3 million LCD televisions, along with other products.

III.2 Second Characteristic

The second characteristic is the traditional strength of Japan's major IDMs in the production of general-purpose semiconductors and related products such as logic ICs, discrete ICs, optical electronics ICs, specific-use ICs, and peripheral LSIs. Except for Japanese-made D-RAM products, IDMs have enjoyed global domination in production. Japan's IDMs are strong in general-purpose semiconductors and peripheral ICs while Intel and Broadcom have competitive superiority in platform LSIs. Even if there might be some rivalry in the final product, Japan's IDMs focus on complementary products that do not clash much with platform LSIs. Japan's IDMs face severe price competition. However, their products have good potential for large-scale production. These products include general-purpose semiconductors such as logic ICs, discrete ICs, and optical electronics ICs, and embedded microcomputers such as dedicated system LSIs that are incorporated into platforms, specific-use ICs, and microcontroller units (MCUs). The biggest share of sales among Japan's IDMs is in peripheral ICs. For example, at Toshiba the NAND Flash rate is high, 38% of sales comes from memory, 42% from LSI products, and 20% from general purpose semiconductors. At Renesas Technology the MCU rate is high, 30% of sales come from MCUs, 60% from general-purpose semiconductors, and 10% from memory.

Figure 2. Electronic device exports (Units: Million \) (Source: Current Production Statistics, Ministry of Economy, Trade and Industry (METI))

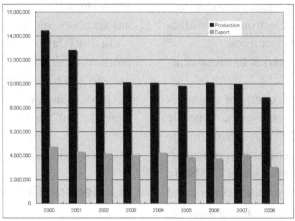

Table 2. Production of main electronic devices (2007)

Product	Production (Millions)
Mobile handset	45
Printer	3.0
LCD TV	7.3
Plasma TV	1.3
Laptop	5.25
Digital camera	46.7

(Source: Current Production Statistics, Ministry of Economy, Trade and Industry (METI))

At Sony sales are concentrated in LSIs (65%) and image sensors (30%).

Table 3 shows trends in the global sales rankings for the three major IDMs

In terms of total sales, these three Japanese IDMs have been ranked in the top 10 of global semiconductor manufacturers for 28 consecutive years starting from 1980. One of the main reasons for this success lies in strong domestic demand for general-purpose semiconductors, not the D-RAM market.

This strength in general-purpose semiconductors has given rise to excessive price competition among Japan's major IDMs, with makers squeezing their margins tighter and tighter (Porter and Takahashi). The reason for this excessive competition is the production of homogeneous general-purpose semiconductors by Japan's major IDMs. Compared to overseas IDMs, Japan's IDMs handle a far greater range of products.

Table 3. Rankings of Japan's 3 largest IDMs (1980-2007) (Units: Million US $)

2008		2007	2006	2005	2004	2003	2002	2001	2000	1999	1998	1992	1986	1980
Company	Revenue	Ranking												
TOSHIBA	10,510	3	3	6	4	7	5	3	2	2	3	4	3	2	6
Renesas	7,849	8	8	8	6	4	3	10	8	8	7	7	5	3	7
NEC	5,889	10			10	8	8	6	6	3	2	2	2	1	4

Renesas (Joint enterprise between the semiconductor divisions of Hitachi and Mitsubishi): Before 2002, this company was called Hitachi Data. (Source: Dataquest)

III.3 Third Characteristic

The third characteristic is that Japan's major IDMs originated from the semiconductor production divisions of general electronics manufacturers. That is true even today, as seen from the joint enterprise between the semiconductor divisions of Hitachi and Mitsubishi (Tani). One important role of an IDM is the way in which a semiconductor business helps bring out strengths in the company's products. Semiconductor differentiation in electronic devices is a key factor in market survival. At the same time, internal demand for semiconductors among general electronics manufacturers—for use in their own products—is a big, stable market. The internal semiconductor divisions of general electronics manufacturers supply from 10 to 20% of the semiconductors used in their companies' products. Demand for semiconductors used in internal products also enables the development of key devices such as system LSIs. The advantage of internal development is that a company can control the sale of system LSIs used in its final products to rival companies. Even in the absence of any control, very few companies use system LSIs developed by a rival's semiconductor division in their own products.

III.4 Fourth Characteristic

The fourth characteristic is the unique distribution system that supports Japan's semiconductor market.

The main channels of distribution in Japan's semiconductor market are Semiconductor distributors (53%), internal demand of major IDMs (26%), and direct sales (21%).

Figure 3 shows distribution rates of semiconductors to various channels in Japan. Excluding the 26% internal demand within major electronics manufacturers from their own semiconductor divisions, most semiconductors clearly go through semiconductor distributors.

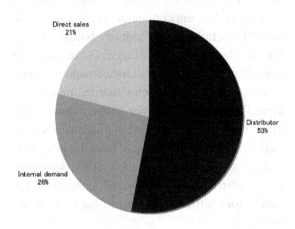

Figure 3. Semiconductor distribution share in Japan

The distinguishing feature of Japan's semiconductor distribution system is the close business relationship between semiconductor distributors, major IDMs, electronics manufacturers, and automobile manufacturers. The distribution system achieves a high level of information sharing on semiconductor demand. Based on semiconductor demand forecasting, the distribution system ensures that the supply is met. The system responds flexibly to fluctuations—including surges and plunges—in the balance of supply and demand and ensures that products are delivered on time.

The system meets the availability and distribution needs of electronics and automobile manufacturers, and the demand and sales channel needs of major IDMs and semiconductor distributors. It is based on practical business relations. As a result, distribution channels and actors are thus fixed, which makes it difficult for overseas semiconductor manufacturers and fabless semiconductor companies to enter the market in Japan.

IV. THE ROLE OF SEMICONDUCTOR DISTRIBUTORS

In earlier analyses of Japan's semiconductor market, the semiconductor distribution system has been seen as playing an important role in the continuous growth of Japan's semiconductor industry, in that semiconductor distributors, as the core of the semiconductor industry, built a network among electronics manufacturers, automobile manufacturers, and semiconductor manufacturers.

In Japan's semiconductor distribution system, by fulfilling three functions semiconductor distributors play a major part in building business networks and serving as a type of modular interface.

Figure 4 gives an overview of the semiconductor distribution system, and semiconductor distributors fulfill three roles as the core of the network.

The three roles of a semiconductor distributors are

1. Inventory: the availability of general-purpose semiconductors, flexibility in responding to fluctuations in the balance of supply and demand, and delivery response times
2. Business promotion: the expansion of product sales and marketing according to customer needs
3. Finance: funding agent

Another distinguishing feature of Japan's semiconductor distributors is excessive price competition due to the production of homogeneous general-purpose semiconductors.

V. CONCLUSION

Japan's semiconductor distribution system achieves efficiency in the procurement of general-purpose semiconductors. This system is not appropriate for the procurement of custom products and product-specific LSIs. The best way for overseas semiconductor manufacturers to enter the Japanese market is with differentiated semiconductor products based on a platform leadership strategy. However, general electronics products use a high proportion of general-purpose semiconductors. The monetary value of these semiconductors is also very large. The distinguishing characteristic of Japan's semiconductor distribution system is the way in which semiconductor distributors fulfill three specific functions and play a major part in building business networks and serving as a type of modular interface.

REFERENCES

Baldwin, E. R. (1994). The impact of the 1986 US – Japan semiconductor agreement. *Japan and the World Economy, 6.*

Borrus, M. (1988). *Competing for control: America's stake in microelectronics.* Cambridge, MA: Ballinger Publishing Company.

Figure 4. The role of semiconductor distributors in Japan

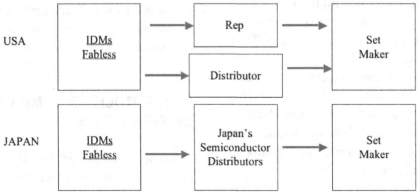

Borrus, M., Millstein, J., & Zysman, J. (1982). U.S. – Japanese competition in the semiconductor industry. In *Policy Papers in International Affairs, 17. Institute for International Studies*. Berkeley, California: University of California.

Borrus, M., Tyson, L. D., & Zyaman, J. (1988). Creating advantage: How government policies shape international trade in the semiconductor industry. In Krugman, P. R. (Ed.), *Strategic trade policy and the new international trade economics*. Cambridge, MA: The MIT Press.

Christensen, C. M. (1997). *The innovator's dilemma*. Harvard Business School Press.

Drysdale, P. (1995). The question of access to the Japanese market. *Pacific Economic Papers, 247*.

Fujimoto, T. (2007). Nihonhatu no Keieigaku ha kanouka? *MMRC Discussion Paper, 148*.

Ito, M. (2003). *Suihei-Bungyouka to Araiansu-Senryaku no Bunseki*. Research Institute for Economics & Business Administration – Kobe Unversity, Discussion Paper Series.

Johnson, C., Tyson, L. D., & Zysman, J. (1989). *Politics and productivity*. Cambridge, MA: Ballinger Publishing Company.

Lawrence, R. Z. (1993). Japan's different trade regime: An analysis with particular reference to Keiretsu. *The Journal of Economic Perspectives, 7*(3).

Lincoln, E. J. (1990). *Japan's unequal trade*. Washington, DC: Brookings Institute.

METI. (2009). *Current production statistics*. Ministry of Economy, Trade and Industry.

Miwa, S. (2001). Semiconductor-Sangyou ni okeru architecture no kakushin. In Fujimoto, T., Takeishi, A., & Aoshima, Y. (Eds.), *Business Architectureshin* (pp. 73–100).

Murayama, M., & Osada, H. (2006). Business system which create differences in corporate profitability: A case study on semiconductor trading companies. *The Journal of Science Policy and Research Management, 21*(2), 183–193.

Ogawa, K. (2007). Wagakuni Electronics-sangyou nimiru Platform keisei mechanism. *MMRC Discussion Paper, 146*.

Okimoto, D. I., Sugano, T., & Weinstein, F. B. (Eds.). (1984). *Competitive edge: The semiconductor industry in the U.S and Japan*. Stanford, CA: Stanford University Press.

Porter, M., & Takahashi, H. (2000). Can Japan compete? *Diamond (Philadelphia, Pa.)*, 130.

Sakakibara, K. (2005). *Innovation no syuuekika*. Yuhikaku.

Sangyo Times Hensyuu-bu. (2008). *Handoutai-gyoukai handbook ver. 2* (pp. 68–81). Toyo Keizai.

Satake, M. (1994). *Sizyou-kaihou o meguru Nitibeiboueki-kousyou: gaikan*. Graduate School of International Cultural Studies Tohoku University Ronsyuu.

Satake, M. (1996). *Nihon no Sizyou ha Heisatekika*. Graduate School of International Cultural Studies Tohoku University Ronsyuu.

Shane, S. (2005). Academic entrepreneurship: University spinoff and wealth creation. (p. 84).

Srinivasan, T. N. (1991). Is Japan an outlier among trading countries? In de Melo, J., & Sapie, A. (Eds.), *Trade theory and economic reform*. Cambridge, MA: B. Blackwell.

Tani, K. (1999). *Handoutai-sangyou no keifu* (p. 235). The Nikkan Kogyu Shimbun.

United States Tariff Commission (USTC). (2005). *Department of Commerce*.

Yoshimoto, T., & Shintaku, J. (2005). Kaigai-Kigyou tono Kyougyou o tosuita Kikan-Buzai to Kanseihin-Jigyou no Renkei-Model. *MMRC Discussion Paper, 49*.

Yunogami, T. (2004). *Competitiveness of Japanese semiconductor industry in technological level*. ITEC.

Yunogami, T. (2009). *Nihon Handoutai Haisen*.

Chapter 11
Modern Diffusion of Products with Complex Network Models

Atsushi Tanaka
Yamagata University, Japan

ABSTRACT

In modern rapid technological change, how some innovation can diffuse all over is a very fascinating subject. In the past diffusion research, the case studies or analyses based on the economic theory have been dominant. The theory with the classification of adopter categories by Rogers is most famous and thought to be a milestone for the former approach. There are rich case studies why it has been accepted widely so far, however the fact that a more than forty-year-old theory still governs the world sounds a little curious. Thus, new diffusion theory for modern network society is required.

In this chapter, some important matters of complex networks and their models are reviewed shortly, and then the modern diffusion of products under the information propagation using multiagent simulation is discussed. The remarkable phenomena like "Winner-Takes-All" and "Chasm" can be observed, and one product marketing strategy is also proposed.

INTRODUCTION

In recent markets, huge amount of new products have got into circulation. Which product will become a big seller and which one will vanish away is a great matter of concern for all consumers. And

DOI: 10.4018/978-1-61520-871-5.ch011

in a bitter format fighting category, which format will remain in competition is a very important issue that connects directly to buying intention. Though diffusion research have been down for tens of years, diffusion of technological or other innovation has been a main concern and there are few researches for products yet. Moreover recent decision process of purchase has changed because of the change of information propagation in modern network society. Thus the construction of modern diffusion model of products in consideration of this point and the search for diffusion conditions is our aim in this chapter.

At first, two important concepts diffusion and complex network are explained and their theory and models are shortly reviewed. Next the construction of product diffusion model is simplified by applying the idea of existing model to the agent-based model. Moreover adding interaction environment using complex networks and some variety of information transfer characteristics, the process of diffusion and the occurrence condition for chasm are inspected and it would be clear that the modeling of product diffusion market by agent-based model is possible and valuable. Finally by extending our model, the effect of network externality in the format competition and its characteristics will be clarified.

BACKGROUND

As you know, recent progress of the Internet is amazing. The penetration of e-commerce and Web 2.0 applications have varied both the form of purchases and the pattern of information propagation. As above, the importance of the relationships between individuals has grown higher. From that point of view, the ideas of complex networks have been required for diffusion research.

In the past diffusion research of products, the case analysis [Anderson, 2006] or the analysis based on the economic theory [Arthur et al., 1996] are dominant. In most of those studies, they suppose the dominant equation which describes the whole phenomena and carry out simulations [Bass, 1969, Rohlfs, 1974]. As opposed to these top-down and macroscopic view, bottom-up and microscopic design approach has been drawing attention these days. Complex system science enabled such a method and it researches the mechanism of the emergence of macro state by

the interaction of a large number of micro states. One of the most effective tool of its analysis is an agent-based model and it has been used in several systems including artificial market.

The study of artificial market using agent-based model is concentrating on financial markets such as stock [Chen et al., 1999] and foreign exchange [Izumi et al., 1999] and there are few studies for product market so far mainly because of the variety of consumers. There have been some studies on consumers themselves [Kats et al., 1955, Rogers, 1995] and the interaction between them [Watts, 2003]. Though some studies on format competition on some product market exist [Iba et al., 2001, Uchida et al., 2008], they assume the products are already well diffused or on the way, and they never discuss the process of diffusion. In real world, all new products are not accepted in consumers and widely diffused, and some are occasionally accepted only to a few enthusiasts, then the diffusion will stop. This phenomenon is called "Chasm" and can be seen very often in real markets [Moore, 1991].

DIFFUSION OF PRODUCTS

Though the research that what product will be purchased by consumers is important for marketing research, it is difficult to determine how to model it or what point of view we should study it. In this section, we define what diffusion is and summarize the diffusion researches in the past and their problems.

What Is Diffusion?

You might wonder what diffusion is in the first place. It is very hard to believe that all the people will come to adopt whatever techniques or products. Then what adoption rate is suitable for enough diffusion.

Rogers, the foremost authority on diffusion research defined it as follows: Diffusion is the process in which an innovation is communicated through channels over time among the members of a social system. That is, it is not considered how widely it is diffused, he considered it as a special type of communication. However in other fields, e.g. in economics it is defined as the spread of an innovation across social groups over time. In any case, it would be interesting for us how much does the diffusion spread. According to the adopter category in diffusion research which is described later, if prudent late majority come to adopt, then it has a majority, and you might think that the diffusion has well spread.

On the other hand, as described in the later section, there is a large gap among adopter categories, and there sometimes happens the phenomenon that the diffusion will stop after that. Crossing the chasm means overcoming the largest hurdle, and they can make it to diffusion with a little efforts after that. Someone may say that exceeding the tipping point means diffusion.

Traditional Diffusion Theory

One of the most important and pioneering researches in the early diffusion field is the work of E. M. Rogers. Though originally his main issue was diffusion of agricultural technology, it has become a great achievement based on huge actual data in several fields like family planning, public health etc. Most famous and best cited core part

in his research is the adopter category. As shown in Figure 1, considering the normal distributed diffusion pattern as an ideal type, he categorized new adopters into five categories: innovators, early Adopters, early majority, late majority and laggards by the timing of new adoption. He also described profiles about characteristics of adopters in each category. This will be explained in detail later. His research is individual description about adopter characteristics and diffusion pattern, and that is not a theoretical model for relationship but empirical general proposition, thus its validity has not validated yet.

Traditional Diffusion Model

Bass model was proposed in 1969 as a analytic model for new demands of consumer durables with long purchase cycle[Bass, 1969]. Though there are generally three kinds of demands: new, additional and alternative ones, a new demand is the most important for the diffusion analysis from the infusion of new product. This is the pioneer model which describes simply the behavior of a new product from the infusion through the growing period. It is based on the distributing information theory and concentrated on the fact that the product information is conveyed through the channels inside and between social systems. It is a combined model of the former Mansfield model[Mansfield, 1961] and the latter Fourt and

Figure 1. The distribution of adopter categories. All consumers are categorized into 5 groups.

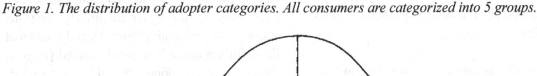
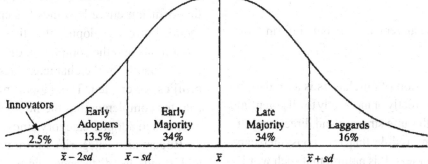

Woodlock model[Fourt et al., 1960], the potential adopters of new products is separated into two kinds: pioneers who act on their own will and imitators who make a wait-and-see decision.

The cumulative number of purchases $N(t)$ in Bass model is given as follows,

$$N(t)=N(t-1)+p(m-N(t-1)) +qN(t-1)$$
$$(m-N(t-1))/m, \quad\quad\quad (1)$$

where m,p and q are an index of market potential, a coefficient of mass media influence and a coefficient of interpersonal influence respectively. The second term of the right hand side describes pioneers who purchase at time t, and the third does imitators. The latter increases proportional to the cumulative purchasers by the time $t-1$. This model shows that the product diffusion curve becomes S-shaped.

Problems of Bass Model

Though Bass model is based on distributing information though, it contradicts real world in many respects because it is too simplified. The main contradictions are summarized as follows.

1. The distributing information from consumers is not considered.

In Bass model, the distributing information between pioneers or imitators is not considered. But we should consider the information exchange between potential purchasers who obtain product information.

2. Every consumer can distribute information mutually.

The information of purchasers is assumed to be distributed directly or indirectly to all potential purchasers with same strength and direction, but it is almost impossible that one consumer can affect all consumers. It is natural that such word-of-mouth communication activities are transacted along their human connections. Therefore the complex network models which can replicate well the structure of human relations are effective.

3. The distributing information rate is homogeneous.

In Bass model, all distributing information are simply assumed to be homogeneous. In real life they are naturally heterogeneous and could change a lot the speed and pattern of the diffusion. This heterogeneity has already studied in detail in the adopter category study by Rogers[Rogers, 1995]. He pays attention to the heterogeneity of the timing of new adoption, so it is very useful to take his theory in our model.

4. The completion of product information is not considered.

The product information is supposed to be complete in Bass model, it means that potential consumers suppose to purchase the product immediately as soon as they receive its information. But in real life, they need to collect more information and complement their information for the purchase, thus the product information should be incomplete.

Adopter Category

Rogers categorized all adopters into five heterogeneous categories by their adoption timing in his adopter category study(Figure 1), and found that the diffusion curve becomes S-shaped [Rogers, 1995]. For each adopter, the distributing information rate and the completion of information is determined from the characteristics and adopter profiles are created. The adopter profiles play a role for complementing the interaction between adopters in adopter category study.

Rogers also categorized information sources and ruled the differences among adopters in distributing information for various information sources. All adopters are categorized into high, medium and low levels of global oriented types from their distributing information rates by paying attention to information transfer characteristics. The amount of completion of information is a trigger of purchase and it can be expressed as a threshold. We categorize consumers in four types: risk favor, respect favor, low verification and high verification. The parameters of adopter profiles in our study are shown in Table 1.

COMPLEX SYSTEMS AND GRAPH THEORY

In this section, an outline of complex systems and graph theory as the basis of complex networks is described. The mutual relationship is important in the interaction which is the source of the representative phenomenon in complex systems "emergence", and its usual method is graph theory. Thus both fields have a strong and deep connection.

Complex Systems and Power Laws

How would several shapes in nature be determined? Since the reductionism is dominant in old-time physics, it was believed that all patterns and phenomena could be clarified if only they observed on the molecular or atomic level. However, reductionism faced the limit, and amazing fact was found that many inforeseeable macroscopic shapes and new functions are emerged from huge amount of microscopic ones, then it has become called complex systems later[Waldrop, 1992].

Chaos and fractal are both its main concepts and powerful methods for understanding it. Fractal was termed by B. Mandelbrot in 1975[Mandelbrot, 1982]. The fact that the scale invariant characteristic, that is the power law, is observed all over the place has attracted a lot of researchers. We can say the scale free characteristic is the commodity of the interactions among individuals, and it was found to be general in not only natural phenomena but also artificial and one and products.

Graph Theory

The origin of graph theory is tracked back to Euler in 17th century. In those days, they dealt with only small neat regular ones. Erdös and Reny defined the concept of random graph long time later, then graph theory made a great progress. Due to not only the randomness but also its extensibility to a large graph, graph theory has become the basis of network science. Though random graph gave a good method for analyzing several kinds of networks in the world, there are still many unexplainable facts, and some concepts of complex networks were expected to appear as described in the next section.

Table 1. Parameters of adopter profiles. Parameters and characteristics of adopters profile. p_i and q_i are information propagation rates from outside and inside respectively. a and b are given in each simulation and a<b.

	%	Contact	p_i	q_i	Type	Threshold
Innovators	2.5	High	0.4	0.1	Risk favor	0
Early adopters	13.5	Medium	0.02	0.45	Respect favor	0
Early majority	34	Medium	0.02	0.45	Low verification	a
Late majority	34	Medium	0.02	0.45	High verification	b
Laggards	16	Low	0.02	0.1	High verification	b

COMPLEX NETWORKS

As described in the former section, complex system is that when huge amount of small futile particles gathers, some unpredictable structures or functions will appear. In that system, mutual relationships are important and considering it as a network gave birth to the research field,complex networks. In this section, two important concepts in complex networks, small world and scale free are explained briefly, and several related models are also reviewed.

Small World Networks

Most people are realized and have experienced that the world is surprisingly small. The term small world is expressed in graph theory as characteristic which the average shortest path length L is small and the average degree of nodes is not so high. Though this characteristic has been confirmed experimentally since long time ago in social science, random graph theory could not have explained this phenomenon. However social experiments tend to be suspected at the point of bias and etc, thus their believability was After a while Watts and Strogatz succeeded in explaining the small world characteristic with a simple model by adding a small amount of randomness(shortcuts) to a regular graph [Watts et al.,1998]. Not only their model is simple enough, but also the transition from regular graph to random one can be observed using only one parameter, the rewiring probability p. Small world is realized at their intermediate state. A little later some modified models are proposed and its analysis has become easy.

Scale Free Networks

In 1999, the next year of the proposal of WS model, another important concept scale free network was proposed by Barabási and Albert[Barabási et al., 1999]. They found that widely seen networks in the world are connected not equally but unequally

with power law as the same as in complex systems. It means that Parate law well-known as social empirical rule consists widely in networks. It has been certified in Internet, ecology, metabolism, citation of academic papers, human relationships, sexual contact and etc. They succeeded in explaining the power law mechanism with a simple model(BA model) and then complex networks have been studied very actively. In their paper, they concluded that the keys of scale free are the growth of network and the preferential attachment. However as described next it is true only in BA model and it has been shown that both characteristics are not always necessary for scale free in several kinds of models.

Some Important Models

Huge amount of models for constructing complex networks have been proposed inspired by the former WS and BA models. Here some especially important ones are briefly reviewed. For more details, refer to the reviews of complex networks[Barabási et al., 2002, Newman, 2003].

(a)   Fitness Model

In BA model, the preferential attachment contributes the most to the appearance of the power law. That is the larger the degree of the node, the easier it can obtain links. If so, the older nodes are easy to become hubs, and new entering nodes have seldom chance of becoming hubs. But there appears new hubs in fact. Barabási et al. introduced the fitness parameter on each node and a kind of values then proposed modes which can explain the phenomenon[Bianconi et al., 2001a, Barabási, 2003]. Higher fitness node can obtain more links and it means the nodes which are flexible and suitable to the situation will develop. It is known that this model can be pretty matched to Bose gas[Bianconi et al., 2001b] and it can explain the Winner-Takes-All phenomenon to be described.

(b) Deactivation Model

Though BA model and its extension, the fitness model realize both small L and power law, the clustering coefficient C remains small and they luck the cluster property. In real world, a friend of one's friend tends to be also his friend, thus the clustering coefficient C is thought to be relatively high. In 2002, Klemm et al. introduced the concept of aging and succeeded in realizing high clustering property[Klemm et al., 2002a, Klemm et al., 2002b]. An aging means that nodes become deactivated according to their ages and stop growing richer. This deactivation mechanism gives young nodes the chance to become hubs instead as a result as the same as the fitness model.

(c) CNN Model

There exists many other modes which show high cluster property. The property of networks depends greatly on which modes are easy to connect each other. That is, the one which is eager to connect which a hub is also a hub or a low degree node. That can be measured by the degree correlation, and the former model has a negative correlation. On the contrary, CNN model was proposed as a positive correlation one[Vázquez, 2003]. In this model, there exists some pseudo-existing links in the neighbor, and some of them will be actualized stochastically.

(d) Hierarchical Model

The former models are all stochastic more or less. Is the probability necessary for the scale free property? To that question, Barabasi et al. proposed a scale free model with the deterministic mechanism[Barabási et al., 2001]. This model has a hierarchical structure and it is easy to calculate analytically. Many of actual networks are hierarchical, and modeled by this model[Ravasz et al., 2002, Ravasz et al., 2003].

(e) Threshold Model

Since BA model was proposed, it has been said that the growth and the preferential attachment are necessary for the appearance of scale free property. However, the threshold model which they determine the links only by the weight between two nodes and has been studied[Caldarelli et al., 2002, Boguñá et al., 2003, Masuda et al., 2004]. It has been said that the competition rule is necessary for the scale free, but it is remarkable that this model is cooperative in some senses[Caldarelli et al., 2002, Boguñá et al., 2003].

NEW MODEL AND SIMULATION

Improvement of Bass Model

In order to solve above problems, it is necessary to introduce both the interaction environment based on the connection between consumers who are distributing information and the heterogeneous information transfer characteristics of consumers. Therefore we use some complex network models for the former, and the adopter category study by Rogers for the latter, and then we improve the model[Tanaka et al., 2009]. Since consumers and advertisers can be described as agents, we can carry out simulations using a multiagent model.

The past studies in the consumers activity theory are very suggestive for our modeling of product diffusion. In our study we adopt the representative EBM model [Tanaka et al., 2009] as a basic framework, then we make the decision making process of each consumer agent using four processes among seven in the original EBM model: need recognition, information search, alternatives evaluation and the purchase. Each process in this model is described as a recognitive mechanism to go from the initial state to the target.

The consumers can recognize the product for the first time by the information from the outer(advertisement) and the inner(word-of-mouth communication) groups. The distributing information probability is given by the adopters profile and we assume that from the inside is proportional to the number of neighbors who have the information. And we define the recognition rates as p_i from the outside and q/k_i from the inside, where k_i is the number of nearest agents of i.

Next we search the necessary information to fill up the need. In our study we search the whole product diffusion rate for the outside group and the product diffusion rate and the product efficiency among neighboring agents for the inside. These rates are defined as p_i and q_i respectively.

We calculate the utility of products from those information. The utility $U_i(t)$ at time t is given as follows,

$$U_i(t) = wF_i^L(t) + (1-w)F_i^G(t) \tag{2}$$

$$F_i^G(t) = \frac{F^G(t) + \sum U_{n(i)}(t)}{k_i + 1}. \tag{3}$$

Here $F_i^L(t)$ is the diffusion rate(Local share) in the neighboring agents of i-th agent $F_i^G(t)$ is the average of the diffusion rate in the whole market $F^G(t)$ and the sum of the utilities of the neighboring agents $n(i)$, which means the utility value of the whole market. w is the rate of local share and can be considered as the sight of consumer.

Finally consumers make a decision for the purchase of product by the estimation of alternatives. In our study if the utility of agent become larger than the threshold of completion, they purchase the product, otherwise they keep searching more information.

Simulation and Basic Results

We construct our model with consumers interaction and information transfer characteristics based on Bass model, and carry out multiagent simula-tions. Parameters are as follows: the agent number M=50 and the product diffusion period N=300. The network models we adopt are WS, BA and CNN. The reason why we adopt CNN is that it provides both the small-world characteristic like WS and the scale-free one like BA [Vázquez, 2003]. As WS model can be expressed continuously from regular(p=0) to random (p=1) only by changing probability p, and we use p=0,0.01,0.1,1.

First of all, we carried out a comparison with existing economic theory in order to validate our model. Figure 2 shows the comparison between Bass model and several network models with $\langle k \rangle$=10. Thresholds of information completion are a=0.2,b=0.4, and we set w=1.0 in order to clarify the difference of network structures.

In each network model, it grows logistically though, a delay occurs compared with Bass model. That is because there needs the time of estimation of products by the completion of product information. It is also found that the higher the randomness of network becomes, the faster the diffusion becomes. Because both the average path length L and the cluster coefficient C are small, the information will not stay in the cluster and propagate to almost every agent. Small or medium cascade means products propagate overall.

DIFFUSION AND CHASM

When we think of diffusion of products, we sometimes encounter the phenomenon which diffusion suddenly stops. In this section this phenomenon chasm is defined and its occurrence conditions are explored numerically.

What Is Chasm?

We all know all new products will not percolate into all the people. However since in traditional diffusion research the adoption of new innovation by all the people is desirable, diffusion to

Figure 2. Comparison of the development of diffusion between Bass model and several network models. WS, BA, CNN, Bass indicate the model name and numbers(0.0,0.01,0.1,1.0) are rewiring rates.

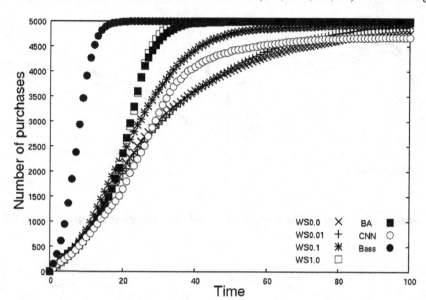

all is premised. That is obviously an impractical assumption, and by contrast Moore pointed out the fact that many diffusion stop in relatively early stage[Moore, 1991]. He thought the large gap between early adopter and early majority is easy to rise and many diffusion stop there, and he called it chasm. He has advised that the keys to cross the chasm and diffuse the innovation are "Exhibition of whole products", "Making Use of the power of word of mouth" and "Becoming a market leader".

Simulation and Results

The reason why the gap between early adopter and early majority come to rise depends mainly on the properties of each category. Thus in order to find its mechanism we search for the diffusion condition in changing $\langle k \rangle$ where $w=1$ and w where $\langle k \rangle=10$ respectively. Three characteristic diffusion are observed in real world: large-scale cascade, small or medium scale cascade and chasm. The large-scale cascade means it propagates to almost every agent. The small or medium scale cascade

means it propagates to any kind of agent but not so much as the former. The chasm is the phenomenon that the diffusion suddenly stops between two categories. It can be often observed in real world especially between early adopters and early majority.

In this simulation we define large-scale cascade and chasm as the diffusion to more than 80% consumers and that to less than 20% respectively, and we search for the occurrence conditions for large-scale cascade and chasm. We select the completion of information as $b=2a$, and carry out 100 times procedures. Since the data behaviors are a little complicated in all the following figures, they are approximated by Bézier curves. Resulting conditions are shown in Figures 3 and 4. The curves in these figures means the minimum threshold of chasm and the maximum one of large-scale cascade. That is, in the former above the curve chasm will occur and in the latter below the curve large-scale cascade will occur.

With respect to the occurrence of chasm, we can see that chasm does not tend to occur above around $\langle k \rangle=3$. That is because of the network

Figure 3. Occurrence condition for chasm in changing average degree ⟨k⟩ and ratio of local share w

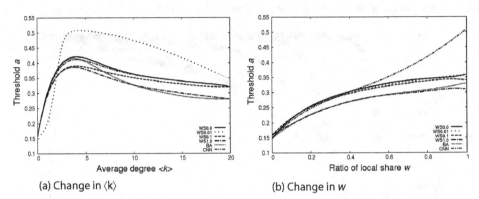

(a) Change in ⟨k⟩   (b) Change in w

Figure 4. Occurrence condition for large-scale cascade in changing average degree ⟨k⟩ and ratio of local share w

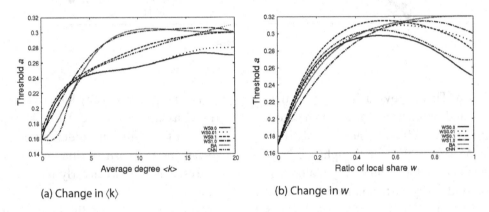

(a) Change in ⟨k⟩   (b) Change in w

structure of CNN model. Since in the model high dense clusters are formed around hubs, it can be easy that small-scale cascade occurs inside. But if randomness becomes higher, a clustering coefficient becomes small and a small-scale cascade does not occur so often, thus chasm occurs easily. On the other hand, if we increase w, there hardly occurs chasm. Since increasing the local share means making the sight of consumers narrow, a small-scale cascade seems to occur easily.

With respect to the occurrence of large-scale cascade, the larger $\langle k \rangle$ is or the higher the randomness of networks is, the easier large-scale cascade occurs. In this case we have to spread the information to all the agents. The highness of the order and the smallness of L seem to be effective. If we change w, there tends to occur large-scale cascade around $w=1$ in high random network. In this case both L and C are so small that the information can spread to many agents even if the sight of consumers is narrow. But if the randomness is low, the information grows stagnant in case of the narrow sight, it is required that we spread the sight up to about $w=0.5$.

NETWORK EXTERNALITY

Since most people would prefer to buy the product which their friends or families have, the sales of products depend on the network structure. In this section the effect of this network externality is observed.

Network Externality Models

The network externality means that the more consumers use the same format, the larger the worth of that format becomes, e.g. telephone, mail software, OS etc. [Katz et al., 1985]. In the strong network externality market, most consumers tend to purchase better diffused products, and that is called "the band wagon effect". It can be also seen that the rapid diffusion occurs over the critical value "the critical mass".

Let us extend the product diffusion model, and construct the model of format competition of the products with network externality. The extension are carried out for each four process of the purchase.

In the requirement recognition process, they recognize not only the products but also the information of the format. In the information research, they search the whole diffusion rate of the format against outside of the group, and they search the diffusion rate among the neighboring agents and the utility of each format against inside. In the estimation of alternatives, we calculate the utility of each format. The utility of i-th agent for the format j at time t, is given as follows,

$$U_{ij}(t) = U_{ij}^A + s[wF_{ij}^L(t) + (1-w)F_{ij}^G(t)] \tag{4}$$

$$F_{ij}^G(t) = \frac{F_j^G(t) + \sum U_{n(i)j}(t)}{k_{ij}+1}. \tag{5}$$

Here U_{ij}^A is self choice function for the format j, and it is given by uniform distribution. F_{ij}^L is the diffusion rate of the format j among the neighboring agents of i. $F_{ij}^G(t)$ is given by the average of the whole diffusion rate $F_j^G(t)$ and the utility of the format j in the neighboring agent $n(i)$, and it means the value of the utility of the whole market. The parameter s is the strength of the network externality. Finally in the purchase pro-

cess they adopt the highest format based on the above estimation. After the purchase they continue searching, and replace the product if another estimation becomes larger. In addition to the same parameters in the previous section, we select the parameters: the formats 2, the strength of the network externality s=2, the thresholds of completion a=0.1, b=0.2, and carry out multiagent simulations.

Winner-Takes-All

There often happens that only one product or format survives in competition, and it is called Winner-Takes-All phenomenon[Frank et al., 1998]. The occurrence conditions for Winner-Takes-All in our simulations are shown in Figure 5. We change (a) $\langle k \rangle$ in w=1 and (b) w in $\langle k \rangle$=10. Each y-axis means the average occurrence probability of Winner-Takes-All in 100 times simulations.

In case of changing w, though there exists Winner-Takes-All in every network at w=0, they can be hardly seen according to approach to w=1. It is especially remarkable in high cluster coefficient networks. That is because in large w, consumers take care of only the diffusion rate in neighboring agents and one format stays in a cluster.

In case of changing $\langle k \rangle$, there never occurs Winner-Takes-All at k=0 because they do not connect with anyone and judge only from the self choice function. Though there never still occurs Winner-Takes-All in low random case, there occurs Winner-Takes-All in high random case when $\langle k \rangle$ becomes large. It can be explained as follows. In small $\langle k \rangle$, targets for searching information are so little that the information of the format is hard to propagate, thus there occurs a stagnation of information.

Effects of Marketing

We also measure the effects of marketing in network externality market. At first we increase

Figure 5. Occurrence condition for Winner-Takes-All in changing average degree ⟨k⟩ and ratio of local share w

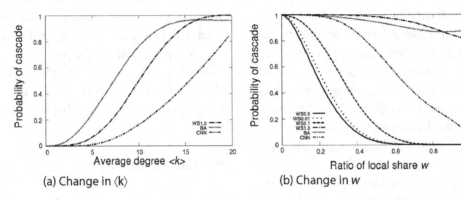

(a) Change in ⟨k⟩   (b) Change in w

advertisements and encouraging word-of-mouth communication for one format. Figure 6 shows the occurrence conditions for Winner-Takes-All when we increase 5% respectively. The effects of marketing can be seen in both cases. Though in advertisement there occurs Winner-Takes-All only in very small *w*, in word-of-mouth communication Winner-Takes-All is outstanding especially in high random network. Next we concentrate 20% advertisements on the hub and observe its effect(Figure 7). In CNN model, the probability of Winner-Takes-All decays monotonically with local share *w* though, in BA model, there is a minimum point of the probability. Their comparison is not simple but word-of-mouth communication

can be more effective in order to produce a lot of marketing effects.

CONCLUSION

In this chapter, we have described the model of product diffusion and some backgrounds using agent-based model. Several states of diffusion such as chasm and large-scale cascade have been observed, and it is found that the interaction environment and the information transfer characteristics affect the condition of diffusion. Moreover we extend the model and analyze the network externality market. It is also clarified that the same two factors are effective in the format

Figure 6. Occurrence condition for Winner-Takes-All in increasing advertisements and word-of-mouth communication by 5% respectively

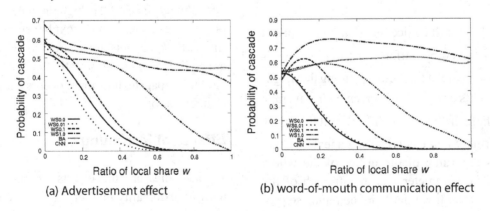

(a) Advertisement effect   (b) word-of-mouth communication effect

Figure 7. Occurrence condition for Winner-Takes-All in concentrating 20% advertisements on a hub

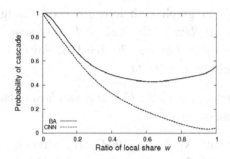

competition and the word-of-mouth communication is confirmed effective for the marketing strategy. Our proposed model enables us to investigate the difference of diffusion by the interaction environment, which cannot be treated with existing macroscopic model, and the effectiveness and the possibility of agent-based model becomes clear.

For future works, it is important to measure the effect of several kinds of marketing activities such as advertisement, monitoring, campaign etc., and induce the optimal marketing method by the cost-effectiveness. Since we know our study has not transcended the framework of modeling, the comparison with real data is indispensable, however it is so difficult to obtain the sale amount data of chasm. If we can confirm the consistency with real data, it can be used for the more effective strategy method for new products.

REFERENCES

Anderson, C. (2006). *The long tail*. Random House Business.

Arthur, W. B., & Lane, D. A. (1996). Increasing contagion. *Structural Change and Economic Dynamics*, *41*, 81–104.

Barabási, A.-L. (2003). *Linked*. Plume, a member of the Penguin Group, Inc.

Barabási, A.-L., & Albert, R. (1999). Emergence of scaling in random networks. *Science*, *286*, 509–512. doi:10.1126/science.286.5439.509

Barabási, A. L., & Albert, R. (2002). Statistical mechanics of complex networks. *Reviews of Modern Physics*, *74*, 47–97. doi:10.1103/Rev-ModPhys.74.47

Barabási, A.-L., Ravasz, E., & Vicsek, T. (2001). Deterministic scale-free networks. *Physica A*, *299*, 559–564. doi:10.1016/S0378-4371(01)00369-7

Bass, F. M. (1969). A new product growth model for consumer durables. *Management Science*, *15*(5), 215–227. doi:10.1287/mnsc.15.5.215

Bianconi, G., & Barabási, A.-L. (2001). Competition and multiscaling in evolving networks. *Europhysics Letters*, *54*(4), 436–442. doi:10.1209/epl/i2001-00260-6

Bianconi, G., & Barabási, A.-L. (2001). Bose-Einstein condensation in complex networks. *Physical Review Letters*, *86*(24), 5632–5635. doi:10.1103/PhysRevLett.86.5632

Boguñá, M., & Pastor-Satorras, R. (2003). Class of correlated random networks with hidden variables. *Physical Review E: Statistical, Nonlinear, and Soft Matter Physics*, *68*, 036112. doi:10.1103/PhysRevE.68.036112

Caldarelli, G., Capocci, A., De Los Rios, P., & Munoz, M. A. (2002). Scale-free networks from varing vertex intrinsic fitness. *Physical Review Letters*, *89*(25), 258702. doi:10.1103/PhysRevLett.89.258702

Chen, S. H., Yeh, C. H., & Liao, C. C. (1999). Testing the rational expectations hypothesis with the agent-based model of stock markets. *Proceedings of, ICAI99*, 381–387.

Engel, J. F., Blackwell, R. D., & Miniard, P. W. (1995). *Consumer behavior* (8th ed.). The Dryden Press.

Erdös, P., & Rényi, A. (1959). On random graphs. *Publicationes Mathematicae, 6,* 290–297.

Fourt, L. A., & Woodlock, J. W. (1960). Early prediction of market success of new grocery products. *Journal of Marketing, 25*(2), 31–48. doi:10.2307/1248608

Frank, R. H., & Cook, P. J. (1998). *The winner take all society.* Penguin Books USA Inc.

Iba, T., Takenaka, H., & Takefuji, Y. (2001). Reappearance of video cassette format competition using artificial market simulation. *Transactions of Information Processing Society of Japan, 42*(14), 73–89.

Izumi, K., & Ueda, K. (1999). Analysis of dealers' processing financial news based on an artificial market approach. *Journal of Computational Intelligence in Finance, 7,* 23–33.

Kats, E., & Lazarsfeld, P. F. (1955). *Personal influence.* Free Press.

Katz, M. L., & Shapiro, C. (1985). Network externalities, competition, and compatibility. *The American Economic Review, 75,* 424–440.

Klemm, K., & Eguíluz, V. M. (2002a). Highly clustered scale-free networks. *Physical Review E: Statistical, Nonlinear, and Soft Matter Physics, 65,* 036123. doi:10.1103/PhysRevE.65.036123

Klemm, K., & Eguíluz, V. M. (2002b). Growing scale-free networks with small-world behavior. *Physical Review E: Statistical, Nonlinear, and Soft Matter Physics, 65,* 057102. doi:10.1103/PhysRevE.65.057102

Mandelbrot, B. B. (1982). *The fractal geometry of nature.* Freeman.

Mansfield, E. (1961). Technical change and the rate of imitation. *Econometrica, 29,* 741–766. doi:10.2307/1911817

Masuda, N., Miwa, H., & Konno, N. (2004). Analysis of scale-free networks based on a threshold graph with intrinsic vertex weights. *Physical Review E: Statistical, Nonlinear, and Soft Matter Physics, 70,* 036124. doi:10.1103/PhysRevE.70.036124

Moore, G. A. (1991). *Crossing the chasm.* Harper Business.

Newman, M. E. J. (2003). The structure and function of complex networks. *SIAM Review, 45,* 167–256. doi:10.1137/S003614450342480

Ravasz, E., & Barabási, A.-L. (2003). Hierarchical organization in complex networks. *Physical Review E: Statistical, Nonlinear, and Soft Matter Physics, 67,* 026112. doi:10.1103/PhysRevE.67.026112

Ravasz, E., Somera, A. L., Mongru, D. A., Oltvai, Z. N., & Barabási, A.-L. (2002). Hierarchical organization of modularity in metabolic networks. *Science, 297,* 1551–1555. doi:10.1126/science.1073374

Rogers, E. M. (1995). *Diffusion of innovations* (4th ed.). Free Press.

Rohlfs, J. (1974). A theory of interdependent demand of a communication service. *The Bell Journal of Economics and Management Science, 42*(9), 16–37. doi:10.2307/3003090

Tanaka, A., & Haga, K. (2009). Multiagent simulation on product diffusion process: From chasm to cascade. *Information, 12*(5).

Uchida, M., & Shirayama, S. (2008). Artificial market simulation with embedded complex network structures. *Transactions of the Japanese Society for Artificial Intelligence, 23*(6A), 485–493. doi:10.1527/tjsai.23.485

Vázquez, A. (2003). Growing network with local rules: Preferential attachment, clustering hierarchy and degree correlations. *Physical Review E: Statistical, Nonlinear, and Soft Matter Physics, 67*, 056104. doi:10.1103/PhysRevE.67.056104

Waldrop, M. M. (1992). *Complexity: The emerging science at the edge of order and chaos*. Simon & Schuster.

Watts, D. J. (2003). *Six degrees: The science of a connected age*. W. W. Norton & Co Inc.

Watts, D. J., & Strogatz, S. H. (1998). Collective dynamics of small-world networks. *Nature, 393*, 440–442. doi:10.1038/30918

KEY TERMS AND DEFINITIONS

Adopter Category: Groups of consumers separated by the timing of adopting new innovation. Rogers defined 5 categories, Innovators, Early adopters, Early majority, Late majority, Laggards.

Chasm: Phenomenon which diffusion of innovation or product suddenly stop at some step. Crossing this chasm is a mandatory requirement for diffusion.

Complex Networks: Networks which is constructed by considering relations among several things as links. Their structures, properties and functions have been actively studied in recent years.

Diffusion: This term has been used differently in two groups. In marketing and communication fields it means the communication of an innovation through the population. On the other hand, in economics and most non-marketing fields, it means the spread of innovation or products. Here we adopt the latter.

Graph Theory: Research field to study graphs theoretically those consist of nodes and their connecting edges. This field has an old history and plays an important role in complex network research.

Multiagent Simulation: Simulation to observe the behavior of the system of many agents who have their individual characteristics independently. It is one of the most effective method in complex system research.

Network Externality: Property which the more people have the same product, the higher the value of it becomes. it can be observed in the market of telephone, E-mail, OS and etc.

Section 3
Intelligent Web Construction and E-Support

Chapter 12
E–Cocreation of Knowledge through Informal Communications

Kazushi Nishimoto
Japan Advanced Institute of Science and Technology, Japan

ABSTRACT

It is pointed out that the 21st century is an era of knowledge creation where productivity of knowledge is more important than the productivity of things. Therefore, improvement of the productivity of knowledge is an urgent demand from public organizations i.e., industry, academia and government as well as personal individuals. As a method to achieve it, knowledge management systems have recently been studied and developed. However, there have been few cases that could successfully improve the productivity of knowledge; many systems have been installed but not used. One of the principal problems of the ordinary attempts is, I think, the unbalanced way for sharing the knowledge. For example, experts are required to voluntarily provide their professional knowledge to create and to maintain a knowledge-base with many efforts so that novices as free riders can readily exploit the knowledge-base without any efforts. In order to solve and/or to avoid this problem, I focused on informal communications by chance as places for sharing knowledge and my laboratory has been constructed various e-cocreation systems to support sharing and creating knowledge in the informal communications. This chapter introduces some of the research efforts conducted in the author's laboratory.

DOI: 10.4018/978-1-61520-871-5.ch012

INTRODUCTION

This chapter will introduce the research that the author's laboratory has been undertaking into establishing venues to promote the sharing and co-creation of knowledge. I and my laboratory members have focused on informal communication as a venue for such knowledge sharing and co-creation. There are various definitions of the phrase "informal communication," but we use the phrase "informal communication" to refer to "communication which is not planned in advance and which arises incidentally without any specific topic of discussion or objectives to be decided, or any ordered process etc." (Kraut et al. 1990)

In response to Nonaka and Takeuchi's claim that productivity of knowledge becomes an important key for enterprises to survive and to develop in the 21st century (Nonaka & Takeuchi 1995), various Knowledge management systems (KM systems, hereafter) have been developed, marketed and installed to many companies to increase the productivity of knowledge. However, most existing KM systems have not yet satisfactorily worked as they were expected up to now. Krogh et al. (Krogh et al. 2000) explained the reason why KM systems did not work well from the organizational viewpoint. To enable knowledge creation in the enterprises, following five factors should be combined and utilized: 1) instilling knowledge vision, 2) managing conversations, 3) mobilizing knowledge activists, 4) creating the right context and 5) globalizing local knowledge. These factors must be always considered to promote knowledge management. Any organizations that do not satisfy or do not attempt to satisfy them shall not success in knowledge management regardless of using the KM systems.

On the other hand, the existing KM systems include an essential problem. Typical KM systems have been grounded on a belief that live and useful knowledge is basically "static" and can be easily captured, transcribed, stored and exchanged by the IT systems. Hori (Hori 2005)

pointed out that this is a wrong belief. Knowledge is dynamic. Each knowledge should be captured and stored with the context, and a new knowledge is reconstructed with considering a new context to which the reconstructed knowledge is applied.

However, it is still difficult to capture knowledge even if we consider the context. Liu pointed out that a computer can manage "data" but not "knowledge."[1] It is also very difficult to adequately reconstruct suitable knowledge that can be applied to a new context. Furthermore, their approach still has a structural defect that the ordinary KM systems had, too. Namely, the providers of the knowledge, i.e., the experts, are imposed heavy labor to input knowledge to the systems and to maintain it, while the users of the knowledge can readily utilize the knowledge in the systems with very light effort. This is the contrary of the common sense, i.e., the benefit principle. We think this structural defect is the most principal reason why the experts are reluctant to provide their valuable knowledge, rather than the poor incentive problem.

We focused spontaneous informal communications as a chance for effective knowledge-sharing and knowledge co-creation. The function that informal communication possesses to promote the sharing and co-creation of knowledge has been the subject of focus for some time, and empirical research into its utility at companies etc. has been undertaken (Kraut et al. 1990). However, every now and again doubts have been expressed as to its efficacy. In other words, there are claims that it is hard to consider communication corresponding to mere conversation as constituting a venue for the sharing or co-creation of meaningful knowledge, and that even if such processes do occasionally take place such a venue is too inefficient. The author also agrees that in some situations, such claims are accurate. If people who do not know one another's names do happen to meet, the probability that communication will arise in this situation is extremely low, and even if some sort of communication should arise, it is difficult to get the contents of such communication to develop much beyond small talk about the weather and the like, or to bring about rich sharing and co-creation of knowledge.

To make informal communication into something meaningful, at least one of the people must surely have the intention of communicating. Furthermore, even if the parties both possess a certain common basis in the sense of having an acquaintance with each other, such as when they are both members of the same department, friends or relatives, it is preferable for them to also have a specific shared topic of conversation.

We are undertaking research which targets a variety of different cases with regard to two points: one method in which we not only provide opportunities for simple communication, but also provide opportunities to a person with a particular intention of communicating, and another method where we provide a common topic of conversation which is likely to form the contents of a rewarding informal conversation that will be brought about. Through these methods, we aim to enhance both the quantity and quality of informal communication.

RELATED WORKS

There have been a lot of efforts to support sharing and co-creation of knowledge in an organization. Answer Garden (Ackerman & Malone 1990), FISH (Seki et al. 1994), and KIDS (Fukui et al. 1998) are systems that support to share experts' knowledge in asynchronous and distributed situations. Answer Garden combines users and experts by creating a knowledge-base of frequently asked questions and answers. FISH integrates the fragments of information stored in a database by using keywords. KIDS allows users to retrieve a knowledge-base that stores semantically-structured knowledge and free format knowledge by using natural language. However, such systems violate the benefit principle; they require experts

to input their professional knowledge into the system data-bases. In addition, they still involve incentive and maintenance problems that are difficult to be solved (Ekbia & Hara 2005) (Semar 2004). i-Land (Streitz 1999) supports cooperative work in face-to-face situations. i-LAND consists of several "roomware (Streitz 1998)" components, i.e., computer-augmented objects that integrate various elements in a room with information devices. However, it is difficult for this kind of system to promote knowledge-sharing beyond the frame of group work.

It is known that informal communication plays an important role in the sharing of knowledge within organizations such as companies, laboratories and schools (Kraut et al. 1990). For example, many people know that major gaps can appear in the degree to which smokers and nonsmokers possess company internal information because of the exchange of information that is going on across organizational boundaries through the informal communication between smokers in smoking rooms. Thus, attempts are being made to promote the sharing of knowledge, particularly of implicit knowledge, through installing recreation rooms inside a company and having managers take the initiative in using them (Desouza 2003).

Therefore, various systems to support informal communications have been proposed. Silhouettell (Okamoto et al. 1998) supports the initiation of conversations in face-to-face situations by projecting user's profile data like a shadow onto a large-sized display as a trigger for the conversation. Silhouettell aims to support small talk in a party, not to support objective-oriented communications. The Meeting Pot (Siio & Mima 2001) is a networked coffee maker. When someone begins to brew coffee in an informal communication space, this event is announced to his/her colleagues in their offices by emitting the aroma of coffee from networked aroma-emission units in the offices. Thus, people gather in the informal communication space. However, they cannot know who desires what kind of information or who has related information. Moreover, it is difficult to have communications beyond a section.

Additionally, in recent years the opportunities for members of the same organization to meet one another have in themselves been decreasing due to the increasing decentralization of offices and the spread of working from home. Thus, a number of studies are being undertaken which attempt to generate informal communication by getting people in separate offices to meet one another in an incidental manner by providing a virtual large room and corridor using a video link between distant offices (Dourish & Bly 1992). Cruiser (Fish et al. 1992) (Cool et al. 1992) and OfficeWalker (Obata & Sasaki 1998) support communications between remote offices mediated by video. Cruiser connects people who are randomly selected. Although it simulated the encounters in a corridor, it gave a sense of sudden invasion. OfficeWalker adopted the metaphor of distance to avoid giving such a sense of invasion. FreeWalk (Nakanishi et al. 1996) provides a three-dimensional virtual space for informal communication where users can walk through using their avatars. Based on casual encounters, they can have informal communications in the space. These systems attempted to promote informal communications by using virtual space. However, the contents of the communications are decided haphazardly as in casual informal communications in the real-world. Moreover, we wonder whether the communications would become poor due to the lack of non-verbal communications.

In this manner, research which has endeavored to promote the sharing and co-creation of knowledge through invigorating informal communication within organizations has shown an expanding trend in recent years. However, as of now there have been few trials that have proactively provided opportunities to people who have the intention of communicating, or provided common topics of conversation.

SUPPORT FOR SHARING AND CO-CREATION OF KNOWLEDGE IN ORGANIZATIONS

This section will first introduce a study case of supporting the informal communications within a single department and on a relatively small scale in terms of laboratory level, which targets an organization composed of members who are acquainted with one another; second, it will introduce a case on the level of an entire building targeting a large-scale organization in which many people were not acquainted with the other members of the organization.

Analysis of Actions and Support in the Shared Communication Space

As in the many cases of research into support of informal communication undertaken previously, we attempted to support the informal communication which already takes place in the communication space. In order to do this, we first carried out an observational analysis of the manner in which informal communication tended to begin in the shared communication space. The results revealed, interestingly, that users of the shared communication space tended to create two kinds of excuse: an "excuse for coming here," and an "excuse for remaining here." (Matsubara et al. 2002)

Whether there was nobody present in the shared communication space or someone was in there already, people who made their way to the shared communication space with the intention of communicating but with no particular person in mind and no specific objective to talk about would refrain from striking up a conversation with the previous arrival, and would instead first pick up one of the newspapers, magazines or casual amusement items (for example, a Rubik cube) placed in the space. They would then gaze at an article in the newspaper or play with the Rubik cube, acting as though this were really their intention in coming to the space. However, it would be evident that they were not absorbed in the activity. This is the "excuse for coming here," which covers up the fact that the person in fact has nothing to do, and provides a justification for coming to the space both for the person themselves and the people around them.

By doing this and continuing such actions, the person justifies their continuing to remain in the space. This is the action that is the "excuse for remaining here." Taking up an action which provides an excuse for remaining in the space makes it possible to wait by oneself for someone else to come if nobody else is there, and enables the person to continue to co-exist in the space without speaking to anyone if there should be someone else already occupying the space (alleviating the pressure of distance). As the person undertakes the action which provides an excuse in this way, they are waiting for some chance that will spark off a dialog with the other person.

Based on the results of the above analysis, we attempted to establish informal communication support media targeting the shared communication space which would make use of an "excuse action." This was Cyber-IRORI (Matsubara et al. 2002). Figure 1 shows what Cyber-IRORI looks like. The system possesses a large-sized display with a horizontally positioned touch panel attached; upon the screen, a number of bubbles represented with computer graphics are shown floating about. Touching the touch panel can cause the bubbles to move or to be broken up. The individual bubbles are set up so as to respond to the URL of the webpage that the members of the same office have recently viewed in reality, so that when the bubbles are broken up, the webpages which respond to the bubbles are displayed on the large-sized upright screen which is connected and set up adjacent to the system. In this way, Cyber-IRORI at the same time as providing an excuse action in the form of playing with the bubbles also aims to provide a topic of conversation that people will start to talk about in the form of the webpages which are displayed from the bubbles that are broken up.

Through verification testing it has been revealed that Cyber-IRORI promotes visits to and staying in the shared space by members, and invigorates communication among them.

Support for the Invigoration of Communication in a Compartmentalized Office

In recent years an increasing number of offices compartmentalize the work space into semi-individual offices with partitions etc. with the objective of enabling individuals to concentrate on their work. However, as a result it has become more difficult for people to see the state of progress of one another's work even when they are in the same room, and people have ended up confining themselves to their own booths as they work. In addition, because this sets up a considerable psychological barrier against visiting another person's booth without a particular reason, it has a negative effect in that it causes deterioration in the communication between people in an office, in spite of the fact that they are all in the same room.

Thus, we established support media to invigorate communication in such compartmentalized offices. This is the Traveling Café (Nakano et al. 2006). Coffee and tea are among the best media for triggering informal communication, as seen when used in the research of (Siio & Mima

Figure 1. What Cyber-IRORI looks like

139

2001). Up until now, attempts have been made to use these to gather people together at shared communication spaces which already exist in a fixed location. However, this will not be effective at drawing into the communicational circle people who are confining themselves to work at their desks. Therefore, we turned this concept on its head and proposed a method which would mobilize the shared communication space by "delivering" the shared communication space to the booths where people remained.

The structure of the Traveling Café system is shown in Figure 2. A coaster equipped with a pressure sensor and ultrasonic sensor is installed in each booth. As these are connected to a server PC via a network, information about the weight of the cup which sits on top of the pressure sensor is uploaded constantly to the server PC. The server PC, upon discovering a person whose cup has remained empty for more than a certain amount of time, displays that person's name on the small display attached to the touch panel which is connected to the coffee maker, and at the same time indicates in a relaxed manner to the people nearby that the person's coffee cup is empty, by causing a lamp to light up. When this takes place, if a person goes to the coffee maker to get some coffee, they can see from the lamp and display whether there is anyone else who might also like some coffee. They can then take the coffee server and go to visit the booth of the office member in question. In this situation, "I've come to pour you some coffee" functions as the "excuse for visiting," alleviating the psychological barriers which stand in the way of people's visiting an individual booth without any particular reason, and enabling people to start informal communication.

In addition, it is possible to know whose booth the coffee server has gone to because the coaster's ultrasonic sensor can detect the signals from the ultrasonic oscillator installed in the coffee server. When this information is sent to the server PC, the server PC sends a notification that "the coffee server has gone to a booth nearby" to the individual PCs of the members in the room who are in booths that are physically close to that booth where the coffee server has gone, and this notification is displayed on their PCs. In this way, the members in the booths near the booth where the coffee server has gone can also be drawn into informal communication. In other words, in the Traveling Café system, the communication space is attached to an object in the form of the coffee server, with each booth within the room becoming

Figure 2. Composition of the Traveling Café system

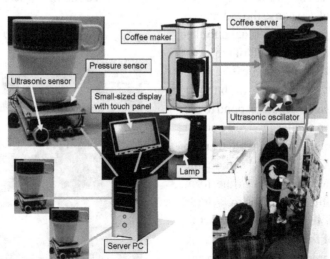

a temporary communication space through the movement of the coffee server.

Only preliminary evaluations have been undertaken as yet for this system, but there are suggestions of effects in terms of making it easier to visit other people's booths, and invigoration of communication as a result of this. Going forward, we aim to create links with the function which gauges the work status of the members in the room, to enable a shift towards smoother informal communication.

"Docta Ignorantia" and the Use of Chance Meetings

In a large-scale organization, there are people with many different kinds of knowledge. If the knowledge which these people possess can be used efficiently, great improvements may be anticipated in the organizational productivity of the organization as a whole. When a knowledge base is established through extracting knowledge possessed by the constituent members, and made searchable on an as-needed basis, this is known as a knowledge management system; in recent years, many such systems have been subjected to research and development and some of them have been realized in a usable form. However, there are few instances of cases of skillful operation of these systems.

The greatest problem of knowledge management systems is that it is difficult to enhance the knowledge base to a sufficient extent, and knowledge thus accumulated rapidly becomes obsolete. The reason for this is that the burden of recording knowledge in the knowledge base and the burden of preserving this in a continually updated form falls entirely on the experts who possess the knowledge, while the merits arising from doing this do not accrue to the experts at all. In general, experts are people at the center of work in their workplaces, so it is difficult for them to put aside the time to maintain such a knowledge base. In addition, there is in specialized knowledge

a high degree of what is called "implicit knowledge" which is hard to put into document form. Finally, because specialized knowledge is the original source of the prerogative of the experts themselves, it is unlikely that experts will accept with good grace requests to publically disclose such information in exchange for next to nothing, however much it is to the benefit of the company as a whole. In other words, it is impossible to use the knowledge management system for the basic concept of creating a knowledge base to gather together expert knowledge. Even in the "know-who" system, people must register profile information relating to their own specialized field, and as a result there are apprehensions that experts will be flooded with questions unrelated to their own work, resulting in an unnecessary burden. As a result, gathering and maintaining know-who information appropriately is difficult.

Thus, we have turned this idea on its head and given up the idea of establishing a knowledge base. Instead, we decided to establish an "docta-ignorantia-base." In other words, rather than accumulating information in terms of "This is what I know," we would accumulate information in terms of "I know that this is what I don't know." Such "docta ignorantia" information, say "unknown knowledge" information, refers to being aware of such information, or wanting such information, in other words. We would then ask as many people as possible in the organization to look at such "unknown knowledge information." This is based on the idea that when people who have some kind of knowledge see "unknown knowledge information" and start to talk (provided, of course, that they have sufficient free time), they will share knowledge as a result.

As a result of this, experts are freed from the cumbersome work of registering and maintaining knowledge in a knowledge base. Instead, the "beneficiaries," who easily obtained useful information from the traditional knowledge management systems of the past, are given the responsibility for establishing the docta-ignorantia-base and the task (described below) of searching for people who know about this. In other words, the "benefit principle," which is accepted without question in human society, is incorporated into knowledge sharing.

In the sense that users publically disclose "what I would like to know," and are instructed by people who do know, the system resembles "knowledge communities." However, our target was the constituent members of organizations who were busy carrying out their work. Hence, even if we were to set up a webpage which catalogs the information asking "could you please tell me this?" few people would take the trouble to browse such a base, and in particular it can hardly be expected that experts, who are very busy, would browse the page. In other words, the media which publically discloses the unknown knowledge information must be not passive "pull"-type media like a website, but an active "push"-type media. Thus, we established two kinds of "push"-type "unknown knowledge information" display systems.

HuNeAS

The first system was the Human Network Activating System (HuNeAS), a system which aims to bring about knowledge-sharing through face-to-face dialog (Nishimoto & Matsuda 2007). An outline of HuNeAS is shown in Figure 3. People who want to learn information first of all register this information at the docta-ignorantia-base. After this, they carry around an RFID tag on a constant basis. In the research department to which the authors are affiliated, 40-inch large-sized plasma displays are set up in various places such as the corridor, elevator hall and break room. An RFID antenna is installed in each display. When someone carrying an RFID tag approaches any of the displays, the RFID antenna reads the person's ID from the tag, and sends the ID information to the docta-ignorantia-base. The docta-ignorantia-base sends the unknown knowledge information which the person has registered in response to the ID,

and displays it on the screen. As a result, a person approaching the display can easily see "what the person who is in front of the display wants to know." In this way, if someone who happens to read the information knows something about this kind of knowledge and is able to take the time to talk, they can exchange information on the spot as they stand around and talk. In other words, this is a form of media which "pushes" unknown knowledge in the places where people come across one another, such as passing one another in the corridor or while waiting for an elevator. Even if dialog is not created at this time, people can see that "this person is interested in such-and-such a thing." This is a useful kind of know-who information.

We started actual operation of HuNeAS and implemented an operational trial lasting around two months. The results showed that the system brought about information exchange through face-to-face dialog by displaying unknown knowledge information. Furthermore, it was revealed that information exchange occurred through face-to-face dialog not only in cases where the people were acquainted with one another but even in cases where the people had never spoken to one another before.

Interactive Fliers

The second system was that of Interactive Flyers (Nishimoto & Nemoto 2006). This is a system which aims to bring about knowledge sharing by non-face-to-face dialog. An outline of Interactive Fliers is shown in Figure 4. Because this system is basically an electronic advertisement system, it describes the information displayed here in the form of an "advertisement"; when the system is operated within an organization, the advertisements are for unknown knowledge information. As might be expected, this promotes knowledge sharing centering on unknown knowledge. As in the case of HuNeAS, the "advertiser" who wishes to transmit unknown knowledge infor-

Figure 3. Outline of HuNeAS

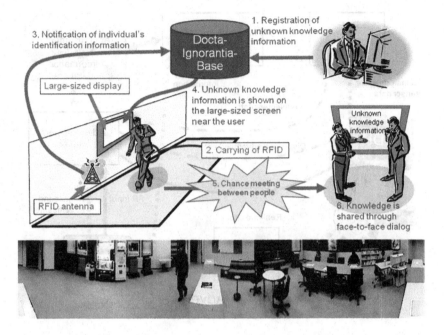

mation first of all registers the information at the docta-ignorantia-base (in Figure 4, this is the advertisement/advertiser information database), along with their own personal information. In this system, a large-sized display is used, as used in HuNeAS. A human detector sensor is installed in the large-sized display. When someone (not necessarily the advertiser) approaches any of the screens, the human detector sensor detects this and notifies the PDP monitoring server. Then the PDP monitoring server sends the read request for the advertisement information to the advertisement server, and thumbnails of 10 advertisements that were registered are displayed on the PDP from among the new advertisements. Browsers can see the details of one of the advertisements by touching the thumbnail of the advertisement they are interested in.

Meanwhile, the PDP monitoring server sends a notification of who is looking at what advertisement to the advertiser-calling server. The advertiser-calling server instantly sends a notification to the advertiser who registered the advertisement, with information along the lines of "Currently,

someone appears to be viewing your advertisement" (using emails sent to cell phones and the like). Advertisers who have received such a notification can add further "soliciting (PR)" information to their own advertisement. Soliciting information is displayed in telop form directly beneath the thumbnail advertisement. In other words, browsers can know that the advertiser is there on the other side of the advertisement where the "soliciting" information is displayed. By touching the thumbnail of the advertisement, the browser can move to a page with more details; as a text chat system is prepared, the browser can immediately exchange information anonymously with the advertiser.

In this way, Interactive Fliers makes it possible to make use of all meetings between people and the several large-sized displays installed in our research department. In those parts where face-to-face dialog is not possible, Interactive Fliers is lacking communication efficiency in some areas comparing to HuNeAS, but in terms of increasing the number of meetings by a large degree, Interactive Fliers is superior to HuNeAS. We put

Figure 4. Outline of interactive fliers

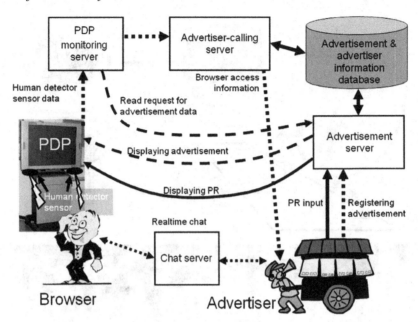

the system into actual operation and carried out experiments. We confirmed that an extremely large number of people came to browse advertisements, and that due to PR and the text chat that was triggered by the PR, actual information exchange was also brought about.

These systems, which make use of "unknown knowledge information" and "instant communication from chance meetings," realize the sharing and co-creation of knowledge in a beneficiary-pays form which does not impose a burden on experts. In addition, there is a high likelihood that people who registered unknown knowledge will obtain information connected with this after a certain period of time has elapsed. Thus, if one conducts a search for unknown knowledge information registered in the past on the docta-ignorantia-base, and looks for the person who registered it, it is likely that they obtained information connected to the problem. In other words, the docta-ignorantia-base is changing naturally into a know-who data base, rather than a system where old knowledge becomes obsolete. Furthermore, no direct burden is imposed on the experts who are the original source of the knowledge. If the person first consults with the

people discovered on the docta-ignorantia-base, and only if it appears that that alone will not solve the problem, the person then finds out the (expert who knows the) original source of the information, and if the person goes to consult with the expert, we believe that it is easy to achieve an appropriate distribution of the burden according to the level of the problem.

INNOVATION IN THE FORM OF COMMUNICATION

We have advanced our research into innovations in the very form of communication. Here, two cases will be presented.

Multithreading Speech Dialog

In recent years, there has been a huge increase in opportunities to communicate online to the rapid enhancement of the network environment. Text chat is one of the forms of online communication media that is used with particular frequency. Instant messaging systems are a communication media which may be described as in essence the same as text chat, although there are some differences. We considered methods for establishing systems using text chat which would support creative meetings (Nishimoto et al. 1996), the establishment of text chat systems which are sensitive to the dialog context on both sides through communicating keystroke vibrations (Yamada et al. 2003), and methods for automatically organizing meeting contents in text chat (Ogura et al. 2004).

One of the characteristics of text chat is that the dialog is multithreaded. This means that a number of dialog threads exist and progress in a parallel manner, and each speaker participates simultaneously in a number of dialog threads. The origin of this situation is the fact that in text chat, the speaker cannot see the status of the dialog in terms of what kind of statement the other person is making about what, or indeed whether the other person is about to make a statement in the first place. Because of this, a number of attempts have been made in the past to make such dialog into a single threaded system in the same manner as face-to-face dialog through communicating the dialog status through some means or other. The research cited above (Yamada et al. 2003) is an example of this. However, in spite of such efforts, it has not proven possible to remove the multithreaded nature of text chat. When we conducted an observational analysis of the behavior of power users in text chat, it was revealed that in fact, power users themselves worked proactively to multithread the dialog. It is believed that the aim behind this is to raise the efficiency of the dialog.

Because speech dialog is an extremely everyday means of communication, we do not think much about its efficiency. On the contrary, there is a strong tendency to assume implicitly that speech dialog is the ideal form of dialog; as a result, attempts are made to somehow make text chat assume the same form as speech dialog. However, in some aspects, speech dialog is extremely inefficient. In speech dialog, essentially only person can speak in any given instant. Although many

participants there are in the dialog, when someone is speaking, the other people should listen to him/her. Furthermore, as it is considered undesirable to change the topic of conversation abruptly, it is impossible to turn a conversation around until it has got to the point where the current topic of conversation is considered to have more or less reached its convergence. As a result, even if an interesting idea springs to someone's mind which is not connected to the current topic of conversation, it is not possible to talk about this right away, and in many cases the person does not in the end get the chance to speak or, worse, may even forget it. This is a huge loss from the perspective of the sharing and co-creation of knowledge.

Thus, we have established ChaTEL, a completely new speech communication media which makes it possible to multithread speech dialog in the same manner as text chat (Ogura et al. 2007). By enabling the multithreading of speech dialog, it enables one to talk about what one wants to talk about when one wants regardless of what anyone else is talking about at the present time, thus resolving the problems described above, and enabling useful knowledge to be shared in an economical manner.

The user interface screen of ChaTEL is shown in Figure 5. The composition of ChaTEL is taken from that of the server client in the same manner as text chat in general. To make a statement, the user presses the "Normal Recording" button shown on the upper left-hand side of Figure 5, and inputs the statement via the microphone. When the input is complete, the voice data is uploaded to the server. When the server receives this voice data, it transmits to all clients the information only of whose statement it is and, simultaneously, the metadata stating that such data has been received. Each client adds the metadata thus received to the bottommost part of the statement log list shown in the center of Figure 5. To listen to the voice statements, one selects the statement one wants to listen to from the log, and double-clicks on this or presses the "Listen to this message" button shown

Figure 5. The user interface screen of ChaTEL

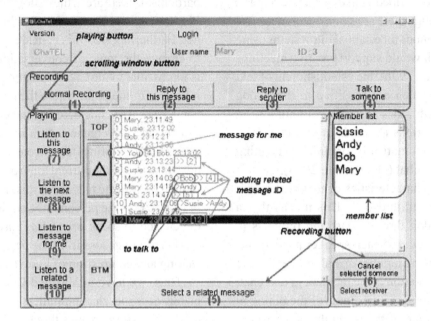

on the left-hand side of Figure 5. This sends a request to the server to download the voice data, and the corresponding voice data package is sent from the server to the client making the request. The above process is the basic method of using ChaTEL. We added two functions to this to make it even easier to undertake multithreaded dialog.

The first function specifies which preceding statement is being responded to. Even in text chat, users who are accustomed to the system not infrequently work to maintain the multithread nature of dialog through voluntarily specifying which preceding statement their own statement is connected with using the following method.

I agree with your opinion, too > The drink-driving problem

ChaTEL allows the ID of the preceding statement to be added to the end of the statement metadata on the log. This can be seen in the center of the log on Figure 5, indicated by "related message ID" for example, >>[2]. In order to add this information, after the preceding statement to which a connection is desired to be placed has

been selected in the log, it is only necessary to press the "Reply to this message" button shown in the upper center of Figure 5, and record the statement. In order to listen to the preceding statement responded to, one presses the "Listen to a related message" button on the lower left-hand side of Figure 5. When this happens, in the event that >>[2], for example, is specified [2] will be played.

The second function specifies which participant(s) the statement is directed to. Once again, this is something which is not infrequently seen in text chat.

Will someone carry this on? > Mr. Koizumi

In ChaTEL, after the person one wishes to nominate has been selected from the "Member list" on the right-hand side of Figure 5, it is only necessary to press the "Talk to someone" button on the upper right-hand side of Figure 5, and record the statement. When one records the statement using this method, the name of the partner nominated is shown at the end of the statement metadata on the log, as >Bob. In the event that one is oneself nominated as a partner by someone else, the indication >>> You: is added to the top of the log data. In the event that one wishes to select and listen to only those statements addressed to oneself, one presses the "Listen to message for me" button on the left-hand side of Figure 5.

When a trial experiment of this system was undertaken, it was revealed that it is possible to multithread speech dialogs. As a result, it was possible to bring about an extremely high-level information exchange using speech which everyday speech dialog was not able to realize. In addition, it was discovered that while "Nominate a partner" (e.g., >Bob) was frequently used in text chat, "Specify preceding statement" (e.g., >>[2]) was used extremely frequently in ChaTEL, and this form of dialog is characterized by the fact that partner nomination is barely used. We aim to conduct further analysis and discussion of such characteristics, and to realize communication media using multithreaded speech dialog which is easier to use.

Communication Media Which Triggers Discussion Using Multiple Modalities

There are several modalities which can be used for communication, and each has advantages and disadvantages. For example, in speech subtle nuances are brought across through nonverbal information such as intonation, but as explained in descriptions of ChaTEL system, speech scores poorly in terms of information exchange efficiency, recordability and reusability. On the other hand, while texting possesses recordability and reusability, communicating subtle nuances is difficult. Thus, if any one problem is discussed using a number of different modalities, it may be anticipated that the advantages of each modality will be exploited, resulting in a deeper and more efficient discussion.

Thus, we established Attractiblog, a new communication media which combines online text-based dialog with offline face-to-face speech dialog (Chiba & Nishimoto 2007). The composition of Attractiblog is shown in Figure 6. Attractiblog uses an intrablog as its text-based communication media. Intrablogs have been introduced at a rapid pace in companies etc. in recent years as an informal communication media for constituent members of an office. We introduced a laboratory intrablog into the laboratory, and have already operated it continuously for over four years, and are attempting activities such as carrying out research progress reports on the blog. As a result, the laboratory intrablog has become firmly established at the laboratory, and with contents across an extremely wide range of fields being continually posted on it, from research topics to recreational topics, the online sharing and co-creation of knowledge is taking place.

Attractiblog induces face-to-face discussion among members in the laboratory by displaying the contents of the laboratory intrablog on a large-sized screen display in the shared communication space set up in the laboratory. To generate discussions more easily, the system detects who is in the shared communication space using the RFID tag which each person continually carries with them, and selectively displays articles of the people in the space and articles by other people in the space commenting on these articles.

The results of this operational trial confirmed cases in which mutual discussion on research contents was triggered by the laboratory intrablog articles shown in the shared communication space. At the current stage, effects of using multiple modalities have not been confirmed; going forward, therefore, we would like to advance our investigative research. In addition, at present only a tendency to induce face-to-face offline dialog from online conversations has been realized; we would like, therefore, to realize a function which will reverse this and induce online dialog from face-to-face dialog.

Figure 6. Composition of Attractiblog

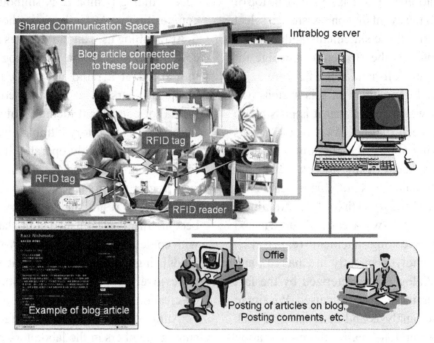

KNOWLEDGE SHARING AND CO-CREATION THROUGH INFORMAL COMMUNICATIONS IN OTHER SETTINGS

Knowledge sharing and co-creation through informal communication are not only effective in business-related settings such as office work. Informal communication also functions effectively in a variety of ways in scenes such as everyday private lives and individual work. In this section, we will introduce two case studies which targeted families and individual pastime activities.

Dining Table Communication Media to Enrich Family Life

In most families, much of family life takes place at the evening meal around the dinner table. However, because each constituent member of the family is active in a different community throughout the day, it is difficult for a family to form a common ground, and it is in fact relatively difficult for people to understand the contents of what others are talking about. In such cases, it is effective to make use of photographs. In particular, with the rapid spread of cell phones with cameras in recent years, it has become a matter of course for people to carry a cell phone with them as they go about their day. Thus, we thought that bringing photographs taken on a cell phone camera to the meal and showing them to others could enrich the family conversation and facilitate understanding, and thus enable closer bonds between family members. Based on such thinking, we established "pHotOluck," a system which enables the sharing and operation of a digital camera at the dining table (Nishimoto et al. 2006). The composition of pHotOluck is shown in Figure 7.

First of all, when a person thinks during their day-to-day life, "This is interesting; I'd like to tell my family about it," they can take a photograph with a cell phone camera, and send the photograph as an email attachment to the photograph server which is installed in the household. A plate specially designated for photograph projection is prepared on the dining table. Three color markers are adhered to the edge of each plate; each indi-

Figure 7. Composition of the pHotOluck system

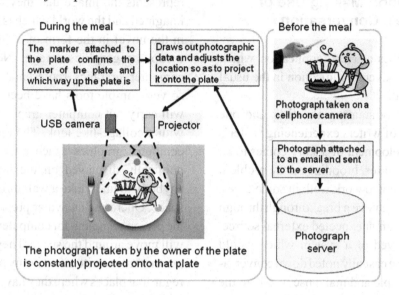

vidual plate and the way up it is placed in can be determined through the combination of colors. A USB camera which constantly films the scene at the dining table and a projector which projects the photographs are installed at the head of the dining table. In this way, the system can be set so that photographs which any person has taken can be continually projected onto the specially designated plate of that person. To switch photographs, the plate is turned over. A specialized marker which shows the underside of the plate is adhered to the underside of the plate; when this is detected, the system recognizes that the plate has been turned over. Hence, each person can display the photographs that they have taken one at a time in order on the surface of their own plate. Because a plate is used as the projection zone, the projection domain of the photograph can be maintained in a sure manner even on a dining table where the plates used for food and the like become mixed up during meals.

In order to evaluate the practicality of this system, we undertook a comparative experiment of two systems: a routine digital photo browser in which thumbnail images are lined up on a liquid crystal display with a touch panel, in which the photograph which one wants to see can be im-

mediately selected by touching the thumbnail; and the situation in which a digital photograph is made into camera-ready copy, which is then transferred to the person who took the photograph. The results showed that the routine digital browser and camera-ready copy photographs were far superior to pHotOluck in terms of the photograph search function, but that in these cases people's behavior went no further than "looking through photographs," and conversations were almost never induced in the end; the results also showed that what might be called "the person with the loudest voice" tended to control the right to speak at any one time. By contrast, it was revealed that in the case of pHotOluck, because when discussion of one's own photograph had finished, selecting the next candidate for the topic of conversation from among one's own photographs immediately was difficult, this resulted in the right to speak being naturally transferred to another person, and individual photographs thus became the topic of conversation in a more even-handed manner. In other words, this indicates that in order to support communication in venues such as families, "slow media" such as pHotOluck functions more effectively than systems which are more "efficient" in the general meaning of the word.

Creative Support Making Use of Other People's Conversation

This case describes a tricky application which differs slightly from communication in the usual sense of the word.

There are many amateur novelists, and one frequently hears of writers experiencing writer's block as the development of a story comes to an impasse. In such cases, brooding on the problem by oneself tends not to work well; in some cases, however, writers achieve a breakthrough through stimulation from an unexpected external source. Thus, we conceived of a system which would gather together the casually noted down conversations of other people and make use of this in the creative process (Kainuma et al. 2006).

A snapshot image of an example of the system in use is shown in Figure 8. First, the novelist

represents the image that they themselves have imagined and the world which is being expressed in the novel in the form of a three-dimensional computer graphics image. Needless to say, computer graphics representation is not easy, so very simple tools have been prepared which will carry out computer graphics representation with a collage-like look. The three-dimensional computer graphics space thus created is then publically displayed on the internet, allowing anybody to undertake a walkthrough through the space. Operating an avatar prepared beforehand, the person searching for computer graphics spaces will move around the space. They can them leave a comment as written text in any place they choose regarding places where they have taken a liking to any objects. In addition, comments posted in the past by other people can be read by anybody who

Figure 8. Image of searching for computer graphics spaces

approaches the place in question, and comments on such comments can also be added.

In other words, this system can serve the function of a spatial, asynchronous online message board, which induces comments on computer graphics spaces in particular. In this manner, it has possibilities for asynchronous communication between searchers, but no explicit communication exists between novelists and searchers. The novelist can go around the space and look at the comments (illusions) casually noted down by searchers enabled by this system, and use them as external inspiration for their own creative processes.

We undertook a comparison using four subjects, which compared a situation in which the system was used, and a situation in which writers were asked to write a novel completely alone without use of the system. In each case, novelists obtained their themes from the experimenters, and in the situations where the system was used, computer graphics in accordance with the theme were prepared beforehand by the experimenters, while separate examiners were asked to search and to post comments. In the results, it was observed that while among the subjects not using the system there were many cases of subjects reaching an impasse soon after starting the experiment, subjects using the system would search the computer graphics space when they reached an impasse and were inspired by the comments of other users, allowing them to continue writing.

In this case, communication is not directly used for the sharing or co-creation of knowledge. However, this case may be said to show that information which can be useful for bringing about new knowledge lies buried in the trail left in the form of the casually-noted communications of other people, and that by using this it is possible to create better-quality knowledge.

CONCLUSION

This chapter has introduced attempts which have been advanced in the author's laboratory to strengthen support for the sharing and co-creation of knowledge based on informal communication. The dialog which takes place in informal communication is a resource of great value. However, at the same time, despite the seams of gold that are to be found in this resource, enormous levels of impurities are also to be found there. We need to strip the impurities away if we are to refine the gold itself. Such technological development is the key to enabling effective use of informal communication. Going forward, we want to advance research and development into technology which will enable the effective use of informal communication in a wide range of situations.

ACKNOWLEDGMENT

This research was partially supported by a research grant of the Mitani foundation for research and development (2008-2009). The author would like to thank all graduates and persons currently active at the Center for Knowledge Science, Japan Advanced Institute of Science and Technology (JAIST) for their cooperation in the execution of the research introduced in this chapter.

REFERENCES

Ackerman, M. S., & Malone, T. W. (1990). Answer garden: A tool for growing organizational memory. *Proceedings of ACM Conference on Office Information Systems (COIS'90)*, 1990.

Chiba, Y., & Nishimoto, K. (2007). An intrablog-based informal communication encouraging system that seamlessly links on-line communications to off-line ones. *The IEICE Transactions on Information and Systems. E (Norwalk, Conn.)*, 90-D(10), 1501–1508.

Cool, C., Fish, R., Kraut, R., & Lowery, C. (1992). Iterative design of video communication systems. *Proceedings of ACM CSCW'92*, (pp. 25-32).

Desouza, K. C. (2003). Facilitating tacit knowledge exchange. *Communications of the ACM, 46*(6), 85–88. doi:10.1145/777313.777317

Dourish, P., & Bly, S. (1992). Portholes: Supporting awareness in a distributed work group. *Proceedings of CHI'92*, (pp. 541-547).

Ekbia, H. R., & Hara, N. (2005). Incentive structures in knowledge management. In Schwartz, D. (Ed.), *Encyclopedia of knowledge management*. Hershey, PA: Idea Group Inc.

Fish, R., Kraut, R., Root, R., & Rice, R. (1992). Evaluating video as a technology for informal communication. *Proceedings CHI, 92*, 37–48.

Fukui, M., Sasaki, K., Shibazaki, Y., Ohtake, Y., & Nakamura, Y. (1998). Practice of know-how sharing in office environment using knowledge and knowledge-sharing system. *IPSJ SIG Notes, 27*(3), 13–18.

Hori, K. (2005). *Do knowledge assets really exist in the world and can we access such knowledge-knowledge evolves through a cycle of knowledge liquidization and crystallization. (LNCS 3359)* (pp. 1–13). Springer.

Kainuma, S., Miyashita, H., & Nishimoto, K. (2006). Analyses of creation processes of novels where others' whims are exploited to inspire an author's imagination. *IPSJ SIG Technical Reports 2006-EC-3, 24*, 113-120.

Kraut, R. E., Fish, R. S., Root, R. W., & Chalfonte, B. L. (1990). Informal communication in organizations: Form, function, and technology. In Oskamp, S., & Spacapan, S. (Eds.), *People's reactions to technology* (pp. 145–199). London, UK: Sage Publications.

Krogh, G. V., Ichijo, K., & Nonaka, I. (2000). *Enabling knowledge creation: How to unlock the mystery of tacit knowledge and release the power of innovation*. Oxford University Press.

Matsubara, T., Sugiyama, K., & Nishimoto, K. (2002). *Raison d'etre object: A cyber-hearth that catalyzes face-to-face informal communication*. Engineering and Deployment of Cooperative Information Systems: First International Conference EDCIS 2002, (LNCS 2480), (pp. 537-546).

Nakanishi, H., Yoshida, C., Nishimura, T., & Ishida, T. (1996). *FreeWalk: Supporting casual meetings in a network*. International Conference on Computer Supported Cooperative Work (CSCW'96), (pp. 308-314).

Nakano, T., Kamewada, K., Sugito, J., Nagaoka, Y., Ogura, K., & Nishimoto, K. (2006). The Traveling cafe: A communication encouraging system for partitioned offices. *CHI2006 Extended Abstract*, (pp. 1139-1144).

Nishimoto, K., Amano, K., & Usuki, M. (2006). pHotOluck: A home-use table-ware to vitalize mealtime communications by projecting photos onto dishes. *Proceedings of The First IEEE International Workshop on Horizontal Interactive Human-Computer Systems (TableTop2006)*, (pp. 9-16).

Nishimoto, K., & Matsuda, K. (2007). Informal communication support media for encouraging knowledge-sharing and creation in a community. [IJITDM]. *International Journal of Information Technology and Decision Making, 6*(3), 411–426. doi:10.1142/S0219622007002551

Nishimoto, K., & Nemoto, H. (2006). Interactive fliers: An electric ad system for a community to facilitate communications between advertisers and audience. *Proceedings of The First International Conference on Knowledge, Information and Creativity Support Systems (KICSS2006)*, (pp. 197-204).

Nishimoto, K., Sumi, Y., & Mase, K. (1996). Toward an outsider agent for supporting a brainstorming session-an information retrieval method from a different viewpoint. *Knowledge-Based Systems, 9*(6), 377–384. doi:10.1016/S0950-7051(96)01050-7

Nonaka, I., & Takeuchi, H. (1995). *The knowledge-creating company: How Japanese companies create the dynamics of innovation*. Oxford University Press.

Obata, A., & Sasaki, K. (1998). OfficeWalker: A virtual visiting system based on proxemics. *Proceedings CSCW, 98*, 1–10.

Ogura, K., Ishizaki, M., & Nishimoto, K. (2004). A method of extracting topic threads towards facilitating knowledge creation in chat conversations. *Proceedings of KES2004*

Ogura, K., Nishimoto, K., & Sugiyama, K. (2007). ChaTEL: A novel voice communication systems based on analyzing text-based chat conversations for multiple topic thread. *Proceedings of the Second IASTED International Conference Human-Computer Interaction* (pp. 49-54).

Okamoto, M., Nakanishi, H., Nishimura, T., & Ishida, T. (1998). Silhouettell: Awareness support for real-world encounter. In Ishida, T. (Ed.), *Community computing and support systems. (LNCS 1519)* (pp. 317–330). Springer-Verlag. doi:10.1007/3-540-49247-X_21

Seki, Y., Yamagami, T., & Shimizu, A. (1994). FISH: Flexible knowledge-sharing and handling system. *Systems and Computers in Japan, 25*(10), 36–46. doi:10.1002/scj.4690251004

Semar, W. (2004). Incentive systems in knowledge management to support cooperative distributed forms of creating and acquiring knowledge. In H. Arabnia, et al. (Eds.), *Proceedings of the International Conference on Information and Knowledge Engineering - IKE'04*, (pp. 406-411).

Siio, I., & Mima, N. (2001). *Meeting pot: Coffee aroma transmitter*. UbiComp 2001: International Conference on Ubiquitous Computing.

Streitz, N. A. (1998). *Roomware for collaborative buildings: Integrated design of architectural spaces and information spaces. Cooperative Buildings. (LNCS1370)* (pp. 4–21). Springer. doi:10.1007/3-540-69706-3_3

Streitz, N. A. (1999). i-LAND: An interactive landscape for creativity and innovation. *Proceedings of ACM Conference on Human Factors in Computing Systems (CHI'99)*, (pp. 120-127).

Yamada, Y., Hirano, T., & Nishimoto, K. (2003). TangibleChat: A chat-system that conveys conversation-context-awareness by transmitting vibration produced by key-stroke-act. *Transactions of the Information Processing Society of Japan, 44*(5), 1392–1403.

ENDNOTE

[1] In his talk at the Sino-Japan Workshop on Meta-synthesis and Creativity Support System, Beijing, China, July, 2005.

Chapter 13
Need and Possible Criteria for Evaluating the Effectiveness of Computer–Mediated Communication

Yi-Chieh Ho
Hwa-Hsia Institute of Technology, Taiwan, R.O.C.

ABSTRACT

Computer-mediated communication (CMC) has been a 'hot' topic in computer-assisted language learning (CALL); however, its effectiveness remains uncertain. This chapter reviews the nature of CMC, pinpoints the advantages and disadvantages of incorporating it into language learning, considers factors that may affect the quality of CMC, and identifies possible directions for future studies. The author argues that sound criteria are lacking for the evaluation of the effectiveness of CMC and attempts to identify a set of possible criteria for classroom-based studies drawing from literature in language teaching and learning. The author also urges engineers to consider these criteria when designing new software, so that end users can conveniently measure its effectiveness and record their own progress.

INTRODUCTION

Technology has been increasingly used for language teaching and learning. However, information technology (IT) engineers have probably invented the technology without taking these purposes into account. As a result, teachers consume passively whatever and whenever new software is out on the market. Studies on CMC have burgeoned in recent years. Both positive and negative results have been found and many factors may contribute to the success or failure

DOI: 10.4018/978-1-61520-871-5.ch013

of CMC. It was therefore pointed out that the effectiveness of CMC remains uncertain (Levy & Stockwell, 2006). It has been challenging for teachers to explore ways to incorporate CMC into their classrooms and engage their students in learning activities derived from it. Also challenging is the requirement to identify ways of measuring the effectiveness of CMC. Therefore, it is argued that sound criteria are needed to evaluate the effectiveness of using CMC in language teaching and learning contexts.

LITERATURE REVIEW

According to Herring (1996, cited in Levy & Stockwell, 2006), CMC is *"communication that takes place between human beings via the instrumentality of computers"* (p. 84). It was "originally developed for deaf education at Gallaudet University in the mid-1980s" (Bruce, et al., cited in Abrams, 2006, p. 182). Due to its successful exploitation in English composition classes, it started to be applied to second language (L2) learning and teaching contexts in the 1990s (Abrams, 2006).

CMC has become a central topic in recent research in CALL. Chun (2007), after examining articles in the two top CALL journals in America (i.e., *CALICO Journal* and *Language, Learning & Technology*) from 2001 to 2006, discovered that "hot" topics during this period included CMC, Web-based instruction, culture, writing, vocabulary, reading, literacy, syntax/grammar, speaking, and listening, in this order.

Distance is no longer a problem for communication. CMC "permits not only one-to-one communication but also one-to-many communication" (Kern & Warschauer, 2000, p. 12). Chapelle (2001) also noted that a synchronous CMC writing activity provides the opportunity for learners to focus on form, and the interaction that happens in real-time might help engage learners in modified interaction, as well as modified output. Now

CMC also engages learners in many-to-many communication and has the capacity to allow not only written but also verbal and visual communication with native speakers or other learners around the world.

Effective communication on the Internet requires Web-literacy. Web-literacy refers to knowledge and skills needed for the use of the World Wide Web. The birth of the World Wide Web originated from a networked information project at CERN (a European organization for nuclear research) by Tim Berners-Lee (CERN, 2007) in October, 1990 (Delcloque, 2000, p. 38). Since learners vary in their knowledge or skills, there are high-literate as well as low-literate users of the Web. Moreover, due to constant and rapid change in the nature of the Web and the Internet, the knowledge and skills required inevitably increase.

To be Web-literate, learners need to be able to browse the Internet to search for information, to locate the information needed, to use references to locate the information needed, to comprehend and process the information found, to evaluate whether the information is what is needed, to understand texts that are accompanied by hyperlinks, sound, animation, graphics, music, and video, etc., and to communicate effectively on the Internet (adapted from Edusoft, 2002).

Online communication has become an essential part of people's lives nowadays. To communicate effectively on the Internet with native speakers or other learners anytime and anywhere, learners need to be equipped with skills such as joining in chat rooms or discussion groups on the forum, sending e-mails, and posting messages on the bulletin board or blogs. The communication can be synchronous and happens in real-time (e.g., chat and instant messages) or asynchronously (e.g., email and forums). Language learners can even use audio- or visual-devices to deliver their voice or images through the Internet. For example, it is popular to use podcasts to create personal radio shows on blogs. Many people nowadays use a web camera and voiced chats to communicate with their faraway families and friends.

The prerequisites for achieving the above goals effectively are: to master English, which is still the current dominant language on the Internet; to understand basic computer technology (e.g., the ability to type, to use the keyboard and various computer applications effectively); to be aware of Web traps (Moro, 2007) such as 'advertisements', 'spyware', and 'spam mail' while browsing various sites, and to know how to avoid 'phishing sites' as well as 'online plagiarism' since the only technique needed is to 'click' and 'paste'. Online etiquette is something that Internet users also need to be aware of. It advocates that when learners communicate with strangers without seeing each other's faces, they need to avoid personal or offensive questions that they normally would not ask in face-to-face communication.

It has been proposed that a form of CALL, i.e., network-based language teaching (NBLT) can encourage learner communication. NBLT is "language teaching that involves the use of computers connected to one another in either local or global networks. [...] NBLT represents a new and different side of CALL, where human-to-human communication is the focus" (Kern & Warschauer, 2000, p.1).

NBLT not only fosters literacy skills but also benefits learners who are usually passive and shy in the traditional language classroom. For example, Warschauer (2000) undertook a longitudinal study of online learning in four college second language and writing classrooms. The sample was comprised of students who were believed to be struggling to obtain access to both language and technology. He found that in these classes computers served as a vehicle to develop new literacy skills. Some students considered the opportunity to use and practice electronic literacy skills as a chance to "overcome communication disadvantages that they might have in an English class" (p.48).

There is no agreed term for the skills needed for networked learning. Nunes et al. (2000, cited in McPherson & Nunes, 2004, p. 83) identified these skills as "networked information and communication literacy skills (NICLS)". Students are not only expected to be trained in low-level skills such as "the basic use of computer-mediated technology, online social skills, online etiquette, web navigation and web searching", but also to develop high cognitive skills such as "negotiation of meaning, life-long learning, reflective analysis and meta cognition." As they pointed out, "[t]hese skills are not only required to succeed in the online learning environment to which learners are exposed, but are also an essential part of all aspects of daily networked activity" (p. 83).

While the Web appears to be suitable for providing students with access to authentic, situated materials and meaningful communication, as well as intercultural understandings, full exploitation for language learning purposes remains a difficult task. As Jager (2004) pointed out, "it involves integrating resources already available on the Web, making use of synchronous and asynchronous communication, and providing other forms of interaction" (p. 33).

The assumption behind CMC is that both synchronous and asynchronous communication can foster negotiation of meaning including corrective feedback from the interlocutors. The process of negotiation enables learners to encounter modified and comprehensible input, and thus produce modified or pushed output in the process of meaning construction. Both trigger learners' noticing of grammar forms, implicitly or explicitly (Pellettieri, 2000).

There is a difference between CALL courseware where the computer is used as a tool and interaction happens between learners and computers and CMC where learners use the computer as a tool to communicate with other learners. Therefore, it has been suggested that the theory that supports CMC should not only include second language acquisition (SLA), but also embrace a wider communication framework that integrates "a sociocultural and multimodal environment" (Hampel & Baber, 2003, p. 172).

Results from several studies revealed that CMC fosters the negotiation of meaning (Pellettieri, 2000; Savignon & Rothmeier, 2004; Wang, 2006), facilitates motivation (Fotos, 2004; Appel & Gilabert, 2004; Jauregi & Banados, 2008), facilitates interaction (Kern & Warschauer, 2000), promotes proficiency (Kinginger, 2000; Fotos, 2004; Jauregi & Banados, 2008), enhances teacher's professional development in terms of communication, collaboration, and reflection (Son, 2004), develops autonomy through reflection (Ushioda, 2000) and raises cultural awareness (Zeiss & Isabelli-Garcia, 2005; Lomicka, 2006; Jauregi & Banados, 2008). After reviewing a number of studies of CMC for L2 learning, Abrams (2006) concluded that

research up to the current time has extensively examined the linguistic and affective benefits of intercultural CMC. These benefits include improved attitudes towards the L2, increased learner-to-learner interactions resulting in a positive learning environment for students, greater student output possibly leading to increased fluency in the L2, and more opportunities for negotiation of meaning fostering successful L2 development. (p. 187)

However, some studies failed to demonstrate the effectiveness of CMC due to a variety of reasons such as the low level of participation, and individual, intercultural and institutional differences (e.g., Hauck, 2007). Stockwell (2003) found that the e-mail interaction between a native speaker and a nonnative speaker was not sustained due to the premature ending of topics. Thus, it is not surprising that the effects of CMC remain uncertain (Towndrow & Vallance, 2004). The key point is that made by Levy and Stockwell (2006):

In a CMC setting where a learner is working with other students or one-to-one with a tutor, clearly the learner's experience will be determined by the

quality of the interaction. Results will vary not because of the technology, but rather according to the quality of the interaction and its value for language learning. (p. 72)

Several factors influence the quality of CMC among learners, for example, whether the communication happens in real time (learners tend to focus more on fluency than accuracy) or is delayed (learners have time to attend to accuracy), whether it is one-to-one (the discourse may be private) or one-to-many (the message may be under public scrutiny), whether the interlocutors are motivated or not (task motivation is co-constructed by the task participants, with one interlocutor either increasing or decreasing the motivation of the other, see Dornyei, 2002), whether the communicators are familiar with each other (the interpersonal relationship factor), and whether the interaction occurs between native speaker (NS)-nonnative speaker (NNS) or NNS-NNS (native speakers may not feel motivated to communicate with nonnative speakers, while nonnative speakers may prefer native speaker interlocutors (see Levy & Stockwell, 2006)).

These factors affect the quality of the interaction and the degree to which the participants are willing to communicate. However, most studies carried out have been small-scale, making it difficult to generalize from results.

Oosterhof, Conrad, and Ely (2008) indicated that higher-level evaluative skills to evaluate media online are lacking. Since the results of past studies may or may not favor CMC and several factors may affect the quality of it, it is clear that the effectiveness of CMC remains uncertain. Equally clear is the fact that explicit and sound criteria for the evaluation of the effectiveness of CMC need to be established.

NEED AND POSSIBLE CRITERIA FOR THE EVALUATION OF THE EFFECTIVENESS OF CMC

Reeder, Heift, Roche, Tabyanian, Schlickau, and Golz (2004) pointed out that there are overall two types of software assessment, i.e., introspective (predictive) and empirical (retrospective) evaluations. They argue that "a new approach is needed for the educational evaluation of language-learning software that falls under the rubrics 'new media', 'multimedia', and 'e-learning' as distinct from previous generations of CALL software". As they explained,

present approaches to the evaluation of CALL software, though reasonably adequate (but not wholly, we note) for earlier generations of CALL programs, are not appropriate for what we show to be a new genre of CALL software distinguished by its shared assumptions about language learning and teaching as well as by its technical design. (p. 256)

Reeder et al. (2004) further suggest that knowledge should be drawn at least from applied linguistics, language pedagogy, and L2 learning to form the basis for the evaluation of language-learning software, if theoretical progress is to continue in that field. Moreover, they identified several shortcomings of current approaches to software evaluation: (a) lack of criteria for the evaluation that measures both learning outcomes and learning processes; (b) validity and generalizability problems in experimental evaluation designs; (c) the fact that current approaches to software evaluation fail to account for educational goals; (d) the need for mutual understanding of the various cultures and literacies presented on the Internet to be taken into account during the design and evaluation of any multimedia learning tool; (e) issues of intercultural communication and sociocultural variation among user groups which have not been appropriately reflected in software

evaluation, and (f) the fact that a less dominant teacher role in the technology enhanced learning environment should be considered to constitute a more efficient evaluative system.

Abrams (2006) pointed out that future studies of CMC should examine "cognitive and interpersonal communicative aspects of learner language development as well as effective pedagogical practices using this medium" (p. 188). Thus, questions such as the following ones need to be asked (see Abrams, 2006, p. 188):

- "Which language skills does CMC affect positively and how?"
- "How is turn taking realized?"
- "What specific discourse management skills are necessary in order to follow a discussion?"
- "To what extent are the tasks used in the studies authentic?"

These suggestions, along with those drawn from SLA and CALL theories constitute possible criteria to conduct an evaluation on CMC:

Non-Verbal Communication

The evidence of the effectiveness of the task might be found through the teacher's noticing that learners engage enthusiastically in performing the task (Ellis, 1997). One way to elicit learners' reactions to the task in the CALL classroom can be through observing their learning behaviors in terms of non-verbal cues such as "body language" or "posture", "facial expression" and "eye contact" (Wikipedia, 2007). For example, smiling and frowning can be the indication of learners' interests in the tasks they are asked to perform. However, in most cases of online communication (e.g., e-mails, instant messaging system, blogs and forums), it is hard to detect what the writers are really thinking from reading between the lines. On the other hand, the writers use devices such as 'Emoticon' in the instant messaging system to express their feelings (e.g., ☺, ☹). As a result, the recording and analysis of these signs may provide some evidence of learners' inner state when communicating online. However, some of the signs are not as obvious as the ones in 'Emoticon'. People who have never encountered this kind of new 'language' need to spend some time learning it.

The string of messages in (1) provides some examples of the non-verbal cues that learners used on a social platform. Here, =) is a smiley face; =D is a laughing face, =*(is a sad and teary face, and > < is like saying 'ugh' or 'ahh'.

(1) Michael advanced to Round 3 after beating the table in a Zynga Poker Shootout Tournament.

A special Buddy Bonus is being shared with Michael's friends for a limited time!

November 6th 2:40 from Texas HoldEm Poker
· message ·excellent / Claim the special bonus

Edison
    mike =) u tooo good at hold em
    November 6th 3:45
Zach
    oh shot, time to fold every turn. that anti will last me a few hundred turns
    November 6th 4:03
Edison
    I dun know anyone, who play poker to stay in the game for hundreds of turns =)
    November 6th 4:06
Zach
    hey hey you there... its not nice to break other's dreams
    November 6th 4:06
Edison
    i thought everyone dream is to make it rich, live long, and have all the pleasures of life =D
    November 6th 4:07
Zach
    hey hey get lost
    November 6th 4:08
Edison
    =*(bye

November 6th 4:09
Zach
    > <
November 6th 4:10

Interaction

Interaction has been considered an important variable in Second Language Acquisition (SLA) theory. It has been suggested that CMC facilitates interaction, because "the written nature of the discussion allows greater opportunity to attend to and reflect on the form and content of the communication" (Kern & Warschauer, 2000, p. 15). It should be noted that interaction in the computer lab somewhat differs to that in the traditional classroom because the focus in the CALL classroom is on learners' interaction with the computer and with other users of the computers. Learners' interaction with the computer can be observed by looking at whether they are concentrated on the computer screen or they are looking around. The interaction between the teacher and the learners is equally important. For example, when learners cannot find the meanings of words or phrases, they will probably ask the teacher for help and this serves as an indication of learners' attempts to focus on form. The following table shows how interaction that leads to learning can be distinguished and measured in the CALL classroom:

Questions arise as to how learners' interaction with other users of the computer can be measured as a result of engaging in CMC activities since all they need is typing and clicking. One possible solution might be drawn from the analysis of learners' discourse in terms of negotiation of meaning and communication strategies (Ellis & Barkhuizen, 2005).

Negotiation of Meaning

Negotiation of meaning is believed to facilitate comprehension (Pica, 1994; Ellis, Tanaka, & Yamazaki, 1994). It involves the "conversational

Table 1. Possible Criteria for the Evaluation of Interactional and Non-Interactional Learning Behaviors in the CALL Classroom

Types of Interaction	Evaluation Criteria	
	Interactional Learning Behaviors	**Non-Interactional Learning Behaviors**
1. learner - computer interaction	Learners concentrate on the computer screen	Learners look around
2. learner - teacher interaction	Asking for help from teacher, e.g., • The operation and features of the CALL course • Vocabulary and phrases in the courses • Translation of the sentences from native language to English	• Very few students ask teacher questions • Reluctance to initiate short response to teacher questions
3. learner-learner interaction	Asking for help from classmates, e.g., Learners ask their classmates questions regarding the operation of the CALL course or the linguistic items	Learners do not talk to each other
4. lack of interaction		• Learners sleep in class

exchanges that arise when interlocutors seek to prevent a communicative impasse occurring or to remedy an actual impasse that has arisen" (Ellis, 1999, p. 3). It should be noted that comprehension does not guarantee acquisition. As Ellis (1999, p. 6) maintains

For acquisition to take place, learners need to attend to the linguistic forms in the input and the meanings they realize and to compare what they notice with their own output. In these ways they can obtain the data they need to restructure their interlanguages. In such cases, acquisition may take place with or without message comprehension.

Examples of meaning negotiation include:

1. Request for clarification
   S1: do you think good English is a key to success in Japan
   S2: what does mean//
   S1: //key of success (.) key//
   S2: //key of success (.) ah…."
   (Bitchener, 1999, p. 125)
2. Confirmation check
   S1: one type is tatua

S2: tatua?
   S1: one name is tatua and ah (.) (.) well I don't re-//
   S2: //ah you cannot remember"
   (Bitchener, 1999, p. 125)
3. Comprehension check
   "'Do you understand?', tag questions and repetition with rising intonation" (Long, 1980, 1983, as cited in Bitchener, 1999, p. 125)
   The conversation in (2) illustrates a request for clarification which focused on the content:

(2) Michael: is running outta juice

Edison
   all nighter or that orange juice i saw last time i came? =)
   November 5th 0:02
Zach
   all nighter
   November 5th 5:18
Edison
   o.O for wat class?
   November 5th 5:43

As shown in (2), the conversation was co-constructed by the wall-owner's friends on a social platform. By visiting it, people can easily track everything that happens to others' lives without having to call or send e-mails. Along with the increasing use of social utilities, people do not need to send text messages over the cell phone either, so it is a convenient way of fitting into busy people's schedules and saving money nowadays. For example,

Kasey
> Hey Michael! I hope to see you tonight at 8 in front of the bookstore for flyering and fun!:D

Michael
> Hey Kasey! I'm so sorry but I probably couldn't make it today

To make the meaning of the messages crossed, learners also need to be able to recognize acronyms frequently used in the instant messaging system. For example, tmrw = tomorrow, gotta = got to, idk = I don't know, b4 = before, btw = by the way. Note that 'gotta' is colloquial English. One might argue the needs for learners to learn a second or foreign language via the instant messaging system since it is informal and sometimes incorrect usage of the target language. However, it is still worthwhile to engage learners in CMC activities since non-native speakers of English usually do not have the chance to learn colloquial English in the EFL context, provided that the teacher should raise students' awareness of the various forms of English usage. Furthermore, CMC activities can provide language learners with authentic situations to communicate and thus result in incidental acquisition. Lastly, since learners have limited capacity to attend to both the form and the meaning while processing the input, "the opportunity to negotiate meaning provides learners with the time they need to attend to form while processing the message content" (Ellis, 1999, p. 8).

Communication Strategies

Communication occurs in situations where "meanings are negotiated through interaction" (Widdowson, 1979, as cited in Butler-Pascoe & Wiburg, 2003, p. 28). Communication strategies are crucial in meaning negotiation where "either linguistic structures or sociolinguistic rules are not shared between a second language learner and a speaker of the target language" (O'Malley & Chamot, 1990, as cited in Zhang, 2007, p. 43). Communication strategies, as one essential element of language learning strategies when learners encounter communication breakdown, have been considerably researched (Zhang, 2007). Drawing from the terms presented by several researchers such as Varadi (1973), Tarone, Cohen and Dumas (1976), as well as Tarone, Frauenfelder, and Selinker (1976), Palmberg (1978) illustrated six basic communication strategies (i.e., avoidance, appeal for assistance, admission of ignorance, paraphrase, transfer, and mime) that learners apply when facing lexical difficulties as well as overgeneralization, prefabricated patterns, and over-elaboration when encountering syntactic difficulties. Whatever the strategies, they represent learners' attempts to stay in a conversation, to compensate for deficiencies of their language competence; therefore, communication strategies are approaches that learners adopt to achieve communicative purposes.

Teachers can enhance learners' linguistic competence by raising their awareness of applying these strategies to communication problems. On the other hand, signs of using these strategies in CMC contexts indicate the extent to which learners are willing to communicate and to engage in meaning negotiation.

Task Engagement

Built-in tracking system for individual learners is needed to provide records on a variety of categories to evaluate learners' engagement in CMC tasks. These categories might include:

- The time learners spend on the tasks both in and out of class. It is possible that some learners leave the computer screen on while they are doing something else. Therefore, the time-on-task record should be judged on whether learners really perform some tasks such as typing words.
- The degree to which learners have completed the tasks.
- The frequency learners visit features of the CMC activities (e.g., forums).
- The monitoring record of learners' engagement in 'on task' activity (e.g., listening, reading, speaking and writing) or 'off task activity' (e.g., chatting with friends online in their mother-tongue, playing computer games and sleeping). It is likely that learners are doing other things while they are having a conversation with another learner online. This might be detected by calculating the time and frequency of the pauses between the lines of the messages.
- The record of the dialogues in instant messaging system so that discourse analysis can be conducted.
- The record of emoticon uses to measure non-verbal communication.
- The Progress Report which traces and summarizes every activity that the learner engages in.

CONCLUSION

In conclusion, criteria needed to determine the effectiveness of CMC may vary for different media online; therefore, further studies are needed. Since learners participating in CMC activities may be culturally diverse, it is important to teach learners to understand and appreciate different cultures and literacies. Although the use of CMC in language education is not necessarily the concern

of engineers who design the software, it would be very beneficial to the teachers if some tools are designed to account for the evaluation of its effectiveness.

ACKNOWLEDGMENT

Part of this chapter derived from the author's PhD thesis of the University of Auckland, New Zealand. The author thanks Professor Rod Ellis for his invaluable feedback on the thesis.

REFERENCES

Abrams, Z. I. (2006). From theory to practice: Intracultural CMC in the L2 classroom. In Ducate, L., & Arnold, N. (Eds.), *Calling on CALL: From theory and research to new directions in foreign language teaching* (Vol. 5, pp. 181–209). CALICO Monograph Series.

Appel, C., & Gilabert, R. (2004). Motivation and task performance in a task-based Web-based tandem project. *ReCALL, 14*(1), 16–31.

Bitchener, J. W. (1999). *The negotiation of meaning by advanced ESL learners: The effects of individual learner factors and task type*. Unpublished PhD thesis of the University of Auckland, New Zealand.

Butler-Pascoe, M. E., & Wiburg, K. M. (2003). *Technology and teaching English language learners*. Pearson Education.

CERN. (2007). *About the World Wide Web*. Retrieved November 14, 2007, from http://www.w3.org/WWW/

Chapelle, C. A. (2001). *Computer applications in second language acquisition: Foundations for teaching, testing and research*. Cambridge, UK: Cambridge University Press.

Chun, D. M. (2007). Come ride the wave: But where is it taking us? *CALICO Journal, 24*(2), 239–252.

Delcloque, P. (2000). *History of CALL*. Retrieved November 8, 2007, from http://www.ict4lt.org/en/History_of_CALL.pdf

Dornyei, Z. (2002). The motivational basis of language learning tasks. In Robinson, P. (Ed.), *Individual differences and instructed language learning* (pp. 137–158). Amsterdam, The Netherlands: John Benjamins.

Edusoft. (2002). *Teacher's guide*. Received as an e-mail attachment on June 25, 2004, from the Taiwan distributor.

Ellis, R. (1997). The empirical evaluation of language teaching materials. *ELT Journal, 51*(1), 36–42. doi:10.1093/elt/51.1.36

Ellis, R. (1999). *Learning a second language through interaction*. John Benjamins B.V.

Ellis, R., & Barkhuizen, G. (2005). *Analysing learner language*. Oxford, UK: Oxford University Press.

Ellis, R., Tanaka, Y., & Yamazaki, A. (1994). Classroom interaction, comprehension, and the acquisition of L2 word meanings. *Language Learning, 44*(3), 449–491. doi:10.1111/j.1467-1770.1994.tb01114.x

Fotos, S. (2004). Writing as talking: E-mail exchange for promoting proficiency and motivation in the foreign language classroom. In Fotos, S., & Browne, C. (Eds.), *New perspectives on CALL for second language classrooms* (pp. 109–129). Mahwah, NJ: Lawrence Erlbaum Associates.

Hampel, R., & Baber, E. (2003). Using Internet-based audio-graphic and video conferencing for language teaching and learning. In Felix, U. (Ed.), *Language learning online: Towards best practice* (pp. 171–191). Lisse, The Netherlands: Swets & Zeitlinger.

Hauck, M. (2007). Critical success factors in a TRIDEM exchange. *ReCALL, 19*(2), 202–223. doi:10.1017/S0958344007000729

Jager, S. (2004). Learning management systems for language learning. In Chambers, A., Conacher, J. E., & Littlemore, J. (Eds.), *ICT and language learning: Integrating pedagogy and practice* (pp. 34–48). UK: The University of Birmingham Press.

Jauregi, K., & Banados, E. (2008). Virtual interaction through video-Web communication: A step towards enriching and internationalizing language learning programs. *ReCALL, 20*(2), 183–207. doi:10.1017/S0958344008000529

Kern, R., & Warschauer, M. (2000). Introduction: Theory and practice of network-based language teaching. In Warschauer, M., & Kern, R. (Eds.), *Network-based language teaching: Concepts and practice* (pp. 1–19). Cambridge, UK: Cambridge University Press.

Kinginger, C. (2000). Learning the pragmatics of solidarity in the networked foreign language classroom. In Hall, J. K., & Verplaetse, L. S. (Eds.), *Second and foreign language learning through classroom interaction* (pp. 23–46). Mahwah, NJ: Lawrence Erlbaum Associates, Inc.

Levy, M., & Stockwell, G. (2006). *CALL dimensions: Options and issues in computer-assisted language learning*. Mahwah, NJ: Lawrence Erlbaum.

Lomicka, L. (2006). Understanding the other: Intercultural exchange and CMC. In Ducate, L., & Arnold, N. (Eds.), *Calling on CALL: From theory and research to new directions in foreign language teaching* (Vol. 5, pp. 211–236). CALICO Monograph Series.

McPherson, M., & Nunes, M. B. (2004). *Developing innovation in online learning: An action research framework*. London, UK: Routledge Falmer. doi:10.4324/9780203426715

Need and Possible Criteria for Evaluating the Effectiveness of Computer-Mediated Communication

Moro, B. (2007). *Web literacy*. Retrieved August 27, 2007, from http://www.ecml.at/ projects/ voll/ literacy/ english/ index.htm

Oosterhof, A., Conrad, R., & Ely, D. P. (2008). *Assessing learners online*. Pearson Education.

Palmberg, R. (1978). Strategies of second-language communication. *CIEFL Bulletin, 14*(2), 1–8.

Pellettieri, J. (2000). Negotiation in cyberspace: The role of chatting in the development of grammatical competence. In Warschauer, M., & Kern, R. (Eds.), *Network-based language teaching: Concepts and practice* (pp. 59–86). Cambridge, UK: Cambridge University Press.

Pica, T. (1994). Research on negotiation: What does it reveal about second-language learning conditions, processes, and outcomes? *Language Learning, 44*(3), 493–527. doi:10.1111/j.1467-1770.1994.tb01115.x

Reeder, K., Heift, T., Roche, J., Tabyanian, S., Schlickau, S., & Golz, P. (2004). Toward a theory of e/valuation for second language learning media. In Fotos, S., & Browne, C. (Eds.), *New perspectives on CALL for second language classrooms* (pp. 255–278). Mahwah, NJ: Lawrence Erlbaum Associates, Inc.

Savignon, S. J., & Rothmeier, W. (2004). Computer-mediated communication: Texts and strategies. *CALICO Journal, 21*(2), 265–290.

Son, J. B. (2004). Teacher development in e-learning environments. In J. B. Son (Ed.), *Computer-assisted language learning: Concepts, contexts, and practices* (pp. 107-122). iUniverse.

Stockwell, G. (2003). Effects of topic threads on sustainability of email interactions between native speakers and nonnative speakers. *ReCALL, 15*(1), 37–50. doi:10.1017/S0958344003000417

Towndrow, P. A., & Vallance, M. (2004). *Using IT in the language classroom: A guide for teachers and students in Asia*. Pearson Education South Asia Pte.

Ushioda, E. (2000). Tandem language learning via email: From motivation to autonomy. *ReCALL, 12*(2), 121–128. doi:10.1017/S0958344000000124

Wang, Y. (2006). Negotiation of meaning in desktop videoconferencing-supported distance language learning. *ReCALL, 18*(1), 122–146. doi:10.1017/S0958344006000814

Warschauer, M. (2000). On-line learning in second language classrooms: An ethnographic study. In Warschauer, M., & Kern, R. (Eds.), *Network-based language teaching: Concepts and practice* (pp. 41–58). Cambridge, UK: Cambridge University Press.

Wikipedia. (2007). *Nonverbal communication*. Retrieved October 20, 2009 from http://en.wikipedia.org/ wiki/ Nonverbal_ communication

Zeiss, E., & Isabelli-Garcia, C. L. (2005). The role of asynchronous computer mediated communication on enhancing cultural awareness. *Computer Assisted Language Learning, 18*(3), 151–169. doi:10.1080/09588220500173310

Zhang, Y. (2007). Communication strategies and foreign language learning. *US-China Foreign Language, 5*(4), 43–48.

Chapter 14
Study on Image Quality Assessment with Scale Space Approach Using Index of Visual Evoked Potentials

Hidehiko Hayashi
Naruto University of Education, Japan

Akinori Minazuki
Naruto University of Education, Japan

ABSTRACT

This chapter presents an objective assessment method of image quality using visual evoked potentials (VEPs) to image engineer field based on multi-disciplinarily approach such as knowledge of neurobiology, image recognition theory, or computer vision. The multi-disciplinarily based objective assessment method applies Gaussian scale-space filtering in order to define a scalar parameter to depict blur image. In the experiment, visual stimuli are provided by the scalar parameter, and subjects are detected using VEPs. Their VEPs are recoded during observation of the checkerboard pattern reversal (PR) stimuli, and are analyzed with a latency of about Negative 145 msec (N145) component. The result of the experiment was that latency of N145 components were long about10-20 msec when parameters were large vale (more blur). This result shows one example of availableness for the multi-disciplinarily based objective assessment of image quality by integrating the pattern reversal visual evoked potential (PR-VEP) and the scale-space theory.

DOI: 10.4018/978-1-61520-871-5.ch014

I. INTRODUCTION

IMAGE communication technology progressions create new image information media environment. Components of image information media environment are roughly divided into three factors (Hayashi & Minazuki, 2010). They are media factor, audio-visual environment factor, viewing audience factor. Media factor has effect by producers or contents. Audio-visual environment factor has effect by display devices, audio-visual conditions and so on. Viewing audience factor has characteristic of personas, audio-visual attitude and so on. These researches of their factors have been advanced independently in general, and have been reported in an individual research field. Therefore, these researches of their factors were efficiently advanced in the research field which had been very limited. However, since image information media environment have been originally integrated, not only an analytical approach but also an integrated approach is necessary in the research. The point is that an integrated research approach should be needed and enhanced in order to solve their problems.

On the other hand affect image information to human bodily performance such as photosensitive epilepsy (PSE) (Fylan & Harding, 1997; Harding & Jeavons, 1994; Harding & Harding, 2008), stress, visual fatigue, amenity are problems of growing concern. These symptoms are one-research topics into which of each is integrated. The affect image information to human bodily performance are many kind of ones such as good affect to connect contents affinity like this strong visuals and realistic, bad affect to lead to physiological distemper like this PSE, and affect to seem large-scale screen image or stereoscopic vision. The research of an objective assessment of image quality is one of their affect researches.

The research of image quality assessment is important on image engineering study (Allnatt, 1980; Mitsuhashi, 1999; Miyahara, 1988; Nakasu

et al, 2008; Narita, 1995; Narita & Sugiura, 1998; Hayashi et al, 1999; Kondo et al, 1997; Rec. ITU-R BT.500-11, 2002; Rec. ITU-R BT.710-4, 1998; Tan et al, 1998; Teunissen, 1996; Ridder & Hamberg, 1997, Yamamoto, 2009; Yuyama et al, 1998). There are many theme in the research area. In general, an image quality assessment is roughly divided into a subjective assessment method and an objective assessment method. In addition, the objective assessment method includes the following two cases (Hayashi et al, 2002). One case is that the assessment object is physical characteristic of the image. Another case is that the assessment object is a physiological characteristic of the person who receives the image. The latter indicates the research of using human bodily performance of image information for the index of the image quality assessment. This chapter allocates the latter case to be objective assessment method if there is especially no explanation.

It is clear that the research of the affect image information to human bodily performance or the objective assessment is important. However, the research does not have an enough covering which becomes the world standard. This reason is that it is difficult to integrate many factors in multidisciplinary field such as engineering, psychology, and physiology. And the reason is that a scientific methodology to an integrated problem such as image information media environment including many factors does not develop enough too. On the other hand, it is said that it is a problem to solve such an integrated problem in the 21st century. It is necessary to develop the methodology. From the above-mentioned this chapter shows one example of integrated research approach and the multi-disciplinarily based objective assessment of image quality.

In the second section, background is described about basic knowledge of each research field of the image quality assessment, the image recognition theory, and the VEPs. In the third section, a blurring parameter is defined by multiple resolution analysis in the scale-space theory. In fourth section, the experiment of VEPs recoding with the bluring parameter is described. In fifth section, the role which this research plays and the problem in the future are presented. The summary is described in sixth section.

II. BACKGROUND: BASIC KNOWLEDGE OF EACH FIELD

A. Image Assessment

In image quality assessment the importance of something like a sharpness or vividness or blurring, know as the psychological characteristic, to subjective assessment of image quality and objective assessment of physical characteristic in image has been widely recognized (Matsui, 2002). However, the research of objective assessment of physiological characteristic of the person who receives the image is very few, and the research is especially little intended for the brain functional mechanism which exceeds the visual characteristic. However, the development of the image quality assessment method in which electroencephalography (EEG) is used is reported though they are very few examples.

Hayashi et al (2000) reported image quality assessment of an extra high-quality image using both electroencephalography (EEG) and assessment word on higher order sensations (Miyahara, 2002; Hayashi et al, 2000). The result showed a new possibility to the image quality assessment using EEG measurement in extra high quality image. The examination which includes the relation between an individual factor to decide the image quality and EEG, however, is not enough in this research. For instance, though the assessment word of the subjective assessment of blurring (vivid impression) obtains a high evaluation in this assessment, this research has not come to show the relation with the objective assessment

using EEG. It is inferred that these reason are no systematization of the image quality including the image contents, and nor there are special circumstances of high-quality image. Moreover, that research was a top down mechanism by which the correspondence of objective assessment of EEG and the subjective assessment was examined. This research pays attention to the blurring, and takes the bottom up mechanism on human brain activity. This research measure not EEG but VEP for bottom up approach in order to be taken a more physiologic interpretation. In addition, the visual stimulus applies the image recognition theory, and forms the base of the multidisciplinary based objective assessment of the image quality.

B. VEP Study

Visual evoked potentials (VEPs) are reaction concerned vision in central nervous system (Barrett et al, 1976; Blumenhardt & Halliday, 1976; Jeffreys, 1971; Jones, 1993; Halliday et al, 1972), and evoked by various optical stimuli to be given the retina. This research has been chiefly advanced up to now in the medical field. Latency and amplitude characteristics of VEPs have been studied extensively by calculation of averaging method in general. The VEP measurement has settled as an established technique in the medical practice. Depending on the stimulation method VEP is divided roughly into flash-VEP (F-VEP) by the flash stimulation and pattern reversal VEP (PR-VEP) by the monochrome cross stripes reversing stimulation.

When PR-VEP is compared with F-VEP, merit of PR-VEP is that view field of control to display, and stability of the shape of waves and the latency. Especially, PR stimulation which uses the checkerboard is the highest reproducibility, and put trust in the medical practice. PR stimulation which uses the checkerboard is reversing of a monochrome cross stripes pattern stimulation. It can easily control fundamental factors of visual stimulus such as brightness, the size, the reversing frequency, the contrast, and view field. Therefore, it is a useful technique for a functional evaluation of the initial visual area and diagnosis of optic paths. However, there are not too a lot of researches by which the blurring is assumed to be a main parameter in the VEP measurement among those fundamental factors. Since the blurring is an important factor for the medical practice or the image quality, it is hoped to control the blurring easily and to elucidate the influence which the blurring gives brain function. In addition, the development in the future can be expected by forming a theoretical frame which handles them as follows.

C. Image Recognition Theory

There is a theory of the image that the blurring and becoming obscure the image are systematically controlled. A pattern recognition theory with which Iijima creates is one of a lot of their theories. The pattern recognition theory has widely adjusted to the character recognition. Moreover, the theory is famous as the scale space theory included the scale space filtering.

The scale space filtering (Witkin, 1993; Witkin, 1984) is one of the multi-resolution analysis. The multi-resolution analysis is a method of dividing image data into some sizes of the small with a specific frequency band in general. Since this technique can extract various features which depend on the resolution in the image, this technique is widely used for image analysis. In image analysis by a multi-resolution, there is a technique which uses the wave let type algorithm, the pyramid type algorithm, and the scale space type algorithm. The scale space type algorithm is a technique which is proposed by Iijima in 1962 and expanded by Ootsu in 1981 (Hayashi, 2003). The theory is a model included visual performance such as blur of the image, the view point, and visual field.

III. BLUR SCALE PARAMETER WITH SCALE SPACE FILTERING

This session explains the method of introducing the blurring parameter by using the Gauss type scale space filtering. This method enables the becoming obscure or blurring degree of the image to be adjusted arbitrarily by controlling the blurring parameter. In this research, Gaussian function is $g(x,y)$ used to filter, the size is 60×60 pixel, the quantization bits number is 8bits/pixel, and shows in Equation (1). In this Equation (1), x and y show the spatial position (x,y) of horizontal and vertical direction of each pixel respectively. In Equation (1), μ is an average of the Gaussian function, and the center location of this function is shown. Since the blurring parameter τ is equal statistical variance and can be controlled arbitrarily, τ is assumed to be a blurring parameter.

$$g(x,y) = \frac{1}{2\pi\tau_x\tau_y} \exp\left\{-\frac{1}{2}\left[\frac{(x-\mu_x)^2}{\tau_x^2} + \frac{(y-\mu_y)^2}{\tau_y^2}\right]\right\}$$

(1)

It is supposed to original image $I(x,y)$ and output image $O(x,y)$: 360×360 pixel, 8bits/pixel. Output image $O(x,y)$ obtained by applying the blurring parameter as shown Equation (2). Equation (2) expresses operation of convolution between the original image $I(x,y)$ and the Gaussian function $g(x,y)$, and can generate the image with a different blurring changing in the blurring parameter τ.

$$O(x,y) = \sum_{k_1=1}^{360}\sum_{k_2=1}^{360} I(x,y) \cdot g(x-k_1, y-k_2)$$

(2)

Figure 1 shows the relation between blurring parameter τ and Gaussian function $g(x,y)$. In Figure 1, it is example for Gaussian function $g(x,y)$ at τ=5 and τ=10, and left side in Figure 1 was displayed by three dimensions, and right side was displayed by the two dimension. The area's where the pixel

Figure 1. Gaussian filtering

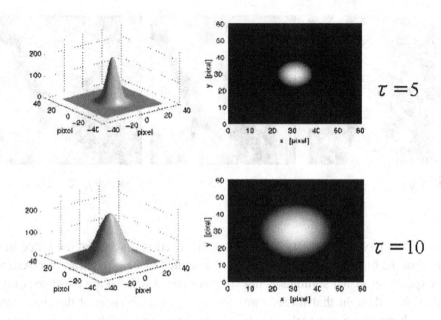

value is diffused as τ increases smoothly extending is understood by display of Gaussian function *g(x,y)* to which the two dimension.

Figure 2 showed the example of the change in the image by which the change in the blurring parameter. It is understood that the obscure or blurring degree of the image is growing as the value of the blurring parameter is increased. Moreover, stripes can be never newly done even if the blurring parameter is raised. This reason is thought that it is guaranteed not to cause a new contour line even if the operation is added in the Gauss type scale space algorithm.

IV. EXPERIMENT OF PR-VEP WITH BLUR SCALE

In this session, the experiment on PR-VEP with blurring parameter is described. The VEPs are measured by using the visual stimulus that applies the blurring parameter which has already been defined. First of all, the hypothesis is generated about blurring affect in PR-VEP based on consideration of a basic factor of the visual stimulus

in conventional research in fourth A session. and fourth B session. And then the verification experiment of the hypothesis is described in fourth C session, fourth D session and fourth E session. The experiment result is discussed in fourth F session.

A. PR-VEP and Blur Scale

It is known that there is a wave form that N75-P100-N145 which has three characteristic peak amplitude in PR-VEP. The P100 component is called most first visual area origins. However, the N145 component does not obtain a united opinion of the source etc. The blurring affect involved N75-P100-N145 in PR-VEP is not clear enough too. It is hoped that the blurring affect in the brain physiology is solved since scale space theory exists obviously included blurring parameter.

There is a VEP study on pattern reversal using checkerboards. Concerning about the blurring parameter they measured VEP when the blurring was changed with a lens, and compared latency in the difference of the blurring (Bobak et al, 1987). As a result, Bobak et al (1987) clarified that latency was long by blurring's lowering. However,

Figure 2. Original image and filtering image

i(x,y)   o(x,y), τ =5   o(x,y), τ =10

this research is large a physical restriction with a lens the control of the blurring. Therefore, the control of the experiment visual stimulus is not easy. In addition, it is thought that there is an influence that the shape of the checkerboards is unnaturally and greatly distorted caused how to give the blurring with lens. Moreover, since the presentation method of using the digital signal processing technology has the advantage of high repeatability, easy improvement etc, image signal processing technology should be used for blurring parameter. From the above-mentioned to one of important problems development of technique with easy control of blurring and experimental verification of the effect.

B. Hypothesis

Some the influences of the vision base stimulation are clear in the measurement of PR-VEP in the conventional research. It is said that space frequency characteristic is greatly to influence reaction of V1 (Tobimatsu, 1994). Therefore, the latency difference and the amplitude change when the check sizes change in case of the checkerboard stimulation. Moreover, delaying the latency was reported when the brightness contrast lowers (Bobak et al, 1987). Moreover, there is a possibility with the relation of becoming obscure the image and hanging of the recognition time of the object, too. There are some researches by which

the reaction time when the space frequency was assumed to be one parameter. As for this, there is a report with taking the shape of the band pass of the characteristic of the space frequency that the reaction time shortens. Moreover, there is an example of causing the delay at the reaction time with blur image as a daily experience. Therefore, it is attempted the hypothesis the latency of VEP is long if the blurring is high. It is attempted the hypothesis of becoming small late at the latency if an objective blurring was low and the verification was attempted by the setting up experiment.

C. Material

The checkerboard stimulation was used as a visual stimulus to obtain the VEP in this research. PR stimulation which uses the checkerboard is reversing of a monochrome cross stripes pattern stimulation. It can control a fundamental factor in visual stimulus such as brightness, the size, the reversing frequency, the contrast, and view field. In addition, it is character without taking place the change in overall average brightness.

In the actual experiment, blurring parameter (τ) and the contrast were set as a changeable parameter. And, the check size of the visual stimulus, the reversing cycle, and the presentation position in the hue, brightness, and view field were set as a fixed parameter. Condition 1 was assumed to be a high contrast condition, whose brightness contrast is 100% in the digital image information, and condition 2 was an image by which the brightness contrast was suppressed to 60% and it was assumed the low contrast condition. In condition 3, the blurring parameter assumed to be $\tau=10$ adjusted to the image of condition 2, and was assumed to be a large blurring condition. How the difference among condition 1, 2, and 3 influences VEP is clarified. The reason to suppress the brightness contrast to 60% is to report on the latency delay by the influence of the contrast (Bobak et al, 1987). The experiment was attempted that the baseline condition become a condition of high contrast (100%) of condition 1.

D. Stimulus, VEP Measure and the Analysis

The visual stimulus was presented by three condition setting by using the monochrome pattern reversing stimulation with the checkerboard for the liquid crystal display for the right half side peripheral visual field. Stimulation presentation condition is that check size is 2°, view area of entire stimulus is 16° and reversing frequency 1Hz. ESA-16 (Brain function laboratory, Inc.) was used to measure the visual evoked potential with 1kHz sampling and high cut filter of 60Hz and time constant: 0.3 sec. The electrode arrangement is based on the international 10-20 system (Jasper, 1957). In Figure 3, The " A" letter is ear lobe, in a similar way "T" is temporal lobe, "F' is Frontal lobe, and "O" is Occipital lobe on the system. It uses Fp1, F3, T3, P3, and O1 for the left hemisphere. On the other hand, Fp2, F4, T4, P3, and O2 are used for the right hemisphere. We analyzed initial visual early area with back of the head which were O1, O2, and OZ in this experiment (Figure 3). Subjects were 5 normal adult, from twenties to thirties, and visual acuity is normal about 1.0. The obtained wavy data used and analyzed the averaging method with down sampling of 400Hz by Matlab (The MathWorks, Inc.).

Figure 3. Electrode arrangement

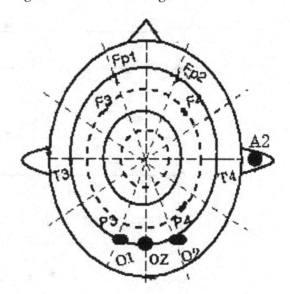

E. Result and Discussion

Figure 4 shows the VEPs experimental result of subject A. In Figure 4, the VEP waveform of O2, OZ, and O1 is sequentially shown from the upper side. A horizontal axis and a vertical axis show sequentially the second and the microvolt. Figure puts a mark in the peaks of P100 and N145 components, which are analyzed the latency and amplitude in general. Figure 5 and Figure 6 show sequentially the results of experiments about subject B and subject C. There are different characters in detail though they have resemblance and each common feature which make a rough estimate of the active P100 component though Figure 4 in their figures.

Since it was right half side peripheral visual field stimulation, a comparatively plain response was observed to O2 on the same side. In the high contrast condition of condition 1 (as shown green dotted line in Figure 4), a plain P100 component at top latency 95ms was observed. In the low contrast condition of condition 2 (as shown blue alternate long and short dash line in Figure 4), the P100 component is suppressed and the N145 component at top amplitude in 147msc latency

Figure 4. Result of VEPs for Subject A (Upper:O2, Median:OZ, Bottom: O1)

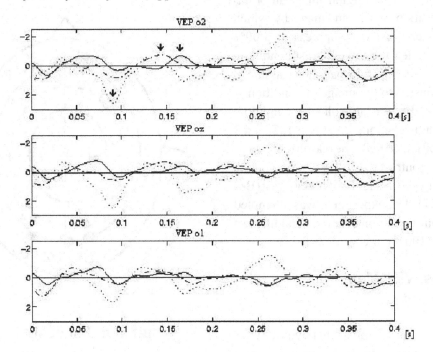

Figure 5. Result of VEPs for Subject B (Upper:O2, Median:OZ, Bottom: O1)

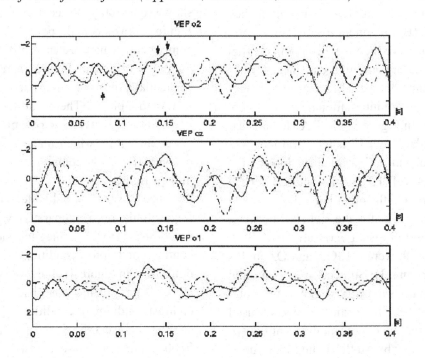

Figure 6. Result of VEPs for Subject C (Upper:O2, Median:OZ, Bottom: O1)

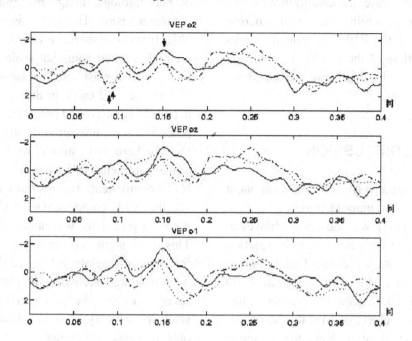

was observed. It was observed that top amplitude in 167ms latency in the condition 3(as shown solid line in Figure 4) which make the becoming obscure degree of the image strong when the blurring is changed. The delay of the latency of about 20msc was observed between condition 2 and condition 3. Their VEPs components through the waveform can be analyzed by focusing on the latency and amplitude as you can see their figures and Table 1 which is summarized the characters of VEPs components.

The latency and the amplitude of each condition were described in Table 1 about the P100 component and the N145 component to consider the experiment result. When the amplitude is lower than $\pm0.5\mu V$, the value of each component is parenthetic or is not described since it is difficult to determine few or no their activity. It was suggested delaying the latency by the difference between condition 2 and condition 3 in N145 when the blurring parameter was strong. Moreover, the P100 component appears, and N145 component of subject's C is not plain in condition 2 as shown

Table 1. Result of latency and amplitude

	①	②	③	④	⑤	⑥	⑥ -⑤
Task Subject	Task 1 P100	Task 2 P100	Task 3 P100	Task 1 N145	Task 2 N145	Task 3 N145	Latency N145
A	95 [ms] 2.59 [μV]	95 0.81	--- ---	(130 -0.57)	**147.5** **-0.74**	**167** **-0.67**	**20** **[ms]**
B	82.5 0.97	--- ---	(117.5 1.56)	117.5 -1.48	**145** **-0.96**	**155** **-1.37**	**10** **[ms]**
C	95 1.13	92.5 1.50	--- ---	147.5 -0.641	--- ---	152.5 -1.24	--- [ms]

in Figure 6. In this case, the condition with low contrast has the possibility that brain function corresponding to the P100 component works as well as the time of the condition with high contrast. Subject C has high contrast sensitivity in possibility.

V. GENERAL DISCUSSION

First of all, a comparatively plain P100 component appeared in the P100 component when a baseline image (condition 1) was observed, however, there was a subject who showed a plain reaction when the image with low contrast (condition 2) was observed, too. Moreover, since the P100 component and other component and so on had not obtained two subject of five, the result was omitted from consideration. Next, the change in the latency by the difference of each condition was obtained about the N145 component. As for the tendency, condition 2 is larger than condition 1, and condition 3 is larger than condition 2. And, it was able to be confirmed that the latency extended compared with high contrast when the contrast was low. When the blurring assumed to be a hypothesis was low, it was obtained result delaying the latency. In a word, the possibility that not only the change in the contrast but also the blurring influences in relation to the N145 component is suggested. This research aimed at the approach by the integration of the visual evoked potential and the image recognition theory, and showed one of new possibilities of the image quality assessment. Covering more work will be necessary in the future.

VI. CONCLUSION

This chapter proposed an objective assessment method of image quality for using visual evoked potentials to image engineer field based on multidisciplinary approach such as knowledge of neurobiology, image recognition theory of computer vision. The multi-disciplinarily based objective assessment method, our proposed method, applied Gaussian scale space filtering in order to consist a scalar parameter to depict blur image, and came in the visual stimuli and detected visual evoked potentials. Visual evoked potentials were measured during observation of the checkerboards stimuli with the change of scalar parameter, and were analyzed latency of N145 component. The result of the experiment was that N145 component were 10-20 msec long during a parameter was large vale (more blur). This result shows one example of availableness for the multi-disciplinarily based objective assessment of image quality by integrating the pattern reversal visual evoked potential (PR-VEP) and the scale-space theory. The multi-disciplinarily based objective assessment method still be many issue to build up the assessment system, i.e., the N145 component of source estimation using something like fMRI and MEG, and theory of scale space with observing point parameter and visual field parameter remained to be solved in the future.

REFERENCES

Allnatt, J. W. (1980). Subjective assessment method for television digital codecs. *Electronics Letters, 16*(12), 450–451. doi:10.1049/el:19800317

Barrett, G., Blumhardt, L., & Halliday, A. M. (1976). A paradox in the lateralisation of the visual evoked response. *Nature, 261*, 253–255. doi:10.1038/261253a0

Blumenhardt, L. D., & Halliday, A. M. (1979). Hemisphere contributions to the composition of the pattern-evoked potential waveform. *Experimental Brain Research, 36*(1), 53–69. doi:10.1007/BF00238467

Bobak, P., Bodis-Wollner, I., & Guillory, S. (1987). The effect of blur and contrast on VEP latency: Comparison between check and sinusoidal grating patterns. *Electroencephalography and Clinical Neurophysiology, 68*(4), 247–255. doi:10.1016/0168-5597(87)90045-1

Fylan, F., & Harding, G. F. A. (1997). The effect of television frame rate on EEG abonormalities in photosensitive and pattern-sensitive epilepsy. *Epilepsia, 38*, 1124–1131. doi:10.1111/j.1528-1157.1997.tb01202.x

Halliday, A. M., McDonald, W. I., & Mushin, J. (1972). Delayed visual evoked response in optic neuritis. *Lancet*, 1982–1985.

Harding, G. F. A., & Harding, P. F. (2008). *Photosensitive epilepsy and image safety. Applied ergonomics*. Elsevier.

Harding, G. F. A., & Jeavons, P. M. (1994). *Photosensitive epilepsy new edition*. London, UK: Mac Keith Press.

Hayashi, H. (2003). *Basic research of inner visual knowledge measurement based on biological measurement*. Doctoral dissertation at School of Knowledge Science in JAIST.

Hayashi, H., Kunifuji, S., & Miyahara, M. (2002). Assessment of extra high quality images using electroencephalography. *The Journal of ITE, 56*(6), 954–962.

Hayashi, H., & Minazuki, A. (2010). Multiple scale of knowledge measurement using sensor technologies of human information processing systems prevent the influence of images upon viewers. *Journal of Electronics & Computer Science, 12*(1), 73–80.

Hayashi, H., Shirai, H., Kunifuji, S., & Miyahara, M. (2000). Assessment of extra high quality images using both EEG and assessment words on high order sensations. *Proceedings of the IEEE, SMC2000*, 289–1294.

Hayashi, H., Torii, K., Kunifuji, S., & Miyahara, M. (1999). *An EEG comparison between extra high quality images and normal quality images*. (Technical report of IEICE, HIP99(186), 7-12).

Jasper, H. H. (1957). Report of the Committee on Methods of Clinical Examination in Electroencephalography. *Electroencephy and Clinical Neurophysiology, 10*(2), 370–375.

Jeffreys, D. A. (1971). Cortical source locations of pattern-related visual evoked potentials recorded from the human scalp. *Nature, 229*, 502–504. doi:10.1038/229502a0

Jones, S. J. (1993). Visual evoked potentials after optic neuritis. Effect of time interval, age and disease dissemination. *Journal of Neurology, 240*(8), 489–494. doi:10.1007/BF00874118

Kondo, C., Kobayashi, Y., & Miyahara, M. (1997). *Analysis of the image assessment words on high order sensation*. (Technical report of IEICE, CQ97(457), 37-44).

Matsui, T. (2002). A new sharpness evaluation method using a cooperative human vision model and its effectiveness. *The IEICE Transactions, J85-A*(8), 867-875.

Mitsuhashi, T. (1999). Subjective assessment techniques of digital image quality. *The Journal of ITE, 53*(6), 1195–1198.

Miyahara, M. (1988). Quality assessments for visual service. *IEEE Communications Magazine, 26*(10), 51–60. doi:10.1109/35.7667

Miyahara, M. (2002). *Extra high quality audio-visual system for creation of future A-V works and two-way presence communication*. JSPS Research Project for Future Program.

Nakasu, E., Kanda, K., Ichigaya, A., Kurozumi, M., & Nishida, Y. (2008). Picture quality assessment test for digitally coded motion pictures in multi-formats. *The Journal of ITE, 62*(2), 262–270. doi:10.3169/itej.62.262

Narita, N. (1995). Comparisons between the DSCQS method and the SSQS method used in absolute evaluation of picture quality-distribution and processing of opinion scores. *The IEICE Transactions, J78-DII*(12), 1899-1910.

Narita, N., & Sugiura, Y. (1998). A consideration of subjective evaluation method for different television systems-on methods of paired comparison with simultaneous presentation. *The IEICE Transactions, J81-A*(2), 269-279.

Recommendation, I. T. U.-R. B. T. (1998). *Subjective assessment methods for image quality in high-definition television* (pp. 710–714). ITU Radiocommunication.

Recommendation, I. T. U.-R. B. T. (2002). *Methodology for the subjective assessment of the quality of television pictures* (pp. 500–511). ITU Radiocommunication.

Ridder, H., & Hamberg, R. (1997). Continuous assessment of image quality. *SMPTE Journal, 106*(2), 123–128.

Tan, K. T., Ghanbari, M., & Pearson, D. E. (1998). An objective measurement tool for MPEG video quality. *Signal Processing, 70*(3), 279–294. doi:10.1016/S0165-1684(98)00129-7

Teunissen, K. (1996). The validity of CCIR quality indicators along a graphical scale. *SMPTE Journal, 105*(3), 144–149.

Tobimatsu, S. (1994). Normative data on reversal visual evoked potentials. *Clinical EEG (Electro-encephalography), 36*(2), 93–97.

Witkin, A. (1984). Scale space filtering: A new approach to multi-scale description. In Ullman, S., & Richards, W. (Eds.), *Image understanding*. New Jersey: Ablex.

Witkin, A. (1993). Scale space filtering. *Proceedings of International Joint Conference on Artificial Intelligence*, Karlsruhe, (pp. 1019-1022).

Yamamoto, T. (2009). Measurement methods and subjective assessment methods for flat panel displays. *The Journal of ITE, 63*(6), 752–757.

Yuyama, I., Nishida, Y., & Nakasu, E. (1998). Objective measurement of compressed digital television picture quality. *SMPTE Journal, 107*(6), 348–352.

Chapter 15
Visual Inspection System and Psychometric Evaluation with Correlation for Multiple Perceptions

Hidehiko Hayashi
Naruto University of Education, Japan

Akinori Minazuki
Naruto University of Education, Japan

ABSTRACT

In this chapter, authors propose a new method for improving detection probabilities of the defect inspection in quality control on the FRP product surface. The proposed method has improved the detection probabilities by using the joint probabilities of dual attributes with correlation for multiple perceptions. In order to obtain the improving detection probability, three kinds of attributes: size, aspect ratio, and color density are prepared in experiments. The experiments were performed by the paired comparison under constant stimuli. The result of our experiment qualitatively shows that the improving ratio of detection probabilities for dual attributes:P12, P23, P31 respectively rise approximately 21%, 26% and 24% for the mean in the case of dual attributes experiments. In addition, detection probabilities to be obtained by the method for multiple perceptions such as using dual attributes experiment were improved approximately 28% in comparison with the detection probability of past single attribute. These results showed this method was effective in raising detection probability for multiple perceptions.

DOI: 10.4018/978-1-61520-871-5.ch015

1. INTRODUCTION

In a progress of a current science and technology, it is no exaggeration to say that the steady development of an instrument to measure or observe something about an object serves an important role. In particular there is the progress of a measuring method for a physical hard object of single attribute such as the measure of length, weight, strength in a material, microscope, telescope, illuminometer, thermometer, and other visibility method. On the other hand, the progress of measuring method or evaluation technique in the soft object such as sensor networks (Delsing & Lindgren, 2005), ubiquitous computing (ubicomp)(Weiser, 1991; Weiser, 1993; Bell & Doursh, 2007), disappearing computer (Streitz et al, 2007), high order sensation of human perception (Hayashi et al, 2000), quality asssessment such as image it (Miyahara, 1988), and decision making for ambient intelligence (Saaty, 1980; Vargas, 1990) need to more strengthen the foundation in soft science and technology.

In addition, recently mixed multiple and conjunction measuring methods from a point of view multiple attribute have been hot issue since the progression for multiple attributes has been later than the single attribute measurement. In this study, drawing focus to multiple perceptions in visual inspection system for defects on the product surface, we propose a new method to measure the multiple attributes for soft science and technology.

Recently, several kinds of image processing method have been applying to the automated visual inspection system for defects on the product surface (Chen & Su, 1996; Chin, 1982; Chin, 1988; Huang et al., 1992; Shirvaikar, 2006). One of the aims of this research is also in the development of the heuristic and simple method that is used in the judgment process in the automated visual inspection system instead of inspector. A sort capacity by human vision is extremely high-performance, therefore such a soft information processing to a sort of images has been regarded unfit on the computer which is good at digital information processing. On the other hand, a visual inspection process has been holding the problem in productivity, since the performance of a precision and a speed will be degraded by fatigue of the inspector. In order to meet these problems, some research works were tried for the standardization of an operation time of visual inspection (Morawski et al, 1992; Arani et al, 1984; Drury, 1972; Spitz & Drury, 1978), though it is not reached to the place which fixes a good evaluation measure, and research of productivity of the production system which consists of a process including such a human being has left lots of problems unresolved.

In the practical situation of quality control on visual inspection, a panel must decide the judgement of the quality by using one's sensitivities for multiple attributes whether the quality of object is good or not. On the other hand, it is required in the field of automated visual inspection system to measure the characteristics of sensitivities for multiple attributes and to evaluate the detective probability when the multiple attributes were used for the judgement of inspection. In this case, it is an important viewpoint to obtain the skill of the professional sense that has the knowledge or skill. In order to meet these problems, a new trial is proposed for the evaluation of human ability on psychometric function. The standard sample was designed by means of paired comparison and constant stimuli. In order to evaluate the visual sensory properties of panel in the practical inspection task, the psychophysical experiment was performed to obtain the psychometric curves to evaluate the distinction probability of target object under the situation of various combinations of mixed dual attributes. This analysis is to obtain the psychometric curve and to estimate the parameters of detectable probability distribution by the experiment of standard sample for single attribute. It is also examined to estimate the correlation among the attributes of figure and to estimate the detection probabilities when the decision was made under the situation of multiple attributes.

2. PSYCHOMETRIC METHOD AND DEFECT INSPECTION

2.1 Psychometric Curve by Single Attribute Experiment

Psychometric curve (Guilford, 1954; Ohyama et al, 1994; Stevens, 1957) is a continuous curve which is made from the detection probability as a function of stimulus strength, when the strength of stimulus is continuously varied over a range of values. Figure 1 shows a psychimetric curve on single attribute. Hirizotal axis is stimulous strength. Vertical axis is the detection probbility. Solid line curvese like "S" letter characteristically in perceptive response of human.

The psychometric curve fit a continuous function $f(x)$.

$$P = f(x) \tag{1}$$

Equation (1) can be derived from the relationship.

$$P = \Phi(y) = \int_{-\infty}^{y_j} \varphi(y)dy, \quad y = \frac{x - \mu_x}{\sigma_x} \tag{2}$$

In Equation (2), $\Phi(\bullet)$ and $\varphi(\bullet)$ is cumulative distribution function and probability density function of the standardized normal distribution

Figure 1. Psychometric curve

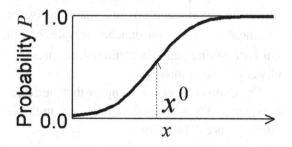

$$\varphi(y) = \frac{1}{\sqrt{2\pi}} e^{-\frac{y^2}{2}} \tag{3}$$

where μ_x and σx is a mean and standard deviation of the strength of stimuli x. If the observation probability $\hat{P}_j$ ($j=1,2,..., m$) that is the ratio of the number n_j to the total number of trials N_j, where n_j is the number of the answer by subject when one answer that j-th degree of strength of stimuli x_j is larger than x_0. The observed probability $\hat{P}_j$ at j-th degree of strength of stimuli x_j is obtained by

$$\hat{P}_j = n_j / Nj \left(j = 1, 2, ..., n\right) \tag{4}$$

The normalized variable $\hat{y}_j$ is defined by the inverse function of $\Phi(\bullet)$ such as:

$$\hat{y}_j = \Phi^{-1}(\hat{P}_j) \tag{5}$$

However, since $\hat{y}_j$ is rewritten by linear relation of stimuli x_j

$$\hat{y}_j = a + bx_j \tag{6}$$

it is noted from Equations (4), (5) and (6)

$$\hat{P}_j = \Phi(a + bx_j) \tag{7}$$

Thus the normalized variable obtained from observed probability from sensory test of single attribute can be formulated by the linear function of j-th degree of strength of stimuli x_j of single attribute.

The estimation of this regression coefficient of a and b will be estimated by the following method. Since it can be assumed that the probability that obtain the number n_j to the total number of trials N_j are distributed by the rule of binomial distribution with the mean P_j and variance $P_j(1-P_j)$, the probability that obtain the set of number $(n_1, n_2, ..., n_n)$ to the total number of trials N_j is given by

$$P(n_1, n_2, ..., n_m) = \prod_{j=1}^{m} \frac{N_j!}{n_j!(N_j - n_j)!} P_j^{n_j} (1 - P_j)^{N_j - n_j}$$

(8)

Therefore, maximum likelihood estimators of a and b are possible to be estimated by partial derivation of the logarithm of likelihood function of Equation (8)

$$L(a,b) = \sum_{j=1}^{l} \log \frac{N_j!}{n_j!(N_j - n_j)!} + \sum_{j=1}^{l} n_j \log P_j + \sum_{j=1}^{l} (N_j - n_j) \log(1 - P_j)$$

(9)

Thus the ML estimators of a and b can be obtained as the solution of the simultaneous equations such as:

$$\frac{\partial l}{\partial a} = 0 \text{ and } \frac{\partial l}{\partial b} = 0$$

(10)

Since this simultaneous equation cannot be soled analytically because of its non-linearity, it is used to solve Equation (10) by a numerical method such as Newton Raphson Method and so on.

One of the way to obtain the solution of Equation (10) is to iterate the sequential calculation such as

$$\begin{bmatrix} a \\ b \end{bmatrix}_{k+1} = \begin{bmatrix} a \\ b \end{bmatrix}_{k} + \begin{bmatrix} \frac{\partial^2 l}{\partial a^2} & \frac{\partial^2 l}{\partial a \partial b} \\ \frac{\partial^2 l}{\partial b \partial a} & \frac{\partial^2 l}{\partial b^2} \end{bmatrix}_{k}^{-1} \begin{bmatrix} \frac{\partial l}{\partial a} \\ \frac{\partial l}{\partial b} \end{bmatrix}_{k}$$

(11)

until the convergence of a and b. This method of obtaining the ML estimators of a and b is called Probit method (Pearson & Hartley, 1962) or Probit analysis (Finney, 1947; Finney, 1978; Hayashi et al, 2007). On the other hand, it is possible to use

regression analysis x_j and temporary candidate of normalized variable

$$y_{wk_j} = \hat{y}_{wk_j} + \frac{1}{\varphi(\hat{y}_{wk_j})} (p - P_{wk_j})$$

(12)

where $\hat{y}_{wk_j}$ is the normalized variable obtained by Equations (8), (9) and (10). The solutions derived by this regression analysis is same as those obtained by Equation (11). An example of this probit analysis is illustrated in Figure 5 where the distinction between initial and probit analyses can be confirmed.

2.2 Approximation Evaluation for Detection Probability of Dual Attribute Experiments

The probability obtained by psychometric curve or by Equation (1) means the probability that one can feel the strength of stimuli of target object larger than specified strength of stimuli such as threshold x^0 in Figure 1. Therefore, this probability is also calculated by Equation (2) as a probability that one can judge that the strength of stimuli of the target sample for paired comparison is larger than that of standard sample as shown in Figure 3. From this discussion, now suppose that this probability is defined by

$$P_i = P(E_i)$$

(13)

where $P(\bullet)$ is an occurrence probability of probability event $\bullet$. E_i means the probability event that a panel judges that the strength of the stimuli of the target sample is less than that of the threshold x_i^0 such as a standard sample for i-th attribute among multiple attributes to express the characteristic of interest.

On the other hand, now suppose that the detection probability P under the situation of multiple attributes are defined by

$$P = P(E_1 \cup E_2 \cdots \cup E_n) \tag{14}$$

In this condition, the confidence interval of detection probability P under multiple attributes can be estimated with upper and lower probability bounds P_L and P_U such as $P_L \leq P \leq P_U$ by the equations (Madsen et al, 1986).

$$P_L = P_1 + (P_2 - P_{12}) + \sum_{k=3}^{n} \max\left\{ P_k - \sum_{l=1}^{k-1} P_{lk}, \ 0 \right\},$$

$$P_U = P_1 + \sum_{k=2}^{k_n} \min\left\{ P_k - P_{lk} \right\}, \ for \ \ l \in \{1, 2, \cdots, k-1\} \tag{15}$$

where $P_1 \geq P_2 \geq \cdots \geq P_n$. In the equation, P_{lk} is the joint probability of the events E_l and E_k

$$P_{lk} = P(E_l \cap E_k) \tag{16}$$

that can be calculated by the integral

$$P_{kl} = \Phi(y_k, y_l) = \int_{-\infty}^{y_k} \int_{-\infty}^{y_l} \varphi\left(y_k, y_l; \rho_{kl}\right) dy_k dy_l \tag{17}$$

where $\varphi(y_k, y_l; \rho_{kl})$ is the density function of bivariate standard normal distribution.

$$\varphi(y_k, y_l; \rho_{kl}) =$$
$$\frac{1}{2\pi\sqrt{1 - \rho_{kl}^2}} \exp\left\{ -\frac{1}{2(1 - \rho_{kl}^2)} \left(y_k^2 - 2\rho_{kl} y_k y_l + y_l^2 \right) \right\} \tag{18}$$

where

$$y_k = \frac{x_k - \mu_k}{\sigma_k}, y_l = \frac{x_l - \mu_l}{\sigma_l}, y_k^0 = \frac{x_k^0 - \mu_k}{\sigma_k}, y_l = \frac{x_l - \mu_l}{\sigma_l},$$

$$\mu_k = \int_{-\infty}^{\infty} \int_{-\infty}^{\infty} x_k \varphi(x_k, x_l) dx_k dx_l,$$

$$\mu_l = \int_{-\infty}^{\infty} \int_{-\infty}^{\infty} x_l \varphi(x_k, x_l) dx_k dx_l,$$

$$\sigma_k^2 = \int_{-\infty}^{\infty} \int_{-\infty}^{\infty} (x_k - \mu_k)^2 \varphi(x_k, x_l) dx_k dx_l,$$

$$\sigma_l^2 = \int_{-\infty}^{\infty} \int_{-\infty}^{\infty} (x_l - \mu_l)^2 \varphi(x_k, x_l) dx_k dx_l,$$

$$\rho_{kl} = \frac{\sigma_{kl}}{\sigma_k \cdot \sigma_l} \tag{19}$$

2.3 Detection Probability of Dual Attribute Experiments for Discrete Quantity

Correlation coefficient in multi attribute experiment is obtained by Equation (19) in a theoretical sense. In the experiment, detection probabilities to calculate correlation coefficient are discretely obtained by actual measurement, hence the calculation of discrete quantity is prepared as follows. Detection probabilities p_{ij} ($i = 1, 2, ..., n, j = 1, 2, ..., m$) are obtained discrete probabilities p_{gij} ($i = 1, 2, ..., n-1, j = 1, 2, ..., m-1$) for each discrete zone of combination i variable and j variable.

$$P_{gij} = \max(p_{ij} - p_{i+1,j} - p_{i,j+1} + p_{i+1,j+1}, 0) \tag{20}$$

where $g_{ki} = (x_{k,i} + x_{k,i+1})/2$, $g_{lj} = (x_{l,j} + x_{l,j+1})/2$. Discrete probabilities p_{gij} ($i = 1, 2, ..., n-1, j = 1, 2, ..., m-1$) is normalized and used gravity point.

The parameters μ_k, μ_l, σ_k^2, σ_l^2, σ_{kl} are calculated using the following equation.

$$\mu_k \fallingdotseq \sum_{i=1}^{n-1} \sum_{j=1}^{m-1} g_{ki} p_{g_{ij}} \quad \mu_l \fallingdotseq \sum_{i=1}^{n-1} \sum_{j=1}^{m-1} g_{lj} p_{g_{ij}}$$

$$\sigma_k^2 \fallingdotseq \sum_{i=1}^{n-1} \sum_{j=1}^{m-1} (g_{ki} - \mu_k)^2 p_{g_{ij}} \quad \sigma_l^2 \fallingdotseq \sum_{i=1}^{n-1} \sum_{j=1}^{m-1} (g_{lj} - \mu_l)^2 p_{g_{ij}}$$

$$\sigma_{kl} \fallingdotseq \sum_{i=1}^{n-1} \sum_{j=1}^{m-1} (g_{ki} - \mu_k)(g_{lj} - \mu_l) p_{g_{ij}} \tag{21}$$

That is approximately obtained from discrete quantity.

3. EXPERIMENT

3.1 Experimental Material: Inspection Data

An attention has been paid on three kinds of attributes such as the size, aspect ratio and color density of object in the sampling image data. These selected attributes are considered from the practical visual inspection image data of FRP product as shown in the left photo in Figure 2.

In the visual inspection, there are many candidates detected from the image data. These candidates are called "object" for judgement whether the quality of object is poor not. For the purpose of this judgement, three kinds of attributes such as the size, aspect ratio and color density of object are selected as the typical qualities that mean geometric characters of the defect or flaw in the surface of FRP product. The size is the first attribute of the object for the judgement that is quantified by area or maximum length of the object. The aspect ratio is the second attribute of the object that is defined by the ratio of the shortest radius to the longest radius. The color density is the third attribute of the object that is quantified by 8bit digits from 0 to 255. Table 1 is mean and standard deviation of three attributes by image processing. There are three statistic parammeter: area sie, aspect ratio, and color density. The parammeters set the experiment which is the stimulus of strength.

For the sensory test, the strength of these attributes must be formulated as the strength of stimuli in order to obtain the psychometric function that is used to evaluate the relation between the detection probability and stimulus threshold for each attribute in the experiment. Some standard samples of objects are captured from the practical

inspection image data of FRP panel in Figure 2. The right side figure in Figure 2 is modeling the object in FRP, Parammter setting in detail is as follows. The properties of the three attributes are investigated statistically. Thus the strength of stimuli x_{1j}, x_1^0 of size as the first attribute is quantified as

$$x_1^0 = \sqrt{\frac{4S}{\pi \mu_R}}, \quad S = 15\mu_A \qquad (22)$$

$$x_{1j} = \sqrt{\frac{4S_j}{\pi \mu_R}}, \quad S_j = 15\left\{\mu_A + \sigma_A h_A \left(j - 3.5\right)\right\} \qquad (23)$$

where $\mu_A, \sigma_A \, \mu_R$ are the mean and the standard deviation of size, and the mean of aspect ratio respectively. The constant value of 15 in Equations (22) and (23) is a scale factor and The h_A is a coefficient for normalization and j is from 1 to 7. Target sample stimuli are 7 levels. Standard sample stimulus is set the centre of the target sample stimuli. In a similar way, the strength of stimuli for the second and third attributes are obtained as follows. The strength of stimuli $x2_j$, x_2^0 of shape of object as the second attribute is defined by

Figure 2. Inspection image data and parameters of sample

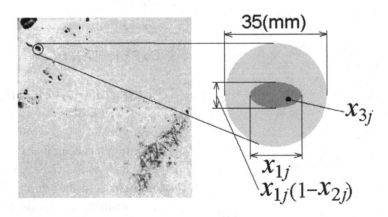

Table 1. Statistics by image processing

	area size (mm²)	aspect ratio	color density
mean	μ_A=5.855	μ_R=0.361	μ_V=0.547
S.D.	σA_19.113	σR_0.197	σV_0.422

$$x_2j=(1-\mu_R)+\sigma_R\,h_R(j\text{-}3.5), x_2^{\,0}=(1-\mu_R) \qquad (24)$$

where constant number σR is the standard deviation of aspect ratio. In this case, the original data of aspect ratio is calculated by $1\text{-}\mu R$ from the standard samples. Finally, the strength of stimuli $x3_j$, $x_3^{\,0}$ of the color density of object as the third attribute is quantified as

$$x_3j=\mu_V+\sigma_V\,h_V(j\text{-}3.5), x_3^{\,0}=\mu_V \qquad (25)$$

where μ_V, σ_V are respectively the mean and the standard deviation of the color density of object as shown in Table 1. The values of coefficients h_A, h_R and h_V are decided by the previous experiments, and are 0.053, 0.055, and 0.028 respectively. In this way, the strength of stimuli x_{ij}, $x_i^{\,0}$ (i=1,2,3, j=1,2,…,7) were set for the paired comparison, then they were presented as shown in Figure 3. In this case, the original data of color density of the object is obtained by capturing from inspection data as 8bit digits from 0 to 255. As the color density, grey scale of that density is defined by Equation (25) is used as the third attribute, since it is well known that the degree of grey scale density is applicable rather than true color scale to judge whether the quality of object is poor or not. From the above definitions of the strength of stimulus of the attributes, it may be possible to evaluate the psychometric curve that means psychometric function of detection probability to strength of stimuli. It is well known that this curve can be obtained by the experiment of the method of constant stimuli. Table 2 shows the value of stimulus strength of standard sample x_{1j}, x_{2j} and x_{3j} and target samples $x_1^{\,0}$, $x_2^{\,0}$ and $x_3^{\,0}$.

In this chapter, the paired comparison method is used to evaluate the psychometric curve for the mentioned attributes as shown in Figure 5. The attribute of standard sample in paired comparison is designated by the right side figure in Figure 2 where an object with heavy density is a sample object with the strength of stimulus of size, aspect ratio and color density. The degrees of these attributes of object can be created by the specified strength of stimuli of attributes and stimulus thresholds such as x_1, x_2 and x_3 as shown in Figure 4.

3.2 Experimental Method

The target sample is located in the centre on background figure that is within a circle with light density as shown in Figure 3. The degree of visual field is about 1 degree from fixation point for target figure and 2 degree for background circle. The paired comparison method is used for standard sample where the allocation of constant and target figures are located on left and right side respectively in the standard sample.

Figure 3. Samples for sensory evaluation experiment

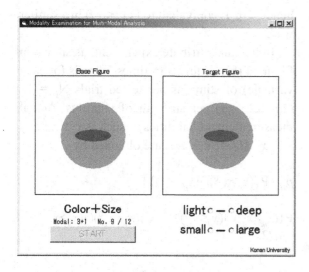

Table 2. Stimuli strength of standard and target samples

i	x_i^0	x_{i1}	x_{i2}	x_{i3}	x_{i4}	x_{i5}	x_{i6}	x_{i7}
1	17.5	16.05	16.63	17.20	17.80	18.38	18.95	19.53
2	0.639	0.611	0.622	0.633	0.644	0.655	0.666	0.677
3	0.547	0.517	0.529	0.541	0.553	0.565	0.577	0.589

Figure 4. Examples of degree of stimuli

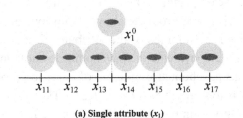

(a) Single attribute (x_1)

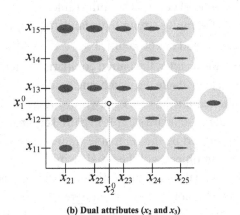

(b) Dual attributes (x_2 and x_3)

Figure 5. Psychometric curves (Subject A)

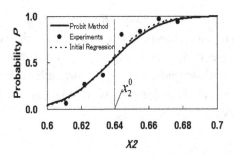

The strength of the visual stimulus is divided into several categories that are dependent on the strength of stimulus. One of the example on the strength of stimulus of attributes such as size and aspect ratio is shown in Figure 4 (a) and (b). It is seen that there are two kinds of standard samples for single and dual attributes.

The answer of subject is performed as a selection from two kinds of candidates, for examples:

1. The size of target sample is larger than that of standard sample.
2. The size of target sample is smaller than that of standard figure.

A subject must answer two kinds of questions simultaneously for the single and dual attributes.

In the single attribute experiment, as shown in Figure 4 (a), 7 levels of stimulus are tested trials N_j=30 (j=1,2,…,7) per strength of stimulus. Actual measurement probabilities p_j are obtained by the experiment of paired comparison which are obtained reaction number n_j under constant stimuli such as:

$$p_j = P(x_{ij} > x_i^0) \ (i=1,2,3, j=1,2,…,7)$$

hence, $1-p_j$ is equivalent to $P(x_{ij} < x_i^0)$ in a similar way.

In the dual attribute experiment, as shown in Figure 4 (b), 25 levels (5 times 5 levels for each variable) of stimulus are tested trials N_{kl} = 15 (k,l=1,2,…,5) per strength of stimulus. Actual measurement probabilities p_{kl} such as $x_{ik} > x_{ij}^0$ and $x_{jl} > x_{ij}^0$ (i,j =1,2,3, $i\neq j$) are obtained by

$$p_{kl} = P\{(x_{ik}>x_{ij}^0)\cap(x_{jl}>x_{ij}^0)\}+$$

$$P\{(x_{ik}>x_{ij}^0)\cap(x_{jl}<x_{ij}^0)\}/2+P\{(x_{ik}<x_{ij}^0)\cap(x_{jl}>x_{ij}^0)\}/2.$$

Hence, $1-p_{kl}$ is proper for $P\{(x_{ik}<x_{ij}^0)\cap(x_{jl}<x_{ij}^0)\}$ and the same probabilities 1/2 are supposed $P\{(x_{ik}>x_{ij}^0)\cap(x_{jl}<x_{ij}^0)\}$ and $P\{(x_{ik}<x_{ij}^0)\cap(x_{jl}>x_{ij}^0)\}$ in balance.

In the experiment, 13 persons from 20 to 28 years old were selected as subjects who have regular class load vehicle licenses with normal vision or corrected normal vision. The size, aspect ratio and color density are selected as the attributes of target sample which strengths of stimuli are represented by the variables x_1, x_2 and x_3.

4. EXPERIMENT RESULTS AND DISCUSSION

4.1 Experimental Results in the Single Attribute Experiment

As an example of psychometric from the single attribute experimet, Figure 5 illustrates the psychometric curve of a subject derived from the data measured by paired comparison test for single attribute of x_2. Horizontal axis is stimulus strength of x_2. Vertical axis is an occurence probability. In Figure 5, dot pattern is experiment data. Dashed line is initial regresion. Solid line is the result of probait method. As can be seen Figure 5, a monotonically increasing function is derived from the ML estimation in the case of all experimental conditions.

Distributions of differences on characteristic of x_1, x_2 and x_3 among 10 subjects are shown in Figure 6. This distribution of PSE can be obtained by method of mean rank in due small order of PSE. From Figure 6, it is known that the mean values of PSE of x_1, x_2 and x_3 are 17.37, 0.647 and 0.548 respectively. Mean values of PSE become close the standard stimuli of x_1^0, x_2^0 and x_3^0. In addition, on the other hand, the coefficients of variation are 0.043, 0.018 and 0.020. Distributions of PSE indicate normality as can be seen to become

Figure 6. Sample distribution of PSE for each attribute

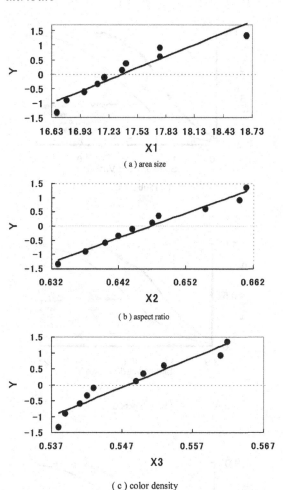

(a) area size

(b) aspect ratio

(c) color density

near straight lines on the plane by normalized variable Y and strength of stimuli x_i.

4.2 Experimental Results in the Multi Attribute Experiment

Experiment of multiple attributes show the result to attain our objective for the improvement of the detection probability. a heavy line shows the experiment of multiple attributes in Figure 7. Gray lines show the experiment of dual attributes. From the result in experiments, the probabilities for dual and multiple attributes are larger than that of single attribute as shown in Figure 7. This tendency is

Figure 7. Example of psychometric curves for multiple perceptions

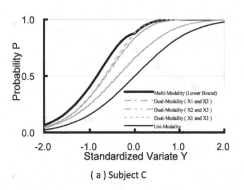

(a) Subject C

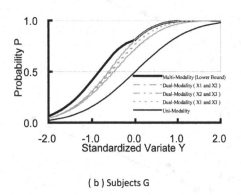

(b) Subjects G

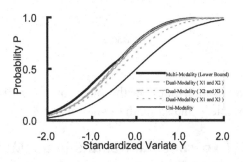

Table 3. Correlation of coefficient

Subject	ρ_{12}	ρ_{23}	ρ_{31}
A	-0.406	-0.426	0.397
B	0.072	0.173	0.1
C	0.545	-0.522	-0.718
D	0.423	-0.042	0.528
E	0.532	-0.249	-0.315
F	0.573	-0.18	0
G	0.177	-0.373	-0.104
H	0.342	0.224	-0.272
I	0.528	0.548	0.048
J	-0.1	0.031	-0.02
K	-0.038	-0.095	0.329
L	-0.062	-0.09	0.346
M	0.144	-0.05	0.539
mean	0.21	-0.081	0.066

coefficient ρ_{12}, ρ_{23} and ρ_{31} are 0.21, –0.081 and 0.066 respectively. On the other hand, Table 4 shows improving ratio of detection probabilities for dual attributes: P12, P23, P31 respectively rise approximately 21%, 26% and 24% for mean in the case of dual attribute experiments. That is to say improving ratio of detection probabilities have a pronounced tendency to depend correlation coefficient. In addition, the improving ratio PL which is obtained by the approximation formula for the multiple attributes rises approximately 28% in comparison with the detection probability of past single attribute.

4.3 Discussions

Apparently, we success the growth of detection probability on the dual attribute experiment more than on the single attribute experiment as shown in results.

Mean values of PSE are close the standard stimuli. Distributions of PSE tend indicate normality as can be seen to become near straight lines on the plane by normalized variable Y and strength of stimuli x_i from single attribute experiment. These

same in all experimental conditions. Increasing amount of detection probability, however, is not same in different ways with the variation of correlation coefficient. In fact, the variation is seen from the correlation coefficient ρ_{12}, ρ_{23} and ρ_{31} for combinations of attributes x_1, x_2 and x_3 in Table 3. In addition, mean values of correlation

Table 4. Improving ratio of detection probability

Subject	P12 (%)	P23 (%)	P31 (%)	PL (%)
A	31.65	32.01	18.5	32.15
B	23.85	22.23	23.41	23.85
C	15.83	33.74	37.76	37.76
D	18.06	25.67	16.14	25.67
E	16.07	29.01	30.11	30.11
F	15.29	27.88	25	27.88
G	22.17	31.08	26.65	31.08
H	19.45	21.41	29.38	29.38
I	16.14	15.78	24.23	24.23
J	26.59	24.51	25.32	26.59
K	25.61	26.51	19.66	26.51
L	25.98	26.43	19.38	26.43
M	22.7	25.8	15.94	25.8
mean	21.49	26.31	23.96	28.27

results suggest that standard stimulus is near the threshold on the detection probability, therefore, target stimulus of setting range is good to obtain psychometric curve.

The detection probabilities for dual and multiple attributes are larger than that of single attribute. This result was expected to follow the theory of proposing our method in section 2.2. It is similar to the improving ratio of detection probabilities depend on correlation coefficient for dual attributes.

A perceptual decision with multiple attributes information possesses qualitatively higher reliability than the perceptual decision with single attribute information in traditional qualitative. In this study it has no small significance that quantitative evaluation, the improving ratio of detection probability or the correlation coefficient based on experimental results, gives a cogent explanation to traditional qualitative property of a perceptual decision with multiple attributes. In addition, it is also similar to be shown quantitatively the improving ratio of detection probabilities depend on correlation coefficient for dual attributes.

5. CONCLUSION

In this study, drawing focus to multiple perceptions evoked multiple attribute stimulus, we proposed a new method for improving detection probability of the defect inspection. We compared the detection probability of single attribute and multiple attributes. The result of our experiment qualitatively showed that the improving ratio of detection probabilities for dual attributes: P12, P23, P31 respectively rose approximately 21%, 26% and 24% for mean in the case of dual attribute experiments. In addition, the improving ratio of multiple attributes rose approximately 28% in comparison with the detection probability of past single attribute. This result showed effective in rising detection probability for multiple perceptions. In addition, the result experimentally showed that improving rate of detection probability depended on various value of correlation coefficient. The diverse correlation coefficient suggests that the detailed standard can be set for the inspection. In other words, we conclude that our method of psychometric evaluation for multiple perceptions is useful for improving detection probability of the defect inspection in quality control on the FRP product surface. In the future we plan to decrease the trial number for dual attribute experiment.

REFERENCES

Arani, T. T., Karwan, M. H., & Drury, C. G. (1984). A variable-memory model of visual search. *Human Factors*, *26*, 680–688.

Bell, G., & Doursh, P. (2007). Yesterday's tomorrows: Notes on ubiquitous computing's dominant vision. *Personal and Ubiquitous Computing*, *11*(2), 133–143. doi:10.1007/s00779-006-0071-x

Chen, F. L., & Su, C. T. (1996). Vision-based automated inspection system in computer-integrated manufacturing. *IJAMT*, *11*(3), 206–213.

Chin, R. T. (1982). Automated visual inspection: A survey. *IEEE Transactions on Pattern Analysis and Machine Intelligence, 4*(6), 557–573. doi:10.1109/TPAMI.1982.4767309

Chin, R. T. (1988). Automated visual inspection: 1981 to 1987. *CVGIP, 41*(3), 346–381.

Delsing, J., & Lindgren, P. (2005). Sensor communication technology towards ambient intelligence. *Measurement Science & Technology, 16*(4), 37–46. doi:10.1088/0957-0233/16/4/R02

Drury, C. G. (1972). The effect of speed of working on industrial inspection accuracy. *Applied Ergonomics*, 42–47.

Finney, D. J. (1947). *Probit analysis* (1st ed.). London, UK: Cambridge University Press.

Finney, D. J. (1978). *Statistical method in biological assay* (3rd ed.). London, UK: Charles Griffin and Co.

Guilford, J. P. (1954). *Psychometric methods*. New York, NY: McGraw-Hill.

Hayashi, H., Nakagawa, M., & Nakayasu, H. (2007). An evaluation method of human property using psychometric function in sensory test. *JCIIE, 24*(4), 259–267.

Hayashi, H., Shirai, H., Kunifuji, S., & Miyahara, M. (2000). Assessment of extra high quality images using both EEG and assessment words on high order sensations. *Proceedings of the IEEE, SMC2000*, 1289–1294.

Huang, C., Cheng, T., & Chen, C. (1992). Color images' segmentation using scale space filter and Markov random field. *Pattern Recognition, 25*(10), 1217–1229. doi:10.1016/0031-3203(92)90023-C

Madsen, H. O., Krenk, S., & Lind, N. C. (1986). *Method of structural safety*. Prentice Hall.

Miyahara, M. (1988). Quality assessments for visual service. *IEEE Communications Magazine, 26*(10), 51–60. doi:10.1109/35.7667

Morawski, T. B., Drury, C. G., & Karwan, M. H. (1992). The optimum speed of visual inspection using a random search strategy. *IIE Transactions, 24*(5), 122–133. doi:10.1080/07408179208964252

Ohyama, T., Imai, S., & Wake, T. (1994). *Handbook of sensory and perception*. Seishin Publisher.

Pearson, E. S., & Hartley, H. O. (1962). *Biometrika tables for statisticians* (1st ed., pp. 4–9). Cambridge, UK: Cambridge University Press.

Saaty, T. L. (1980). *The analytic hierarchy process*. McGraw Hill.

Shirvaikar, M. V. (2006). Trends in automated visual inspection. *Real Time IP, 1*(1), 41–43. doi:10.1007/s11554-006-0009-6

Spitz, G., & Drury, C. G. (1978). Inspection of sheet materials: Test of model prediction. *Human Factors, 20*, 521–528.

Stevens, S. S. (1957). On the psychophysical law. *Psychological Review, 64*, 158–181. doi:10.1037/h0046162

Streitz, N., Kameas, A., & Mavrommati, I. (Eds.). (2007). *The disappearing computer: Interaction design, system infrastructures and applications for smart environments*. Springer.

Vargas, L. G. (1990). An overview of the analytic hierarchy process and its applications. *European Journal of Operational Research, 48*(1), 2–8. doi:10.1016/0377-2217(90)90056-H

Weiser, M. (1991). The computer for the 21st Century. *Scientific American, 265*(3), 66–75. doi:10.1038/scientificamerican0991-94

Weiser, M. (1993). Some computer science problems in ubiuitous computing. *Communications of the ACM, 36*(7), 75–84. doi:10.1145/159544.159617

Chapter 16
Improvement of Lecture Speech Recognition by Using Unsupervised Adaptation

Tetsuo Kosaka
Yamagata University, Japan

Takashi Kusama
Yamagata University, Japan

Masaharu Kato
Yamagata University, Japan

Masaki Kohda
Yamagata University, Japan

ABSTRACT

The aim of this work is to improve the recognition performance of spontaneous speech. In order to achieve the purpose, the authors of this chapter propose new approaches of unsupervised adaptation for spontaneous speech and evaluate the methods by using diagonal-covariance and full-covariance hidden Markov models. In the adaptation procedure, both methods of language model (LM) adaptation and acoustic model (AM) adaptation are used iteratively. Several combination methods are tested to find the optimal approach. In the LM adaptation, a word trigram model and a part-of-speech (POS) trigram model are combined to build a more task-specific LM. In addition, the authors propose an unsupervised speaker adaptation technique based on adaptation data weighting. The weighting is performed depending on POS class. In Japan, a large-scale spontaneous speech database "Corpus of Spontaneous Japanese (CSJ)" has been used as the common evaluation database for spontaneous speech and the authors used it for their recognition experiments. From the results, the proposed methods demonstrated a significant advantage in that task.

DOI: 10.4018/978-1-61520-871-5.ch016

1. INTRODUCTION

High recognition accuracy has been achieved for read speech with a large vocabulary continuous speech recognition (LVCSR) system. The recognition accuracy higher than 95% has been reported using the state-of-the-art speech recognition system (Furui, 2005a). However, it is well known that rather poor performance is reported for spontaneous speech recognition. Compared with read speech, spontaneous speech has repairs, hesitations, filled pauses, unknown words, unclear pronunciation, and so on, and those phenomenon cause poor performance.

In order to improve the recognition performance of spontaneous speech, it is necessary to develop more accurate acoustic and language models which are suitable for spontaneous speech. Since difference between read speech and spontaneous speech is very large, it is difficult to use these models developed for read speech as models for spontaneous speech. Currently, state-of-the-art speech recognition systems use statistical-based models for both acoustic and language modeling. Development of accurate statistical models requires a large amount of training data. For this reason, a large-scale spontaneous speech corpus, Corpus of Spontaneous Japanese (CSJ) was developed and released in 2004 (Maekawa, 2003). By taking this opportunity, the research on this field becomes active in Japan.

The development of CSJ has brought steady progress in the research of Japanese spontaneous speech recognition. However, the absolute performance of recognition is still insufficient. This might result from that utterances of spontaneous speech have a vast variation both acoustically and linguistically. Even if accurate language and acoustic models are created by using a large amount of training data such as the CSJ, it is difficult to cover such an acoustic and linguistic variation in spontaneous speech.

In order to solve the problem, adaptation techniques for acoustic or language models have been investigated. These techniques are referred to as acoustic model (AM) adaptation or language model (LM) adaptation respectively. Many efforts have been made with these issues over the years. For example, maximum-likelihood linear regression (MLLR) technique is well known as the effective speaker adaptation method (Leggetter et al., 1995; Gales, 1998). Regarding the language model adaptation, class-based language model adaptation methods have been proposed to cope with the sparseness of language model space (Moore et al., 2000; Yamamoto et al., 2001).

The adaptation techniques can be classified into two categories. One is supervised adaptation and the other is unsupervised adaptation. In general, the adaptation techniques require both utterance data and transcription data in which the contents of utterances are described by speech units such as phonemes. Since the transcription data does not provide in the unsupervised mode, recognition results are used in place of them. Then, the performance of the unsupervised adaptation is lower than that of the supervised adaptation because of the influence of recognition errors. Generally the transcription data cannot be obtained in advance. Then, the unsupervised adaptation technique can be used for wide range of application areas.

The aim of this work is to improve the performance of spontaneous speech recognition by using both AM adaptation and LM adaptation techniques in the unsupervised mode. This chapter focuses on recognizing lecture speech. However, the proposed methods described below are expected to be applicable to another speaking style. We have an assumption that the recognition is performed off-line. After recognizing the lecture speech data, the model adaptation is carried out and the data are recognized again by using the adapted models. This kind of adaptation is called batch-type adaptation.

For the unsupervised adaptation, it is important to reduce the adverse effect of recognition errors. In order to solve the problem, we investigate two types of approaches for the unsupervised adaptation. First, we investigate effective combination techniques of AM and LM adaptation. Secondly, we propose a novel approach of unsupervised adaptation based on the adaptation data weighting. Those adaptation techniques are evaluated in lecture speech recognition experiments. From the experiments, we describe the effectiveness of our approaches.

This chapter is organized as follows. Section 2 describes the background of this work. The related works are introduced briefly. Section 3 explains the CSJ which is used for model training and the evaluation of proposed approaches. Section 4 explains our proposed approaches of unsupervised adaptation. Section 5 describes the experimental conditions. In Section 6, we describe and discuss the results of recognition experiments. Section 7 describes future research directions and we conclude our work in Section 8.

2. BACKGROUND

Recently, research on LVCSR systems for spontaneous speech makes steady progress. A large-scale speech corpus consisting of 0.9 - 1.4 billion words with a total speech length of 2100 - 2300 hours is available for research organizations participating in DARPA EARS program now. Using such a large-scale speech corpus, those organizations address some challenges such as expansion of phone context (quinphone, septaphone) (Chen, 2003), modification of Gaussian model (full-covariance), improvement of parameter estimation by discriminative training (MPE, fMPE) (Povey et al., 2002) (Povey et al., 2005), expansion of word N-gram (4-gram, 5-gram), accurate LM using class 3-gram, cross-adaptation (Giuliani et al., 2006), system combination (CNC, ROVER) (Mangu et al. 2000; Fiscus, 1997), and so on. In consequence, an average word error rate (WER) of around 15% could be obtained on conversational telephone speech recognition task (Chen

et al., 2006; Matsoukas et al., 2006; Evermann et al., 2005).

In Japan, the research activity on this field began in earnest by releasing the CSJ in 2004. Nakamura et al. developed the LVCSR system in which hidden Markov models (HMMs) with full covariance matrix Gaussians based on the minimum classification error (MCE) training algorithm (Juang et al., 1992) were used as acoustic models (Nakamura et al., 2006). The paper reported that a WER of about 19% could be obtained. Mimura et al. (Mimura et al., 2007) reported that the minimum phone error training (MPE) showed better performance than standard maximum likelihood training (ML) on a CSJ evaluation set. A WER of around 20% was obtained by MPE.

Despite years of efforts to improve the performance of spontaneous speech recognition, it is still not sufficient. It is considered that adaptation technique is indispensable factor to solve the problem. There are two major research areas involved: the acoustic model adaptation and the language model adaptation. The former copes with an acoustic mismatch between input and recognition data. There are some reasons for this mismatch, but one of the main problems is speaker characteristics. Many techniques have been proposed concerning speaker adaptation. The adaptation methods based on linear mapping are one of the major techniques in this field. Some techniques of bias elimination have been proposed (Ohkura et al., 1992; Shinoda et al., 1991). In these methods, signal bias is removed with a certain type of smoothing in order to compensate lack of adaptation data. The techniques based on maximum-likelihood linear regression (MLLR) introduced Section 1 are popular and effective methods for speaker adaptation (Leggetter et al., 1995; Gales, 1998). In these methods, feature parameters are transformed by transform matrices calculated on the basis of maximum likelihood.

Adaptive language modeling copes with the problem of a variety of natural language sources (Bellegarda, 2004). In the general LM adaptation framework, parameters of LM are updated by adaptation data which are relevant to the current recognition task. Interpolation-based approaches are most well known and popular approaches for LM adaptation. The simplest way of interpolation is at the model level. Alternatively, the interpolation is done at the frequency count level rather than the model level. Typical techniques are based on *the maximum a posteriori* (MAP) criterion (Federico, 1996; Masataki et al., 1997).

3. CORPUS OF SPONTANEOUS JAPANESE

We conducted the evaluation of the method on more difficult task. In Japan, a large-scale spontaneous speech database 'Corpus of Spontaneous Japanese (CSJ)" has been used as the training set of models and common evaluation database for spontaneous speech. This corpus consists of roughly 7M words with a total speech length of 650 hours. In the corpus, monologues such as academic presentations and extemporaneous presentations have been recorded. The recordings were carried out by a headset microphone with relatively little background noise. It is well known that the recognition of this task is too difficult because those presentations are real and the spontaneity is high. For example, word error rate of 25.3% was reported in (Furui et al., 2005).

4. UNSUPERVISED ADAPTATION

4.1 Overview

In the unsupervised adaptation, recognition results are used for the adaptation data and this is a major cause of the low performance of the unsupervised adaptation. Then, it is important to reduce the adverse effect of recognition errors. To cope with the problem, two approaches are described in this section.

First, we describes the effective combination techniques of AM and LM adaptation. Generally, the adaptation procedure is carried out iteratively until the improvement of performance is converged. In the iterative adaptation, the same recognition errors tend to be repeated in each iteration step. In order to avoid the problem, the cross adaptation technique has been proposed (Giuliani et al., 2006). In the method, multiple systems which have different trends of recognition error are used for the adaptation. Giuliani et al. combined different AM adaptation methods and the results showed that the performance was better than the conventional system combination technique. In this section, we described new cross adaptation in which both AM and LM adaptation are used iteratively in order to reduce the adverse effect of recognition errors. Four types of iterated adaptation methods, i.e., (a) Sequential adaptation, (b) Parallel adaptation, (c) Parallel adaptation with decode and rescoring and (d) Parallel adaptation with rescoring, are compared in both recognition performance and processing time. Those methods are described in Section 4.4. The last two methods exploit a rescoring technique to save processing time.

Secondly, we describe a novel approach of the unsupervised adaptation based on adaptation data weighting. Compared with supervised adaptation, the performance of the unsupervised mode is insufficient. This is because that recognition errors in the adaptation data cause adverse effect. In order to solve the problem, we propose the method of adaptation data weighting based on part-of-speech (POS) class. The basic idea is that only the speech segments which have low degree of confidence are omitted from the adaptation data. The details of this technique are described in Section 4.5.

4.2 Acoustic Model Adaptation

In the recognition experiments, we employ standard maximum-likelihood linear regression (MLLR) technique for speaker adaptation

(Gales, 1998). The number of regression classes is determined automatically based on the amount of adaptation data. The adaptation data of more than 16 seconds per class are guaranteed. The maximum number of classes is 33 (= #phoneme classes). For diagonal covariance models, mixture weights, mean and variance are adapted. While mixture weights and mean are adapted for block-diagonal covariance models.

4.3 Language Model Adaptation

Figure 1 shows the overview of the class-based unsupervised language model (LM) adaptation which is used in our experiments. Words are categorized based on part-of-speech (POS) tagging. The language model adaptation method consists of the following steps.

1. A baseline N-gram is trained by using a large amount of training texts. Also, the frequency of occurrence of POS sequences is counted from them.
2. Whole utterances of adaptation data are recognized by using the baseline N-gram. The recognition results are used for the adaptation. Note that recognition errors are included in the results.

Figure 1. An overview of the class-based language model adaptation

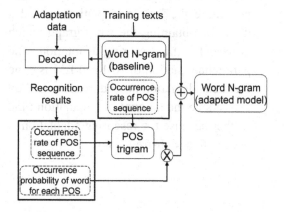

3. The occurrence of POS sequences is counted from the recognition results.
4. POS N-gram language model is calculated by using the count of occurrences of POS sequences from both step (1) and step (3). The N-gram probability of POS sequences is calculated as follows:

$$P(c_i \mid c_{i-N+1} \cdots c_{i-1}) = \frac{N_0(c_{i-N+1} \cdots c_i) + W \cdot N(c_{i-N+1} \cdots c_i)}{N_0(c_{i-N+1} \cdots c_{i-1}) + W \cdot N(c_{i-N+1} \cdots c_{i-1})},$$

(1)

where $N_0()$ and $N()$ are the number of POS sequences counted from training texts and recognition results, respectively. W is a linear interpolation coefficient and is determined on a trial basis.

5. An adapted language model is created by linearly interpolating the baseline LM obtained at step (1) and the POS LM obtained at step (4) as follows:

$$P'(w_i \mid w_{i-N+1} \cdots w_{i-1}) = \lambda P(w_i \mid w_{i-N+1} \cdots w_{i-1}) + (1 - \lambda) P(w_i \mid c_i) P(c_i \mid c_{i-N+1} \cdots c_{i-1}).$$

(2)

The first term of the right hand side is the probability of word N-gram and the second term is that of POS N-gram. $P(w_i | c_i)$ is the occurrence probability of word for each POS class and λ indicates a linear interpolation coefficient. From the results of a preliminary experiment, λ is set to 0.7 and the number of POS classes is set to 316 considering both type and form of inflection.

4.4 Iterated Adaptation for Acoustic Model and Language Model

Figure 2 shows the iterated adaptation methods for acoustic model and language model. The details of these methods are as follows:

Figure 2. Four types of acoustic and language model adaptation

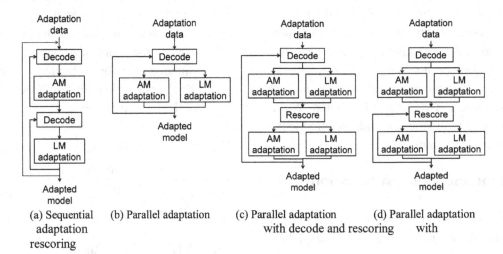

(a) Sequential adaptation rescoring

(b) Parallel adaptation

(c) Parallel adaptation with decode and rescoring

(d) Parallel adaptation with

a. **Sequential adaptation.** First, acoustic model (AM) adaptation is done iteratively. After the adaptation, language model adaptation is carried out iteratively. Finally, those two steps (AM and LM adaptation procedures) are iteratively carried out until performance improvement is converged. By comparing the AM and LM adaptation procedures, we can see that the performance of the AM adaptation overcomes that of the LM adaptation. That is the reason why the AM adaptation is done first. For both the AM and LM adaptation, the recognition results by using decoder are used for the adaptation data.

b. **Parallel adaptation.** The adaptation data are shared by both AM adaptation and LM adaptation. At the first iteration, both updated AM and LM are obtained in parallel. The parallel procedure is carried out iteratively. For the parallel adaptation, the recognition results by the decoder are used for the adaptation data.

c. **Parallel adaptation with decode and rescoring.** This method is similar to that described in b). Both AM and LM are adapted in parallel. However, unlike the method b), both the recognition results by the decoder and the rescoring results are used as adaptation data alternately. We label the former as decode adaptation, and the latter as rescoring adaptation. A word graph created from the decoder in 1st pass is rescored by using adapted AM and LM in the rescoring adaptation procedure and the recognition results are obtained. Compared with the decode adaptation, computational cost can be reduced to one-fifth in the rescoring adaptation.

d. **Parallel adaptation with rescoring.** In this method, the rescoring adaptation is repeatedly carried out with the exception of the first adaptation procedure. In the first procedure, the decode adaptation method is done for obtaining the word graph which is used for the rescoring adaptation. The parallel adaptation of AM and LM is done for each adaptation procedure. The method can reduce the amount of calculation time further because the rescoring adaptation is used with a high-frequency.

4.5 Adaptation Data Weighting Based on POS Class

In the unsupervised speaker adaptation, recognition results are used for the data of adaptation. Since the results contain recognition errors, the performance of the unsupervised adaptation is lower than that of the supervised adaptation. In order to improve the performance of unsupervised adaptation, the use of confidence measures has been proposed in some previous works (Kemp et al., 1999; Wallhoff et al., 2000; Ogata et al., 2002). The basic idea is that only the speech segments which have high degree of confidence are used for adaptation data. In the confidence measure based approach, posterior probabilities are sometimes used for calculating the measure (Ogata et al., 2002).

In this chapter, we propose a novel approach of unsupervised speaker adaptation based on POS class for spontaneous speech recognition. Unlike read speech, irregular expressions such as repairs, hesitations, filled pauses, unclear pronunciation and so on are observed in spontaneous speech. These irregularities do not appear in a sentence randomly, but the statistical bias of the appearance position can be found. For example, fillers and interjections appear frequently at the beginning of a sentence. In a similar way, unclear pronunciation is observed frequently in particular POS segments. Table 1 shows an occurrence rate and a phoneme error rate for each POS class. The phoneme error rate from 6.94% to 15.05% was obtained for 8 POS classes. However, a worse error rate for 3 classes (filler, interjection and prefix) was obtained. Since the occurrence rate of these 3 classes is low for read speech, the problem is not significant. However, that is a problem for spontaneous speech in which unclear pronunciation is observed frequently.

In order to solve the problem, we propose the method of adaptation data weighting based on POS class. In this method, POS classes which indicate high error rates are omitted from adapta-

Table 1. Occurrence rate and phoneme error rate for each POS class

ID	Part of speech	Occurrence rate (%)	Phoneme error rate (%)
1	Noun	33.36	11.95
2	Particle	26.63	12.19
3	Verb	12.61	11.91
4	Auxiliary verb	8.49	6.94
5	Pre-noun adjectival	2.31	10.11
6	Adverb	2.08	13.96
7	Conjunction	1.82	15.05
8	Adjective	0.95	11.82
9	Filler	3.78	30.74
10	Interjection	2.70	34.33
11	Prefix	0.87	26.09
	(Deletion error)	4.38	-

tion data or given low weights for adaptation. This will enable to reduce the problem of recognition errors. Since the information of POS classes is obtained from the recognition results, it may be mistaken. However, the error rates of POS classes are much lower than those of word classes because the number of POS classes is very small.

5. EXPERIMENTAL CONDITIONS

5.1 System Configuration

In the recognition experiments, a two-pass search decoder using word 2-gram and 3-gram is used. In the first pass, word graphs are generated with acoustic models and 2-gram language model. In the second pass, 3-gram language model is applied for re-scoring the word graphs and recognition results are obtained. Decoding is conducted by a one-pass algorithm in which a frame-synchronous beam search and a tree-structured lexicon are applied in the first pass.

In the speech analysis module, a speech signal is digitized at a sampling frequency of 16kHz and at a quantization size of 16bits with the Hamming window. The length of the analysis frame is 25ms and the frame period is set to 8ms. The 13-dimensional feature (12-dimensional MFCC and log power) is derived from the digitized samples for each frame. Additionally, the delta and delta-delta features are calculated from MFCC feature and log power. Then the total number of dimensions is 39. The 39-dimentional parameters are normalized by the cepstral mean normalization (CMN) method which can reduce the adverse effect of channel distortion.

A set of shared state triphones is used as acoustic model. The topology of it is represented by a hidden Markov network (HM-Net) which has been proposed by (Takami et al., 1992). The HM-Net is a network efficiently representing context dependent left-to-right HMMs which have various state lengths and share their states each other. Each node of the network is corresponding to an HMM state and has following information:

- state number,
- acceptable context class,
- lists of preceding states and succeeding states,
- parameters of the output probability density distribution,
- state transition probabilities.

When the HM-Net is given, a model corresponding to a context can be derived by concatenating states which can accept the context from the starting node to the ending node. The structure of HM-Net is determined by the state clustering-based method proposed by (Hori et al., 1998).

The acoustic models we used are 2000 or 3000-state HM-Nets. The number of mixture components is 16. Both block-diagonal covariance and diagonal covariance HM-Nets are used. In the former, correlations between static, delta or delta-delta coefficients are assumed to be zero, however, the information of other correlations is used. In the latter, no correlation of coefficients is considered.

5.2 Training and Evaluation Data

The CSJ consists of monologues such as academic presentations and extemporaneous presentations. In our experiments, academic presentations are used for training and test data. The set of training data consisted of 203 hours speech data uttered by 963 speakers and is used for parameter estimation of acoustic models. The evaluation set we use is 'testset1' which consisted of 10 male speakers. This is one of the standard test sets in CSJ corpus.

Language model is trained from 2,668 lectures' worth of text data in the CSJ and the total number of words is 6.86M. Those lectures consist of both academic presentations and extemporaneous presentations. Trained language model have 47,099 word-pronunciation entries. As we described above, trigram and bigram language models are used in the system. Witten-Bell discounting method is used to compute back-off coefficients.

The evaluation sets have been pre-segmented by detecting sentences with the power lower than given threshold. For read speech, it is relatively easy to detect a sentence by using a pause segment. However, the pause segment does not always appear only at the end of a sentence in spontaneous speech. Since it sometimes appears everywhere in the sentence, there is a possibility that the detected segment does not match sentence expression.

6. RECOGNITION EXPERIMENTS

6.1 Baseline Performance of Acoustic Models

The recognition performance of baseline systems is shown in Table 2. This table shows the word error rate (WER) for various kinds of acoustic models. The number of iteration was five for parameter estimation of the diagonal covariance models. For the training of block-diagonal covariance models, parameters were estimated twice or four times additionally by setting the diagonal covariance models as initial models. The number of mixture components was set to 16 for each model. The block-diagonal system shows better performance than that of diagonal system.

6.2 Recognition Results of Iterated Adaptation

Before we investigated the iterated adaptation techniques, we conducted the preliminary experiments concerning the weights of the occurrence of POS sequences. In the equation (1), W is a linear interpolation coefficient for combining the information from training data and adaptation data. To find an optimal W, some recognition experiments were conducted varying the value. From the results, the best performance could be achieved by setting W to zero. This means that the information from the training data is important regarding the POS class. Then, W was set to zero for following experiments.

Figure 3 indicates the performance comparison of the four iterated adaptation techniques. We compared the performance in terms of processing speed and WER. WERs of both the diagonal covariance model and the block-diagonal covariance model

Table 2. Comparison between diagonal and block-diagonal models (WER%). The number of mixture components was 16

#states	Diagonal	Block-diagonal
#iterations	5	+2
2000	21.91	20.19
3000	20.79	19.32
#iterations	-	+4
3000	-	19.17

are shown in the figure. The method (a) (sequential adaptation) achieved the best performance in WER. WERs of 14.73% by the block-diagonal covariance model and 16.11% by the diagonal covariance model could be obtained respectively. However, it requires a large computational cost. In the comparison of the diagonal covariance model and the block-diagonal covariance model, the block-diagonal one shows better performance in WER for every experiment.

Although the method (c) requires much less calculation cost than the method (b), both the methods indicate similar recognition performance. The reason why the method (c) could save the calculation cost was that the rescoring adaptation which could reduce the calculation time by about 80% compared with the decode adaptation was used in every other iteration step. However, the method (d) in which the rescoring adaptation was used in every iteration step showed the worst recognition performance among all methods. A word graph derived from the decoder is rescored by using adapted AM and LM in the rescoring adaptation method. In the method (d), the word graph was created by the decoder with an initial AM which was not adapted. Then, the word graph was considered to contain more recognition errors and this is the reason why the performance of the method (d) is low.

6.3 Recognition Results of Adaptation Data Weighting

From the investigation results of Table 1, various weights were added to eight classes out of eleven POS classes. For the other three classes (filler, interjection and prefix), weight was set to one respectively. This is because the recognition performance of these three classes is insufficient. By adding the smaller weights to these classes, adverse affect of recognition errors can be reduced. In the experiments, we used the adapted model by the sequential adaptation method as an initial model. Another one iteration of adaptation with

Figure 3. Performance comparison among four iterated adaptation methods. (a): Sequential adaptation. (b): Parallel adaptation. (c): Parallel adaptation with decode and rescoring. (d): Parallel adaptation with rescoring.

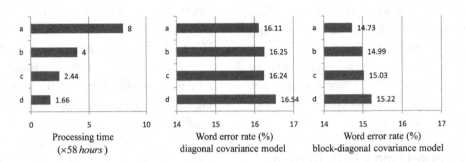

data weighting was carried out by using the initial model. Table 3 shows the recognition results of the adaptation data weighting method. Both the diagonal and block-diagonal models were used for adaptation. The weights were varied from 1.0 to 9.0 to find the optimal performance. The best performance is indicated by boldface. The lowest error rate of 15.82% was achieved at the weight of 5.0 by using the diagonal model and 14.55% at the weight of 7.0 by using the block-diagonal model. The total occurrence rate of the three classes which had lower weights was only 7.35%. However, the results have demonstrated the effects of the data weighting method.

6.4 Recognition Results of Supervised Adaptation

In order to investigate the upper limit of the performance of the unsupervised adaptation, we conducted recognition experiments by using a supervised adaptation technique. Unlike the un-supervised adaptation, the correct transcription is given in the supervised adaptation. Then, there is no adverse effect of recognition errors and the results by the supervised mode are considered to be the upper limit of the recognition performance. Table 4 shows the results of performance comparison between the unsupervised and supervised modes. In this table, Graph Error Rate (GER) indicates the error rate of a word graph generated by 1st pass. Since there are several word hypotheses in the word graph, the GER indicates a smaller number than WER. Word Graph Density (WGD) is defined as the number of word hypotheses per spoken word in the word graph. WER in the table indicates the word error rate for 2nd pass. From the results, we found that the difference in performance between unsupervised and supervised modes remains relatively large. Thus, the unsupervised adaptation leaves much to be improved. Note that WGD can be reduced by both the adaptation modes. For example, a WGD of 62 could be reduced to 23 by the unsupervised adaptation procedure with a diagonal covariance model. This means that word hypotheses can be

Table 3. Word error rates of the method of adaptation data weighting (%)

	Baseline	Weights				
		1.0	3.0	5.0	7.0	9.0
Diagonal	16.11	16.05	15.87	**15.82**	-	-
Block-diagonal	14.73	14.70	14.58	14.56	**14.55**	14.56

Table 4. Performance comparison between unsupervised and supervised adaptation

	w/o adaptation	unsupervised	supervised
Diagonal			
GER (%)	7.06	6.33	3.09
WGD	62	23	27
WER (%)	20.79	16.11	9.90
Block-diagonal			
GER (%)	6.63	5.73	2.87
WGD	57	23	27
WER (%)	19.17	14.73	9.38

narrowed down, and then a highly-accurate graph can be obtained.

7. FUTURE RESEARCH DIRECTIONS

In order to improve the performance of spontaneous speech recognition, we described a new approach of unsupervised adaptation. The research field of spontaneous speech recognition itself should be considered at an early or middle stage. Mainly we dealt with lecture speech recognition in this chapter. In the lecture speech recognition, only one speaker is a target of recognition. Meanwhile there are many types of spontaneous speech including lectures, meetings, broad cast news, face-to-face conversation, conversation through telephone, and so on. Spontaneity or informality of speech differs among these speech types. Also, the number of speakers differs among them. Furthermore, there is a large variety of spontaneity among speakers, even if the speech style is same. In Japan, the CSJ is available for the research of spontaneous speech recognition. However, there are not so many speech corpora for this research field. The CSJ mainly consists of lecture or presentation speech. For more complex recognition task such as meetings, face-to-face conversation and so on, adaptation techniques

are very important because rich Japanese speech corpus for developing the recognition system of these speech styles are not available now.

From the comparison results between the unsupervised and supervised adaptation modes, we can see that the difference in performance between the two remains large. This means that recognition errors of the adaptation data cause adverse effect. Based on this point of view, techniques of adaptation data selection or weighting are crucial. In order to recognize more difficult speech task in which the variety of spontaneity or informality is significant, we plan to develop more effective data selection and weighting methods.

8. CONCLUSION

In this chapter, we described the unsupervised adaptation techniques in order to improve the performance of spontaneous speech recognition. It is well known that recognition accuracy drastically decreases for spontaneous speech compared with the performance of read speech. Utterances of spontaneous speech have a vast variation both acoustically and linguistically. They have hesitations, filled pauses, unknown words, unclear pronunciation, and so on.

In order to increase the performance of spontaneous speech recognition, we proposed several methods of unsupervised adaptation for LVSCR and evaluated the methods by using diagonal-covariance and full-covariance HMMs. A mismatch between trained acoustic / language models and input utterances is a major reason of poor performance. Then, we investigated both techniques of LM adaptation and AM adaptation. In the adaptation procedure, both the techniques were combined in several ways. Four types of iterated adaptation methods, i.e., (a) Sequential adaptation, (b) Parallel adaptation, (c) Parallel adaptation with decode and rescoring and (d) Parallel adaptation with rescoring, were compared in both recognition performance and processing time. From the results, we found that the use of rescoring results in iterated adaptation procedure could save processing time without significant performance degradation.

Unlike supervised adaptation, correct transcription is not given in unsupervised adaptation. Instead of the correct transcription, recognition results are used for the transcription in the unsupervised mode. Then, the adaptation performance of the unsupervised mode is lower than that of the supervised mode. In order to decrease the adverse effect, we proposed a new weighting method of adaptation data. For this problem, confidence measures based on posterior probabilities are used to select adaptation data in general. In contrast, our proposed method is based on POS class. In the proposed method, the POS classes with higher error rates of recognition have low weights for adaptation. This is because unclear pronunciation is observed frequently in particular POS segments in spontaneous speech. From the recognition results, the method that smaller weights were given to three POS classes (filler, interjection and prefix) was effective.

This chapter has focused on unsupervised adaptation for lecture speech recognition. However, the techniques discussed in this chapter are expected to be applicable to more difficult spontaneous speech task such as meetings, face-to-face conversation and so on. We plan to challenge these difficult tasks by using the unsupervised acoustic and language adaptation.

REFERENCES

Bellegarda, J. R. (2004). Statistical language model adaptation: Review and perspectives. *Speech Communication*, *42*(1), 93–108. doi:10.1016/j.specom.2003.08.002

Chen, S. F. (2003). Compiling large-context phonetic decision trees into finite-state transducers. [Geneva, Switzerland.]. *Proceedings of Interspeech*, *2003*, 1169–1172.

Chen, S. F., Kingsburg, B., Mangu, L., Povey, D., Saon, G., Saltau, H., & Zweig, G. (2006). Advances in speech transcription at IBM under the DARPA EARS program. *IEEE Transactions in Audio. Speech and Language Processing*, *14*(5), 1596–1608. doi:10.1109/TASL.2006.879814

Evermann, G., Chan, H. Y., Gales, M. J. F., Jia, B., Mrva, D., Woodland, P. C., & Yu, K. (2005). Training LVCSR systems on thousands of hours of data. [Philadelphia, PA.]. *Proceedings of, ICASSP2005*, 209–212.

Federico, M. (1996). Bayesian estimation methods for N-gram language model adaptation. [Philadelphia, PA.]. *Proceedings of, ICSLP96*, 240–243.

Fiscus, J. G. (1997). A post-processing system to yield reduced word error rates: Recognizer output voting error reduction (ROVER). *Proceedings 1997 IEEE Workshop on Automatic Speech Recognition and Understanding* (pp.347-352). Santa Barbara, CA.

Furui, S. (2005a). Recent progress in corpus-based spontaneous speech recognition. *IEICE Transactions on Information and Systems. E (Norwalk, Conn.)*, *88-D*(3), 366–375.

Furui, S., Nakamura, M., Ichiba, T., & Iwano, K. (2005b). Analysis and recognition of spontaneous speech using corpus of spontaneous Japanese. *Speech Communication*, *47*, 208–219. doi:10.1016/j.specom.2005.02.010

Gales, M. J. F. (1998). Maximum likelihood linear transformations for HMM-based speech recognition. *Computer Speech & Language*, *12*(2), 75–98. doi:10.1006/csla.1998.0043

Giuliani, D., & Brugnara, F. (2006). Acoustic model adaptation with multiple supervisions, *Proceedings of the TC-STAR Workshop on Speech-to-Speech Translation* (pp.151-154). Trento, Italy.

Hori, T., Katoh, M., Ito, A., & Kohda, M. (1998). A study on a state clustering-based topology design method for HM-Nets. *IEICE Transactions on Information and Systems, J81-D-II*(10), 2239-2248.

Juang, B. H., & Katagiri, S. (1992). Discriminative learning for minimum error classification. *IEEE Transactions on Signal Processing, 40*(12), 3043–3054. doi:10.1109/78.175747

Kemp, T., & Waibel, A. (1999). Unsupervised training of a speech recognizer: Recent experiments. *Proceedings of Eurospeech99* (pp. 2725-2728). Budapest, Hungary.

Leggetter, C. J., & Woodland, P. C. (1995). Maximum likelihood linear regression for speaker adaptation of continuous-density hidden Markov models. *Computer Speech & Language, 9*, 171–185. doi:10.1006/csla.1995.0010

Maekawa, K. (2003). Corpus of spontaneous Japanese: Its design and evaluation. *Proceedings of IEEE-ISCA Workshop on Spontaneous Speech Processing and Recognition* (pp. 7-12). Tokyo, Japan.

Mangu, L., Brill, E., & Stolcke, A. (2000). Finding consensus in speech recognition: Word error minimization and other applications of confusion networks. *Computer Speech & Language, 14*, 373–400. doi:10.1006/csla.2000.0152

Masataki, H., Sagisaka, Y., Hisaki, K., & Kawahara, T. (1997). Task adaptation using MAP estimation in N-gram language model. [Munich, Germany.]. *Proceedings of, ICASSP97*, 783–786.

Matsoukas, S., Gauvain, J.-L., Adda, G., Colthurst, T., Kao, C.-L., & Kimball, O. (2006). Advances in transcription of broadcast news and conversational telephone speech within the combined EARS BBN/LIMSI system. *IEEE Transactions in Audio. Speech and Language Processing, 14*(5), 1541–1556. doi:10.1109/TASL.2006.878257

Mimura, M., & Kawahara, T. (2007). Effect of minimum phone error training for spontaneous speech recognition tasks. *Proceedings of Acoustical Society of Japan 2009 Autumn Meeting*, (p. 134). Kofu, Japan.

Moore, G., & Young, S. (2000). Class-based language model adaptation using mixtures of word-class weights. [Beijing, China.]. *Proceedings of, ICSLP2000*, 512–515.

Nakamura, A., Oba, T., Watanabe, S., Ishizuka, K., Fujimoto, M., & Hori, T. ... Minami Y. (2006). *Evaluation of the SOLON speech recognition system: 2006 benchmark using the corpus of spontaneous Japanese.* (IEICE Technical Report, SP2006-127), (pp. 73-78). Nagoya, Japan.

Ogata, J., & Ariki, Y. (2002). Unsupervised acoustic model adaptation based on phoneme error minimization. [Denver, CO.]. *Proceedings of, ICSLP2002*, 1429–1432.

Ohkura, K., Sugiyama, M., & Sagayama, S. (1992). Speaker adaptation on transfer vector field smoothing with continuous mixture density HMMs. [Banff, Canada.]. *Proceedings of, ICSLP92*, 369–372.

Povey, D., Kingsbury, B., Mangu, L., Saon, G., Soltau, H., & Zweig, G. (2005). fMPE: Discriminatively trained features for speech recognition. [Philadelphia, PA.]. *Proceedings of, ICASSP2005*, 961–964.

Povey, D., & Woodland, P. C. (2002). Minimum phone error and I-smoothing for improved discriminative training. [Orlando, FL.]. *Proceedings of, ICASSP2002*, 105–108.

Shinoda, K., Iso, K., & Watanabe, T. (1991). Speaker adaptation for demi-syllable-based continuous-density HMM. [Toronto, Canada.]. *Proceedings of, ICASSP91*, 857–860.

Takami, J., & Sagayama, S. (1992). A successive state splitting algorithm for efficient allophone modeling. [San Francisco, CA.]. *Proceedings of, ICASSP92*, 573–576.

Tsutsumi, R., Katoh, M., Kosaka, T., & Kohda, M. (2006). Lecture speech recognition using pronunciation variant modeling. *IEICE Transactions on Information and Systems, J89-D*(2), 305-313 (in Japanese).

Wallhoff, F., Willett, D., & Rigoll, G. (2000). Frame-discriminative and confidence-driven adaptation for LVCSR. [Istanbul, Turkey.]. *Proceedings of, ICASSP2000*, 1835–1838.

Yamamoto, H., & Sagisaka, Y. (2001). A language model adaptation using multiple varied corpora. [Trento, Italy.]. *Proceedings of, ASRU2001*, 389–392.

Yokoyama, T., Shinozaki, T., Iwano, K., & Furui, S. (2003). Unsupervised language model adaptation using word classes for spontaneous speech recognition. *Proceedings of IEEE-ISCA Workshop on Spontaneous Speech Processing and Recognition* (pp. 71-74). Tokyo, Japan.

KEY TERMS AND DEFINITIONS

Hidden Markov Model (HMM): A statistical model represented by Markov chain whose internal state is not observed directly. It is well known for the application in temporal pattern recognition.

Large Vocabulary Continuous Speech Recognition (LVCSR): A speech recognition system operates on speech in which words are connected together. The size of vocabulary that can be recognized is large (tens of thousands of words).

Multi-Pass System: A speech recognizer which uses multi-pass decoding algorithms in order to speed up the search. In the algorithms, each pass prepares information of word hypotheses for the next one to reduce the size of search space.

Speaker Adaptation: A variety of speaker characteristics sometimes causes adverse effect on the performance of speech recognition. In order to learn speaker characteristics, acoustic model parameters are re-estimated on small quantities of speech data. This process is referred to as speaker adaptation.

Speech Corpus: State-of-the-art speech recognition systems use HMMs as acoustic models and N-gram based language models. In order to train these statistical models, a large amount of speech and text data is required. Speech corpora have been developed to provide the training data. They are also used for system evaluation.

Word Graph Rescoring: A word graph incorporates a large number of recognition hypotheses. In a second pass decoding, the best word sequence is obtained by using some kind of constraints such as language models. This process is referred to as a word graph rescoring.

Word Graph: In the multi-pass system, information of word hypotheses is prepared at each pass. The output format for the intermediate results is referred to as a word graph or lattice.

Chapter 17
Benefits and Challenges of E–Learning:
University Student Perspectives

Su-Chen Wang
National Cheng-Kung University, Taiwan

ABSTRACT

E-learning has altered, and will continue to affect teaching and learning contexts in universities and tertiary education worldwide, including in Taiwan. Many universities in Taiwan have moved to offer courses that include both face-to-face and e-learning but very little research has been undertaken on student perspectives. The issue about whether e-learning can bring benefits to improve student learning or students will face more challenges is a concern of many researchers and educators. This chapter explores the benefits and challenges of e-learning support from student perspectives in a national research-oriented university in Taiwan. An interpretive paradigm with quantitative and qualitative methods was adopted as the basis for the research methodology. This chapter outlines the findings from a survey of nearly 400 different college students and focus group discussions with over thirty students about their perceptions and experiences of e-learning in blended learning courses. SPSS were used to analyze the data of the questionnaires and interviews. The findings suggest that students experience benefits and challenges relating to their personal perception of e-learning, learning attitude, personal expertise with ICT, use and access to the requisite technology. Students perceived the benefits of e-learning as arising from being able to preview and follow up on face-to-face lectures and to discuss ideas and issues with peers and instructors given that class sizes are large, typically over a hundred students. Respondent students indicated e-learning might help them change their learning attitudes to become more active and diligent learners and also improve their personal time management and organizational ability. However, the findings from questionnaires and interviews also identified students face personal and technological challenges. The researcher expects the findings can contribute to enhancing the university e-learning practice and improving instructor teaching and student learning in e-learning. The university and instructors need to identify the perceived benefits and challenges of e-learning and provide practical support for student learning. Students also need to change their perceptions and learning attitude to e-learning.

DOI: 10.4018/978-1-61520-871-5.ch017

I. INTRODUCTION

The use of ICT can remove time and place constraints on teaching and learning to provide the convenience and flexibility that many tertiary students, particularly graduate students, are now demanding (Collis & Moonen, 2001; Lao & Gonzales, 2005; Schrum, 2000; Tallent-Runnels, Thomas, Lan, Cooper, & et al., 2006). E-learning is a key component of blended learning and was the catalyst for the rapid growth in this form of learning (Mackay & Stockport, 2006). Currently many institutions are opting for the blended learning delivery of courses (Stubbs, Martin, & Endlar, 2006).

Broadly speaking, e-learning is a network technology-based mode of education that uses a mix of computer and other ICTs, across time and place constraints to deliver instruction and provide access to information resources (OECD, 2005; Wallhaus, 2000). It can involve delivery systems such as videotape, interactive audio-video, CD-ROMs, DVDs, video-conferencing, Video on Demand (VOD), e-mail, live chat, use of the Web, television and satellite broadcasts. Access to these resources means students can do coursework at a time of their convenience, so learning may happen synchronously or asynchronously (Stuart, 2004; Wallhaus, 2000). Blended learning involves a combination of traditional face-to-face and online technology-based learning (Masie, 2001; Singh, 2003; Stubbs, Martin, & Endlar, 2006; Tallent-Runnels, Thomas, Lan, Cooper, *et al.*, 2006; Welker & Berardino, 2005). Shoniregun and Gray (2004) argue that institutions are opting for the blended learning delivery of courses to the extent that it is 'the quiet secret' of e-learning (Masie, 2001). Almost every tertiary institution does more blended learning than is talked about.

Blended courses has been offered in universities in Taiwan but very little research has been undertaken on the perceived benefits and challenges for university students of a blend of e-learning and face-to-face instruction. E-learning allows the delivery of teaching materials electronically and provides students with an anytime/anyplace independent learning environment. This has altered, and will continue to affect, teaching and learning contexts in universities and tertiary education (Salmon & Jones, 2004). The Taiwan government has built up a good ICT infrastructure and encouraged universities to develop e-learning systems but questions such as, "What are the benefits and challenges of e-learning practice for students and instructors?", and, "What are the factors associated with these benefits and challenges?" are being asked by educators in Taiwan.

All teaching and learning, including that in courses delivered solely through or supported by e-learning, relies on significant student participation (Sevilla & Wells, 2000). What are the factors that influence their participation? Research indicates the range of student personal factors important to student experiences of e-learning include student learning attitude, learning approach, sense of learning community, student personal technical knowledge and skills, and perceptions of the convenience and flexibility of e-learning (Berge, 2005; Crabtree, 2006; Motteram, 2006; Shank, 2005). This chapter outlines the study research design and findings from a survey of 376 different college students and focus group discussions with thirty-three students about their perceptions and experiences of e-learning in blended learning courses.

II. THE RESEARCH STUDY

Research has elaborated the benefits of using e-learning suggesting it has the potential to increase institutional reputations, improve quality of teaching and learning, and provide for more flexibility in student learning (e.g., Henderson, 2003). Daugherty & Funke (1998) considered students had been able to expand their learning and knowledge beyond the limitations of knowledge found in the textbook and presented lectures. Also, the students appeared impressed by the variety, quality and flexibility of learning materials offered via the Web (Daugherty & Funke, 1998). Tiene (2000) found students responded positively to the asynchronous aspect of the online class discussions. Asynchronous online discussions allowed students to participate at their own convenience when they had the time to read the comments and the time to develop their own response. There was also time to think about the points made by their peers and time to decide how they felt about certain issues. This self-regulated, self-paced quality of the online discussion experience was one of its most attractive features (Tiene, 2000). Some students prefer asynchronous discussion as it allows them to make more considered responses, while others find a disadvantage in a lack of immediacy (Ellis, 2001; Tiene, 2000). Palloff and Pratt (2001) found those students who "need time to think and reflect before responding to questions and ideas" might be best suited to learn online. In addition, students also find that easy to access resources via the Internet and the institution's library databases rather than memorizing those resources (Spender, 2002) support their independent learning and enhance their learning (Hase & Ellis, 2001; Khoo, Forret, & Cowie, 2003). In sum, research suggests students appreciate the opportunities that online or e-learning offers for them to read, study and reflect any time, any place and at their own pace. They find this motivating and consider it enhances their learning.

Some qualitative research studies have identified student personality traits as influences on their participation in e-learning (Crabtree, 2006; Ellis, 2003; Kim & Schniederjans, 2004). These five personality dimensions may influence student engaged in various e-learning activities in different ways. For example, extraversion has traits such as sociable, gregarious, talkative, and active that is perhaps suitable for online interaction. This implies that student's will to achieve (i.e. conscientiousness) and being responsible, trusting, tolerant and self-controlled are important

personality traits in student learning attitudes which affect their participation and performance in e-learning. Crabtree (2006) found many students prefer to take a passive learning attitude and considered instructors should provide them the knowledge and entertain them in the learning process. Students with passive attitudes wanted more lecture notes and supporting handouts and expressed a preference for tutorials to go over the lecture notes to better ensure they could get good results or marks (Crabtree, 2006). In contrast, students who had an more active view of learning only considered they needed "a brief outline" and related links (rather than handouts) and felt that, ideally, tutorials should provide an opportunity for group work or whole class discussion (Crabtree, 2006). Moreover, Crabtree (2006) also found both groups of students recognized the need for a change in learning approach and the challenge of acquiring the necessary independent learning skills when using e-learning even although students who took an active approach to learning had accepted personal responsibility for their own learning. The main benefits of e-learning are the individualized and self-paced learning processes so student personality traits need to be considered (Crabtree, 2006).

E-learning facilitates this as resources are no longer confined to libraries but are instead more universally accessible via the Internet. However, e-learning also presents several challenges. It requires reliable technological infrastructure and efficient technical support services. Instructors must also adopt different pedagogical approaches and develop the skills needed to work with new media (e.g., Abel, 2005). Similarly, online learning also presents students with a number of challenges. These can include limited access to hardware and software, limited technical knowledge and expertise and a lack of recognition of the need to 'attend' online classes (Lao & Gonzales, 2005). Thus, student views are also important to consider if they are to be the beneficiaries of e-learning practice. Studies of student attitudes and perceptions of e-learning, particularly blended learning are relatively uncommon. In line with this gap in the literature, the research reported here is designed to explore the benefits and challenges of e-learning from student perspectives and also to suggest ways to enhance the practice of e-learning in tertiary education in Taiwan.

III. THE RESEARCH DESIGN AND METHOD

An interpretive paradigm with quantitative and qualitative methods was adopted as the basis for the research methodology because the intention was to capture the richness of participants' experience and perceptions of e-learning practice (Cohen, Manion, & Morrison, 2000). The data for this chapter was obtained from 376 e-learning students' questionnaires which included closed and open-ended questions and from eight focus group interviews of thirty-three students. The questions for the questionnaire and interview were designed and then piloted (by six students in Taiwan) to check for the validity, reliability and practicability of the questions. Seven e-learning instructors have helped to distribute 480 copies of the questionnaire to their students in class. In total, 399 students have returned their completed questionnaire. However, of these, 23 students only answered the first section of the questionnaire but did not answer the remaining sections. For reliability and validity reasons, the researcher did not count those respondents. Thus, the response rate is 78% (=376/480). The questionnaire for students contained a mix of closed, quantitative and open-ended, qualitative questions. Data received from the questionnaire were put onto computer disks for further analysis. The qualitative responses were coded and categorized in an interpretive manner and were also quantified.

With the written permission of all the participants, each interview was audio taped and lasted 60-110 minutes. Open-ended and leading questions were mutually employed in the interviews in order to allow freedom of expression and lead to increased focus on the study. In the interviews 33 volunteer students from different colleges within eight focus groups were asked to describe benefits and challenges they faced and the factors influencing their use of e-learning. Each participating group was asked the same questions however as the interviews were open not all focus groups discussed the questions in the same depth. The interviews and data in the open-ended questions in the questionnaire were transcribed verbatim by the researcher and the transcripts were verified by two other people who volunteered to check its validity and reliability and by the researcher through a comparison with the audio tapes and notes from the interview session. The researcher read the transcripts and manually highlighted the quotes that fitted into categories. Each response in the interviews and open-ended questions of questionnaires was coded against these categories. Some responses were counted in two or more categories. SPSS and Excel were used to analyze the data of the questionnaires and interviews. All data collected and reported was coded to provide a reference to the data and to protect the anonymity of the data source. All percentages in the quantitative data analysis are rounded to the nearest full percent, therefore totals do not always add to 100% in the results. The major themes regarding student personal benefits and challenges of e-learning raised by students in the questionnaires and interviews were identified and are presented below.

IV. THE FINDINGS

E-learning in this study refers to the online component of blended learning. As such it has its own benefits and challenges. The aim of this focus was to obtain students' perceptions and experiences of the benefits and challenges of e-learning and these will be considered as factors influencing their use of e-learning. This section describes student perceived benefits and challenges of e-learning practice from the quantitative questionnaire and qualitative interview data.

1. Student Perceived Benefits

Data on the benefits of using e-learning came from closed questions in the student questionnaire and the focus-group interviews. Questionnaire students were asked to select benefits from a list and then go back to put a second tick beside the benefits they considered important for their use of e-learning. They could tick as many categories as applied. Of the 376 respondents to the question-naire, 363 answered the question asking them to select the benefits of the e-learning in a blended learning course format. Three hundred and fifty-two of these respondents also indicated which benefits they found important. Based on the data analysis of student selections of e-learning ben-efits from the questionnaires and the descriptions from the focus-group interviews, five categories

of e-learning benefits were identified: flexibility of learning, increased ICT knowledge and skills, better student learning and learning outcomes, improvement of interaction and savings in course cost and time. The questionnaire and interview responses are summarized in Table 1.

(1) Flexibility of Learning

Flexibility of learning was the benefit of e-learning most commonly perceived by students. A majority (92%-334) of questionnaire students and all eight student focus groups identified flexibility of time and place of learning a benefit of their use of e-learning resources. Seventy-seven percent rated it as the most important benefit. The flexibility of e-learning offers greater ongoing access to course materials for student review any time, any place and at their own pace. As has been discussed, students reported e-learning as a convenient way for them to verify and familiarize themselves with course materials and content, particularly before exams. Online material was also helpful if students

Table 1. Frequencies of benefits for the students and found important

Category	Benefit	Respondents (questionnaire)		Found important		Number of groups (Interview)
		N1 (=363)	% of N1	N2 (=352)	% of N2	N3 (=8)
Flexibility of learning	Flexibility of learning at time and place	334	92%	271	77%	8
Increased ICT knowledge and skills	Improve ability to adapt to the infor-mation age	251	69%	175	50%	6
Improve student learning and learning outcomes	Easily manage assignments or reports	240	66%	154	44%	5
	Help to identify their understanding	168	46%	102	29%	
	Improve their learning quality	154	42%	103	29%	
	Improve motivation	127	35%	76	22%	
Improvement of interac-tion	Improve interactions with instructors	173	48%	115	33%	4
	Improve participation and coopera-tion	142	39%	91	26%	
	Improve interactions with peers	139	38%	89	25%	

N1: Questionnaire respondent students

N2: Questionnaire respondent students found this important

N3: Number of focus interview student groups

were absent from class. A student from Focus Group C summarized these benefits:

We can review the course content at our convenience. Sometimes we could be absent from class and review unfamiliar parts of class work after class or before a test... especially for the theory course, we could not remember or understand all the procedures of a proof or solution processes so we needed to review the video files after class. (SgCi.2.6.1)

(2) Increased ICT Knowledge and Skills

Over three fifths (69%-251) of students and six groups of interviewees regarded the improvement in their ability to use technology adaptable to the information age as a benefit arising from their use of e-learning. Overall, half (50%-175) of the students said it was important. Interviewees said e-learning could help students increase their ICT knowledge and skills to adapt to the current information age and become life-long learners. As a student from Focus Group C said:

The application of e-learning includes many kinds of learning activities online and it needs high literacy of technical knowledge and skills to engage in. Our instructors provide us various online course materials and different types of interactions so we need to learn how to use different sorts of computer technologies and multimedia facilities to access them. We think e-learning could increase our ICT knowledge and skills to adapt to the current 'information age' or 'knowledge economy age'. Although many e-contents are not related to our current course study, we are very interested on them and we hope we can learn them for a lifelong. (SgCi.4.6.8)

(3) Improve Student Learning and Learning Outcomes

The benefits included ease in managing assignments or reports; help in identifying their particular areas of understanding; improving the learning quality; and improving motivation were identified. Sixty percent (240) and five groups of interviewees noted e-learning made it easier for them to manage their homework or reports with 44% (154) respondents saying this was important for them. Interviewees said the e-learning system allowed them to submit their homework or reports online and their instructor often required them to submit it before the due date. They noted this benefit forced them to manage their study program and improve their learning outcomes. They said they could keep all their academic work online. Nearly half (46%-168) of the students indicated greater opportunities for self assessment, which had in turn helped them identify content areas they understood poorly. They could then do more relevant study. Twenty-nine percent (102) of students said this was important to them. Some students identified an improvement in student learning quality (42%-152), with 103 (29%) saying this was an important benefit. Respondents also reported e-learning could improve student motivation to study (35%-127), with 76 saying this was an important benefit of their use of e-learning. These benefits suggested e-learning could provide students with different sorts of independent learning approaches and help them become more active, self-motivated and self-managed learners and, as a result, they thought their learning outcomes were better.

(4) Improvement of Interaction

Nearly half (48%-173) of the questionnaire respondents and four focus groups reported e-learning had improved their interactions with course instructors, with 44% (154) questionnaire respondents saying this was important. Respondent interviewees said they often asynchronously (e.g., email) or synchronously (e.g., online discussion) interacted with their instructor outside the class. Nearly two fifths (39%-142) of questionnaire respondents noted e-learning had improved their class participation and cooperation. A quarter (26%-91) reported it was an important benefit. Interviewees noted their instructor provided collaborative projects or online group discussions to motivate student participation and cooperation in e-learning. Some students reported improved interaction with their peers (38%-139), with 25% (89) describing this as important for them. Interviewees reported e-learning provided them with more opportunities and different sorts of interactions with their instructors and peers than face-to-face instruction, especially after class.

(5) Savings in Course Costs and Time

Focus group students reported another benefit of the online quizzes, tests and assignments associated with e-learning was that they could save students money on course paper. Students also noted that they received online answers and results immediately after they submitted them so they did not need to print out the question and answer sheets. Furthermore, students indicated e-learning could save instructors time and effort in printing out and distributing lecture notes, question and answer sheets for the quizzes, tests and assignments and it also saved the university money. This benefit is significant for the university, instructors and students in terms of money and time. There was also an implication that students were motivated to learn because of the immediate response of answers to assignments, quizzes, and tests.

All benefits mentioned above were synthesized from a question asking students to select e-learning benefits from a list in the questionnaire and the descriptions of benefits from focus-group interviews. In sum, student perceived e-learning benefits were e-learning offered flexibility in time and place and own pace of learning; increased ICT knowledge and skills appropriate for the current information age and learn long-life learning; helped the use of more active, diligent and independent learning approaches; provided more opportunities and different sorts of interactions; and saved money and time for students, instructors and the university.

2. Perceived Challenges

This section sets out the descriptions of the challenges students faced in their e-learning courses. The data is from eight groups of students in interviews and the 221 students who responded to an open-ended question in the questionnaire. Based on respondent descriptions and the literature, sub-categories were synthesized from questionnaire and interview responses. Five dominant categories shown in Table 2 were grouped from those sub-categories and will be described in more detail next.

(1) Learning Attitudes

Over two thirds (69%) of questionnaire students and all eight focus groups noted that they needed to change their learning attitudes and roles in the e-learning environment because e-learning demands they become more active, diligent and self-managed learners. Some students from the questionnaire noted they found e-learning's demand for self discipline challenging with requirements of good time management (43%) and good personal organization ability (22%). Some students in the questionnaire reported they did not have an active and diligent learning attitude, so if the online component was not required for course completion (31%), or assessed (24%), they might not use e-learning resources. Some illustrative comments were:

Table 2. Frequencies of challenges students faced

Perceived challenges	N1 (=221)	% of N1	N2 (=8)
Learning attitudes	152	69%	8
Learning approaches	107	48%	5
Interaction approaches	72	33%	4
Technology	50	23%	6
Learning environment	19	9%	3

N1: Questionnaire respondent students
N2: Number of focus interview student groups

E-learning is different from face-to-face learning. The instructor has changed their teaching approaches and role in e-learning so we also need to change our learning attitude, role and learning approaches to adapt to the e-learning. Usually students are passive and lazy in their study. However, e-learning often demands students need to become more active and diligent and have good time management and organization ability because it always takes students much time and effort to engage in the online learning activities. So we need to change our learning attitude and manage our study program well otherwise we will face many challenges in our e-learning. (QS.20.298)

Our instructor often uses many different effective strategies to motivate our engagement in e-learning such as course assignment completion before the due day or assessing our performance in online discussion, so we need to become more active and diligent to meet our e-learning course requirement. (QS.20.352)

All eight focus groups listed the necessity of a course credit for their degree as well as personal interest and learning attitudes to e-learning as factors that influenced their decision to take courses involving e-learning resources because they knew e-learning required extra time and effort to study before or after class. Students feared they were not diligent and active learners, thus in some cases sought to avoid e-learning courses, particularly when instructors rigorously required participation in online discussion, quizzes, tests or assignments, and asked students to preview or review audios/videos. They noted their learning outcomes were reduced if they were not active and diligent learners. A typical comment was:

We face the challenge of a role change for students and instructors. Personal learning attitude is different from that in the traditional F2F instruction. Students must become more active and diligent learners. The information we learned is not just from the instructors but also from others. We need to have self-controlled ability to manage our e-learning time and progress. (SgCi.5.3.2)

(2) Learning Approaches

A new learning approach was required because e-learning instructors adopted different pedagogical approaches to work with the new media in e-learning. Nearly half (48%) of questionnaire students and five focus groups noted that learning approaches such as new teaching and learning methods or assessment change, were the most problematic. Six focus groups reported their instructor usually explained faster than usual in their science e-learning courses because he/she had already put all the formulae statements on PowerPoint files. Students noted they needed to get used to various types of e-content and differences in course attributes influenced their use of e-learning. In addition, the assessment of their learning outcomes was often different from that in F2F instruction. They also worried about the dishonesty and unfairness on their online tests or assignments because some students used cut and paste methods to copy peers' answers.

Students considered the provision of comprehensive e-content might decrease their attendance and or concentration on lectures in class. They also noted increased pressure to keep up with their peers as they were able to observe their progress online through, for example, progress in online assignments or discussions. Conversely, they reported a reduction in pressure from their instructors (e.g. roll-call in class) and felt this could be de-motivating, perhaps allowing them to become lazy. Therefore, students noted they needed to actively manage their e-learning time and programme well. Students in six of the eight focus groups suggested online discussion could become uninteresting and ineffective if their instructors did not make full student engagement in online discussion compulsory. Four groups of students also doubted the effect of awarding additional marks for student performance in online discussion. They noted students in Taiwan seldom actively ask questions but instead wait for others' questions. They proposed students might not know how to ask questions. Combined, these issues suggest students perceived their learning approach impacts upon their use of e-learning, particularly with respect to the need to be more pro-active and organized.

(3) Interaction Approaches

One third (33%) of respondents and four focus groups noted the need for a new interaction approach as a challenge. Some questionnaire respondents indicated they felt uncomfortable facing inhuman computers to ask questions or have discussions with their instructors and or peers. They noted they missed being able to monitor facial expressions and voice tone. A student noted, "In e-learning interaction or discussion, we only can communicate by using words but no facial expressions or body or tone language" (QS.14.36). The students from the focus group interview indicated they experienced two new kinds of interactions in their e-learning courses which were synchronous and asynchronous interactions. Synchronous interactions included online discussions or chat (online group discussion). Asynchronous interactions included online feedback from their instructors or peers on their projects or reports or interactions via email, a bulletin board, or online Q and A. Some issues, such as time-match problems in online group discussion, lacked privacy in some e-learning courses, possible embarrassment or harassment by peers, difficulty including figures, formulae and symbols in their contributions to online discussions, no prompt response, slow and incorrect access, and different demands in communication methods and quality were concerned. Some typical comments were:

The interactions among instructors and peers within e-learning became fewer and worse than the interactions in F2F because the e-learning instructors cannot always respond in a timely manner and the current technologies do not allow the interactions access correctly and fast enough to up-to-date (SgBi.4.3.5).

When we ask questions or discuss with instructors and peers online, it is difficult to express our questions or ideas clearly, especially for mathematical formulae expressions or science symbols (SgEi.5.2.6).

(4) Technology

Technological challenges are defined as challenges surrounding issues of familiarity with new technology and technical problems faced by students, for example, network bandwidth, computer facilities and storage and technology operation. Students commented they encountered four categories of technological challenges: easy access to necessary computer equipment, technical skills to access computer technology and e-learning system, technical skills for communication, and the quality of e-learning computer facilities and technology.

Nearly a quarter (23%-50) of the questionnaire respondents found the technological requirements challenging due to a lack of familiarity with the university e-learning system and the recently updated ICT facilities, as well as with multimedia operation. Similarly, six of the student focus groups reported their peers had difficulties using e-learning systems due to a lack of technical skills. Typically, students reported overcoming these problems by asking peers for help. Some respondents indicated the technology such as a fast speed of network and Internet led them to learn more and easily search more online course or test related information to improve their learning on other non-major subject fields. While access and quality of access was identified as an issue by most students, the nature of access and quality issues was not universal. Students in the focus groups who had an up-to-date laptop requested a wireless environment, whereas others who could not afford to buy laptops hoped the university could provide the advanced technology. Some students indicated miscellaneous multimedia accessories were necessary to improve their learning efficiency and quality such as video-recorders, scanners, and multimedia or audio-visual facilities for interaction or online Q and A.

(5) Learning Environment

Student questionnaire and focus group responses indicate students do indeed believe e-learning resources may aid their learning. However, accessing and using these resources can be time consuming, particularly if the resources are badly organized. Students noted they needed to spend time viewing the videos of lectures, course materials and participating in online discussions. Furthermore, students also concerned about the nature and extent of e-learning course materials and their instructor attitude to the copyright of e-content. Some students had psychological barriers and challenges due to their preference of face-to-face instruction and preference to work from hard copies of resources. Some also mentioned the importance of instructor role in efficiently helping them to overcome learning barriers and solve problems when challenges arose.

Science students indicated they had heavy learning loads in science e-learning because their instructors provided additional e-content. They noted they needed to repeatedly review videos of lessons after class, especially for formulae based lessons, because abstract concepts were not easily understood although their instructors explained the ideas one by one in class.

A stable, reliable, easy-use, fully functional and high performance e-learning system was considered necessary. A high quality network for e-learning practice involving a high enough network bandwidth, fast speed for image presentation, good network management, and enough computer storage space was also considered important.

V. DISCUSSION AND IMPLICATIONS

E-learning in this study has emerged as an alternative mode of teaching and learning and a substantial supplement to traditional face-to-face teaching. As the use of e-learning becomes a mainstream, it has become more important to understand the opportunities to development and barriers in this field. This chapter has described student perceptions of the benefits and challenges of e-learning that were related to personal, pedagogical and technological issues. All benefits and challenges mentioned above were synthesized from student responses to the questionnaire and the focus-group interviews.

A majority of students indicated the main benefit of e-learning for the students is the flexibility of learning. They noted instructors put course materials and audios/videos online before and after class and provided more opportunities for synchronous and asynchronous interactions so they could learn more flexibly in time and place. This finding parallels those of Lao and Gonzales (2005) and Tiene (2000) who found students appreciated being able to view and review e-content at their convenience and at their own pace. The students, however, noted that the flexibility of learning could adversely affect the learning outcomes of any lazy and passive students because they may not attend class and or view e-content before and after class. Respondent students asserted e-learning could benefit and increase student motivation to learn and teach students the importance of self-discipline, learning accountability, and good time management skills. The finding that students need to be self-motivated and organize their own learning including making provision for the time, space and equipment necessary in their use of e-learning is supported by the work of Daugherty and Funke (1998) and Tang (2000). Simultaneously, a majority of students noted e-learning could provide more opportunities and different sorts of interactions to enhance their interactions with instructors and peers and it also could motivate their participation and cooperation in their learning. Moreover, e-learning could increase student ICT knowledge and skills to adapt to the current information age and learn to become life-long learners. These findings are supported by many studies (e.g., Churach & Fisher, 2001;

Focus on Internet News & Data [FIND], 2003). Again, some of participants from focus group noted e-learning could save students much money and time in printing the answer sheets, project reports and or lecture notes. In sum, the findings indicate e-learning can help students have a different but more active and independent learning approach and attitude to improve their learning outcomes and increase their self-managed capacity to be a life-long learner.

A majority of students noted they needed to spend considerable time to preview/review e-content and interact with their instructors and peers online. This was said to lead to learning overload. Along with this, the findings indicate e-learning is considered most beneficial for active and diligent students with a high degree of self-management ability and good technical skills for online access and interaction. These findings resemble those studies by Berge and Lin (2001), Geisman (2001) and Crabtree (2006) in emphasizing student personal learning attitude and capacity could be challenges for student use of e-learning. Furthermore, even though the Taiwan government has worked to provide widespread public access to computers over the last decade, students in both the questionnaire and focus group interviews noted they had experienced difficulties accessing the requisite technology for participation in e-learning. A personal lack of easy access to these technologies, as well as a lack of skills necessary to use available computer and communication technology, had hindered student use of e-learning resources. Some students also faced other technological challenges such as typing formulae and science symbols and putting figures or graphs online. In sum, the findings indicate student individuals saw student learning overload, passive learning attitude, poor capacity of self-management and poor technical skills as personal challenges, and lack of easy and quality access as technological challenges. The need for new learning approaches, course attributes and assessment change were the most problematic pedagogical challenges. Students reported they needed assistance to learn how to use e-learning systems and online course materials, particularly online chatting and discussion functions. This is consistent with Vygotskian theories which emphasize the importance of guided participation (Rogoff, 1991).

There is no one simple solution or best way to provide for e-learning in a blended learning course. When designing and preparing online course material, instructors need to balance the benefits students could gain from reviewing previous materials and considering supplementary ideas with the time this will take students. Not only to read and view the material but also find their way around it if it is not well organized. Instructors would be advised to include guidance for students on how to use and navigate the online component of their course in order to reduce the students' learning load. University administrators would be wise to recognize the benefits and challenges identified here and provide the necessary policy and practical support to minimize those factors that inhibit student use of e-learning practice. Learning via e-learning is not required for all students at this stage, especially for those who have restricted access to computer technologies. However, how to entice more students into e-learning is likely to be a future challenge to university administrators. Understanding each other by among administrators, instructors and students will help in eliminating challenges. Consequently providing more technical and individual support for e-learning practice could motivate students to endeavour to use e-learning.

REFERENCES

Abel, R. (2005). *Achieving success in Internet-supported learning in higher education: Case studies illuminate success factors, challenges, and future directions*. Retrieved April 20, 2005, from http://www.a-hec.org/ research/study_reports/IsL0205/TOC.html

Berge, Z. L. (2005). Taking the distance out of distance education. In Kearsley, G. (Ed.), *Online learning: Personal reflections on the transformation of education*. Englewood Cliffs, NJ: Educational Technology Publications.

Berge, Z. L., & Lin, M. (2001). *Obstacles faced at various stages of capability regarding distance education in institutions of higher education: Survey results*. Retrieved July 9, 2004, from http://www.emoderators.com /barriers/hghred_stgs.shtml

Churach, D., & Fisher, D. (2001). Science students surf the Web: Effects on constructivist classroom environments. *Journal of Computers in Mathematics and Science Teaching, 20*(2), 221–247.

Cohen, L., Manion, L., & Morrison, K. (2000). *Research methods in education* (5th ed.). London, UK: Routledge-Falmer. doi:10.4324/9780203224342

Collis, B., & Moonen, J. (2001). *Flexible learning in a digital world: Experience and expectations*. London, UK: Kogan Page.

Crabtree, H. (2006). *The impact of student centered learning: An evaluation of tutor and student experiences*. 3rd Education in a Changing Environment Conference, University of Salford, UK. Retrieved June 12, 2007 from http://www.edu.salford.ac.uk/ her/proceedings/ papers/hc_06.rtf

Daugherty, M., & Funke, B. L. (1998). University faculty and student perceptions of Web-based instruction. *Journal of Distance Education, 13*(1), 21–39.

Ellis, A. E. (2001). *Student-centred collaborative learning via face-to-face and asynchronous online communication: What's the difference?* Paper presented at the Meeting at the Crossroads: Proceedings of the Eighteenth Annual Conference of the Australasian Society for Computers in Learning in Tertiary Education (ASCILITE), Melbourne, Australia, December 2001, (pp. 169-177).

Ellis, A. E. (2003). Personality type and participation in networked learning environments. *Educational Media International, 40*(1-2), 101–114.

Focus on Internet News & Data. (2003). *Schools online in Taiwan 2002*. Retrieved May 25, 2004, from http://www.find.org.tw/ eng/news.asp?msgid=14& subjectid=4&pos=0

Geisman, J. (2001). I*f you build it, will they come? Overcoming human obstacles to e-learning*. Retrieved May 3, 2004, from http://www.learningcircuits.org/ 2001/mar2001/ elearn.html

Hase, S., & Ellis, A. (2001). Problems with online learning are systemic, not technical. In Stephenson, J. (Ed.), *Teaching and learning online: Pedagogies for new technologies* (pp. 27–34). London, UK: Kogan Page.

Henderson, A. J. (2003). *The e-learning questions and answer book*. New York, NY: Amacom.

Khoo, E. G. L., Forret, M., & Cowie, B. (2003). *Extricating the web of learning: Identifying the characteristics of effective learning environments*. Paper presented at the 34th Australasian Science Education Research Association [ASERA] Conference, 9-12 July, 2003, Melbourne, Australia.

Kim, E. B., & Schniederjans, M. J. (2004). The role of personality in Web-based distance education courses. *Communications of the ACM, 47*(3), 95–98. doi:10.1145/971617.971622

Lao, D., & Gonzales, D. (2005). Understanding online learning through a qualitative description of professors' and students' experiences. *Journal of Technology and Teacher Education, 13*(3), 459–474.

Mackay, S., & Stockport, G. J. (2006). Blended learning, classroom and e-learning. *Business Review (Federal Reserve Bank of Philadelphia), 5*(1), 82–88.

Masie, E. (2001). The real truth about e-learning's future. *IT Training*. Retrieved July 2, 2005, from http://www.train-net.co.uk/ news/full_news.cfm ?ID=2994

Motteram, G. (2006). Blended education and the transformation of teachers: A long-term case study in postgraduate UK higher education. *British Journal of Educational Technology*, *37*(1), 17–30. doi:10.1111/j.1467-8535.2005.00511.x

OECD. (2005). E-learning in tertiary education: Brief policy. *Organization for Economic Co-operation and Development [OECD]: Education-tertiary education*. Retrieved June 25, 2007, from http://www.oecd.org/ dataoecd/55/25/35961132.pdf

Palloff, R. M., & Pratt, K. (2001). *Lessons from the cyberspace classroom: The realities of online teaching*. San Francisco, CA: Jossey-Bass.

Rogoff, B. (1991). Social interaction as apprenticeship in thinking: Guidance and participation in spatial planning. In Resnick, L. B., Levine, J. M., & Teasley, S. D. (Eds.), *Perspectives on socially shared cognition* (pp. 349–364). Washington, DC: American Psychological Association. doi:10.1037/10096-015

Salmon, D., & Jones, M. (2004). Higher education staff experiences of using Web-based learning technologies. *Journal of Educational Technology & Society*, *7*(1), 107–114.

Schrum, L. M. (2000). Guarding the promise of online learning. *Education Digest*, *66*(4), 43–50.

Sevilla, C., & Wells, T. (2000). Converting to web-based training: Choices and trade-offs. *Learning Circuits*. Retrieved May 3, 2004, from http://www.learningcircuits.org/ 2000/may2000/Sevilla.htm

Shank, P. (2005). New social interaction tools for online instruction. *Instructional Technology Forum*. Retrieved January 20, 2006, from http://it.coe.uga.edu/itforum /paper81/paper81.html

Shoniregun, C. A., & Gray, S.-J. (2004). *Is e-learning really the future or a risk?* Retrieved May 3, 2004, from http://www.distance-educator.com/dnews/ Article11123.phtml

Singh, H. (2003). Building effective blended learning programs. *Educational Technology*, *43*(6), 51–54.

Stuart, A. (2004). *Virtual classrooms, actual education*. Retrieved April 02, 2004, from http://www.inc.com/partners /sbc/articles/elearning.html

Stubbs, M., Martin, I., & Endlar, L. (2006). The structuration of blended learning: Putting holistic design principles into practice. *British Journal of Educational Technology*, *37*(2), 163–175. doi:10.1111/j.1467-8535.2006.00530.x

Tallent-Runnels, M. K., Thomas, J. A., Lan, W. Y., & Cooper, S. (2006). Teaching courses online: A review of the research. *Review of Educational Research*, *76*(1), 93–125. doi:10.3102/00346543076001093

Tang, B. A. (2000). *10 tips to optimize your e-learning*. Retrieved May 3, 2004, from http://www.learningcircuits.org/2000/nov2000/ nov2000_el-earn.html

Tiene, D. (2000). Online discussions: A survey of advantages and disadvantages compared to face-to-face discussions. *Journal of Educational Multimedia and Hypermedia*, *9*(4), 371–384.

Wallhaus, R. A. (2000). E-learning: From institutions to providers, from students to learners. In Katz, R. N., & Oblinger, D. G. (Eds.), *The "E" is for everything: E-commerce, e-business, and e-learning in the future of higher education* (*Vol. 2*, pp. 21–54). San Francisco, CA: Jossey-Bass.

Welker, J., & Berardino, L. (2005). Blended learning: Understanding the middle ground between traditional classroom and fully online instruction. *Journal of Educational Technology Systems*, *34*(1), 33–55. doi:10.2190/67FX-B7P8-PYUX-TDUP

Chapter 18
E–Mail Based Mobile Communication System for Interactive Lecture Support

Toshiyuki Maeda
Hannan University, Japan

Tadayuki Okamoto
Ehime University, Japan

Yae Fukushige
Osaka University, Japan

Takayuki Asada
Osaka University, Japan

ABSTRACT

The authors of this chapter present an e-mail based mobile communication system for interactive lecture support. This system consists of: attendance management subsystem, attendance history management subsystem, short examination management subsystem, questionnaire subsystem, and assignment delivery subsystem. Both students and teachers mainly use only e-mail functions and it can access the server. This system can be used regardless of terminal models only if mails can be sent and received through the Internet. In this chapter, the outline of this system is described, and the functions and effects are discussed.

1 INTRODUCTION

One of the major problems at universities in Japan is reduction of 18 year-old population. The rate of aged people is getting higher and higher, and accordance with the changes of this population composition, 18 year-old population is decreasing as well. The population of 18 year-old was 1,773,000 in 1995(*Summary of First Basic Complete Tabulation Results*, (2010)), and it is predicted that the population of 18 year-old will be 1,260,000 at the end of year 2008(*Population of High School Graduates*, (2010)). Thus the decreasing rate of the population of 18 year-old will be around 30 percent, and the population

DOI: 10.4018/978-1-61520-871-5.ch018

decrement of 18 year-old significantly influences education of universities in Japan.

The most significant effect is that average academic abilities of students are falling down(*Education Revolution*, (2010), *Falling Down of Academic Ability*, (2010)). Therefore teaching staffs should work variously because of various levels of students. Teachers have to arrange contents of lectures corresponding to the various levels. Lectures should be cared for various abilities along with keeping general academic level. Teachers thus should make variant lectures. Especially, keeping up motivation of students is very important in education at universities. Network-based learning(Warschauer & Kern, 2000, Trentin, 2001, Levin & Waugh, 1998) may be a solution to keep the motivation of the students with various abilities. In addition, students should be provided various education opportunities not only in school time but also in any time.

There are other aspects in universities. Lectures in universities have been advanced technically in these years. Blackboards were replaced by overhead projectors and later those were substituted by video projectors and electronic whiteboards. In these days many lecture rooms are settled with computers as well as video and audio systems, allowing the integration of every possible type of media into lectures. Nonetheless the basic paradigm is not changed so much throughout this time: teachers give presentations with several different media to show topics of the lecture. For large classes in the order of more than 100 students, where spontaneous interaction is no longer possible, this leads to unidirectional communication and a lack of interactivity between the students and teachers.

Teachers often try to solve this problem on making questionnaires to hook feed-backs on how well the students have understood the presented material, as well as provoke them to actively participate(Bligh, 2000). For large number of students this is a very big problem as only a small fraction of students can interact with the teacher

in this way. The majority will not follow this form of interactivity and remain inactive.

Spontaneous questions asked by students and replies by teachers at lectures make good relationship with each other, leading higher understanding level of students. At lectures in a large classroom this is often difficult. First, not all students Can ask questions because of time constraints. Second, many students do not dare to ask questions in front of a large audience. Finally, if questions are taken only at certain times, the questions are out of context of being naturally asked. All three problems does not cause students to interact at all.

Another problem arises when the teacher wants to get feedback on how the lecture is accepted by the students and what he or she can do to improve the lecture. In lectures with a small audience the teacher can typically deduce this information from social cues, e.g., the students look bored or are inattentive. For large audiences this information is usually gathered by passing out feedback questionnaires to the students at the end of a lecture period. Unfortunately this approach is rather coarse-grained and does not allow the assessment of individual elements contained in a lecture. Furthermore it is not possible for the teacher to quickly react to problems.

These issues have gained even more importance over the last few years by the rapid spreading of synchronous distance education. In an environment where a lecturer has to pay attention not only to a local audience but also to remote students, all of the problems mentioned above increase dramatically.

We have therefore researched several systems (for instance (Maeda, Tomo, & Asada, 2004, Maeda, Okamoto, Fukushige, & Asada, 2006, Maeda, Okamoto, Miura, Fukushige, & Asada, 2007, Maeda, Okamoto, Fukushige, & Asada, 2008, 2009b, 2009a)), and here present an e-mail based learning support system. This system consists of attendance management subsystem, attendance history management subsystem, short examination management subsystem, the questionnaire subsystem, and the assignment delivery subsystem. All of students and teachers use whole system functions by e-mails, including mobile phone messages. Regardless of carriers, messages can be used if those can be sent and received through Internet.

We have examined the system and we found that the management of lecture sequence is important for continuous and habitual study. Therefore we need a sequence management function using e-mail communication, and so we introduce session-based communication architecture.

In the following, the outline of this system is described, and the functions and effects are discussed.

2 RELATED WORKS

There are many useful various education systems supported by computers.

Rodger (Rodger, 1995) describe their positive experiences in teaching sophomore-level computer science courses in an interactive lecture format with a computer in the classroom, As students get more out of an interactive lecture than a passive lecture because they are given time to think, and this time allows them to determine if they understand a concept, and if not to ask questions and so understanding is crucial when concepts build on one another.

In (Hoppe, Luther, Mühlenbrock, Otten, & Tewissen, 1999) Hoppe et al. claim that aim is to gracefully integrate interactive whiteboards and pen-based input with the presentation of prepared electronic documents. Particular attention is given to minimizing the effort for providing both presentation material for the lecturer and electronic WWW scripts for the students, and to smoothly integrating the results of free pen-based elaboration with the scripts.

Shigenobu et al. (Shigenobu, Noda, Yoshino, & Munemori, 2004) have developed a flexible lecture support system using PDAs and wireless LAN, named SEGODON-PDA. A conventional fixed lecture support system has been carried out only in the classroom such as a computer room. The problem is the trouble of management. PDAs are comparatively cheap and their portability is good. A flexible system can be built using PDAs. The system can support two types of lectures. We applied SEGODON-PDA to a lecture-type class. Students could download the contents for the lecture using a wireless LAN in class and could write something on a blackboard while carrying and seeing a PDA. They could do their homework outside of the classroom.

In (Steinert & Snell, 1999), Steinert et al. assert that interactive lecturing involves an increased interchange between teachers, students and the lecture content. The use of interactive lectures can promote active learning, heighten attention and motivation, give feedback to the teacher and the student, and increase satisfaction for both. The article describes a number of interactive techniques that can be used in large group presentations as well as general strategies that can promote interactivity during lectures.

In (Wang & Higgins, 2005), authors describe the weaknesses inherent in, and some non-viable factors of mobile phone learning (PDA and other mobile devices are not included). Our conclusion is that while e-learning has only just been accepted by educators and is increasingly being put into extensive and effective use for learning, m-learning, especially its main delivery system, mobile phone learning, will have a long way to go before it can or will be effectively, extensively used or accepted for learning purposes, by either educators or the general public, unless the problems raised in this article are solved.

In (Qiu & Riesbeck, 2004), Problem-based learning (PBL) is a pedagogical strategy that centers learning activities around the investigation and development of solutions to complex and ill-structured authentic problems. It requires additional support and resources for students and instructors to use it in schools. Computer-based interactive learning environments have been used to provide students authentic and supportive settings for PBL. These systems, however, require significant up-front development effort before they can be put into use. In this chapter, we describe an incremental model that allows instructors to author the learning environment during real use. In our model, an instructor is part of the feedback loop, complementing system feedback and collecting materials to be incorporated into the system. By working within the system, the instructor can observe detailed traces of student learning activities in the system and provide individualized coaching and critiquing. We describe our experience in developing Corrosion Investigator, a Web-based learning environment, as an exemplar of our model. We focus on how the system is designed to facilitate instructor involvement and support incremental authoring. We present empirical results showing materials collected through use and benefits to the students and teachers.

In (Sharples, 2000), Sharples presents a framework for the design of a new genre of educational technology - personal (handheld or wearable) computer systems that support learning from any location throughout a lifetime and set out a theory of lifelong learning mediated by technology and indicate how it can provide requirements for the software, hardware, communications and interface design of a handheld learning resource, or HandLeR. The chapter concludes with a description and formative evaluation of a demonstrator system for children aged 7 - 11.

There is another research (Thornton & Houser, 2004) which they present three projects in mobile learning. First, they polled 333 Japanese university students regarding their use of mobile devices. 100% reported owning a mobile phone. 99% send email on their mobile phones, exchanging some 200 email messages each week. 66% email peers about classes; 44% email for studying. In contrast, only 43% email on PCs, exchanging an average of only 2 messages per week. Only 20% had used a PDA. Second, they emailed 100-word English vocabulary lessons at timed intervals to the mobile phones of 44 Japanese university students, hoping to promote regular study. Compared with students urged to regularly study identical materials on paper or Web, students receiving mobile email learned more (p<0.05). 71% of the subjects preferred receiving these lessons on mobile phones rather than PCs. 93% felt this a valuable teaching method. Third, they created a Web site explaining English idioms. Student-produced animation shows each idiom's literal meaning; a video shows the idiomatic meaning. Textual materials include an explanation, script, and quiz. 31 college sophomores evaluated the site using video-capable mobile phones, finding few technical difficulties, and rating highly its educational effectiveness.

The research (Tan & Liu, 2004) develops a mobile-based interactive learning environment (MOBILE) for aiding elementary school English learning. The MOBILE consists of a mobile learning server and mobile learning tools, which is able to support in- or outdoor learning activities. Several theme-based mobile learning activities including body parts learning and creation of species are conducted. Experimental results obtained from post-tests and questionnaire indicate that the MOBILE can significantly increase students' interest and effect in learning English as compared to the traditional manner.

There are also many researches for learning support systems as network application. For instance, a virtual collaboration space EVE (Educational Virtual Environment) has been developed including synchronous and asynchronous e-learning services (Bouras, Giannaka, & Tsiatsos, 2003). A laboratory has been built around a web-based digital model railroad platform controlled by a client-server system for education of computer science (Sanchez, Alvarez, Iborra, Fernandez-Merono, & Pastor, 2003). Also, a web-based system has been developed for control engineering education (Schmid & Ali, 2002).

To put communication skills into engineering curriculum, a web-based system to integrate workplace has been developed. The purpose of the web-based systems is to establish efficient education, and to communicate sufficiently among teachers and students. In various education areas, various education problems are solved using web-based systems (Hanakawa, Goto, Maeda, & Akazawa, 2004).

The most critical problem is, however, that web-based systems cannot use lecture rooms where computers are not settled for all students, and is essential for many cases. We have thus developed an e-mail based system using mobile phones, which almost all students have in Japan. There are only few e-mail based systems for similar purpose, such as (Johansen, Renesse, & Schneider, 1996).

3 SYSTEM CONCEPT

Figure 1 is the general system flow of our system. This system consists of attendance management subsystem, attendance history management subsystem, short examination management subsystem, the questionnaire subsystem, and the assignment delivery subsystem. All of students and teachers use whole system functions by e-mails, including mobile phone messages. Regardless of carriers, messages can be used if those can be sent and received through Internet.

There is positive correlation between attendance frequency and marking result of students, and a lot of teachers want to check attendance for each class as usual as possible. Not a few teachers require to check attendance every time because they think it may improve the study achievement level. With the view of higher educational service, teachers confirm attendance and the execution of the questionnaire as one of the educational policies is in increasing tendency as well. It is expected that the number of universities that make the classification according to the proficiency, and that increases basic subjects (e.g. science course).

Interactivity in a class improves students' motivation though it is not so easy to improve interactivity especially at a large classroom. Equipments such as response analyzer, etc. improve

Figure 1. General System flow

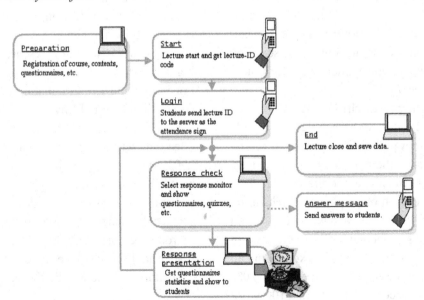

interactivity in the class though it is economically difficult to introduce those equipments.

For example, to check attendance, usage of attendance cards spends much time and so reduce equivalent teaching time. Moreover, data collection and procedure may cause mistakes of checking participants. Furthermore, teachers cannot get the current attendance situation in real time in any way. Cost of questionnaires are almost same as that of collection and analysis, and real-time information is not obtained as well. It is difficult for both teachers and students to understand the study achievement level, the motivation, and the problem in real time.

As a prototype, the concept of our system is that a mobile phone is used as an input device. It includes several subsystem and utilizes in university anytime, and solves some sort of problems previously shown.

Ideal system must be cost-effective and be fair in any places in a classroom because neither the personal computer nor the equipment of information processing on networks are needed. A wide application must be possible to the field of a basic education by the repetition study and improving the proficiency, and so on. Integration with various subsystems including the educational evaluation system must be easy. It is possible to fit needs of students of seat reservation at the library etc.

It cannot be expected to make students use information instruments in lectures in a large classroom though the introduction of educational support system. It is easy to some degree, and already has various systems in a classroom where personal computers are maintained. It may be possible that it takes time for the data collection and the arrangement when cards are used for the attendance check and short examinations, etc. in case of such lectures and a mistake may be caused. Moreover, the possibility of illegal registration comes out for independent short examinations as well.

Control of short examinations, synchronized attendance data, etc. are integrated as switching function using only e-mail messages from mobile phones. Because almost all of university students have mobile phones, extra cost (payment) of each student is not necessary at all. As for communication of this system, it requires at most several tens characters, and so the cost doesn't take so much. The annual cost is a few hundred yen, and the packet transmission of the fixed charge plan will emerged and then the cost will be negligible in the near future.

E-mail is a simultaneous medium, and it processes by students' attendance, short examinations and the questionnaires using the mobile phone mail. Then the system immediately replies the result to each student. Teachers also send the instruction to the server by using the mail function of mobile phones, and receive the result of the total result with each system by the mobile phone. The personal computer is not required and so this system is applicable for all classrooms. It is only required a mobile phone as a terminal that can send and receive e-mails, though teachers may use personal computers.

Figure 2 is a sample page of the manual on this system. This page shows how to register a student to the class in this system with an e-mail sending by himself. In this figure,

1. is a title of this manual page, which means "Student ID Registration Mail".
2. means "a mail sent by a student for student ID registration".
3. shows "Address".
4. means "the mail does not require Subject: header".
5. means "message body".
6. means "the body contains the student name, the student ID, the password, and the keyword of the day, separated by '#'".
7. is an example of the above explanation.
8. shows the note that "the body part should be written in ASCII characters except the student name".

Figure 2. Sample of manual page (in Japanese)

3.1 Attendance Management Subsystem

Because sending mails by students themselves automatically does attendance check, teachers can understand the situation in real time. It is recorded in the attendance database that the teacher receives, not only attendance and absence but also students' registration, and because it can be received as the registration order list of names, it can be used for the nomination etc. in the class. Moreover, latecomer(s) can be easily recognized by a reverse-order list (order with late registration) of student names. Attendance can be confirmed in the registration result because it individually replies to an individual student.

Moreover, if the mistake is found in sending mails, the student gets replies of error mail, and the registration mistake is not generated because the attendance registration can be done again. Using it together with Short examination and Questionnaire subsystem can prevent injustice.

3.2 Short Examination Subsystem

Teachers make short examinations by using Short examination subsystem, as delivering as e-mails or printing the necessary number of copies. As for printed matters, when short examinations are executed, printed matters are turned upside down and distributed. The answer begins simultaneously for all students. Students fill in the student ID number, the short examination ID number, and the answer in the text of e-mail by one line and send the answer result to the server. The server automatically makes the grade and replies the result.

Because students can challenge questions repeatedly until getting full marks. They can put the order of examinations in the short examinations management subsystem, working on examinations for the student in a game-like sense, and as a result the improvement of the understanding level can be expected. It is possible to study short examinations at home after the lecture time even when missing it, and then contentiousness of study can be maintained.

3.3 Lecture Sequence

As management of lecture sequence is important for continuous and habitual study, we introduce a sequence management function using e-mail communication. In this function, session-based communication architecture is used, where e-mail

Figure 3. E-mail session management

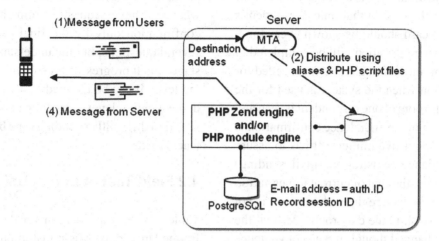

addresses themselves are used as pseudo "cookie" data. That means, confirmation of sequence is treated as sending to and receiving from the same address which is regarded as user-identification.

Our system manages a leaning session, which is regarded as a sequence (several stages) in one lecture. The flow of the session management is as follows.

- Our system use various addresses and messages from students are sorted by the addresses.
- The system uses a e-mail address of each student as "session ID", and through a lecture the address is marked as ID.
- The system stores and maintains communication data within a lecture databases, where e-mail addresses are continuously checked and followed as ID.
- Responses are sent to each addresses, and in this way communication are kept until the end of the lecture.

3.4 Session Management Flow

As figure 3 shows, session management flow in our system is described as follows;

- Distribution by destination e-mail address: Each destination address is delivered into various functions.
- Start of session by above e-mail using address as authentication ID.
- Reserving session data: Continual data (used by several mails) are processed and saved in records corresponding to effective session ID.
- Delivery of results to each user by e-mails.

4 DISCUSSION

We have already used some variations of this system for a couple of years and we have got some experimental data from students. In this section we discuss those.

4.1 Field Test at Matsuyama University

Table 1 shows a situation on the field test at Matsuyama University. The attendance confirmation is executed only with the system at this course. Each student who doesn't have a mobile phone or whose mobile phone runs out of battery charge submits the attendance by a paper card, and the number of those students is averagely about four students in each class. At that time, the student's identification card should be shown every time. The attendance registration will be completed in about three minutes, though time was needed for the explanation when the system is used for the first time. The room of one respondent is seen and the registration of the attendance confirmation is possible for about five minutes. It has to assure secure attendance registration (mail sending) time while doing the chat of current topics and so on. related to the lecture theme because it is not necessary to stroll in the classroom. At first, the system was changed though it was convenience of the procedure of the school register registration to the system, and there was a case where the attendance of students was not able to register in some cases, which were occurred when the Chinese character of student's name was not able to be input on the mobile phone. In this course over ten short examinations are presented.

At this field test, attendance management are mainly used. However, this system should be effective when the questionnaire and the short examinations are actually executed. It can know whether the understanding of which part is difficult according to the low degree of the correct answer rate of the exercise judged to be natural understanding without permission.

The combination ratio of parts where time should be emphatically spent in the explanation and others can be changed if it is necessary to evaluate not the original evaluation of attendance to the target from the doubt to the evaluation what you have requested from the attendance confirmation only by the final examination of several questions, but the understanding of each stage, and it progresses for student's understanding level. It can be finished easily to confirm the understanding level every time under the present situation difficultly spending time by judging the teacher side.

4.2 Field Test at Ehime University

Table 2 shows a situation on the field test at Ehime University. Mis-registration happens frequently at the first time, limited as input mistake in the destination address and/or input mistake of normal-width and em-size (Zenkaku) characters in Japanese character sets. Carrying operation is confused for the inexperienced student (input method of "@", "#" and other special characters). Dissatisfied mails issued by student's attendance system are not certified. Mis-registration happens by input time limit as well. The previous mail can be sent again edited shortly.

For above problems, the examples of input mistake that happens frequently are described in the user manual. The portable operation method for this system is described in the user manual as well. It explains the advantage which can offer the registration confirmation and the attendance history management of students in real time.

Examples of questionnaire replies are as follows;

Table 1. Situation at Matsuyama University

Period	1 term (half year)
Number of students	150
Subject	engineering accounting
Methods	lecture with text and syllabus, test, and questionnaire
Used systems	attendance management and questionnaire

Table 2. Situation at Ehime University

Periods	4 days
Number of students	15
Subject	cost accounting
Methods	lecture with text and syllabus, test, questionnaire
Used systems	attendance management, questionnaire

- The system that confirmed attendance and the questionnaire by using carrying was good. I think that it demonstrates considerable power if the number of people is more.
- Because the attendance registration and the questionnaire by carrying become shortening time, I think it is good.
- It took time to get the point of lecture (the spoken content) clearly.

4.3 Field Test at Osaka University

Table 3 shows a situation on the field test at Osaka University. This field test leads the followings ;

- Some of receiving and/or sending reaction must be ill operated in carrying, because the sensitivity of the reception and the communications antenna of mobile phone is not enough affected as the user environment (microwave strength, etc.).
- A lecture attended though the student attitude in the class is quiet by posture, and that lacks the questioned posture and is passive.
- The lecture syllabus copies each one, and uses it. It is a half of students to buy the textbook.
- 90% of students submit the reports. The answer is along the content case explained by the lecture abundantly.

Table 3. Test condition at Osaka University

Period	1 month
Number of students	93
Subject	management accounting
Methods	lecture with text and syllabus, short examinations, questionnaire
Used systems	attendance management, short examination, questionnaire

4.4 Questionnaires

Table 4 shows some comments about students' mobile phone charges. In Japan, fixed-charge fare plan is spreading and so cost problem is getting negligible.

Table 5 shows how students feel about attendance management function.

Table 6 shows how students feel about questionnaire & short examination.

Table 7 shows students' opinions about attendance registration. Students make it by registering from the beginning as long as the attendance record is seen to fixation. Illegal attendance or late attendance of students are always monitored.

Table 8 shows opinions about short examination.

These results imply that;

- This system deals with some sensitive questions, which is hard for students to make their own opinions public in classes,

Table 4. Phone Charges

	Jan-05	Jul-05	Jan-06	Jul-06
Fixed charge	13%	16%	30%	44%
Up to inclusive basic charge	23%	18%	28%	22%
Limit to some arbitrary price	13%	6%	6%	2%
Don't care	51%	60%	36%	31%
(Blank)	1%	0%	0%	1%

Table 5. Attendance Management function

	Jan-05	Jul-05	Jan-06	Jul-06
Useful	15%	10%	31%	63%
Interesting	13%	32%	15%	-
No problem	33%	48%	44%	29%
Troublesome	29%	8%	9%	-
Unnecessary	8%	0%	0%	5%
(Blank)	2%	2%	0%	3%

Table 6. Questionnaire & short examination

	Jan-05	Jul-05	Jan-06	Jul-06
Useful	8%	6%	7%	40%
Interesting	12%	38%	15%	-
No problem	42%	40%	50%	42%
Troublesome	26%	10%	24%	-
Unnecessary	7%	4%	4%	15%
(Blank)	5%	2%	0%	2%

- Students can recognize gaps between other students' understandings,
- Teachers can pick up unveiled dissatisfaction of students.

The correlation with the understanding level by the examination result (final examination and short examinations) must be investigated.

This system stimulates the participation motivation for attendance. If it is monitored, the deterrent effect is high even though some students try

Table 7. About attendance registration (multiple answers allowed)

	Jan-05	Jul-05	Jan-06	Jul-06
Good to register by oneself	34%	56%	54%	67%
Good to check the attendance statistics by oneself	47%	46%	54%	64%
Good to be surplus attendance point	28%	16%	24%	38%
Interesting as a IT tool	23%	52%	19%	35%
Seems more interesting if improved	20%	24%	28%	40%
Need to proceed strictly about unfair registration	30%	12%	20%	21%
Dislike because of troublesome registration	20%	8%	9%	2%
Seems unnecessary on university lectures	16%	4%	6%	1%
Get harder to escape from lectures	6%	6%	4%	4%
Good to use this system at other lectures	15%	24%	24%	30%
(Others)	9%	4%	0%	0%

Table 8. About short examination

	Jan-05	Jul-05	Jan-06	Jul-06
Good to check understanding level	15%	34%	46%	51%
Good to know other students' levels and thoughts	37%	46%	37%	25%
Wants more frequently	6%	12%	6%	23%
Seems more interesting if arranged use	23%	28%	22%	38%
Interesting as a IT tool	18%	28%	11%	20%
Seems more interesting if improved	14%	24%	20%	36%
Dislike because of troublesome use	23%	10%	17%	16%
Seems unnecessary on university lectures	8%	4%	6%	5% 2
Interesting rather than talk-only lectures	17%	18%	15%	18%
Good to use this system at other lectures	3%	12%	11%	16%
(Others)	3%	6%	2%	0%

illegal attendance temporarily. It becomes a chance to change lecture style by touching off students because of interactive class performance. Even if teachers prepare many questionnaires, that is not a heavy task. The problem is that of the intention of teachers who try to use.

Furthermore, especially in a large classroom, it is very hard to check understanding levels of students without this system, as it is very difficult to add up answers of short examinations.

This system also makes stimuli of answering for students, because the system lets students avoid pending to answer and motivate to answer quickly and correctly.

5 CONCLUSION

We present an e-mail based interactive mobile communication system and discuss some field tests, or feasibility experiments. We certify the effectiveness of our system, which consists of several subsystems.

Ad future work, we need more field tests to refine our system, and concurrently improve each subsystems, for instance, short examination functions, and so on, and we are planning to improve this system as e-learning common platform. Furthermore, we are aiming to apply this mobile communication system for health care support.

ACKNOWLEDGMENT

This research is partially supported by the Ministry of Education, Science, Sports and Culture, Japan; Grant-in-Aid for Scientific Research (A), 19201032 (2007-2009). Part of this research is also supported and collaborated by A-Live Co., Ltd. The authors greatly appreciate those.

REFERENCES

Bligh, D. (2000). *What's the use of lectures?* Jossey-Bass Publishers.

Bouras, C., Giannaka, E., & Tsiatsos, T. (2003). Virtual collaboration spaces: The EVE community. In *Proceedings of the 2003 International Symposium on Applications and the Internet* (pp. 48–55). Orlando, FL (USA).

Education Revolution. (2010). http://www.mext. go.jp/ a_menu/shougai/kaikaku /pdf/p150.pdf

Falling Down of Academic Ability. (2010). http:// ja.wikipedia.org/ wiki/%E5%AD%A6%E5% 8A%9B%E4%BD %8E%E4%B8%8B

Hanakawa, N., Goto, K., Maeda, T., & Akazawa, Y. (2004). Discovery learning for software engineering –a Web based total education system: HInT–. In *Proceedings of The International Conference on Computers in Education (ICCE 2004)* (pp. 1929–1939). Melbourne (Australia).

Hoppe, H. U., Luther, W., Mühlenbrock, M., Otten, W., & Tewissen, F. (1999). Interactive presentation support for an electronic lecture hall-a practice report. In Cumming, G. (Eds.), *Advanced research in computers and communications in education* (pp. 923–930).

Johansen, D., van Renesse, R., & Schneider, F. B. (1996). Supporting broad Internet access to TACOMA. In *Proceedings of the 7th SIGOPS European Workshop* (pp. 55–58). Connemara, Ireland.

Levin, J., & Waugh, M. (1998). Teaching teleapprenticeships:Electronic network-based educational frameworks for improving teacher education. *Interactive Learning Environments Journal*, *6*(1-2), 39–58. doi:10.1076/ilee.6.1.39.3612

Maeda, T., Okamoto, T., Fukushige, Y., & Asada, T. (2006). Interactive e-learning environment using mobile phone messages. In [Dublin, Ireland.]. *Proceedings of IADIS International Conference Mobile Learning, 2006*, 374–378.

Maeda, T., Okamoto, T., Fukushige, Y., & Asada, T. (2008). Learning session management with e-mail communication. In *Proceedings of World Conference on Educational Multimedia, Hypermedia & Telecommunications (ED-MEDIA 2008)* (pp. 1787–1792). Vienna, Austria.

Maeda, T., Okamoto, T., Fukushige, Y., & Asada, T. (2009a). Learning session management with e-mail communication. In *Proceedings of World Conference on Educational Multimedia, Hypermedia & Telecommunications (ED-MEDIA 2009)* (pp. 1156–1161). Honolulu, HI, USA.

Maeda, T., Okamoto, T., Fukushige, Y., & Asada, T. (2009b). Session management of mobile communication for learning support environment. In [Barcelona, Spain.]. *Proceedings of IADIS International Conference Mobile Learning, 2009*, 217–221.

Maeda, T., Okamoto, T., Miura, T., Fukushige, Y., & Asada, T. (2007). Interactive lecture support using mobile-phone messages. In *Proceedings of World Conference on Educational Multimedia, Hypermedia & Telecommunications (ED-MEDIA 2007)* (pp. 3659–3665). Vancouver, Canada.

Maeda, T., Tomo, M., & Asada, T. (2004, 7). Integrated lecture-support system using e-mail. In *Proceedings of National University Symposium on Information Education Methods* (pp. 26–27). Tokyo, Japan.

Population of High School Graduates. (2010). http://www.mext.go.jp/ b_menu/toukei/001/ 08072901/003/sanzu07.pdf

Qiu, L., & Riesbeck, C. (2004). An incremental model for developing computer-based learning environments for problem-based learning. In. *Proceedings of IEEE International Conference on Advanced Learning Technologies, 2004*, 171–175.

Rodger, S. H. (1995). An interactive lecture approach to teaching computer science. In *Proceedings of the 26th SIGCSE Technical Symposium on Computer Science Education* (pp. 278–282). Nashville, Tennessee, USA.

Sanchez, P., Alvarez, B., Iborra, A., Fernandez-Merono, J., & Pastor, J. (2003). Web-based activities around a digital model railroad platform. *Journal of IEEE Transaction on Education, 46*(2), 302–306. doi:10.1109/TE.2003.811040

Schmid, C., & Ali, A. (2002). A Web-based system for control engineering education. In *Proceedings of the 2002 American Control Conference* (pp. 3463–3467). Chicago, IL (USA).

Sharples, M. (2000). The design of personal mobile technologies for lifelong learning. *Computers & Education, 34*, 177–193. doi:10.1016/S0360-1315(99)00044-5

Shigenobu, T., Noda, T., Yoshino, T., & Munemori, J. (2004). Flexible lecture support system using wireless LAN and PDAs. *Transactions of Information Processing Society of Japan, 45*(1), 255–266.

Steinert, Y., & Snell, L. S. (1999). Interactive lecturing: Strategies for increasing participation in large group presentations. *Medical Teacher, 21*(1), 37–42. doi:10.1080/01421599980011

Summary of First Basic Complete Tabulation Results. (2010). http://www.stat.go.jp/ english/ data/kokusei/ 1995/1513.htm

Tan, T. H., & Liu, T. Y. (2004). The mobile-based interactive learning environment (MOBILE) and a case study for assisting elementary school English learning. In. *Proceedings of IEEE International Conference on Advanced Learning Technologies, 2004*, 530–534.

Thornton, P., & Houser, C. (2004). Using mobile phones in education. In *Proceedings in The 2nd IEEE International Workshop on Wireless and Mobile Technologies in Education 2004* (pp. 3–10).

Trentin, G. (2001). From formal training to communities of practice via network-based learning. *Educational Technology, 41*, 5–14.

Wang, S., & Higgins, M. (2005). Limitations of mobile phone learning. In *Proceedings of IEEE International Workshop on Wireless and Mobile Technologies in Education (WMTE'05)* (pp. 179–181).

Warschauer, M., & Kern, R. G. (2000). *Network-based language teaching: Concepts and practice.* Cambridge University Press.

Compilation of References

Abel, R. (2005). *Achieving success in Internet-supported learning in higher education: Case studies illuminate success factors, challenges, and future directions.* Retrieved April 20, 2005, from http://www.a-hec.org/ research/study_reports/ IsL0205/TOC.html

Abrams, Z. I. (2006). From theory to practice: Intracultural CMC in the L2 classroom. In Ducate, L., & Arnold, N. (Eds.), *Calling on CALL: From theory and research to new directions in foreign language teaching* (*Vol. 5*, pp. 181–209). CALICO Monograph Series.

Ackerman, M. S., & Malone, T. W. (1990). Answer garden: A tool for growing organizational memory. *Proceedings of ACM Conference on Office Information Systems (COIS'90)*, 1990.

Adamides, E. D., & Karacapilidis, N. (2006). Information Technology support for the knowledge and social processes of innovation management. *Technovation, 26*, 50–59. doi:10.1016/j.technovation.2004.07.019

Agrawal, R., Imielinski, T., & Swami, A. (1993). Database mining: A performance perspective. *IEEE Transactions on Knowledge and Data Engineering, 5*(6), 914–925. doi:10.1109/69.250074

Agrawal, R., & Shafer, J. C. (1996). Parallel mining of association rules. *IEEE Transactions on Knowledge and Data Engineering, 8*(6), 962–969. doi:10.1109/69.553164

Akimoto, T., Suenaga, Y., & Wallace, R. (1993). Automatic creation of 3D facial models. *IEEE Computer Graphics and Applications, 13*(5), 16–22. doi:10.1109/38.232096

Al-Lawati, A., Lee, D., & McDaniel, P. (2005). *Blocking-aware private record linkage.* IQIS 2005, International Workshop on Information Quality in Information Systems, 17 June 2005, Baltimore, Maryland, USA (SIGMOD 2005 Workshop)

Allnatt, J. W. (1980). Subjective assessment method for television digital codecs. *Electronics Letters, 16*(12), 450–451. doi:10.1049/el:19800317

Amit, R., & Schoemaker, P. J. (1993). Strategic assets and organizational rent. *Strategic Management Journal, 14*(1), 33–46. doi:10.1002/smj.4250140105

An, D., Woodward, A., Delmas, P., Gimel'farb, G., & Morris, J. (2006). Comparison of active structure lighting mono and stereo camera systems: Application to 3D face acquisition. *ENC'06: Proceedings of the Seventh Mexican International Conference on Computer Science*, (pp. 135-141). Washington, DC: IEEE Computer Society.

Anderson, C. (2006). *The long tail.* Random House Business.

Ando, T., Mashitani, K., Higashino, M., Kanayama, H., Murata, H., & Funazou, Y. (2005). Multiview image integration system for glassless 3D display. *SPIE, 5664*(1), 158–166. doi:10.1117/12.596849

Appel, C., & Gilabert, R. (2004). Motivation and task performance in a task-based Web-based tandem project. *ReCALL, 14*(1), 16–31.

Araki, K., Shimizu, M., Noda, T., Chiba, Y., Tsuda, Y., & Ikegaya, K. (1995). A high-speed and continuous 3d measurement system. *Machine Vision and Applications, 8*(2), 79–84. doi:10.1007/BF01213473

Arani, T. T., Karwan, M. H., & Drury, C. G. (1984). A variable-memory model of visual search. *Human Factors, 26*, 680–688.

Arthur, W. B., & Lane, D. A. (1996). Increasing contagion. *Structural Change and Economic Dynamics, 41*, 81–104.

Arvanitis, S. (2005). Computerization, workplace organization, skilled labour and firm productivity: Evidence for the Swiss business sector. *Economics of Innovation and New Technology*, *14*(4), 225–249. doi:10.1080/1043859042000226257

Baldwin, E. R. (1994). The impact of the 1986 US – Japan semiconductor agreement. *Japan and the World Economy*, 6.

Barabási, A.-L., & Albert, R. (1999). Emergence of scaling in random networks. *Science*, *286*, 509–512. doi:10.1126/science.286.5439.509

Barabási, A. L., & Albert, R. (2002). Statistical mechanics of complex networks. *Reviews of Modern Physics*, *74*, 47–97. doi:10.1103/RevModPhys.74.47

Barabási, A.-L., Ravasz, E., & Vicsek, T. (2001). Deterministic scale-free networks. *Physica A*, *299*, 559–564. doi:10.1016/S0378-4371(01)00369-7

Barabási, A.-L. (2003). *Linked*. Plume, a member of the Penguin Group, Inc.

Barney, J. B. (1991). Firm resources and sustained competitive advantage. *Journal of Management*, *7*, 99–120. doi:10.1177/014920639101700108

Barrett, G., Blumhardt, L., & Halliday, A. M. (1976). A paradox in the lateralisation of the visual evoked response. *Nature*, *261*, 253–255. doi:10.1038/261253a0

Bass, F. M. (1969). A new product growth model for consumer durables. *Management Science*, *15*(5), 215–227. doi:10.1287/mnsc.15.5.215

Bell, G., & Doursh, P. (2007). Yesterday's tomorrows: Notes on ubiquitous computing's dominant vision. *Personal and Ubiquitous Computing*, *11*(2), 133–143. doi:10.1007/s00779-006-0071-x

Bellegarda, J. R. (2004). Statistical language model adaptation: Review and perspectives. *Speech Communication*, *42*(1), 93–108. doi:10.1016/j.specom.2003.08.002

Berge, Z. L. (2005). Taking the distance out of distance education. In Kearsley, G. (Ed.), *Online learning: Personal reflections on the transformation of education*. Englewood Cliffs, NJ: Educational Technology Publications.

Berge, Z. L., & Lin, M. (2001). *Obstacles faced at various stages of capability regarding distance education in institutions of higher education: Survey results*. Retrieved July 9, 2004, from http://www.emoderators.com /barriers/ hghred_stgs.shtml

Bharadwaj, A. S. (2000). A resource-based perspective on Information Technology capability and firm performance: An empirical investigation. *Management Information Systems Quarterly*, *24*(1), 169–196. doi:10.2307/3250983

Bhatt, G. D., & Grover, V. (2005). Types of Information Technology capabilities and their role in competitive advantage: An empirical study. *Journal of Management Information Systems*, *22*(2), 253–277.

Bhatt, G. D., Gupta, J. N. D., & Kitchens, F. (2005). An exploratory study of groupware use in the knowledge management process. *Journal of Enterprise Information Management*, *8*(1), 28–46. doi:10.1108/17410390510571475

Bhowmick, S. S., Gruenwald, L., Iwaihara, M., & Chatvichienchai, S. (2006). Private-iye: A framework for privacy preserving data integration. In ICDEW '06: *Proceedings of the 22nd International Conference on Data Engineering Workshops* (ICDEW'06), Washington, DC: IEEE Computer Society.

Bianconi, G., & Barabási, A.-L. (2001). Competition and multiscaling in evolving networks. *Europhysics Letters*, *54*(4), 436–442. doi:10.1209/epl/i2001-00260-6

Bianconi, G., & Barabási, A.-L. (2001). Bose-Einstein condensation in complex networks. *Physical Review Letters*, *86*(24), 5632–5635. doi:10.1103/PhysRevLett.86.5632

Bickel, B., Lang, M., Botsch, M., Otaduy, M. A., & Gross, M. (2008). *Pose-space animation and transfer of facial details*. ACM SIGGRAPH Symposium on Computer Animation, (pp. 57-66).

Bitchener, J. W. (1999). *The negotiation of meaning by advanced ESL learners: The effects of individual learner factors and task type*. Unpublished PhD thesis of the University of Auckland, New Zealand.

Bligh, D. (2000). *What's the use of lectures?* Jossey-Bass Publishers.

Blumenhardt, L. D., & Halliday, A. M. (1979). Hemisphere contributions to the composition of the pattern-evoked potential waveform. *Experimental Brain Research, 36*(1), 53–69. doi:10.1007/BF00238467

Blundell, B. G., & Schwarz, A. J. (2005). *Creative 3-D display and interaction interfaces: A trans-disciplinary approach*. Wiley-Interscience. doi:10.1002/0471764078

Bobak, P., Bodis-Wollner, I., & Guillory, S. (1987). The effect of blur and contrast on VEP latency: Comparison between check and sinusoidal grating patterns. *Electroencephalography and Clinical Neurophysiology, 68*(4), 247–255. doi:10.1016/0168-5597(87)90045-1

Boguñá, M., & Pastor-Satorras, R. (2003). Class of correlated random networks with hidden variables. *Physical Review E: Statistical, Nonlinear, and Soft Matter Physics, 68*, 036112. doi:10.1103/PhysRevE.68.036112

BoIA (Bureau of Industry Affairs). (2007). *M-Taiwan application promotion plan – VoIP application service interoperation specification*. Taiwan: Ministry of Economy.

Borrus, M. (1988). *Competing for control: America's stake in microelectronics*. Cambridge, MA: Ballinger Publishing Company.

Borrus, M., Millstein, J., & Zysman, J. (1982). U.S. – Japanese competition in the semiconductor industry. In *Policy Papers in International Affairs, 17. Institute for International Studies*. Berkeley, California: University of California.

Borrus, M., Tyson, L. D., & Zyaman, J. (1988). Creating advantage: How government policies shape international trade in the semiconductor industry. In Krugman, P. R. (Ed.), *Strategic trade policy and the new international trade economics*. Cambridge, MA: The MIT Press.

Bose, R. (2009). Sensor networks- motes, smart spaces, and beyond. *IEEE Pervasive Computing / IEEE Computer Society [and] IEEE Communications Society, 8*(3), 84–90. doi:10.1109/MPRV.2009.55

Bouras, C., Giannaka, E., & Tsiatsos, T. (2003). Virtual collaboration spaces: The EVE community. In *Proceedings of the 2003 International Symposium on Applications and the Internet* (pp. 48–55). Orlando, FL (USA).

Brynjolfsson, E., & Hitt, L. M. (2000). Beyond computation: Information Technology, organizational transformation and business performance. *The Journal of Economic Perspectives, 14*(4), 23–48. doi:10.1257/jep.14.4.23

Butler-Pascoe, M. E., & Wiburg, K. M. (2003). *Technology and teaching English language learners*. Pearson Education.

Caldarelli, G., Capocci, A., De Los Rios, P., & Munoz, M. A. (2002). Scale-free networks from varing vertex intrinsic fitness. *Physical Review Letters, 89*(25), 258702. doi:10.1103/PhysRevLett.89.258702

Camarillo, G., Roach, A. B., Peterson, J., & Ong, L. (2002). *Integrated services digital network (ISDN) user part (ISUP) to session initiation protocol (SIP) mapping*. (IETF RFC 3398).

Carneiro, A. (2000). How does knowledge management influence innovation and competiteveness? *Journal of Knowledge Management, 4*(2), 87–98. doi:10.1108/13673270010372242

Carr, N. (2003). IT doesn't matter. *Harvard Business Review*, (May): 41–49.

CERN. (2007). *About the World Wide Web*. Retrieved November 14, 2007, from http://www.w3.org/WWW/

CGLX Project. (2010). Retrieved from http://vis.ucsd.edu/~cglx

Chan, M., Delmas, P., Gimel'farb, G., & Leclercq, P. (2005). *Comparative study of 3D face acquisition techniques: Computer analysis of images and patterns*. (LNCS 3691), (pp. 740-747).

Chapelle, C. A. (2001). *Computer applications in second language acquisition: Foundations for teaching, testing and research*. Cambridge, UK: Cambridge University Press.

Chen, S. H., Yeh, C. H., & Liao, C. C. (1999). Testing the rational expectations hypothesis with the agent-based model of stock markets. *Proceedings of, ICAI99*, 381–387.

Chen, F. L., & Su, C. T. (1996). Vision-based automated inspection system in computer-integrated manufacturing. *IJAMT, 11*(3), 206–213.

Chen, S. F. (2003). Compiling large-context phonetic decision trees into finite-state transducers. [Geneva, Switzerland.]. *Proceedings of Interspeech, 2003*, 1169–1172.

Chen, S. F., Kingsburg, B., Mangu, L., Povey, D., Saon, G., Saltau, H., & Zweig, G. (2006). Advances in speech transcription at IBM under the DARPA EARS program. *IEEE Transactions in Audio. Speech and Language Processing, 14*(5), 1596–1608. doi:10.1109/TASL.2006.879814

Chiba, Y., & Nishimoto, K. (2007). An intrablog-based informal communication encouraging system that seamlessly links on-line communications to off-line ones. *The IEICE Transactions on Information and Systems. E (Norwalk, Conn.), 90-D*(10), 1501–1508.

Chin, R. T. (1982). Automated visual inspection: A survey. *IEEE Transactions on Pattern Analysis and Machine Intelligence, 4*(6), 557–573. doi:10.1109/TPAMI.1982.4767309

Chin, R. T. (1988). Automated visual inspection: 1981 to 1987. *CVGIP, 41*(3), 346–381.

Chiu, R., Yeh, Y., & Chi, S. (2009). *Kaohsiung county broadband mobile network. IWEA2009/ACIS-SNPD2009 proceedings. C-IE-5011_0. (2007). Broadband wireless communication system conformance test technical specifications. National Communications Commission.* Taiwan: NCC.

Christen, P. (2008). Febrl: An open source data cleaning, de-duplication and record linkage system with a graphical user interface. *KDD, 2008*, 1065–1068.

Christensen, C. M. (1997). *The innovator's dilemma.* Harvard Business School Press.

Chun, D. M. (2007). Come ride the wave: But where is it taking us? *CALICO Journal, 24*(2), 239–252.

Churach, D., & Fisher, D. (2001). Science students surf the Web: Effects on constructivist classroom environments. *Journal of Computers in Mathematics and Science Teaching, 20*(2), 221–247.

Churches, T., & Christen, P. (2004). Blind data linkage using n-gram similarity comparisons. *PAKDD, 2004*, 121–126.

C-IS2045_0. (2007). *Broadband wireless communication base station transmission equipment technical specifications.* National Communications Commission (NCC), Taiwan. C-IT-5040_0. (2007). *Broadband wireless communication base station conformance test specifications.* National Communications Commission (NCC), Taiwan.

Cleland-Huang, J., Settimi, R., Romanova, E., Berenbach, B., & Clark, S. (2007). Best practices for automated traceability. *IEEE Computer, 40*(6), 27–35.

Clemons, E. K., & Row, M. C. (1991). Sustaining IT advantage: The role of structural differences. *Management Information Systems Quarterly, 15*(3), 275–292. doi:10.2307/249639

Clifton, C., Kantarcioğlu, M., Doan, A., Schadow, G., Vaidya, J., Elmagarmid, A., & Suciu, D. (2004). Privacy-preserving data integration and sharing. In DMKD '04: *Proceedings of the 9th ACM SIGMOD Workshop on Research Issues in Data Mining and Knowledge Discovery*, (pp. 19-26). New York, NY: ACM.

Cohen, L., Manion, L., & Morrison, K. (2000). *Research methods in education* (5th ed.). London, UK: RoutledgeFalmer. doi:10.4324/9780203224342

Collis, B., & Moonen, J. (2001). *Flexible learning in a digital world: Experience and expectations.* London, UK: Kogan Page.

Cool, C., Fish, R., Kraut, R., & Lowery, C. (1992). Iterative design of video communication systems. *Proceedings of ACM CSCW'92*, (pp. 25-32).

Crabtree, H. (2006). *The impact of student centered learning: An evaluation of tutor and student experiences.* 3rd Education in a Changing Environment Conference, University of Salford, UK. Retrieved June 12, 2007 from http://www.edu.salford.ac.uk/ her/proceedings/ papers/ hc_06.rtf

Craig, A., Sherman, W. R., & Will, J. D. (2009). *Developing virtual reality applications: Foundations of effective design.* Morgan Kaufmann.

Cruz, I. F., Tamassia, R., & Yao, D. (2007). Privacy-preserving schema matching using mutual information. In *Proceedings of the 21th Annual IFIP WG 11.3 Working Conference on Data and Applications Security* (DBSec '07). Redondo Beach, CA. July 2007.

Cruz-Neira, C., Sandin, D. J., & DeFanti, T. A. (1993). Surround-screen projection-based virtual reality: The design and implementation of the CAVE. *SIGGRAPH*, *93*, 135–142.

Cyranoski, D. (2001). Japan's first BSE case fuels fears elsewhere. *Nature*, *413*, 337. doi:10.1038/35096710

Datta, S., Giannella, C., & Kargupta, H. (2005). *K-means clustering over peer-to-peer networks*. In the 8th International Workshop on High Performance and Distributed Mining. IEEE.

Daugherty, M., & Funke, B. L. (1998). University faculty and student perceptions of Web-based instruction. *Journal of Distance Education*, *13*(1), 21–39.

Delcloque, P. (2000). *History of CALL*. Retrieved November 8, 2007, from http://www.ict4lt.org/en/History_of_CALL.pdf

Delsing, J., & Lindgren, P. (2005). Sensor communication technology towards ambient intelligence. *Measurement Science & Technology*, *16*(4), 37–46. doi:10.1088/0957-0233/16/4/R02

Desouza, K. C. (2003). Facilitating tacit knowledge exchange. *Communications of the ACM*, *46*(6), 85–88. doi:10.1145/777313.777317

Devaraj, S., & Kholi, R. (2003). Performance impacts of Information Technology: Is actual usage the missing link? *Management Science*, *49*(3), 273–289. doi:10.1287/mnsc.49.3.273.12736

Dickinson, D. L., & Bailey, D. V. (2002). Meat traceability: Are U.S. consumers willing to pay for it? *Journal of Agricultural and Resource Economics*, *27*(2), 348–364.

Dornyei, Z. (2002). The motivational basis of language learning tasks. In Robinson, P. (Ed.), *Individual differences and instructed language learning* (pp. 137–158). Amsterdam, The Netherlands: John Benjamins.

Dourish, P., & Bly, S. (1992). Portholes: Supporting awareness in a distributed work group. *Proceedings of CHI'92*, (pp. 541-547).

Doyle, J., & Philips, J. (1989). *Manual on experimental stress analysis* (5th ed.). Society for Experimental Mechanics.

Drury, C. G. (1972). The effect of speed of working on industrial inspection accuracy. *Applied Ergonomics*, 42–47.

Drysdale, P. (1995). The question of access to the Japanese market. *Pacific Economic Papers, 247*.

Du, W., & Atallah, M. (2000). *Protocols for secure remote database access with approximate matching*. 7th ACM Conference on Computer and Communications Security (ACMCCS 2000), The First Workshop on Security and Privacy in E-Commerce. November 2000, Athens.

Ebara, Y., Nabuchi, T., Sakamoto, N., & Koyamada, K. (2006). *Study on eye-to-eye contact by multi-viewpoint videos merging system for tele-immersive environment.* IEEE International Workshop on Network-based Virtual Reality and Tele-existence, (pp. 647-651).

Education Revolution. (2010). http://www.mext.go.jp/a_menu/shougai/kaikaku /pdf/p150.pdf

Edusoft. (2002). *Teacher's guide*. Received as an e-mail attachment on June 25, 2004, from the Taiwan distributor.

Ekbia, H. R., & Hara, N. (2005). Incentive structures in knowledge management. In Schwartz, D. (Ed.), *Encyclopedia of knowledge management*. Hershey, PA: Idea Group Inc.

Ellis, R. (1997). The empirical evaluation of language teaching materials. *ELT Journal*, *51*(1), 36–42. doi:10.1093/elt/51.1.36

Ellis, R. (1999). *Learning a second language through interaction*. John Benjamins B.V.

Ellis, R., & Barkhuizen, G. (2005). *Analysing learner language*. Oxford, UK: Oxford University Press.

Ellis, R., Tanaka, Y., & Yamazaki, A. (1994). Classroom interaction, comprehension, and the acquisition of L2 word meanings. *Language Learning*, *44*(3), 449–491. doi:10.1111/j.1467-1770.1994.tb01114.x

Ellis, A. E. (2003). Personality type and participation in networked learning environments. *Educational Media International*, *40*(1-2), 101–114.

Ellis, A. E. (2001). *Student-centred collaborative learning via face-to-face and asynchronous online communication: What's the difference?* Paper presented at the Meeting at the Crossroads: Proceedings of the Eighteenth Annual Conference of the Australasian Society for Computers in Learning in Tertiary Education (ASCILITE), Melbourne, Australia, December 2001, (pp. 169-177).

Elmagarmid, A. K., Ipeirotis, P. G., & Verykios, V. S. (2007). Duplicate record detection: A survey. *IEEE Transactions on Knowledge and Data Engineering, 19*(1), 1–16. doi:10.1109/TKDE.2007.250581

Enciso, R., Li, J., Fidaeo, D., Noh, T. Y., & Neumann, U. (1999). Synthesis of 3d faces. *Proceedings of the International Workshop Digital and Computational Video*, Florida.

Engel, J. F., Blackwell, R. D., & Miniard, P. W. (1995). *Consumer behavior* (8th ed.). The Dryden Press.

Erdös, P., & Rényi, A. (1959). On random graphs. *Publicationes Mathematicae, 6*, 290–297.

Essa, I. A. (1994). *Visual interpretation of facial expressions using dynamic modeling.* Unpublished doctoral dissertation, MIT.

Estrin, D., Culler, D., Pister, K., & Sukhatme, G. (2002). Connecting the physical world with pervasive networks. *IEEE Pervasive Computing / IEEE Computer Society [and] IEEE Communications Society, 1*(1), 59–69. doi:10.1109/MPRV.2002.993145

Evermann, G., Chan, H. Y., Gales, M. J. F., Jia, B., Mrva, D., Woodland, P. C., & Yu, K. (2005). Training LVCSR systems on thousands of hours of data. [Philadelphia, PA.]. *Proceedings of, ICASSP2005*, 209–212.

Fa, T., Pi, C., & Peng, Y. (2006). Multiple labels associative classification. *Knowledge and Information Systems, 9*(1), 109–129. doi:10.1007/s10115-005-0213-x

Falling Down of Academic Ability. (2010). http://ja.wikipedia.org/ wiki/%E5%AD%A6%E5%8A%9B%E4%BD %8E%E4%B8%8B

Faugeras, O. (1993). *Three-dimensional computer vision.* Cambridge, MA: The MIT Press.

Federico, M. (1996). Bayesian estimation methods for N-gram language model adaptation. [Philadelphia, PA.]. *Proceedings of, ICSLP96*, 240–243.

Finkenzeller, K. (1999). *RFID handbook: Radio-frequency identification fundamentals and applications.* John Wiley & Sons.

Finn, K. E., Sellen, A. J., & Wilbur, S. B. (1997). *Video-mediated communication.* Lawrence Erlbaum Assoc Inc.

Finney, D. J. (1947). *Probit analysis* (1st ed.). London, UK: Cambridge University Press.

Finney, D. J. (1978). *Statistical method in biological assay* (3rd ed.). London, UK: Charles Griffin and Co.

Fiscus, J. G. (1997). A post-processing system to yield reduced word error rates: Recognizer output voting error reduction (ROVER). *Proceedings 1997 IEEE Workshop on Automatic Speech Recognition and Understanding* (pp.347-352). Santa Barbara, CA.

Fish, R., Kraut, R., Root, R., & Rice, R. (1992). Evaluating video as a technology for informal communication. *Proceedings CHI, 92*, 37–48.

Focus on Internet News & Data. (2003). *Schools online in Taiwan 2002.* Retrieved May 25, 2004, from http://www.find.org.tw/ eng/news.asp? msgid=14& subjectid=4&pos=0

Fotos, S. (2004). Writing as talking: E-mail exchange for promoting proficiency and motivation in the foreign language classroom. In Fotos, S., & Browne, C. (Eds.), *New perspectives on CALL for second language classrooms* (pp. 109–129). Mahwah, NJ: Lawrence Erlbaum Associates.

Fourt, L. A., & Woodlock, J. W. (1960). Early prediction of market success of new grocery products. *Journal of Marketing, 25*(2), 31–48. doi:10.2307/1248608

Frank, R. H., & Cook, P. J. (1998). *The winner take all society.* Penguin Books USA Inc.

Frazelle, E. H. (2001). *Transportation and distribution management, supply chain strategy: The logistics of supply chain management* (pp. 169–223). McGraw-Hill.

Frick, H., Leonhardt, H., & Starck, D. (1991). *Human anatomy* (*Vol. 1*). Stuttgart, Germany: Thieme Medical Publishers.

Froehlich, B., Deisinger, J., & Bullinger, H. J. (2001). *Immersive projection technology and virtual environments*. Springer.

Frohlich, M. T. (2002). E-integration in the supply chain: Barriers and performance. *Decision Sciences, 33*(4), 537–555. doi:10.1111/j.1540-5915.2002.tb01655.x

Frohlich, M. T., & Westbrook, R. (2002). Demand chain management in manufacturing and services: Web-based integration, drivers and performance. *Journal of Operations Management, 20*(6), 729–745. doi:10.1016/S0272-6963(02)00037-2

Fujimoto, T. (2007). Nihonhatu no Keieigaku ha kanouka? *MMRC Discussion Paper, 148*.

Fukui, M., Sasaki, K., Shibazaki, Y., Ohtake, Y., & Nakamura, Y. (1998). Practice of know-how sharing in office environment using knowledge and knowledge-sharing system. *IPSJ SIG Notes, 27*(3), 13–18.

Furui, S. (2005a). Recent progress in corpus-based spontaneous speech recognition. *IEICE Transactions on Information and Systems. E (Norwalk, Conn.), 88-D*(3), 366–375.

Furui, S., Nakamura, M., Ichiba, T., & Iwano, K. (2005b). Analysis and recognition of spontaneous speech using corpus of spontaneous Japanese. *Speech Communication, 47*, 208–219. doi:10.1016/j.specom.2005.02.010

Fylan, F., & Harding, G. F. A. (1997). The effect of television frame rate on EEG abonormalities in photosensitive and pattern-sensitive epilepsy. *Epilepsia, 38*, 1124–1131. doi:10.1111/j.1528-1157.1997.tb01202.x

Gales, M. J. F. (1998). Maximum likelihood linear transformations for HMM-based speech recognition. *Computer Speech & Language, 12*(2), 75–98. doi:10.1006/csla.1998.0043

Gao, J., Jiang, G., Chen, H., & Han, J. (2009). *Modeling probabilistic measurement correlations for problem determination in large-scale distributed systems*. In International Conference. on Distributed Computing Systems (pp. 623-630). Montreal, Quebec, Canada: ICDCS.

Geisman, J. (2001). I*f you build it, will they come? Overcoming human obstacles to e-learning*. Retrieved May 3, 2004, from http://www.learningcircuits.org/ 2001/ mar2001/ elearn.html

Gibbs, S. J., Arapis, C., & Breitender, C. J. (1999). TELEPORT-towards immersive copresence. [Springer-Verlag]. *Multimedia Systems, 7*, 214–221. doi:10.1007/s005300050123

Giuliani, D., & Brugnara, F. (2006). Acoustic model adaptation with multiple supervisions, *Proceedings of the TC-STAR Workshop on Speech-to-Speech Translation* (pp.151-154). Trento, Italy.

Gray, H. (1985). *Anatomy of the human body* (29th ed.). Philadelphia, PA: Lea Febiber.

Grayson, D. M., & Monk, A. F. (2003). Are you looking at me? Eye contact and desktop video conferencing. *ACM Transactions on Computer-Human Interaction, 10*(3), 221–243. doi:10.1145/937549.937552

Guan, H. (1995). Technical approaches of real-time control based on multiprocessor systems. *IEE International Computing & Control Engineering Journal, 6*(2), 75–78. doi:10.1049/cce:19950203

Guan, H. (1996a). Construction and implementation of the parallel computing model of DBP learning algorithm. *Journal of Software, 7*(2), 111–118.

Guan, H., & Cheung, T. (2000). Efficient approaches for constructing a massively parallel processing system. *Journal of Systems Architecture, 46*, 1185–1190. doi:10.1016/S1383-7621(00)00019-9

Guan, H., & Ip, H. (2007). A study of parallel data mining in a peer-to-peer network. *Concurrent Engineering: Research and Applications, 15*(3), 281–289. doi:10.1177/1063293X07083088

Guan, H., Ip, H., & Zhang, Y. (1998). Java-based approaches for accessing databases on Internet and a JDBC-ODBC implementation. *IEE International Computing & Control Engineering Journal, 9*(2), 71–78. doi:10.1049/cce:19980204

Guan, H., & Li, C. (1997). Generalized stochastic petri net technology modelling MPP system. *MINI-MICRO Systems, 18*(3), 34–41.

Guan, H., & Sun, Y. (1992). The parallel programming techniques based on transputers. *MINI-MICRO Systems, 13*(9), 1–8.

Guan, H., & Sun, Y. (1993). Design and implementation of a reconfigurable system of multi-transputer network. *Journal of Computers, 16*(7).

Guan, H., Yu, S., & Ip, H. (2006). *A parallel algorithm for mining association rules in a distributed system. In the 3rd International Workshops on Software Development Methodologies of Distributed Systems* (pp. 23–30). IEEE.

Guan, H. (1996b). *Technical approaches for supporting multimedia communication in a distributed network of multiple servers*. In 1996 IEEE International Conference on Commuincation Systems (pp. 1483-1487). Singapore. IEEE.

Guan, H., & Cheung, T. (1996). *A belief logic system and associative plan method based on goal*. In 1996 IEEE International Conference on Systems, Man and Cybernetics (pp. 2653-2658). IEEE.

Guan, H., & Li, C. (1995). *An associative plan method based on goal and construction of a belief logic system*. In 1995 IEEE International Conference on Intelligent Control & Instrumentation (pp. 358-363). Singapore, IEEE.

Guan, H., Cheung, T., Li, C., & Yu, S. (1997). *Parallel design and implementation of SOM neural computing model in PVM environment of a distributed system*. In IEEE the 1997 Advances in Parallel and Distributed Computing Conference (pp. 26-31). APDC. IEEE.

Guan, H., Li, C., & Chan, W. (1995). *A parallel implementation of BP neural network on a multiple processor system*. In 1995 IEEE International Symposium on Artificial Neural Networks. Taipei, Taiwan: IEEE.

Guan, H., Li, C., & Cheung, T. (1996). *A generalized stochastic petri net approach for modeling multi-processor parallel processing system*. In IEEE 2nd International Conference on Algorithms & Architectures for Parallel Processing (pp. 413-420). Singapore.

Guenter, B. (1992). *A system for simulating human facial expression: State of the art in computer animation* (pp. 191–202). Springer-Verlag.

Guilford, J. P. (1954). *Psychometric methods*. New York, NY: McGraw-Hill.

Hair, J. F., Anderson, R. E., Tatham, R. L., & Black, W. C. (1998). *Multivariate data analysis with readings*. New Jersey: Prentice-Hall.

Halliday, A. M., McDonald, W. I., & Mushin, J. (1972). Delayed visual evoked response in optic neuritis. *Lancet*, 1982–1985.

Hamel, G. (2002). *Leading the revolution*. New York, NY: Plume.

Hampel, R., & Baber, E. (2003). Using Internet-based audio-graphic and video conferencing for language teaching and learning. In Felix, U. (Ed.), *Language learning online: Towards best practice* (pp. 171–191). Lisse, The Netherlands: Swets & Zeitlinger.

Han, J., & Kamber, M. (2006). *Data mining: Concepts and techniques* (2nd ed.). Morgan Kaufmann.

Hanakawa, N., Goto, K., Maeda, T., & Akazawa, Y. (2004). Discovery learning for software engineering –a Web based total education system: HInT–. In *Proceedings of The International Conference on Computers in Education (ICCE 2004)* (pp. 1929–1939). Melbourne (Australia).

Handley, M., Jacobson, V., & Perkins, C. (2006). *SDP: Session Description Protocol*. (IETF RFC 4566).

Harding, G. F. A., & Harding, P. F. (2008). *Photosensitive epilepsy and image safety. Applied ergonomics*. Elsevier.

Hase, S., & Ellis, A. (2001). Problems with online learning are systemic, not technical. In Stephenson, J. (Ed.), *Teaching and learning online: Pedagogies for new technologies* (pp. 27–34). London, UK: Kogan Page.

Hauck, M. (2007). Critical success factors in a TRI-DEM exchange. *ReCALL, 19*(2), 202–223. doi:10.1017/S0958344007000729

Hautakorpi, J., Camarillo, G., Penfield, R., Hawrylyshen, A., & Bhatia, M. (2008). *Requirement from SIP (Session Initiation Protocol) session border control developments*.

Hayashi, H., & Minazuki, A. (2010). Multiple scale of knowledge measurement using sensor technologies of human information processing systems prevent the influence of images upon viewers. *Journal of Electronics & Computer Science, 12*(1), 73–80.

Hayashi, H., Shirai, H., Kunifuji, S., & Miyahara, M. (2000). Assessment of extra high quality images using both EEG and assessment words on high order sensations. *Proceedings of the IEEE*, SMC2000, 289–1294.

Hayashi, H., Nakagawa, M., & Nakayasu, H. (2007). An evaluation method of human property using psychometric function in sensory test. *JCIIE, 24*(4), 259–267.

Hayashi, H. (2003). *Basic research of inner visual knowledge measurement based on biological measurement.* Doctoral dissertation at School of Knowledge Science in JAIST.

Hayashi, H., Torii, K., Kunifuji, S., & Miyahara, M. (1999). *An EEG comparison between extra high quality images and normal quality images.* (Technical report of IEICE, HIP99(186), 7-12).

Hempell, T. (2003). *Do computers call for training? Firm-level evidence on complementarities between ICT and human capital investments.* (ZEW Discussion Paper No. 03-20, Mannheim).

Henderson, A. J. (2003). *The e-learning questions and answer book.* New York, NY: Amacom.

Herzog, T. N., Scheuren, F. J., & Winkler, W. E. (2007). *Data quality and record linkage techniques.* Springer.

Hipp, J., Guntzer, U., & Nakaeizadeh, G. (2000). *Algorithms for association rule mining-a general survey and comparison.* In the 36th ACM SIGKDD International Conference on Knowledge Discovery and Data mining. ACM.

Hoopes, D. G., Madsen, T. L., & Walker, G. (Eds.). (2003). Guest editors' introduction to the special issue: Why is there a resource-based view? Toward a theory of competitive heterogeneity. *Strategic Management Journal, 24*(10), 889–902. doi:10.1002/smj.356

Hoppe, H. U., Luther, W., Mühlenbrock, M., Otten, W., & Tewissen, F. (1999). Interactive presentation support for an electronic lecture hall-a practice report. In Cumming, G. (Eds.), *Advanced research in computers and communications in education* (pp. 923–930).

Hori, K. (2005). *Do knowledge assets really exist in the world and can we access such knowledge-knowledge evolves through a cycle of knowledge liquidization and crystallization. (LNCS 3359)* (pp. 1–13). Springer.

Hori, T., Katoh, M., Ito, A., & Kohda, M. (1998). A study on a state clustering-based topology design method for HM-Nets. *IEICE Transactions on Information and Systems, J81-D-II*(10), 2239-2248.

HP Technology INC. (2008). *Three mystic mountain M-Kaohsiung contract project management and acceptance procedure, system integration plan.* Taiwan: Kaohsiung County Government, Fengshan, Kaohsiung County.

HP Technology INC. (2009). *Three mystic mountain M-Kaohsiung contract project management and acceptance test report.* Taiwan: Kaohsiung County Government, Fengshan, Kaohsiung County.

Huang, M. (2006). *Wireless Taipei, the future is now – The birth of the world's first wireless capital.* Taipei City Government Publication.

Huang, C., Cheng, T., & Chen, C. (1992). Color images' segmentation using scale space filter and Markov random field. *Pattern Recognition, 25*(10), 1217–1229. doi:10.1016/0031-3203(92)90023-C

Humphreys, G., Houston, M., Ng, Y., Frank, R., Ahern, S., Kirchner, P., & Klosowski, J. T. (2002). *Chromium: A stream-processing framework for interactive rendering on clusters.* The 29th Annual Conference on Computer Graphics and Interactive Techniques SIGGRAPH '02, (pp. 693-702).

Husemann, D. (1999). The smart card: Don't leave home without it. *IEEE Concurrency, 7*(2), 24–27. doi:10.1109/4434.766959

Iba, T., Takenaka, H., & Takefuji, Y. (2001). Reappearance of video cassette format competition using artificial market simulation. *Transactions of Information Processing Society of Japan, 42*(14), 73–89.

IEEE 1012. (1998). *IEEE standard for software verification and validation.* IEEE Standard.

IEEE 730. (2002). *IEEE standard for software quality assurance plans.* IEEE Standard.

IEEE 802.16-2004. (2004). *Air interface for fixed broadband wireless access system.* IEEE Standard for Local and metropolitan area networks.

IEEE 802.16e-2005. (2005). *Air interface for fixed and mobile broadband wireless access systems.* IEEE Standard for Local and metropolitan area networks.

IEEE 829. (1998). *IEEE standard for software test documentation.* IEEE Standard.

Inan, A., Kantarcioglu, M., Bertino, E., & Scannapieco, M. (2008). A hybrid approach to private record linkage. In *Proceedings of the 24th International Conference on Data Engineering*, 7–12 April 2008; Cancun, Mexico. (pp. 496-505). Los Alamitos, CA: IEEE.

Ito, M. (2003). *Suihei-Bungyouka to Araiansu-Senryaku no Bunseki*. Research Institute for Economics & Business Administration – Kobe Unversity, Discussion Paper Series.

ITRI (Industrial Technology Research Institute). (2008a). *Network, operation, and VoIP acceptance test procedure standard*. Taiwan: Bureau of Industry Affairs, Ministry of Economy.

ITRI (Industrial Technology Research Institute). (2008b). *Application service acceptance test procedure*. Taiwan: Bureau of Industrial Affairs, Ministry of Economy.

Itsuki, R., Shibata, H., Ikkai, Y., & Komoda, N. (2003). The autonomous Information System design for item management using rewritable RFID tags in supply chain. *Proceedings of 2003 IEEE International Conference on Emerging Technologies and Factory Automation* (ETFA 2003), (pp. 27-34).

Izumi, K., & Ueda, K. (1999). Analysis of dealers' processing financial news based on an artificial market approach. *Journal of Computational Intelligence in Finance, 7*, 23–33.

Jager, S. (2004). Learning management systems for language learning. In Chambers, A., Conacher, J. E., & Littlemore, J. (Eds.), *ICT and language learning: Integrating pedagogy and practice* (pp. 34–48). UK: The University of Birmingham Press.

Jasper, H. H. (1957). Report of the Committee on Methods of Clinical Examination in Electroencephalography. *Electroencephy and Clinical Neurophysiology, 10*(2), 370–375.

Jauregi, K., & Banados, E. (2008). Virtual interaction through video-Web communication: A step towards enriching and internationalizing language learning programs. *ReCALL, 20*(2), 183–207. doi:10.1017/S0958344008000529

Jeffreys, D. A. (1971). Cortical source locations of pattern-related visual evoked potentials recorded from the human scalp. *Nature, 229*, 502–504. doi:10.1038/229502a0

Jeong, B., Renambot, L., Jagodic, R., Singh, R., Aguilera, J., Johnson, A., & Leigh, J. (2006). *High-performance dynamic graphics streaming for scalable adaptive graphics environment*. ACM/IEEE Conference on Supercomputing 2006, (p. 24).

Johansen, D., van Renesse, R., & Schneider, F. B. (1996). Supporting broad Internet access to TACOMA. In *Proceedings of the 7th SIGOPS European Workshop* (pp. 55–58). Connemara, Ireland.

Johnson, C., Tyson, L. D., & Zysman, J. (1989). *Politics and productivity*. Cambridge, MA: Ballinger Publishing Company.

Johnston, A., Donovan, S., Sparks, R., Cunningham, C., & Summers, K. (2003a). *Session initiation protocol basic call flow examples*. (IETF RFC 3665).

Johnston, A., Donovan, S., Sparks, R., Cunningham, C., & Summers, K. (2003b). *SIP public switched telephone network-PSTN call flows*. IETF RFC 3666.

Jones, S. J. (1993). Visual evoked potentials after optic neuritis. Effect of time interval, age and disease dissemination. *Journal of Neurology, 240*(8), 489–494. doi:10.1007/BF00874118

Juang, B. H., & Katagiri, S. (1992). Discriminative learning for minimum error classification. *IEEE Transactions on Signal Processing, 40*(12), 3043–3054. doi:10.1109/78.175747

Kainuma, S., Miyashita, H., & Nishimoto, K. (2006). Analyses of creation processes of novels where others' whims are exploited to inspire an author's imagination. *IPSJ SIG Technical Reports 2006-EC-3, 24*, 113-120.

Kamvar, S., Schlosser, M., & Garcia-Molina, H. (2003). T*he eigentrust algorithm for reputation management in p2p networks*. In the 12th International Conference on World Wide Web (WWW) (pp. 640-651). IEEE.

Kantarcioglu, M., Jiang, W., & Malin, B. (2008). *A privacy-preserving framework for integrating person-specific databases*. Privacy in Statistical Databases Conference, (pp. 298-314).

Kaplan, S., & Sawhney, M. (2000). E-hubs: The new B2B marketplaces. *Harvard Business Review, 70*(1), 71–79.

Karakasidis, A., & Verykios, V. S. (2009). Privacy preserving record linkage using phonetic codes. In BCI '09: *Proceedings of the 4th Balkan Conference in Informatics.* Thessaloniki, Greece, 2009, (pp.101-106).

Kargupta, H., Han, J., Yu, P., Motwani, R., & Kumar, V. (Eds.). (2008). *Next generation of data mining.* Taylor & Francis.

Kats, E., & Lazarsfeld, P. F. (1955). *Personal influence.* Free Press.

Katz, M. L., & Shapiro, C. (1985). Network externalities, competition, and compatibility. *The American Economic Review, 75,* 424–440.

Kauff, P., & Schreer, O. (2002). An immersive 3D videoconferencing system using shared virtual team user environments. *Proceedings of the 4th International Conference on Collaborative Virtual Environments,* (pp. 105-112).

Kelshikar, N., Zabulis, X., Mulligan, J., Daniilidis, K., Sawant, V., & Sinha, S. ... Huntoon, G. (2003). *Real-time terascale implementation of teleimmersion.* International Conference on Computation Science, (pp. 33-42).

Kemp, T., & Waibel, A. (1999). Unsupervised training of a speech recognizer: Recent experiments. *Proceedings of Eurospeech99* (pp. 2725-2728). Budapest, Hungary.

Kern, R., & Warschauer, M. (2000). Introduction: Theory and practice of network-based language teaching. In Warschauer, M., & Kern, R. (Eds.), *Network-based language teaching: Concepts and practice* (pp. 1–19). Cambridge, UK: Cambridge University Press.

Kessler, E. H. (2003). Leveraging e-R&D processes: A knowledge-based view. *Technovation, 23,* 905–915. doi:10.1016/S0166-4972(03)00108-1

Kette, R., & Schluns, K. (1998). *Computer vision–three-dimensional data from images.* Springer-Verlag.

Kettinger, W. J., Grover, V., Guha, S., & Segars, A. H. (1994). Strategic Information Systems revisited: A study insustainability and performance. *Management Information Systems Quarterly, 18,* 31–58. doi:10.2307/249609

Khoo, E. G. L., Forret, M., & Cowie, B. (2003). *Extricating the web of learning: Identifying the characteristics of effective learning environments.* Paper presented at the 34th Australasian Science Education Research Association [ASERA] Conference, 9-12 July, 2003, Melbourne, Australia.

Kim, E. B., & Schniederjans, M. J. (2004). The role of personality in Web-based distance education courses. *Communications of the ACM, 47*(3), 95–98. doi:10.1145/971617.971622

Kinginger, C. (2000). Learning the pragmatics of solidarity in the networked foreign language classroom. In Hall, J. K., & Verplaetse, L. S. (Eds.), *Second and foreign language learning through classroom interaction* (pp. 23–46). Mahwah, NJ: Lawrence Erlbaum Associates, Inc.

Klemm, K., & Eguíluz, V. M. (2002a). Highly clustered scale-free networks. *Physical Review E: Statistical, Nonlinear, and Soft Matter Physics, 65,* 036123. doi:10.1103/PhysRevE.65.036123

Klemm, K., & Eguíluz, V. M. (2002b). Growing scale-free networks with small-world behavior. *Physical Review E: Statistical, Nonlinear, and Soft Matter Physics, 65,* 057102. doi:10.1103/PhysRevE.65.057102

Kondo, C., Kobayashi, Y., & Miyahara, M. (1997). *Analysis of the image assessment words on high order sensation.* (Technical report of IEICE, CQ97(457), 37-44).

Kowalczyk, W., Jelasity, M., & Eiben, A. (2003). *Towards data mining in large and fully distributed peer-to-peer overlay networks.* In BNAIC'03 (pp. 203-210).

Kowtha, N. R., & Choon, T. W. I. (2001). Determinants of website development: A study of electronic commerce in Singapore. *Information & Management, 39*(3), 227–242. doi:10.1016/S0378-7206(01)00092-1

Kraut, R. E., Fish, R. S., Root, R. W., & Chalfonte, B. L. (1990). Informal communication in organizations: Form, function, and technology. In Oskamp, S., & Spacapan, S. (Eds.), *People's reactions to technology* (pp. 145–199). London, UK: Sage Publications.

Krogh, G. V., Ichijo, K., & Nonaka, I. (2000). *Enabling knowledge creation: How to unlock the mystery of tacit knowledge and release the power of innovation.* Oxford University Press.

Kukimoto, N., Ebara, Y., & Koyamada, K. (2004). Voice communication library for collaborative virtual environment. (IPSJ Technical report, 109).

Lai, P. K. Y., Yiu, S. M, Chow, K. P., Chong, C. F., &Hui, L. C. K. (2006). An efficient Bloom filter based solution for multiparty private matching. *Security and Management*, 286-292

Lao, D., & Gonzales, D. (2005). Understanding online learning through a qualitative description of professors' and students' experiences. *Journal of Technology and Teacher Education, 13*(3), 459–474.

Lawrence, R. Z. (1993). Japan's different trade regime: An analysis with particular reference to Keiretsu. *The Journal of Economic Perspectives, 7*(3).

Lawson, S. (2006). *Can metro Wi-Fi beat cellular?* PC World.

Leclercq, P., Liu, J., Chan, M., Woodward, A., Gimel'farb, G., & Delmas, P. (2004). Comparative study of stereo algorithms for 3D face reconstruction. *Proceedings of the Conference of Advanced Concepts for Intelligent Vision Systems*, (pp. 690-704).

Lederer, A. L., Mirchandani, D. A., & Sims, K. (2001). The search for strategic advantage from the World Wide Web. *International Journal of Electronic Commerce, 5*(4), 117–133.

Lee, H. L., & Billington, C. (1992). Managing supply chain inventory: Pitfalls and opportunities. *Sloan Management Review, 33*, 65–73.

Lee, Y., Terzopoulos, D., & Waters, K. (1995). Realistic modeling for facial animation. ACM Conference on SIGGRAPH (ACM Computer Graphics), (pp. 55-62).

Leggetter, C. J., & Woodland, P. C. (1995). Maximum likelihood linear regression for speaker adaptation of continuous-density hidden Markov models. *Computer Speech & Language, 9*, 171–185. doi:10.1006/csla.1995.0010

Leigh, J., DeFanti, T. A., Johnson, A. E., Brown, M. D., & Sandin, D. J. (1997). Global tele-immersion: Better than being there. *Proceedings in ICAT, 97*, 10–17.

Levin, J., & Waugh, M. (1998). Teaching teleapprenticeships:Electronic network-based educational frameworks for improving teacher education. *Interactive Learning Environments Journal, 6*(1-2), 39–58. doi:10.1076/ilee.6.1.39.3612

Levy, M., & Stockwell, G. (2006). *CALL dimensions: Options and issues in computer-assisted language learning.* Mahwah, NJ: Lawrence Erlbaum.

Lincoln, E. J. (1990). *Japan's unequal trade.* Washington, DC: Brookings Institute.

Lomicka, L. (2006). Understanding the other: Intercultural exchange and CMC. In Ducate, L., & Arnold, N. (Eds.), *Calling on CALL: From theory and research to new directions in foreign language teaching* (Vol. 5, pp. 211–236). CALICO Monograph Series.

Loukis, E., Pazalos, K., & Georgiou, St. (2009). An empirical investigation of the moderating effects of BPR and TQM on ICT business value. *Journal of Enterprise Information Management, 22*(5), 564–586. doi:10.1108/17410390910993545

LP002. (2007). *Low power transmitter electrical specifications. National Communications Commission.* Taiwan: NCC.

Luczak, H. (2002). Computer supported collaborative work -making information aware. *International Journal of Human-Computer Interaction.* Lawrence Erlbaum Assoc Inc.

Mackay, S., & Stockport, G. J. (2006). Blended learning, classroom and e-learning. *Business Review (Federal Reserve Bank of Philadelphia), 5*(1), 82–88.

Madsen, H. O., Krenk, S., & Lind, N. C. (1986). *Method of structural safety.* Prentice Hall.

Maeda, T., Okamoto, T., Fukushige, Y., & Asada, T. (2006). Interactive e-learning environment using mobile phone messages. In [Dublin, Ireland.]. *Proceedings of IADIS International Conference Mobile Learning, 2006*, 374–378.

Maeda, T., Okamoto, T., Fukushige, Y., & Asada, T. (2009b). Session management of mobile communication for learning support environment. In [Barcelona, Spain.]. *Proceedings of IADIS International Conference Mobile Learning, 2009*, 217–221.

Maeda, T., Okamoto, T., Fukushige, Y., & Asada, T. (2008). Learning session management with e-mail communication. In *Proceedings of World Conference on Educational Multimedia, Hypermedia & Telecommunications (ED-MEDIA 2008)* (pp. 1787–1792). Vienna, Austria.

Maeda, T., Okamoto, T., Miura, T., Fukushige, Y., & Asada, T. (2007). Interactive lecture support using mobile-phone messages. In *Proceedings of World Conference on Educational Multimedia, Hypermedia & Telecommunications (ED-MEDIA 2007)* (pp. 3659–3665). Vancouver, Canada.

Maeda, T., Tomo, M., & Asada, T. (2004, 7). Integrated lecture-support system using e-mail. In *Proceedings of National University Symposium on Information Education Methods* (pp. 26–27). Tokyo, Japan.

Maekawa, K. (2003). Corpus of spontaneous Japanese: Its design and evaluation. *Proceedings of IEEE-ISCA Workshop on Spontaneous Speech Processing and Recognition* (pp. 7-12). Tokyo, Japan.

Mandelbrot, B. B. (1982). *The fractal geometry of nature.* Freeman.

Mangu, L., Brill, E., & Stolcke, A. (2000). Finding consensus in speech recognition: Word error minimization and other applications of confusion networks. *Computer Speech & Language, 14*, 373–400. doi:10.1006/csla.2000.0152

Mansfield, E. (1961). Technical change and the rate of imitation. *Econometrica, 29*, 741–766. doi:10.2307/1911817

Masataki, H., Sagisaka, Y., Hisaki, K., & Kawahara, T. (1997). Task adaptation using MAP estimation in N-gram language model. [Munich, Germany.]. *Proceedings of, ICASSP97*, 783–786.

Masie, E. (2001). The real truth about e-learning's future. *IT Training.* Retrieved July 2, 2005, from http://www.train-net.co.uk/ news/full_news.cfm ?ID=2994

Masuda, N., Miwa, H., & Konno, N. (2004). Analysis of scale-free networks based on a threshold graph with intrinsic vertex weights. *Physical Review E: Statistical, Nonlinear, and Soft Matter Physics, 70*, 036124. doi:10.1103/PhysRevE.70.036124

Mata, F. J., Fuerst, W. L., & Barney, J. B. (1995). Information Technology and sustained competitive advantage: A resource-based analysis. *Management Information Systems Quarterly, 19*(4), 487–505. doi:10.2307/249630

Matsoukas, S., Gauvain, J.-L., Adda, G., Colthurst, T., Kao, C.-L., & Kimball, O. (2006). Advances in transcription of broadcast news and conversational telephone speech within the combined EARS BBN/LIMSI system. *IEEE Transactions in Audio. Speech and Language Processing, 14*(5), 1541–1556. doi:10.1109/TASL.2006.878257

Matsubara, T., Sugiyama, K., & Nishimoto, K. (2002). *Raison d'etre object: A cyber-hearth that catalyzes face-to-face informal communication.* Engineering and Deployment of Cooperative Information Systems: First International Conference EDCIS 2002, (LNCS 2480), (pp. 537-546).

Matsui, T. (2002). A new sharpness evaluation method using a cooperative human vision model and its effectiveness. *The IEICE Transactions, J85-A*(8), 867-875.

McPherson, M., & Nunes, M. B. (2004). *Developing innovation in online learning: An action research framework.* London, UK: Routledge Falmer. doi:10.4324/9780203426715

Mehyar, M., Spanos, D., Pongsajapan, J., Low, S., & Murray, R. (2005). *Distributed averaging on a peer-to-peer network.* In IEEE Conference on Decision and Control. IEEE.

Melucci, M., & Castiglion, R. (2005). *A weighing, framework for information retrieval in peer-to-peer networks.* In 16th International Workshop on Database and Expert Systems Applications (pp. 374-378). Copenaghen. IEEE.

Meroño-Cerdan, A. L., & Soto-Acosta, P. (2007). External Web content and its influence on organizational performance. *European Journal of Information Systems, 16*(1), 66–80. doi:10.1057/palgrave.ejis.3000656

Meroño-Cerdan, A. L., Soto-Acosta, P., & Lopez-Nicolas, C. (2008a). Analyzing collaborative technologies' effect on performance through intranet use orientations. *Journal of Enterprise Information Management, 21*(1), 39–51. doi:10.1108/17410390810842246

Meroño-Cerdan, A. L., Soto-Acosta, P., & Lopez-Nicolas, C. (2008b). How do collaborative technologies affect innovation in SMEs? *International Journal of e-Collaboration*, *4*(4), 33–50. doi:10.4018/jec.2008100103

METI. (2009). *Current production statistics*. Ministry of Economy, Trade and Industry.

Mimura, M., & Kawahara, T. (2007). Effect of minimum phone error training for spontaneous speech recognition tasks. *Proceedings of Acoustical Society of Japan 2009 Autumn Meeting*, (p. 134). Kofu, Japan.

Mitsuhashi, T. (1999). Subjective assessment techniques of digital image quality. *The Journal of ITE*, *53*(6), 1195–1198.

Miwa, S. (2001). Semiconductor-Sangyou ni okeru architecture no kakushin. In Fujimoto, T., Takeishi, A., & Aoshima, Y. (Eds.), *Business Architectureshin* (pp. 73–100).

Miyahara, M. (1988). Quality assessments for visual service. *IEEE Communications Magazine*, *26*(10), 51–60. doi:10.1109/35.7667

Miyahara, M. (2002). *Extra high quality audio-visual system for creation of future A-V works and two-way presence communication*. JSPS Research Project for Future Program.

Mo, J. P. T., Sheng, Q. Z., Li, X., & Zeadally, S. (2009). RFID infrastructure design: A case study of two Australian RFID projects. *IEEE Internet Computing*, *13*(1), 14–21. doi:10.1109/MIC.2009.18

Moore, G. A. (1991). *Crossing the chasm*. Harper Business.

Moore, G., & Young, S. (2000). Class-based language model adaptation using mixtures of word-class weights. [Beijing, China.]. *Proceedings of, ICSLP2000*, 512–515.

Morawski, T. B., Drury, C. G., & Karwan, M. H. (1992). The optimum speed of visual inspection using a random search strategy. *IIE Transactions*, *24*(5), 122–133. doi:10.1080/07408179208964252

Moro, B. (2007). *Web literacy*. Retrieved August 27, 2007, from http://www.ecml.at/projects/voll/literacy/english/index.htm

Motteram, G. (2006). Blended education and the transformation of teachers: A long-term case study in postgraduate UK higher education. *British Journal of Educational Technology*, *37*(1), 17–30. doi:10.1111/j.1467-8535.2005.00511.x

Mukhopadhyay, T., Kekre, S., & Kalathur, S. (1995). Business value of Information Technology: A study of electronic data interchange. *Management Information Systems Quarterly*, *19*(2), 137–156. doi:10.2307/249685

Murayama, M., & Osada, H. (2006). Business system which create differences in corporate profitability: A case study on semiconductor trading companies. *The Journal of Science Policy and Research Management*, *21*(2), 183–193.

Nakamura, A., Oba, T., Watanabe, S., Ishizuka, K., Fujimoto, M., & Hori, T. … Minami Y. (2006). *Evaluation of the SOLON speech recognition system: 2006 benchmark using the corpus of spontaneous Japanese*. (IEICE Technical Report, SP2006-127), (pp. 73-78). Nagoya, Japan.

Nakanishi, H., Yoshida, C., Nishimura, T., & Ishida, T. (1996). *FreeWalk: Supporting casual meetings in a network*. International Conference on Computer Supported Cooperative Work (CSCW'96), (pp. 308-314).

Nakano, T., Kamewada, K., Sugito, J., Nagaoka, Y., Ogura, K., & Nishimoto, K. (2006). The Traveling cafe: A communication encouraging system for partitioned offices. *CHI2006 Extended Abstract*, (pp. 1139-1144).

Nakasu, E., Kanda, K., Ichigaya, A., Kurozumi, M., & Nishida, Y. (2008). Picture quality assessment test for digitally coded motion pictures in multi-formats. *The Journal of ITE*, *62*(2), 262–270. doi:10.3169/itej.62.262

Narasimhan, S., Koppal, S., & Yamazaki, S. (2008). *Temporal dithering of illumination for fast active vision*. European Conference on Computer Vision, 4, (pp. 830-844).

Narita, N. (1995). Comparisons between the DSCQS method and the SSQS method used in absolute evaluation of picture quality-distribution and processing of opinion scores. *The IEICE Transactions, J78-DII*(12), 1899-1910.

Narita, N., & Sugiura, Y. (1998). A consideration of subjective evaluation method for different television systems-on methods of paired comparison with simultaneous presentation. *The IEICE Transactions, J81-A*(2), 269-279.

Newman, M. E. J. (2003). The structure and function of complex networks. *SIAM Review, 45,* 167–256. doi:10.1137/S003614450342480

Ni, T., Schmidt, G. S., Staadt, O. G., Livingston, M. A., Ball, R., & May, R. (2006). *A survey of large high-resolution display technologies, techniques, and applications.* The IEEE Conference on Virtual Reality 2006, (pp. 223-236).

Nirnimesh, H. P., & Narayanan, P. J. (2007). Garuda: A scalable tiled display wall using commodity PCs. *IEEE Transactions on Visualization and Computer Graphics, 13*(5), 864–877. doi:10.1109/TVCG.2007.1049

Nishimoto, K., & Matsuda, K. (2007). Informal communication support media for encouraging knowledge-sharing and creation in a community. [IJITDM]. *International Journal of Information Technology and Decision Making, 6*(3), 411–426. doi:10.1142/S0219622007002551

Nishimoto, K., Sumi, Y., & Mase, K. (1996). Toward an outsider agent for supporting a brainstorming session-an information retrieval method from a different viewpoint. *Knowledge-Based Systems, 9*(6), 377–384. doi:10.1016/S0950-7051(96)01050-7

Nishimoto, K., & Nemoto, H. (2006). Interactive fliers: An electric ad system for a community to facilitate communications between advertisers and audience. *Proceedings of The First International Conference on Knowledge, Information and Creativity Support Systems (KICSS2006),* (pp. 197-204).

Nishimoto, K., Amano, K., & Usuki, M. (2006). pHotO-luck: A home-use table-ware to vitalize mealtime communications by projecting photos onto dishes. *Proceedings of The First IEEE International Workshop on Horizontal Interactive Human-Computer Systems (TableTop2006),* (pp. 9-16).

Nonaka, I., & Takeuchi, H. (1995). *The knowledge-creating company: How Japanese companies create the dynamics of innovation.* Oxford University Press.

Obata, A., & Sasaki, K. (1998). OfficeWalker: A virtual visiting system based on proxemics. *Proceedings CSCW, 98,* 1–10.

Ochiai, S. (2003). *DXF handbook.* Tokyo, Japan: Ohmsha Ltd.

OECD. (2005). E-learning in tertiary education: Brief policy. *Organization for Economic Co-operation and Development [OECD]: Education-tertiary education.* Retrieved June 25, 2007, from http://www.oecd.org/dataoecd/55/25/ 35961132.pdf

Ogata, J., & Ariki, Y. (2002). Unsupervised acoustic model adaptation based on phoneme error minimization. [Denver, CO.]. *Proceedings of, ICSLP2002,* 1429–1432.

Ogawa, K. (2007). Wagakuni Electronics-sangyou ni-miru Platform keisei mechanism. *MMRC Discussion Paper, 146.*

Ogi, T., & Sakai, M. (2006). Communication in the networked immersive environment. *ASIAGRAPH, 2006,* 67–72.

Ogura, K., Ishizaki, M., & Nishimoto, K. (2004). A method of extracting topic threads towards facilitating knowledge creation in chat conversations. *Proceedings of KES2004*

Ogura, K., Nishimoto, K., & Sugiyama, K. (2007). Cha-TEL: A novel voice communication systems based on analyzing text-based chat conversations for multiple topic thread. *Proceedings of the Second IASTED International Conference Human-Computer Interaction* (pp. 49-54).

Ohkura, K., Sugiyama, M., & Sagayama, S. (1992). Speaker adaptation on transfer vector field smoothing with continuous mixture density HMMs. [Banff, Canada.]. *Proceedings of, ICSLP92,* 369–372.

Ohyama, T., Imai, S., & Wake, T. (1994). *Handbook of sensory and perception.* Seishin Publisher.

Okamoto, M., Nakanishi, H., Nishimura, T., & Ishida, T. (1998). Silhouettell: Awareness support for real-world encounter. In Ishida, T. (Ed.), *Community computing and support systems. (LNCS 1519)* (pp. 317–330). Springer-Verlag. doi:10.1007/3-540-49247-X_21

Okimoto, D. I., Sugano, T., & Weinstein, F. B. (Eds.). (1984). *Competitive edge: The semiconductor industry in the U.S and Japan.* Stanford, CA: Stanford University Press.

Oosterhof, A., Conrad, R., & Ely, D. P. (2008). *Assessing learners online.* Pearson Education.

Opara, L. U. (2003). Traceability in agriculture and food supply chain: A review of basic concepts, technological implications, and future prospects. *Food. Agriculture & Environment, 1*(1), 101–106.

P.862. (2001). *Perceptional evaluation of speech quality (PESQ): An objective method for end-to-end speech quality assessment of narrow-band telephone network and speech codecs.* International Telecommunication Union (ITU) recommendation.

Palloff, R. M., & Pratt, K. (2001). *Lessons from the cyberspace classroom: The realities of online teaching.* San Francisco, CA: Jossey-Bass.

Palmberg, R. (1978). Strategies of second-language communication. *CIEFL Bulletin, 14*(2), 1–8.

Park, K. S., Kapoor, A., Scharver, C., & Leigh, J. (2000). Exploiting multiple perspectives in tele-immersion. *Proceedings of Immersive Projection Technology Workshop.*

Pearson, E. S., & Hartley, H. O. (1962). *Biometrika tables for statisticians* (1st ed., pp. 4–9). Cambridge, UK: Cambridge University Press.

Pellettieri, J. (2000). Negotiation in cyberspace: The role of chatting in the development of grammatical competence. In Warschauer, M., & Kern, R. (Eds.), *Network-based language teaching: Concepts and practice* (pp. 59–86). Cambridge, UK: Cambridge University Press.

Pica, T. (1994). Research on negotiation: What does it reveal about second-language learning conditions, processes, and outcomes? *Language Learning, 44*(3), 493–527. doi:10.1111/j.1467-1770.1994.tb01115.x

Pooler, V. H., & Pooler, D. J. (1997). *Purchasing and supply management creating the vision.* Chapman & Hall. RFID news. (2003). Hitachi unveils smallest RFID chip. *RFID Journal.* Retrieved January 31, 2011, from http://www.rfidjournal.com/article/view/337/1/1

Population of High School Graduates. (2010). http://www.mext.go.jp/ b_menu/toukei/001/ 08072901/003/sanzu07.pdf

Porter, M., & Takahashi, H. (2000). Can Japan compete? *Diamond (Philadelphia, Pa.),* 130.

Povey, D., Kingsbury, B., Mangu, L., Saon, G., Soltau, H., & Zweig, G. (2005). fMPE: Discriminatively trained features for speech recognition. [Philadelphia, PA.]. *Proceedings of, ICASSP2005,* 961–964.

Povey, D., & Woodland, P. C. (2002). Minimum phone error and I-smoothing for improved discriminative training. [Orlando, FL.]. *Proceedings of, ICASSP2002,* 105–108.

Powell, T. C., & Dent-Micallef, A. (1997). Information Technology as competitive advantage: The role of human, business, and technology resources. *Strategic Management Journal, 18*(5), 375–405. doi:10.1002/(SICI)1097-0266(199705)18:5<375::AID-SMJ876>3.0.CO;2-7

Q.737. (1997). *Specifications of signaling system no. 7 – ISDN supplementary services.* International Telecommunication Union (ITU) recommendation.

Q.764. (1999). *Signaling system no. 7: ISDN user part signaling procedure.* International Telecommunication Union (ITU) recommendation.

Q.931. (1998). *ISDN user-network interface layer 3 specification for basic call control.* International Telecommunication Union (ITU) recommendation.

Qiu, L., & Riesbeck, C. (2004). An incremental model for developing computer-based learning environments for problem-based learning. In. *Proceedings of IEEE International Conference on Advanced Learning Technologies, 2004,* 171–175.

Ravasz, E., & Barabási, A.-L. (2003). Hierarchical organization in complex networks. *Physical Review E: Statistical, Nonlinear, and Soft Matter Physics, 67,* 026112. doi:10.1103/PhysRevE.67.026112

Ravasz, E., Somera, A. L., Mongru, D. A., Oltvai, Z. N., & Barabási, A.-L. (2002). Hierarchical organization of modularity in metabolic networks. *Science, 297,* 1551–1555. doi:10.1126/science.1073374

Ravichandran, T., & Lertwongsatien, C. (2005). Effect of Information Systems resources and capabilities on firm performance: A resource-based perspective. *Journal of Management Information Systems, 21*(4), 237–276.

Ravikumar, P., Cohen, W., & Fienberg, S. E. (2004). *A secure protocol for computing string distance metrics.* WPSADM 2004.

Recommendation, I. T. U.-R. B. T. (1998). *Subjective assessment methods for image quality in high-definition television* (pp. 710–714). ITU Radiocommunication.

Recommendation, I. T. U.-R. B. T. (2002). *Methodology for the subjective assessment of the quality of television pictures* (pp. 500–511). ITU Radiocommunication.

Reeder, K., Heift, T., Roche, J., Tabyanian, S., Schlickau, S., & Golz, P. (2004). Toward a theory of e/valuation for second language learning media. In Fotos, S., & Browne, C. (Eds.), *New perspectives on CALL for second language classrooms* (pp. 255–278). Mahwah, NJ: Lawrence Erlbaum Associates, Inc.

Renambot, L., Jeong, B., Jagodic, R., Johnson, A., Leigh, J., & Aguilera, J. (2006). *Collaborative visualization using high-resolution tiled displays.* CHI 06 Workshop on Information Visualization and Interaction Techniques for Collaboration Across Multiple Displays.

Renambot, L., Rao, A., Singh, R., Jeong, B., Krishnaprasad, N., & Vishwanath, V. … Johnson, A. (2004). *SAGE: The Scalable Adaptive Graphics Environment.* Workshop on Advanced Collaborative Environments.

Ridder, H., & Hamberg, R. (1997). Continuous assessment of image quality. *SMPTE Journal, 106*(2), 123–128.

Rodger, S. H. (1995). An interactive lecture approach to teaching computer science. In *Proceedings of the 26th SIGCSE Technical Symposium on Computer Science Education* (pp. 278–282). Nashville, Tennessee, USA.

Rogers, E. M. (1995). *Diffusion of innovations* (4th ed.). Free Press.

Rogoff, B. (1991). Social interaction as apprenticeship in thinking: Guidance and participation in spatial planning. In Resnick, L. B., Levine, J. M., & Teasley, S. D. (Eds.), *Perspectives on socially shared cognition* (pp. 349–364). Washington, DC: American Psychological Association. doi:10.1037/10096-015

Rohlfs, J. (1974). A theory of interdependent demand of a communication service. *The Bell Journal of Economics and Management Science, 42*(9), 16–37. doi:10.2307/3003090

Rosenberg, J., & Schulzrinne, H. (2002a). Session initiation protocol – locating SIP servers. (IETF RFC 3263).

Rosenberg, J., & Schulzrinne, H. (2002b). *An offer/answer model with the session description protocol* (SDP). (IETF RFC 3264).

Rosenberg, J., Schulzrinne, H., Camarillo, G., Johnston, A., Peterson, J., Sparks, R., …Schooler, E. (2002). *Session initiation protocol.* (IETF RFC 3261).

Roussos, G., Duri, S. S., & Thompson, C. W. (2009). RFID meets the Internet. *IEEE Internet Computing, 13*(1), 11–13. doi:10.1109/MIC.2009.19

Saaty, T. L. (1980). *The analytic hierarchy process.* McGraw Hill.

Sadagic, A., Towles, H., Holden, L., Daniilidis, K., & Zeleznik, B. (2001). *Tele-immersion portal: Towards an ultimate synthesis of computer graphics and computer vision systems.* 4th Annual International Workshop on Presence, (pp. 21-23).

Sakakibara, K. (2005). *Innovation no syuuekika.* Yuhikaku.

Sakamura, K. (2009). *Ubiquitous ID technologies 2009.* Retrieved January 31, 2011, from http://www.uidcenter.org/ wp-content/themes/wp.vicuna/pdf/UID910-W001-090511_en.pdf

Salmon, D., & Jones, M. (2004). Higher education staff experiences of using Web-based learning technologies. *Journal of Educational Technology & Society, 7*(1), 107–114.

Sanchez, P., Alvarez, B., Iborra, A., Fernandez-Merono, J., & Pastor, J. (2003). Web-based activities around a digital model railroad platform. *Journal of IEEE Transaction on Education, 46*(2), 302–306. doi:10.1109/TE.2003.811040

Sander, P. V., Snyder, J., Gortler, S. J., & Hoppe, H. (2001). *Texture mapping progressive meshes.* ACM SIGGRAPH Symposium on Computer Graphics.

Sangyo Times Hensyuu-bu. (2008). *Handoutai-gyoukai handbook ver. 2* (pp. 68–81). Toyo Keizai.

Santhanam, R., & Hartono, E. (2003). Issues in linking Information Technology capability to firm performance. *Management Information Systems Quarterly, 27*(1), 125–153.

Satake, M. (1994). *Sizyou-kaihou o meguru Nitibeiboueki-kousyou: gaikan.* Graduate School of International Cultural Studies Tohoku University Ronsyuu.

Satake, M. (1996). *Nihon no Sizyou ha Heisatekika.* Graduate School of International Cultural Studies Tohoku University Ronsyuu.

Savignon, S. J., & Rothmeier, W. (2004). Computer-mediated communication: Texts and strategies. *CALICO Journal, 21*(2), 265–290.

Sawhney, M., & Prandelli, E. (2000). Communities of creation: Managing distributed innovation in turbulent markets. *California Management Review, 42*(4), 24–54.

Scannapieco, M., Figotin, I., Bertino, E., & Elmagarmid, A. K. (2007). Privacy preserving schema and data matching. In SIGMOD '07: *Proceedings of the 2007 ACM SIGMOD international conference on Management of data.* (pp. 653-664). New York, NY: ACM.

Scharstein, D., & Szeliski, R. (2002). A taxonomy and evaluation of dense two-frame stereo correspondence algorithms. *International Journal of Computer Vision, 47*(1), 7–42. doi:10.1023/A:1014573219977

Schmid, C., & Ali, A. (2002). A Web-based system for control engineering education. In *Proceedings of the 2002 American Control Conference* (pp. 3463–3467). Chicago, IL (USA).

Schnell, R., Bachteler, T., & Reiher, J. (2009). Privacy-preserving record linkage using bloom filters. *BMC Medical Informatics and Decision Making, 9*(1), 41. doi:10.1186/1472-6947-9-41

Schreer, O. Kauff, P. & Sikora, T. (2005). *3D video communication: Algorithms, concepts and real-time systems in human centred communication.* Wiley.

Schroeder, R., & Axelsson, A. (2006). *Avatars at work and play: Collaboration and interaction in shared virtual environments (computer supported cooperative work).* Springer.

Schrum, L. M. (2000). Guarding the promise of online learning. *Education Digest, 66*(4), 43–50.

Schulze, W. S. (1992). *The two resource-based models of the firm: Definitions and implications for research* (pp. 37–41). Academy of Management Best Papers Proceedings.

Schuster, E. W., Brock, D. L., & Allen, S. J. (2010). *Global RFID: The value of the EPCglobal network for supply chain management.* Springer.

Seki, Y., Yamagami, T., & Shimizu, A. (1994). FISH: Flexible knowledge-sharing and handling system. *Systems and Computers in Japan, 25*(10), 36–46. doi:10.1002/scj.4690251004

Semar, W. (2004). Incentive systems in knowledge management to support cooperative distributed forms of creating and acquiring knowledge. In H. Arabnia, et al. (Eds.), *Proceedings of the International Conference on Information and Knowledge Engineering - IKE'04,* (pp. 406-411).

Sevilla, C., & Wells, T. (2000). Converting to web-based training: Choices and trade-offs. *Learning Circuits.* Retrieved May 3, 2004, from http://www.learningcircuits.org/ 2000/may2000/Sevilla.htm

Shane, S. (2005). Academic entrepreneurship: University spinoff and wealth creation. (p. 84).

Shank, P. (2005). New social interaction tools for online instruction. *Instructional Technology Forum.* Retrieved January 20, 2006, from http://it.coe.uga.edu/itforum / paper81/paper81.html

Sharples, M. (2000). The design of personal mobile technologies for lifelong learning. *Computers & Education, 34,* 177–193. doi:10.1016/S0360-1315(99)00044-5

Shigenobu, T., Noda, T., Yoshino, T., & Munemori, J. (2004). Flexible lecture support system using wireless LAN and PDAs. *Transactions of Information Processing Society of Japan, 45*(1), 255–266.

Shinoda, K., Iso, K., & Watanabe, T. (1991). Speaker adaptation for demi-syllable-based continuous-density HMM. [Toronto, Canada.]. *Proceedings of, ICASSP91,* 857–860.

Shirvaikar, M. V. (2006). Trends in automated visual inspection. *Real Time IP, 1*(1), 41–43. doi:10.1007/s11554-006-0009-6

Shoniregun, C. A., & Gray, S.-J. (2004). *Is e-learning really the future or a risk?* Retrieved May 3, 2004, from http://www.distance-educator.com/dnews/Article11123.phtml

Siio, I., & Mima, N. (2001). *Meeting pot: Coffee aroma transmitter.* UbiComp 2001: International Conference on Ubiquitous Computing.

Simchi-Levi, D., Kaminsky, P., & Simchi-Levi, E. (2003). *Designing and managing the supply chain concepts, strategies, and case studies.* McGraw Hill.

Singh, H. (2003). Building effective blended learning programs. *Educational Technology, 43*(6), 51–54.

Sobolewski, M., & Kolonay, R. M. (2006). Federated Grid computing with interactive service-oriented programming. *Concurrent Engineering, 14*(1), 55–66. doi:10.1177/1063293X06064148

Soga, S., Hiroshige, Y., Dobashi, A., Okumura, M., & Kusuzaki, T. (1999). Products lifecycle management system using radio frequency identification technology. *Proceedings of 1999 IEEE International Conference on Emerging Technologies and Factory Automation (ETFA'99),* (pp. 1459-1468).

Son, J. B. (2004). Teacher development in e-learning environments. In J. B. Son (Ed.), *Computer-assisted language learning: Concepts, contexts, and practices* (pp. 107-122). iUniverse.

Song, D.-X., Wagner, D., & Perrig, A. (2000). *Practical techniques for searches on encrypted data.* IEEE Symposium on Security and Privacy. Berkeley, CA, May 14–17, 2000.

Soto-Acosta, P. (2008). The e-business performance measurement in SMEs. *International Journal of Enterprise Network Management, 2*(3), 268–279. doi:10.1504/IJENM.2008.018781

Soto-Acosta, P., & Meroño-Cerdan, A. (2009). Evaluating Internet technologies business effectiveness. *Telematics and Informatics, 26*(2), 211–221. doi:10.1016/j.tele.2008.01.004

Soto-Acosta, P., & Meroño-Cerdan, A. L. (2008). Analyzing e-business value creation from a resource-based perspective. *International Journal of Information Management, 28*(1), 49–60. doi:10.1016/j.ijinfomgt.2007.05.001

Spitz, G., & Drury, C. G. (1978). Inspection of sheet materials: Test of model prediction. *Human Factors, 20,* 521–528.

Srinivasan, T. N. (1991). Is Japan an outlier among trading countries? In de Melo, J., & Sapie, A. (Eds.), *Trade theory and economic reform.* Cambridge, MA: B. Blackwell.

Steinert, Y., & Snell, L. S. (1999). Interactive lecturing: Strategies for increasing participation in large group presentations. *Medical Teacher, 21*(1), 37–42. doi:10.1080/01421599980011

Steinfield, C., Mahler, A., & Bauer, J. (1999). Electronic commerce and the local merchant: Opportunities for synergy between physical and Web presence. *Electronic Markets, 9,* 51–57.

Stevens, S. S. (1957). On the psychophysical law. *Psychological Review, 64,* 158–181. doi:10.1037/h0046162

Stockwell, G. (2003). Effects of topic threads on sustainability of email interactions between native speakers and nonnative speakers. *ReCALL, 15*(1), 37–50. doi:10.1017/S0958344003000417

Streitz, N. A. (1998). *Roomware for collaborative buildings: Integrated design of architectural spaces and information spaces. Cooperative Buildings. (LNCS1370)* (pp. 4–21). Springer. doi:10.1007/3-540-69706-3_3

Streitz, N., Kameas, A., & Mavrommati, I. (Eds.). (2007). *The disappearing computer: Interaction design, system infrastructures and applications for smart environments.* Springer.

Streitz, N. A. (1999). i-LAND: An interactive landscape for creativity and innovation. *Proceedings of ACM Conference on Human Factors in Computing Systems (CHI' 99),* (pp. 120-127).

Stuart, A. (2004). *Virtual classrooms, actual education.* Retrieved April 02, 2004, from http://www.inc.com/partners /sbc/articles/elearning.html

Stubbs, M., Martin, I., & Endlar, L. (2006). The structuration of blended learning: Putting holistic design principles into practice. *British Journal of Educational Technology, 37*(2), 163–175. doi:10.1111/j.1467-8535.2006.00530.x

Summary of First Basic Complete Tabulation Results. (2010). http://www.stat.go.jp/ english/data/kokusei/ 1995/1513.htm

Sun, Y., Yu, Y., & Han, J. (2009). *Ranking-based clustering of heterogeneous information networks with star network schema*. In 2009 ACM SIGKDD International Conference on Knowledge Discovery and Data Mining (KDD'09). Paris, France: ACM.

Takami, J., & Sagayama, S. (1992). A successive state splitting algorithm for efficient allophone modeling. [San Francisco, CA.]. *Proceedings of, ICASSP92*, 573–576.

Takaragi, K., Usami, M., Imura, R., Itsuki, R., & Satoh, T. (2001). *An ultra small individual recognition security chip* (pp. 43–49). IEEE MICRO, Nov.-Dec.

Takemura, M., & Ohta, Y. (2005). *Generating high-definition facial video for shared mixed reality*. IAPR Conference on Machine Vision Applications, (pp. 422-425).

Tallent-Runnels, M. K., Thomas, J. A., Lan, W. Y., & Cooper, S. (2006). Teaching courses online: A review of the research. *Review of Educational Research, 76*(1), 93–125. doi:10.3102/00346543076001093

Tallon, P., Kraemer, K., & Gurbaxani, V. (2000). Executives' perceptions of the business value of Information Technology: A process-oriented approach. *Journal of Management Information Systems, 16*(4), 137–165.

Tan, P.-N., Steinbach, M., & Kumar, V. (2006). *Introduction to data mining*. Pearson Addison-Wesley.

Tan, K. T., Ghanbari, M., & Pearson, D. E. (1998). An objective measurement tool for MPEG video quality. *Signal Processing, 70*(3), 279–294. doi:10.1016/S0165-1684(98)00129-7

Tan, T. H., & Liu, T. Y. (2004). The mobile-based interactive learning environment (MOBILE) and a case study for assisting elementary school English learning. In. *Proceedings of IEEE International Conference on Advanced Learning Technologies, 2004*, 530–534.

Tanaka, A., & Haga, K. (2009). Multiagent simulation on product diffusion process: From chasm to cascade. *Information, 12*(5).

Tang, B. A. (2000). *10 tips to optimize your e-learning*. Retrieved May 3, 2004, from http://www.learningcircuits. org /2000/nov2000/ nov2000_elearn.html

Tani, K. (1999). *Handoutai-sangyou no keifu* (p. 235). The Nikkan Kogyu Shimbun.

Tarini, M., Yamauchi, H., Haber, J., & Seidel, H. P. (2002). *Texturing faces*. Parco. Graphics Interface.

Teunissen, K. (1996). The validity of CCIR quality indicators along a graphical scale. *SMPTE Journal, 105*(3), 144–149.

Thornton, P., & Houser, C. (2004). Using mobile phones in education. In *Proceedings in The 2nd IEEE International Workshop on Wireless and Mobile Technologies in Education 2004* (pp. 3–10).

Tiene, D. (2000). Online discussions: A survey of advantages and disadvantages compared to face-to-face discussions. *Journal of Educational Multimedia and Hypermedia, 9*(4), 371–384.

Tobimatsu, S. (1994). Normative data on reversal visual evoked potentials. *Clinical EEG (Electroencephalography), 36*(2), 93–97.

Towles, H., Chen, W., Yang, R., Kum, S., Fuchs, H., & Kelshikar, N. … Lanier, J. (2002). *3D tele-collaboration over Internet*. International Workshop on Immersive Telepresence.

Towles, H., Kum, S., Sparks, T., Sinha, S., Larsen, S., & Beddes, N. (2003). *Transport and rendering challenges of multi-stream 3D tele-immersion data*. NSF Lake Tahoe Workshop on Collaborative Virtual Reality and Visualization.

Towndrow, P. A., & Vallance, M. (2004). *Using IT in the language classroom: A guide for teachers and students in Asia*. Pearson Education South Asia Pte.

Traub, K., et al. (2005). *The EPCglobal architecture framework*. Retrieved January 31, 2011, from http://autoid.mit.edu/CS/files/folders/specifications/entry5.aspx

Trentin, G. (2001). From formal training to communities of practice via network-based learning. *Educational Technology, 41*, 5–14.

Trepetin, S. (2008). Privacy-preserving string comparisons in record linkage systems: A review. *Information Security Journal: A Global Perspective, 17*, 253-266.

Tsutsumi, R., Katoh, M., Kosaka, T., & Kohda, M. (2006). Lecture speech recognition using pronunciation variant modeling. *IEICE Transactions on Information and Systems, J89-D*(2), 305-313 (in Japanese).

Uchida, M., & Shirayama, S. (2008). Artificial market simulation with embedded complex network structures. *Transactions of the Japanese Society for Artificial Intelligence, 23*(6A), 485–493. doi:10.1527/tjsai.23.485

United States Tariff Commission (USTC). (2005). *Department of Commerce.*

Ushioda, E. (2000). Tandem language learning via email: From motivation to autonomy. *ReCALL, 12*(2), 121–128. doi:10.1017/S0958344000000124

Van Eycken, E., Haustermans, K., Buntinx, F., Ceuppens, A., Weyler, J., & Wauters, E. (2000). Evaluation of the encryption procedure and record linkage in the Belgian National Cancer Registry. *Archives of Public Health, 58*, 281–294.

Vargas, L. G. (1990). An overview of the analytic hierarchy process and its applications. *European Journal of Operational Research, 48*(1), 2–8. doi:10.1016/0377-2217(90)90056-H

Vázquez, A. (2003). Growing network with local rules: Preferential attachment, clustering hierarchy and degree correlations. *Physical Review E: Statistical, Nonlinear, and Soft Matter Physics, 67*, 056104. doi:10.1103/PhysRevE.67.056104

Verykios, V. S., Bertino, E., Fovino, I. N., Provenza, L. P., Saygin, Y., & Theodoridis, Y. (2004). State-of-the-art in privacy preserving data mining. *SIGMOD Record, 33*(1), 50–57. doi:10.1145/974121.974131

Verykios, V. S., Karakasidis, A., & Mitrogiannis, V. K. (2009). Privacy preserving record linkage approaches. *International Journal of Data Mining. Modelling and Management, 1*(2), 206–221.

Waldrop, M. M. (1992). *Complexity: The emerging science at the edge of order and chaos.* Simon & Schuster.

Wallhaus, R. A. (2000). E-learning: From institutions to providers, from students to learners. In Katz, R. N., & Oblinger, D. G. (Eds.), *The "E" is for everything: E-commerce, e-business, and e-learning in the future of higher education* (*Vol. 2*, pp. 21–54). San Francisco, CA: Jossey-Bass.

Wallhoff, F., Willett, D., & Rigoll, G. (2000). Frame-discriminative and confidence-driven adaptation for LVCSR. [Istanbul, Turkey.]. *Proceedings of, ICASSP 2000*, 1835–1838.

Wang, Y. (2006). Negotiation of meaning in desktop videoconferencing-supported distance language learning. *ReCALL, 18*(1), 122–146. doi:10.1017/S0958344006000814

Wang, S., & Higgins, M. (2005). Limitations of mobile phone learning. In *Proceedings of IEEE International Workshop on Wireless and Mobile Technologies in Education (WMTE'05)* (pp. 179–181).

Wang, Z., Guan, H., Niu, J., & Hung, S. (1999). *An online slack stealing algorithm for jointly scheduling aperiodic and periodic tasks in fixed-priority preemptive system.* In the 20th IEEE Real-time Systems Symposium (pp. 60-64). Phoenix.

Warneke, B., Last, M., Liebowitz, B., & Pister, K. S. J. (2001). Smart dust: Communicating with a cubic-millimeter computer. *IEEE Computer, 34*(1), 44–51.

Warschauer, M., & Kern, R. G. (2000). *Network-based language teaching: Concepts and practice.* Cambridge University Press.

Warschauer, M. (2000). On-line learning in second language classrooms: An ethnographic study. In Warschauer, M., & Kern, R. (Eds.), *Network-based language teaching: Concepts and practice* (pp. 41–58). Cambridge, UK: Cambridge University Press.

Watts, D. J. (2003). *Six degrees: The science of a connected age.* W. W. Norton & Co Inc.

Watts, D. J., & Strogatz, S. H. (1998). Collective dynamics of small-world networks. *Nature, 393*, 440–442. doi:10.1038/30918

Weiser, M. (1991). The computer for the 21st Century. *Scientific American, 265*(3), 66–75. doi:10.1038/scientificamerican0991-94

Weiser, M. (1993). Some computer science problems in ubiuitous computing. *Communications of the ACM, 36*(7), 75–84. doi:10.1145/159544.159617

Welker, J., & Berardino, L. (2005). Blended learning: Understanding the middle ground between traditional classroom and fully online instruction. *Journal of Educational Technology Systems, 34*(1), 33–55. doi:10.2190/67FX-B7P8-PYUX-TDUP

Wells, D. C., Greisen, E. W., & Harten, R. H. (1981). FITS: A Flexible Image Transport System. *Astronomy & Astrophysics, 44*, 363–370.

Wheeler, A. (2007). Commercial applications of wireless sensor network using ZigBee. *IEEE Communications Magazine, 45*(4), 70–77. doi:10.1109/MCOM.2007.343615

Wikipedia (2010). *Distributed computing*. Retrieved from http://en.wikipedia.org/wiki/Distributed_computing

Wikipedia. (2007). *Nonverbal communication*. Retrieved October 20, 2009 from http://en.wikipedia.org/wiki/Nonverbal_communication

Wikipedia. (2010). *Data mining*. Retrieved from http://en.wikipedia.org/wiki/Data_mining

WiMAX. (2006a). *Mobile WiMAX - part I: A technical overview and performance evaluation*. WiMAX Forum.

WiMAX. (2006b). *Mobile WiMAX – part II: A comparative analysis*. WiMAX Forum.

WiMAX. (2007). *M-Taiwan program – a WiMAX ecosystem*. WiMAX Forum.

Witkin, A. (1984). Scale space filtering: A new approach to multi-scale description. In Ullman, S., & Richards, W. (Eds.), *Image understanding*. New Jersey: Ablex.

Witkin, A. (1993). Scale space filtering. *Proceedings of International Joint Conference on Artificial Intelligence*, Karlsruhe, (pp. 1019-1022).

Wittig, R. D., & Chow, P. (1996). One chip: An FPGA processor with reconfigurable logic. *Proceedings of IEEE Symposium on FPGAs for Custom Computing Machines*, (pp. 126-135).

Woodward, A., & Delmas, P. (2004). Toward a low cost realistic human face modeling and animation framework. *Proceedings of the International Conference on Image and Vision Computing*, (pp. 11-16). New Zealand

Woodward, A., An, D., Gimel'farb, G., & Delmas, P. (2006). A comparison of 3-D facial reconstruction approaches. *Proceedings of the IEEE International Conference on Multimedia and Expo*, (pp. 9-12). Canada.

Wu, F., Mahajan, V., & Balasubamanian, S. (2003). An analysis of e-business adoption and its impacts on business performance. *Journal of the Academy of Marketing Science, 31*(4), 425–447. doi:10.1177/0092070303255379

Yakout, M., Atallah, M., & Elmagarmid, A. (2009). *Efficient private record linkage*. 2009 IEEE International Conference on Data Engineering, (pp. 1283-1286).

Yamada, Y., Hirano, T., & Nishimoto, K. (2003). TangibleChat: A chat-system that conveys conversation-context-awareness by transmitting vibration produced by key-stroke-act. *Transactions of the Information Processing Society of Japan, 44*(5), 1392–1403.

Yamamoto, T. (2009). Measurement methods and subjective assessment methods for flat panel displays. *The Journal of ITE, 63*(6), 752–757.

Yamamoto, H., & Sagisaka, Y. (2001). A language model adaptation using multiple varied corpora. [Trento, Italy.]. *Proceedings of, ASRU2001*, 389–392.

Yang, Q., & Wu, X. (2008). 10 challenging problems in data mining research. *International Journal of Information Technology Decision Making, 5*(4), 597–604. doi:10.1142/S0219622006002258

Yokoyama, T., Shinozaki, T., Iwano, K., & Furui, S. (2003). Unsupervised language model adaptation using word classes for spontaneous speech recognition. *Proceedings of IEEE-ISCA Workshop on Spontaneous Speech Processing and Recognition* (pp. 71-74). Tokyo, Japan.

Yoshimoto, T., & Shintaku, J. (2005). Kaigai-Kigyou tono Kyougyou o tosuita Kikan-Buzai to Kanseihin-Jigyou no Renkei-Model. *MMRC Discussion Paper, 49*.

Young, M., Beeson, E., Davis, J., Rusinkiewicz, S., & Ramamoorthi, R. (2007). *Viewpoint coded structured light*. IEEE Conference on Computer Vision and Pattern Recognition, (pp. 1-8).

Yunogami, T. (2004). *Competitiveness of Japanese semiconductor industry in technological level*. ITEC.

Yunogami, T. (2009). *Nihon Handoutai Haisen.*

Yuyama, I., Nishida, Y., & Nakasu, E. (1998). Objective measurement of compressed digital television picture quality. *SMPTE Journal, 107*(6), 348–352.

Zeiss, E., & Isabelli-Garcia, C. L. (2005). The role of asynchronous computer mediated communication on enhancing cultural awareness. *Computer Assisted Language Learning, 18*(3), 151–169. doi:10.1080/09588220500173310

Zhang, Y. (2007). Communication strategies and foreign language learning. *US-China Foreign Language, 5*(4), 43–48.

Zhang, Y., Sim, T., & Tan, C. T. (2004). Rapid modeling of 3D faces for animation using an efficient adaptation algorithm. *Proceedings of the 2nd International Conference on Computer Graphics and Interactive Techniques in Austrasia and South East Asia,* (pp. 173-181).

Zhu, K., & Kraemer, K. (2002). E-commerce metrics for net-enhanced organizations: Assessing the value of e-commerce to firm performance in the manufacturing sector. *Information Systems Research, 13*(3), 275–295. doi:10.1287/isre.13.3.275.82

Zhu, K., & Kraemer, K. (2005). Post-adoption variations in usage and value of e-business by organizations: Cross-country evidence from the retail industry. *Information Systems Research, 16*(1), 61–84. doi:10.1287/isre.1050.0045

Zhu, K., Kraemer, K., & Xu, S. (2003). Electronic business adoption by European firms: A cross-country assessment of the facilitators and inhibitors. *European Journal of Information Systems, 12*(4), 251–268. doi:10.1057/palgrave.ejis.3000475

Zorin, D. (2006). *Modeling with multiresolution subdivision surfaces.* ACM SIGGRAPH 2006 Course, (pp. 30-50).

Zytkow, J. M., & Quafafou, M. (1998). *Principles of data mining and knowledge discovery.* (LNAI 1510).

About the Contributors

Tokuro Matsuo (Ph.D., M.S., and B.Edu.) is an associate professor at Graduate School of Science and Engineering in Yamagata University since 2006. He graduated from School of Culture and Education of Saga University in 2001 and from School of Knowledge Science of Japan Advanced Institute of Technology in 2003. He received his Ph.D. from Department of Computer Science at Nagoya Institute of Technology in 2006. He is a visiting researcher in University California, Irvine (2010-2011) and a research fellow of Software Engineering and Information Technology Institute of Central Michigan University (2010-2012). His current research interests include career service system, safety service for disaster recovery, designs on secure electronic commerce systems and robust e-auction protocols, qualitative reasoning and simulations, polymer chemical material design system, and travel support systems. Some of his researches are presented in top-leveled international conference including AAAI, IEEE CEC, AAMAS, and WWW. He created and organized 26 international conferences and workshops including Pacific Rim International Workshop on E-Commerce 2006, Conference on Software Engineering, Network, Parallel and Distributed Computing 2009, IEEE/ACIS International Conference on Computer and Information Science 2010, IEEE International Workshop on e-Activity 2007-2011, and International Workshop on Automated Complex Agent-based Negotiation 2005-2011. He received over 40 awards and research grants from research foundations, company, and government. He is commissioned as Adviser of Information Promotion from the Japanese Government. He also is a chairperson of the Investigation Committee on Tourist Information System in the Institute of Electrical Engineers of Japan from 2011.

Takayuki Fujimoto (Ph.D., M.S., B.Edu.) received the Doctor degree of Informatics (Ph.D.) from Graduate School of Science and Engineering in Yamagata University in 2007. He also received Master degree of Science in Japan Advanced Institute of Science and Technology in 2003 and Bachelor degree of Education in Waseda University in 2001. Currently, he is a lecturer of Dep. of Computational Science and Engineering, Toyo University. His main area of study includes information design, artificial intelligence, and electronic education, e-learning support systems, university information support systems based on information reuse and integrations, and e-activity. He is a member of IEEE, and several others. He is a conference organizing IEEE IWEA 2007.

* * *

Takayuki Asada is a professor of Accounting in Graduate school of Economics at Osaka University in Japan since September 1st 1995. Prior to this he had a position of Associate Professor of Accounting in University of Tsukuba. He belongs to several academic associations, The Accounting Association of Japan, Japanese Management Accounting Association, The International Association of Project and Program and American Accounting Association. He also has worked with Osaka Gus Company and also has teaching and consultancy experience in Japanese service and manufacturing companies. He is a regular speaker at some international conferences and holds visiting lecturer's experience in UK and France. Also, he got a distinguished research funds from Fulbright Committee and Japanese Foundation in 1985 and 1999 and got a paper award from IMA in 1999.

Ran-Fun Chiu has his BS degree from national Taiwan University, and MS, PhD degrees from University of Houston, all in electrical engineering. From 1970 to 1981, he was with Racal-Milgo designing high-speed modems and other digital transmission equipment. He joined Hewlett Packard Laboratories to work on network products and systems in 1981. Currently he is a distinguished technologist. His works include LANs, IP routers, network management, HFC data delivery systems (cable modem), LMDS, VoIP, and network security. In the past 10 years he has been working on large scale mobile networks, including the M-Taipei, and the M-Taiwan projects.

Ricardo Colomo-Palacios is an Associate Professor at the Computer Science Department of the Universidad Carlos III de Madrid. His research interests include applied research in Information Systems, software project management, people in software projects and social and Semantic Web. He received his PhD in Computer Science from the Universidad Politécnica of Madrid. He also holds a MBA from the Instituto de Empresa. He has been working as software engineer, project manager, and software engineering consultant in several companies, including Spanish IT leader, INDRA. He is also an Editorial Board Member and Associate Editor for several international journals and conferences and Editor in Chief of the International Journal of Human Capital and Information Technology Professionals.

Nashwan Dawood, BEng, MPhil, PhD is currently the director of Technology Future Institute (TFI) and director and creator of the Centre for Construction Innovation & Research (CCIR) at Teesside University, UK. He has spent many years as an academic, practitioner, and a researcher within the field of project and construction management and the application of IT/VR in the construction process. This has ranged across a number of research topics including sustainability, ICT for energy efficient buildings, Information Technologies and Systems (nD, VR, Integrated databases), planning and management of off-site production, risk management, and intelligent decision support systems. This has resulted in over 200 published papers in refereed international journals and conferences, research grants from European Union FP7, British Council, Industry, Engineering Academy, EPSRC, DTI UK Department Trade and Industry, construction industry companies and knowledge transfer partnership, totalling about 4,500,000 in cash. Prof. Dawood has been invited for keynote presentations around the world, and he is the creator of CONVR (Construction Application of VR) conference series. He is a major contributor to BIM implementation strategies in the UK. Prof. Dawood's research projects are multi-disciplinary in nature and complementary knowledge and expertise within his research centre, national and international research institutions, and collaboration with the UK and EU construction industry has led to successful research bids and exciting research projects.

Yasuo Ebara received M.S. and Ph.D. degrees in the Graduate School of Information Science, Tohoku University, Sendai, Japan, in 1997 and 2000. Since 2000, he has been with Kyoto University, where he is an assistant professor. Since 2008, he has been with Central Office for Information Infrastructure at Osaka University, where he is an associate professor. His research interests include tele-immersion technology, network computing, and application of information communication system. He is a member of IEEE Computer Society.

Yae Fukushige is an associate professor at the Graduate School of Commerce at Otaru University of Commerce, Japan. She received Bachelor of Law from Shimane University, Master of Law from Osaka Gakuin University, Master of Economics and Ph.D in Economics from Osaka University. After being a part-time lecturer and a research assistant at Hannan University, since 2010 she is an Associate Professor at Otaru University of Commerce. She is a member of Japan Society for Intellectual Production, Japanese Society for Information and Systems in Education, Japan Academic Society of Ventures and Entrepreneurs.

Huiwei Guan received PhD degree in computer science from Shanghai Jiao Tong University of China in 1993. He was an Associate Professor of Computer Engineering & Science School of Shanghai University in China. From 1995, he worked as a research fellow in Department of Electronic Engineering of Hong Kong Polytechnic University, and from 1996 to 1997 he worked as a senior research fellow in Department of Computer Science, City University of Hong Kong. From 1998 to 1999, he joined German National Research Center for Information Technology (GMD-IPSI) in Germany as a senior international scientist. From 1999 to 2001, he was the principal researcher and the director of Advanced Technology Department of Primeon Inc., USA. From 2001, he joined the faculty of Computer Science, North Shore Community College, USA and presently he is a tenured full professor there. He is also a certified national IT professional in USA. Dr. Guan is the author of more than 80 research contributions to international journals and international conferences. He is a referee of IEE International Computing & Control Engineering Journal, International Journal of Cooperative Information Systems, Journal of Computer Science and Technology, International Journal of Computing and Informatics, International Journal of Advanced Technology for Learning, and Journal of China Science. He is a PC member and referee of IEEE International Conference on Algorithms & Architectures for Parallel Processing, IEEE International Symposium on High-Performance Distributed Computing, IEEE Real-Time Systems Symposium, IEEE International Conference on Systems, Man and Cybernetics, International Symposium on Database, Web and Cooperative Systems, and International Symposium on Cooperative Database Systems for Advanced Applications. His current research topics are parallel processing system and parallel algorithms, and network security and network applications.

Hidehiko Hayashi is currently an associate professor in the Department of Technology and Information Education, Naruto University of Education, Tokushima, Japan. He received his MS in Information Science and PhD degree in Knowledge Science from Japan Advanced Institute of Science and Technology (JAIST) in 2000 and 2003, respectively. His research interests are Information and knowledge Science, brain computer interface, medical information, & evaluation of human information processing mechanism.

Yi-Chieh Ho received her PhD degree in Language Teaching and Learning from the Department of Applied Language Studies and Linguistics of the University of Auckland, New Zealand. She is currently Assistant Professor at Hwa-Hsia Institute of Technology in Taiwan. Her research interests include program evaluation, CALL, curriculum development, and effective teaching and learning.

Naohiro Ishii received the BE and ME degrees and the PhD degree in Electrical and Communication Engineering from Tohoku University, Japan, in 1963,1965 and 1968, respectively. He was a professor in Computer Science in Nagoya Institute of Technology, Japan. Since 2003, he has been a professor of Information Science in Aichi Institute of Technology. His research interests include computer systems, artificial intelligence, and Web applications. He is a member of IEEE, ACM, and ACIS.

Rei Itsuki received the Master degree in mechanical engineering from Waseda University in 1987 and the Doctor degree of engineering from Osaka University in 2000. He joined Hitachi, Ltd. in 1987. In 2002, he joined Hiroshima International University, where he is currently a professor in the Department of Information and Communication Technology, Faculty of Engineering. His research interests include man machine interface, Internet of Things, RFID application, sensor network, and ubiquitous computing. He is a member of the IEEE, the IEEJ, and the JSAI.

Alexandros Karakasidis received his BS degree from the Department of Computer Science at the University of Ioannina in Greece, in 2002. He received his MSc from the same department in 2005. Currently, he is a PhD candidate in the Department of Computer and Communication Engineering at the University of Thessaly, in Volos, Greece. His main research interests include privacy and security in advanced database systems, data mining, and data quality. He has published papers in refereed journals and international conferences and workshops. He has served as a reviewer for international journals and conferences.

Masaharu Kato was born in Osaka, Japan, in 1969. He received B.E., and M.E. degrees from Yamagata University, Yamagata, Japan, in 1991 and 1993 respectively. He also received Ph.D. degrees from Tohoku University, Miyagi, Japan, in 2010. Since 1993, he has been with Yamagata University, where he is currently an Assistant Professor at Graduate School of Science and Engineering. His research interests include speech recognition. He is a member of the Acoustical Society of Japan.

Masaki Kohda was born in Aichi, Japan in 1942. He received B.E., M.E., and Ph.D. degrees from Nagoya University, in 1965, 1967, and 1979 respectively. In 1967, he joined Electrical Communication Laboratories of Nippon Telegraph and Telephone Corporation, Tokyo, Japan. Since 1987, he has been with Yamagata University, where he is currently an Emeritus Professor. His research interests include speech recognition, speaker recognition, speech synthesis, speech coding, and language modeling. He is a member of the Information Processing Society of Japan, the Acoustical Society of Japan, the Japanese Society for Artificial Intelligence, and the Association for Natural Language Processing.

Tetsuo Kosaka was born in Miyagi, Japan, in 1960. He received B.E., M.E., and Ph.D. degrees from Tohoku University, Miyagi, Japan, in 1984, 1986, and 1997 respectively. In 1986, he joined CANON Inc., Tokyo, Japan. From 1991 to 1995, he was a researcher at ATR Interpreting Telephony Research Laboratories, Kyoto, Japan. Since 2002, he has been working at Yamagata University, Yamagata, Japan, where he is currently an Associate Professor at Graduate School of Science and Engineering. His research interests include speech processing and its applications. He received the Paper Award of the Institute of Electronics, Information and Communication Engineers (IEICE), Japan, in 1996. He is a member of the IEICE, the IEEE, and the Acoustical Society of Japan.

Takashi Kusama was born in Miyagi, Japan, in 1984. He received B.E. and M.E. degrees from Yamagata University, Yamagata, in 2006 and 2008, respectively. He has currently been working with PFU Ltd. His research interests include speech recognition.

Euripidis Loukis is an Assistant Professor of Information Systems and Decision Support Systems in the Department of Information and Communication Systems Engineering at the University of the Aegean, Greece. Formerly he has been Information Systems Advisor at the Ministry to the Presidency of the Government of Greece, Technical Director of the Program of Modernization of Greek Public Administration of the Second Community Support Framework and National Representative of Greece in the programs Telematics for Administrations and IDA (Interchange of Data between Administrations) of the European Union. He is the author of numerous scientific articles in international journals and conferences; one of them has been honoured with the International Award of the American Society of Mechanical Engineers Controls and Diagnostics Committee. His current research interests include Information Systems value/impacts and internal/external determinants, e-government, e-participation, and medical decision support systems.

Toshiyuki Maeda is a professor of network communication at the Faculty of Management Information at Hannan University, Japan. He graduated MSc (1984), MSc (1986) from Kyoto University, Ph.D in Computer Science from Osaka Prefecture University in 2004. He joined as a researching engineer in Matsushita Electric Industrial Co., Ltd. from 1986 until 1997, engaged in computer-aided design, knowledge information processing, multimedia communication, et cetera. He was a lecturer from 1999 until 2003 at Fukuyama Heisei University, and from 2003 an associate professor at Hannan University, and from 2008 a professor at Hannan University to present. He is a member of IEEE, Information Processing Society of Japan, Japanese Society of Artificial Intelligence, and so on. He is currently interested in network communication, educational engineering, and medical risk management system.

Akinori Minazuki is currently a professor and a director of Center for Information and Technology and System, Kushiro Public University, Hokkaido, Japan. He received his PhD degree in Knowledge Science from Japan Advanced Institute of Science and Technology, Japan (JAIST) in 2003. His research interests are Information and knowledge Science, Information Technology for Socail systems, information education, emergency medical service & medical information.

Kazushi Nishimoto received his B.Eng. and M.Eng. from Kyoto University, Japan, in 1985 and 1987, respectively, and received Dr.Eng. from Osaka University, Japan, in 1998. He worked for Matsushita Electric Industrial Co., Ltd. from 1987 to 1992. He was a researcher of ATR Communication Systems Research Laboratories from 1992 to 1995, and was a visiting researcher of ATR Media Integration & Communications Research Laboratories from 1995 to 1999. He was made an associate professor in the Center for Knowledge Science at Japan Advanced Institute of Science and Technology in 1999, and he was promoted to a full professor in 2007. He is currently also the director of Center for Knowledge Science as well as a vice trustee of the research and international division, JAIST. His research interests include creativity support, musical information processing and informal communication support. He is a member of IEEE CS, ACM, Information Processing Society of Japan, Japanese Society for Artificial Intelligence, and Japan Human Interface Society.

Akihiko Nagai is a doctoral course student in Tokyo Institute of Technology Graduate School of Innovation Management since 2007. He was in the School of Knowledge Science at Japan Advanced Institute of Science and Technology (JAIST) as a master course student from 2004 to 2006. He received his Master degree of Knowledge Science from JAIST. His major area of study is "sharing and using knowledge of inter-organization."

Yousuke Okada is a bachelor course student of Information Science in Aichi Institute of Technology.

Tadayuki Okamoto is an associate professor of Cost Accounting at the Faculty of Law and Letters at Ehime University, Ehime, Japan. He graduated from Osaka University with undergraduate majors in economics, and received Master of Economics degrees from Osaka University in 1991. He currently teaches Cost Accounting, Management Accounting and Accounting Information Analysis. His major research interests are in agency problems in outsourcing contracts at public sector and mobile-learning. Since 2004, he has been used mobile-learning systems for undergraduate classes at Ehime University and Matsuyama University (Ehime, Japan), which uses mobile phone messages.

Manabu Onogi is a bachelor course student of Information Science in Aichi Institute of Technology.

Ali Selamat is currently an Associate Professor at Faculty of Computer Science and Information System, Universiti Teknologi Malaysia (UTM) and Manager of Information Technology at UTM Graduate School. He is a member of ACM and IEEE. He received a B.Sc. (Hons.) in IT from Teesside University, U.K. and M.Sc. in Distributed Multimedia Interactive Systems from Lancaster University, U.K. in 1997 and 1998, respectively. He obtained his Ph.D. degree from Osaka Prefecture University, Japan in 2003. His research interests include software engineering, software agents, web engineering, and information retrieval, artificial intelligence and sofcomputing. He can be contacted at aselamat@utm.my or selamat.ali@gmail.com.

Pedro Soto-Acosta is a Professor of Management at the University of Murcia (Spain). He holds a PhD in Management Information Systems (MISs) and a Master's degree in Technology Management from the University of Murcia. He received his BA in Accounting and Finance from the Manchester Metropolitan University (UK) and his BA in Business Administration from the University of Murcia. He attended Postgraduate Courses at Harvard University (USA). His work has been published in journals such as the European Journal of Information Systems, the International Journal of Information Management, the Information Systems Management, and the Journal of Enterprise Information Management, among others. He is also an Editorial Board Member and Associate Editor for several international journals and Chairman of various international conferences.

Koji Tanabe is a professor at Tokyo Institute of Technology Graduate School of Innovation Management from 2005. He received the Doctor degree of Engineering from Dept. of Innovation at Tokyo Institute of Technology in 2005. His major area of study was analysis of innovation.

Atsushi Tanaka is an Associate Professor in Graduate School of Science and Engineering, Yamagata University. He received B.S., M.E, D.E degrees from Tohoku University, Sendai, Japan in 1886, 1988,, and 1991, respectively. From 1991 to 1998, he was an Assistant Professor in the department of Electrical and Information Engineering, Faculty of Engineering, Yamagata University. From 1998 to 2003, he was an Associate Professor in the Computing Service Center, Yamagata University. His research interests include complex systems and pattern formation in nature. He has been analyzing the structures in complex networks in many fields including physics, informatics, sociology, and so on and modeling their mechanisms in recent years.

Muhammad Tarmizi Lockman is currently a graduate researcher at Faculty of Computer Science and Information System, Universiti Teknologi Malaysia (UTM). He received a B.Eng from Universiti Putra Malaysia. His research interests include embedded systems and real-time software engineering.

Takanori Terashima received PhD (2001), MS (1998) and BS (1994) in Engineering from Muroran Institute of Technology, Japan. After he worked for several university--Hokkaido University, University of Teesside, etc.-- as a researcher, he settled at his current position. His major is production and information systems engineering, particularly he has experience with designing 3D graphics applications for construction and metal mold industry. He has interest in data visualization on 3D space. The contribution to "E-Activity and Intelligent Web Construction: Effects of Social Design" is about an application of construction planning tool which visualizes the work progress from given materials such as CAD and project schedule data. He is trying to apply 3D visualization to any kind of industries. Other works are visualizing the structure of crawling Web pages for the intuitive display method of data search on the Net. Also he is studying the applications on the sports science. The range of this study covers from the human extraction from moving pictures to playback the flow line of the players for game strategy, or offering the educational material from junior club to referee training course. His recent contribution to the academic society is a conference local arrangement chair of IEEE/ACIS International Conference on Computer and Information science 2010, and of the International Conference on Construction Applications of Virtual Reality 2011. He also served a program committee of IEEE IWEA 2007 – 2010, etc.

Ippei Torii received B.F.A degree in sculpture of fine arts from Nihon University, Tokyo, Japan in 1982. From 1982 to1984, he was at the school of fine arts in Nihon University. From 2007, he has been an associate professor in Aichi Institute of Technology, Japan. From 2008, he has been a PhD course student. His research interests include computer graphics, visual design and drawing. He is a member of ACM SIGGraph, IEEE and ACIS.

Vassilios S. Verykios received the Diploma degree in Computer Engineering from the University of Patras in Greece in 1992, and the MS and the PhD degrees from Purdue University in 1997 and 1999, respectively. In 1999, he joined the Faculty of Information Systems in the College of Information Science and Technology at Drexel University in Pennsylvania, as a tenure track assistant professor. Since 2005 he has been an assistant professor in the Department of Computer and Communication Engineering at the University of Thessaly, in Volos, Greece. Dr. Verykios has served on various visiting positions in Athens Information Technology Center, Hellenic Open University and University of Patras, in Greece. His main research interests include knowledge based systems, privacy, security and anonymity in advanced database systems, data mining, data reconciliation, privacy preserving record linkage, parallel computing, and performance evaluation of large scale parallel systems. He has published over 50 papers in major referred journals and in the proceedings of international conferences and workshops, and he has coauthored a monograph on Association Rule Hiding for Data Mining by Springer. He has served in the program committees of several international scientific events and he has consulted for Telcordia Technologies, ChoiceMaker Technologies, Intracom SA, and SingularLogic SA. He has also been a visiting researcher to CERIAS, the Department of Computer Sciences at Purdue University, the US Naval Research Laboratory and the Research and Academic Computer Technology Institute in Patras, Greece.

Su-Chen Wang-- After receiving her Master of Education degree in Computer-Assisted Instruction from University of Illinois at Urbana- Champaign, USA in 1983, she worked at the Computer and Network Center, National Cheng-Kung University (NCKU) in Taiwan. She is a former Director of Administration and Consultant Division and former Director of Campus Information Management Division at the Computer and Network Center, NCKU for nine years. She has taught many courses in the field of Educational Technology and Computer Science at NCKU and some government institutes for over 20 years. She obtained her Ph.D. in Science and Technology Educational Research from University of Waikao, New Zealand in 2008. She is an assistant professor at NCKU. Her research interests include e-learning, e-business, and information management system. She has presented many national and international conference papers and has been session chairs in the international conferences. She has published some journal papers, book chapters, and technical reports.

Index